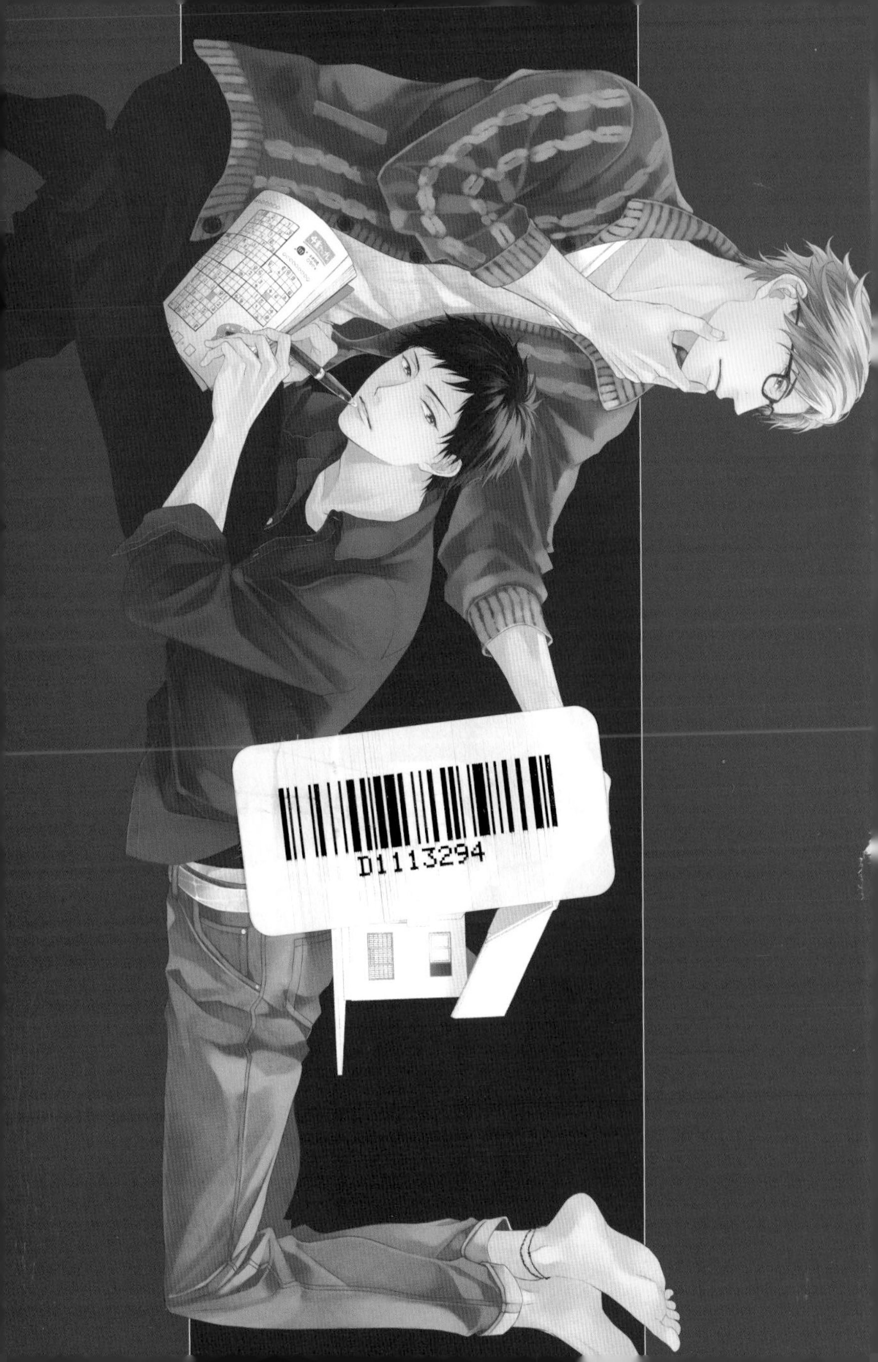

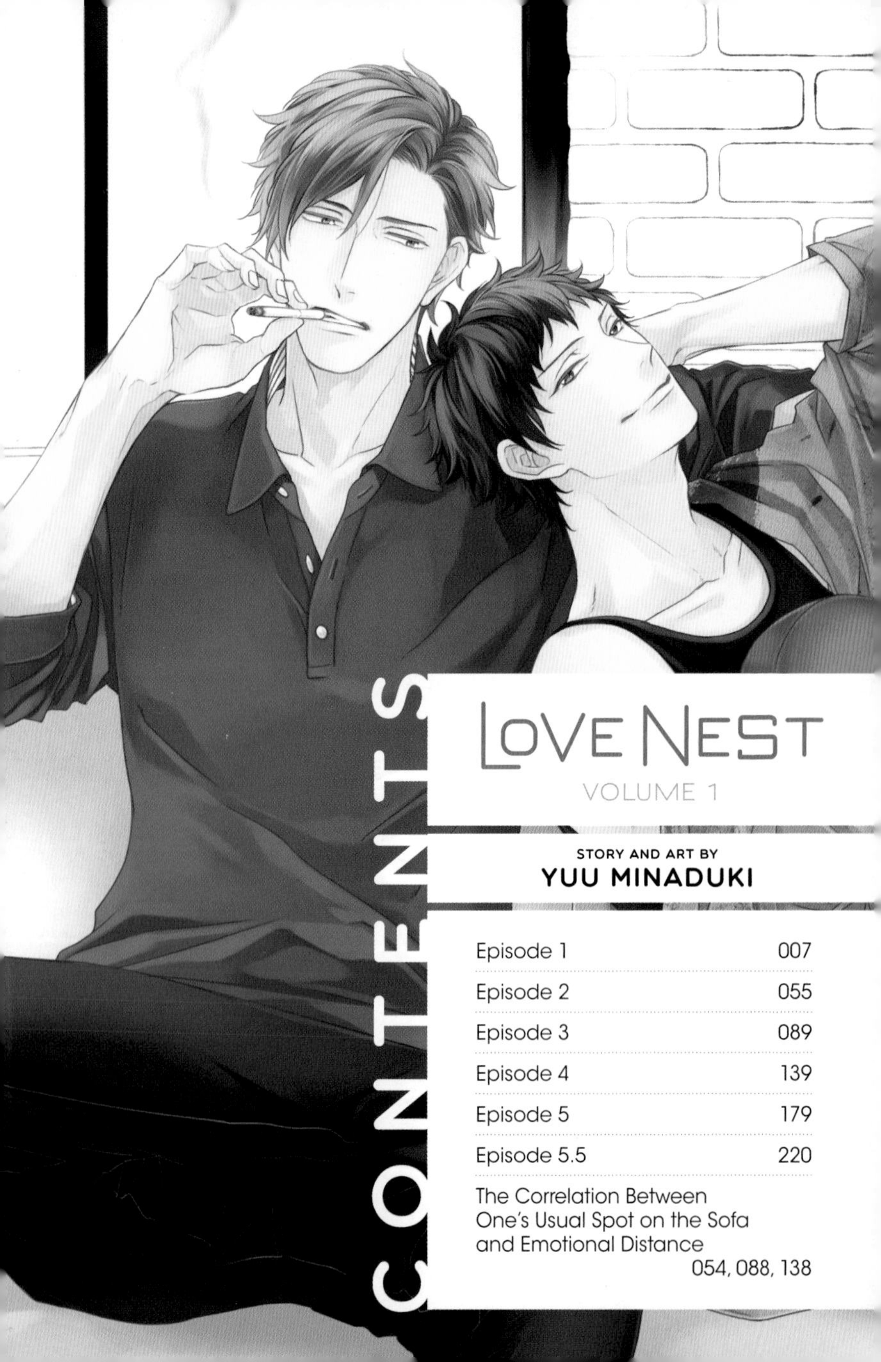

CONTENTS

LOVE NEST

VOLUME 1

STORY AND ART BY
YUU MINADUKI

LOVE NEST

STORY AND ART BY
YUU MINADUKI

1

FIRST THERE WAS *SAYONARA GAME*, AND THEN CAME *CHANGE WORLD*, AND NOW IT'S *LOVE NEST*.

MASATO HOZUMI

A 30-year-old system engineer currently assigned to Yotsutomo. He's mischievous and friendly, but a wound from a past relationship never healed, making it difficult for him to have a boyfriend.

CHANGE WORLD
YUU MINADUKI
1
CHANGE WORLD
YUU MINADUKI
2

CHANGE WORLD VOL. 1 & VOL. 2

Taking place one year after the events in *Sayonara Game*, Arimura's old college classmate, Masato, comes back into his life, causing Arimura and Yosuke's relationship to enter a critical stage...

IKUO ARIMURA

A 28-year-old department store employee. He's an old college classmate of Masato's that Masato had a crush on. He has a cheerful, positive personality, but when it comes to Yosuke, he's been known to lose control.

YOSUKE ITO

A 26-year-old Yotsutomo employee. After his past run-ins with Masato, he basically looks upon him with hostility. He was Arimura's classmate in high school and harbored a longtime secret crush on him that has finally bore fruit. He now enjoys his life with him.

MARIE KURODA

30 years old, she was Masato's college classmate and is his current beard. She understands Masato very well. She currently lives with her girlfriend.

Currently available from SuBLime!

SAYONARA GAME
After five years of harboring a secret crush on Arimura, his old high school upperclassman, Yosuke's reunited with him, spurring their story to start again.

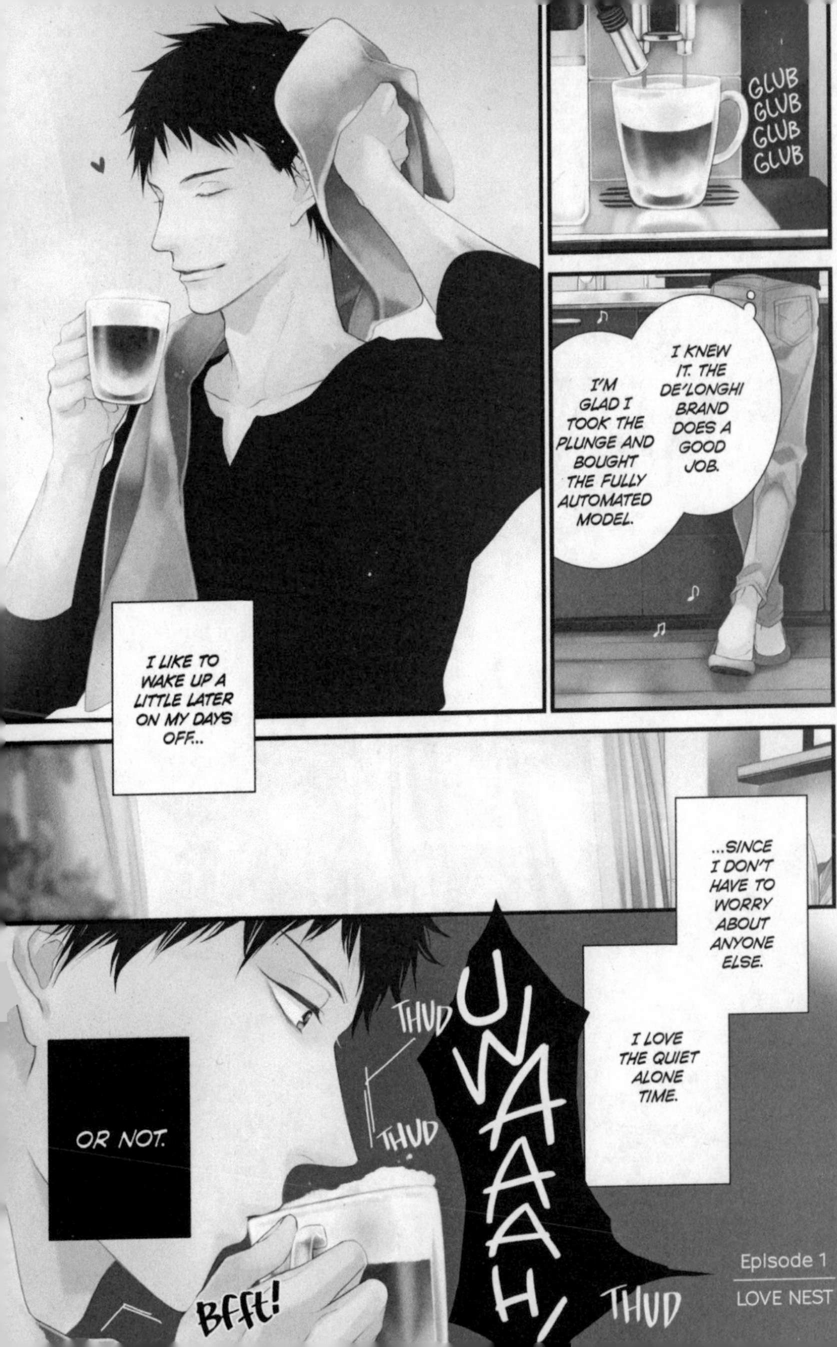
GLUB GLUB GLUB GLUB
I KNEW IT. THE DE'LONGHI BRAND DOES A GOOD JOB.
I'M GLAD I TOOK THE PLUNGE AND BOUGHT THE FULLY AUTOMATED MODEL.
I LIKE TO WAKE UP A LITTLE LATER ON MY DAYS OFF...
...SINCE I DON'T HAVE TO WORRY ABOUT ANYONE ELSE.
I LOVE THE QUIET ALONE TIME.
THUD
UWAAAH!
THUD
OR NOT.
THUD
BFFT!

Episode 1

LOVE NEST

LOVE NEST

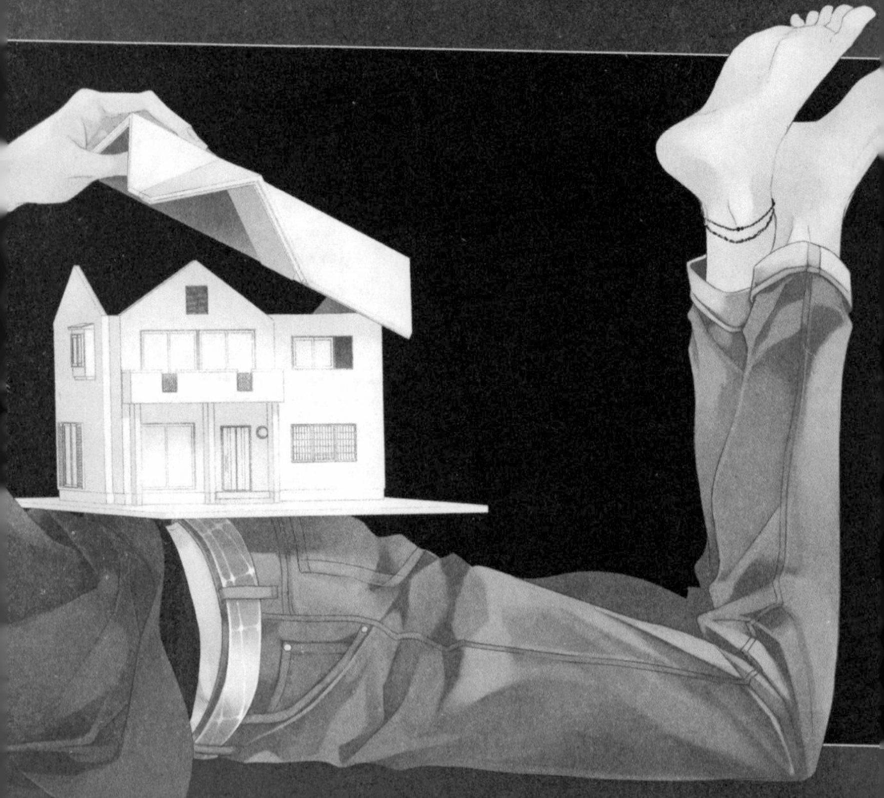

Episode 1

LOVE NEST

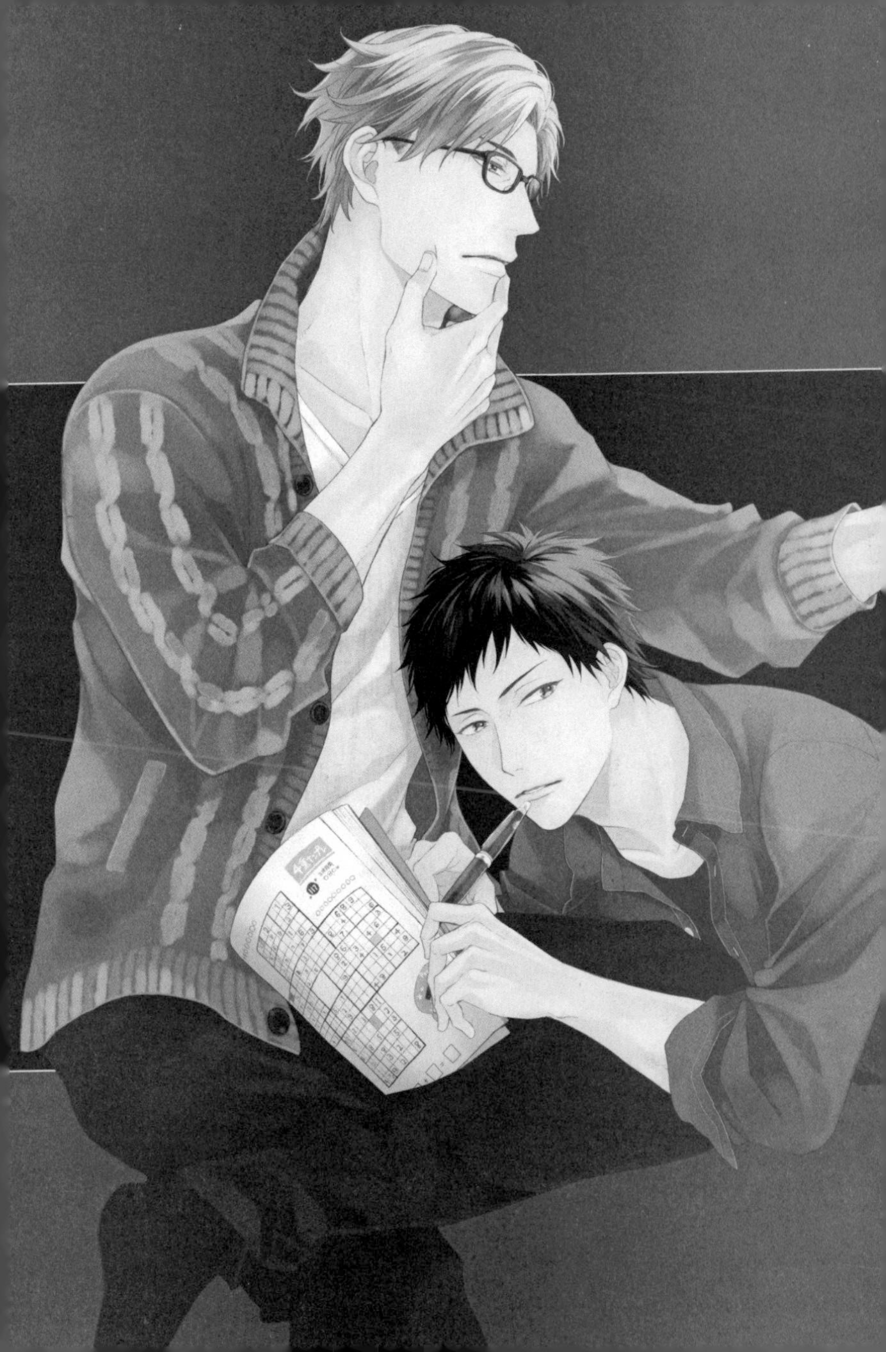

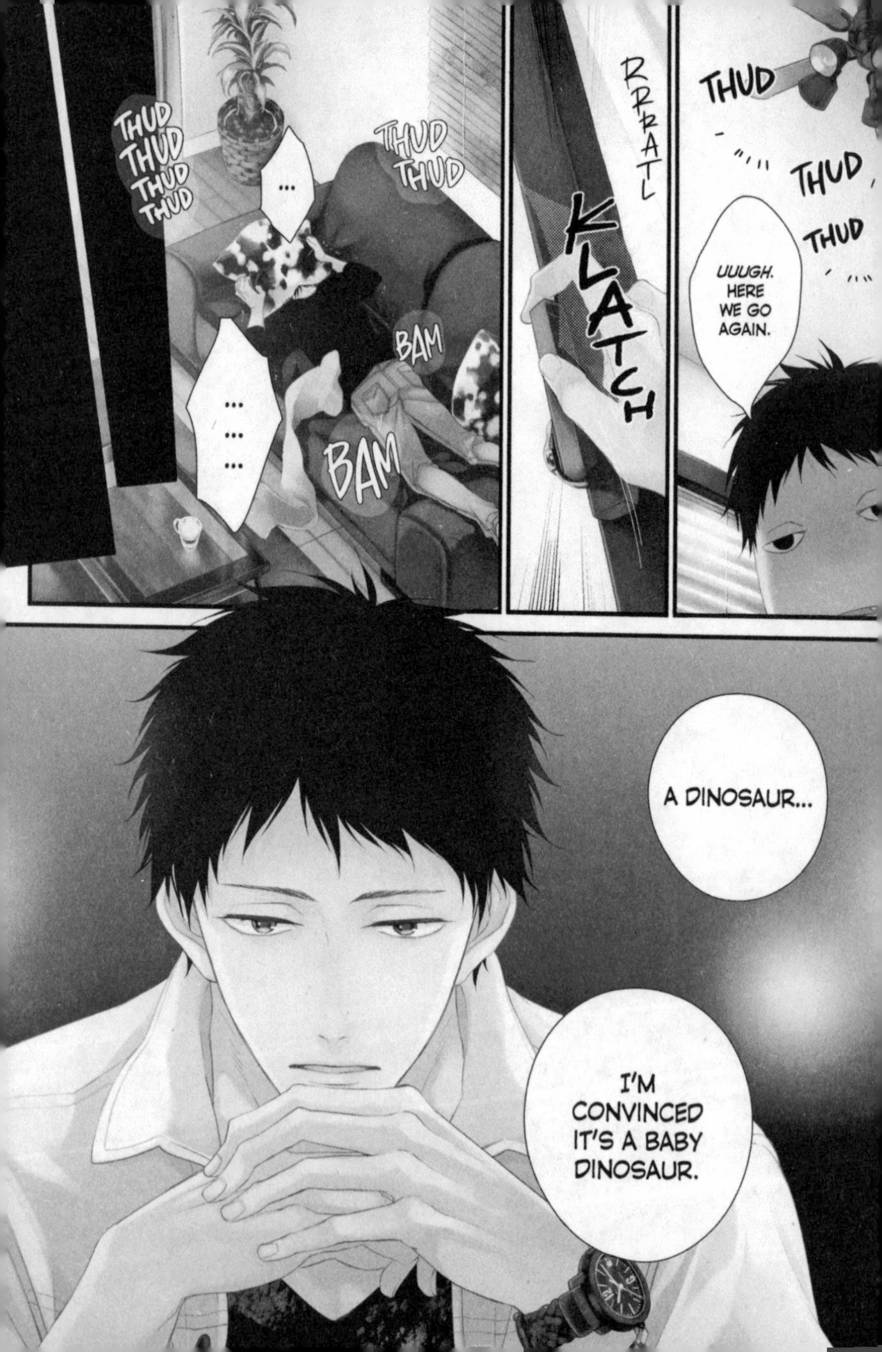

THUD
THUD
THUD
UUUGH. HERE WE GO AGAIN.
RRRATL
KLATCH
THUD THUD
...
THUD THUD THUD THUD
BAM
... ...
BAM
A DINOSAUR...
I'M CONVINCED IT'S A BABY DINOSAUR.

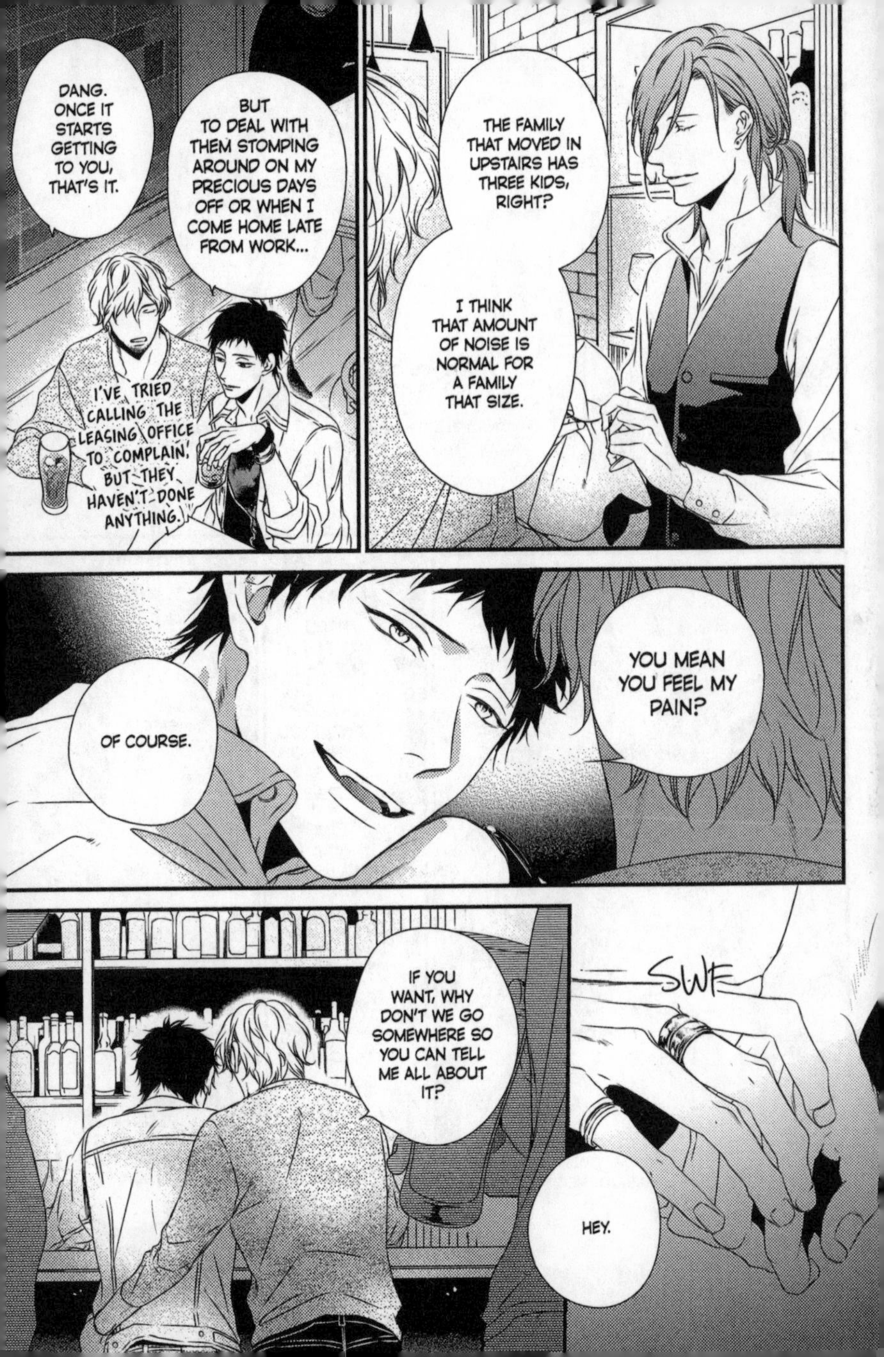
THE FAMILY THAT MOVED IN UPSTAIRS HAS THREE KIDS, RIGHT?
I THINK THAT AMOUNT OF NOISE IS NORMAL FOR A FAMILY THAT SIZE.
BUT TO DEAL WITH THEM STOMPING AROUND ON MY PRECIOUS DAYS OFF OR WHEN I COME HOME LATE FROM WORK...
DANG. ONCE IT STARTS GETTING TO YOU, THAT'S IT.
I'VE TRIED CALLING THE LEASING OFFICE TO COMPLAIN, BUT THEY HAVEN'T DONE ANYTHING.
YOU MEAN YOU FEEL MY PAIN?
OF COURSE.
SWF
HEY.
IF YOU WANT, WHY DON'T WE GO SOMEWHERE SO YOU CAN TELL ME ALL ABOUT IT?

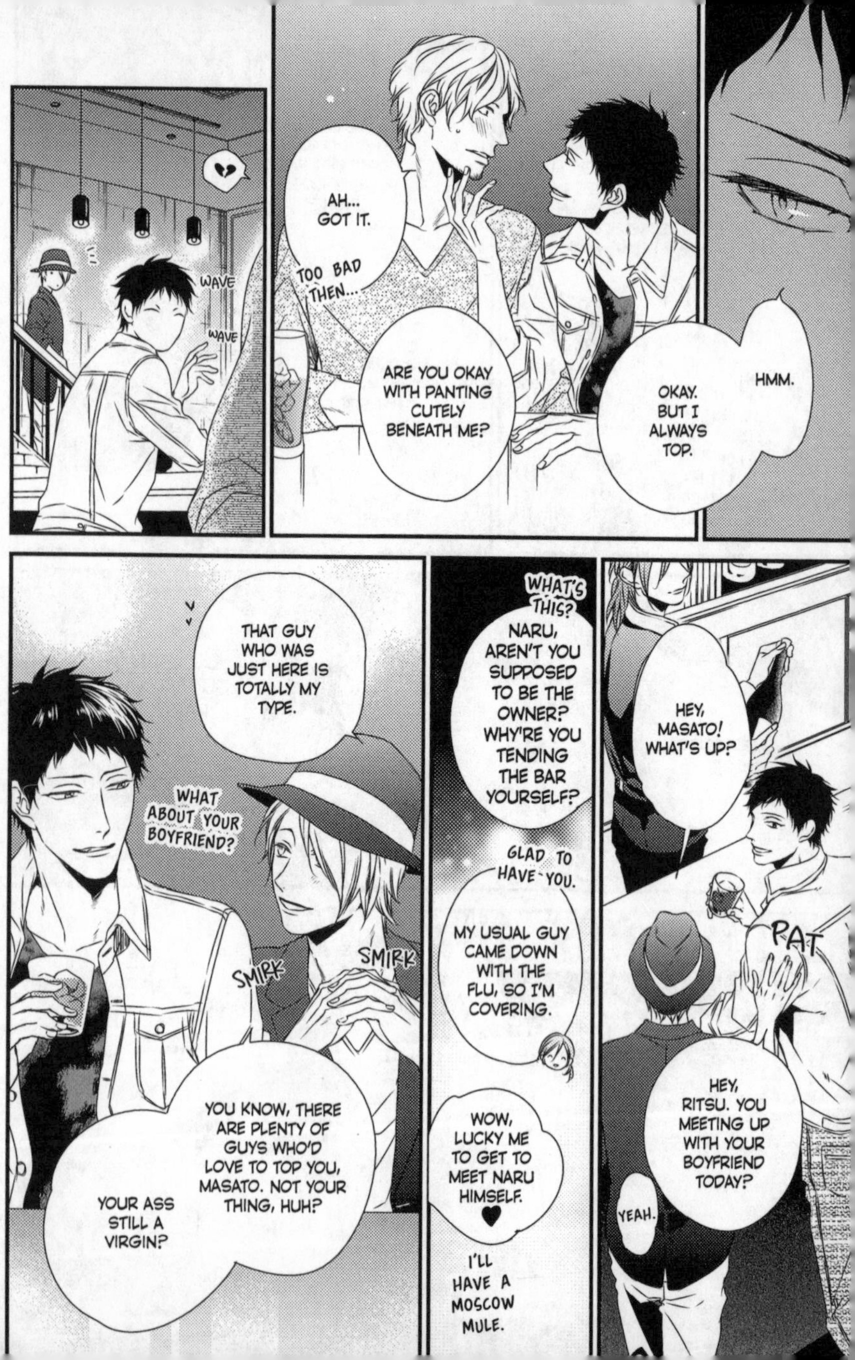
HMM.
OKAY. BUT I ALWAYS TOP.
ARE YOU OKAY WITH PANTING CUTELY BENEATH ME?
AH... GOT IT.
TOO BAD THEN...
WAVE
WAVE
HEY, MASATO! WHAT'S UP?
PAT
HEY, RITSU. YOU MEETING UP WITH YOUR BOYFRIEND TODAY?
YEAH.
WHAT'S THIS?
NARU, AREN'T YOU SUPPOSED TO BE THE OWNER? WHY'RE YOU TENDING THE BAR YOURSELF?
GLAD TO HAVE YOU.
MY USUAL GUY CAME DOWN WITH THE FLU, SO I'M COVERING.
WOW, LUCKY ME TO GET TO MEET NARU HIMSELF. ♥
I'LL HAVE A MOSCOW MULE.
THAT GUY WHO WAS JUST HERE IS TOTALLY MY TYPE.
WHAT ABOUT YOUR BOYFRIEND?
SMIRK
SMIRK
YOU KNOW, THERE ARE PLENTY OF GUYS WHO'D LOVE TO TOP YOU, MASATO. NOT YOUR THING, HUH?
YOUR ASS STILL A VIRGIN?

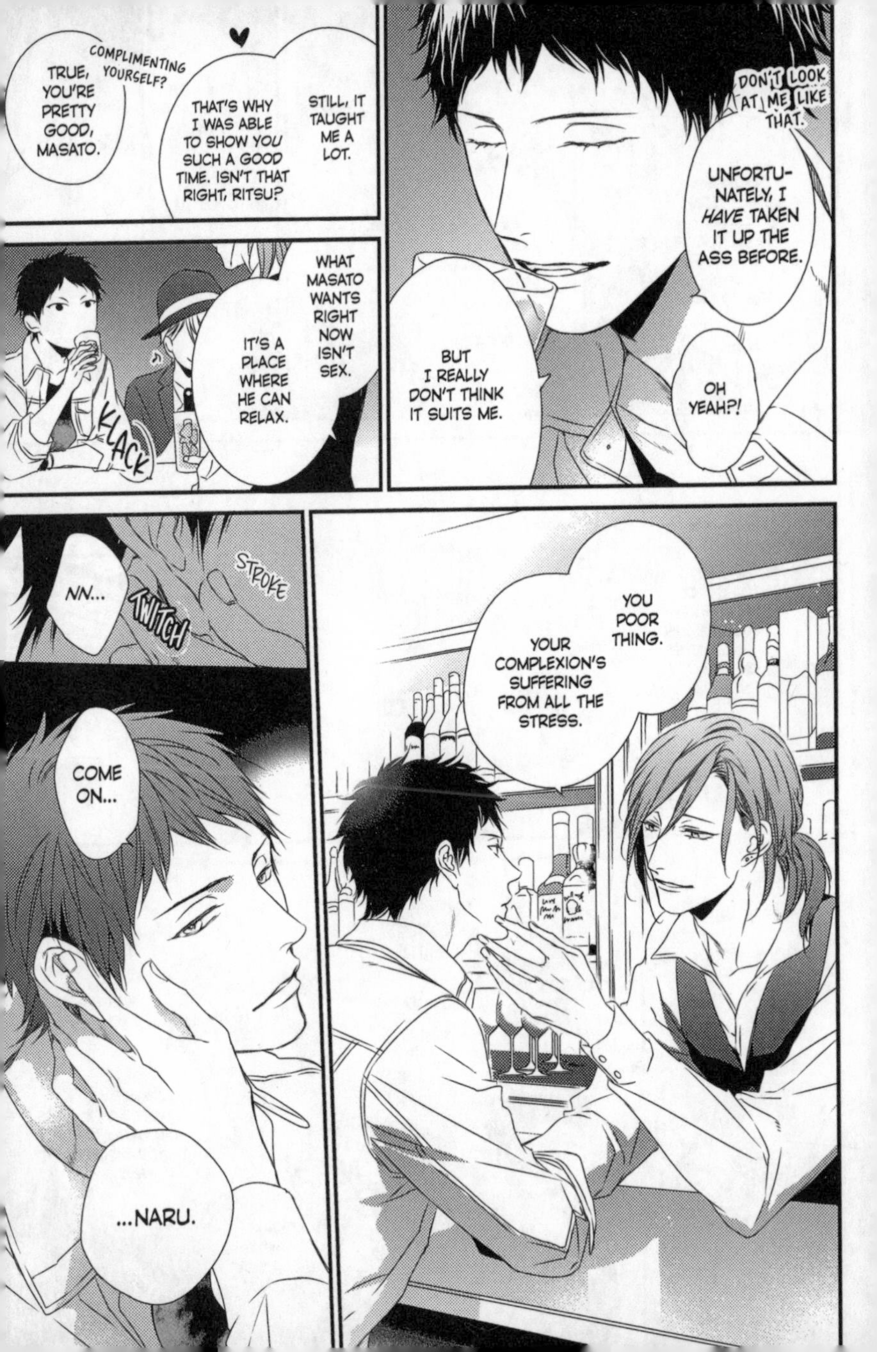
DON'T LOOK AT ME LIKE THAT.
UNFORTUNATELY, I *HAVE* TAKEN IT UP THE ASS BEFORE.
OH YEAH?!
BUT I REALLY DON'T THINK IT SUITS ME.
STILL, IT TAUGHT ME A LOT.
THAT'S WHY I WAS ABLE TO SHOW *YOU* SUCH A GOOD TIME. ISN'T THAT RIGHT, RITSU?
COMPLIMENTING YOURSELF?
TRUE, YOU'RE PRETTY GOOD, MASATO.
WHAT MASATO WANTS RIGHT NOW ISN'T SEX.
IT'S A PLACE WHERE HE CAN RELAX.
KLACK
YOU POOR THING.
YOUR COMPLEXION'S SUFFERING FROM ALL THE STRESS.
STROKE
NN...
TWITCH
COME ON...
...NARU.

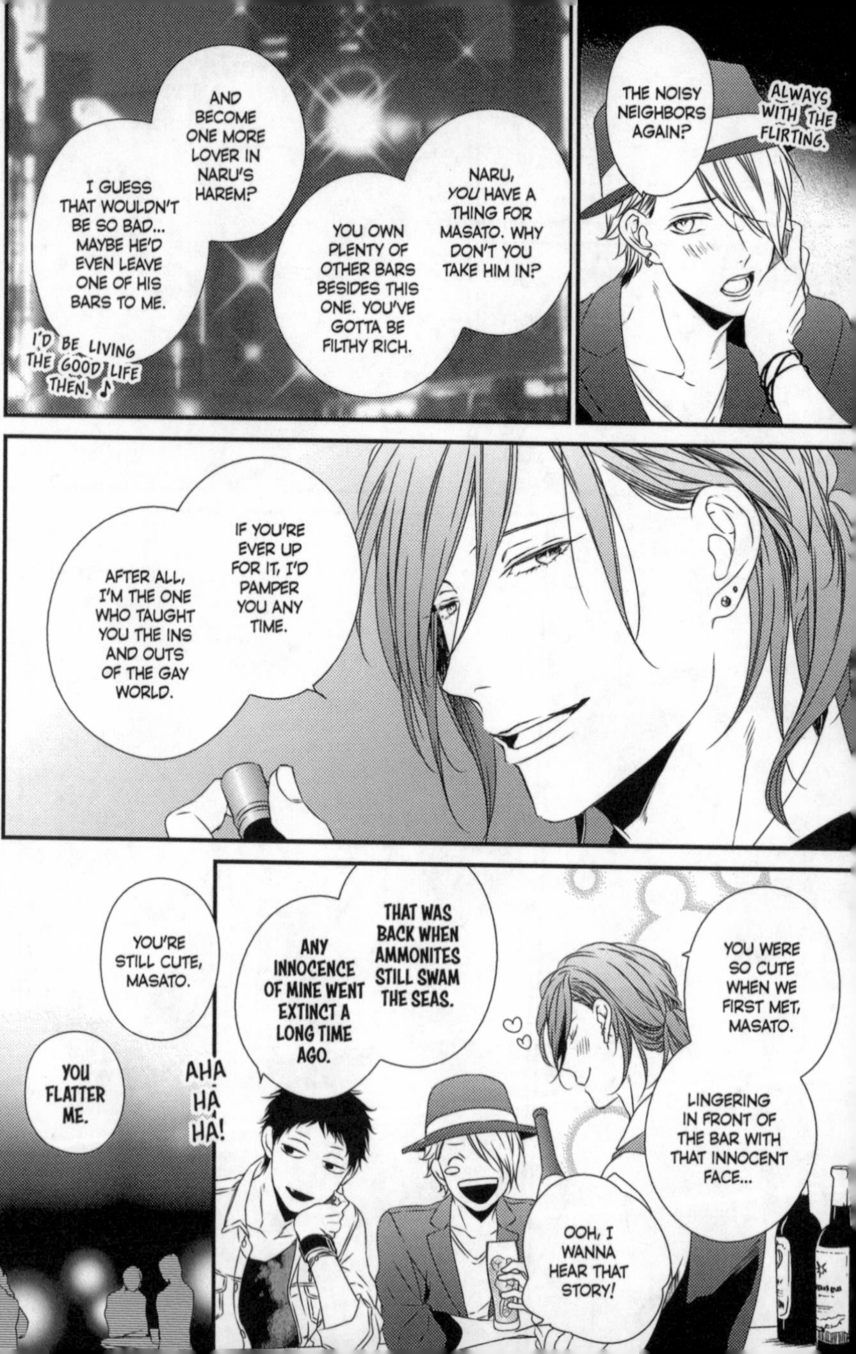
THE NOISY NEIGHBORS AGAIN?
ALWAYS WITH THE FLIRTING.
NARU, *YOU* HAVE A THING FOR MASATO. WHY DON'T YOU TAKE HIM IN?
YOU OWN PLENTY OF OTHER BARS BESIDES THIS ONE. YOU'VE GOTTA BE FILTHY RICH.
AND BECOME ONE MORE LOVER IN NARU'S HAREM?
I GUESS THAT WOULDN'T BE SO BAD... MAYBE HE'D EVEN LEAVE ONE OF HIS BARS TO ME.
I'D BE LIVING THE GOOD LIFE THEN. ♪
IF YOU'RE EVER UP FOR IT, I'D PAMPER YOU ANY TIME.
AFTER ALL, I'M THE ONE WHO TAUGHT YOU THE INS AND OUTS OF THE GAY WORLD.
YOU WERE SO CUTE WHEN WE FIRST MET, MASATO.
LINGERING IN FRONT OF THE BAR WITH THAT INNOCENT FACE...
OOH, I WANNA HEAR THAT STORY!
THAT WAS BACK WHEN AMMONITES STILL SWAM THE SEAS.
ANY INNOCENCE OF MINE WENT EXTINCT A LONG TIME AGO.
AHA HA HA!
YOU'RE STILL CUTE, MASATO.
YOU FLATTER ME.

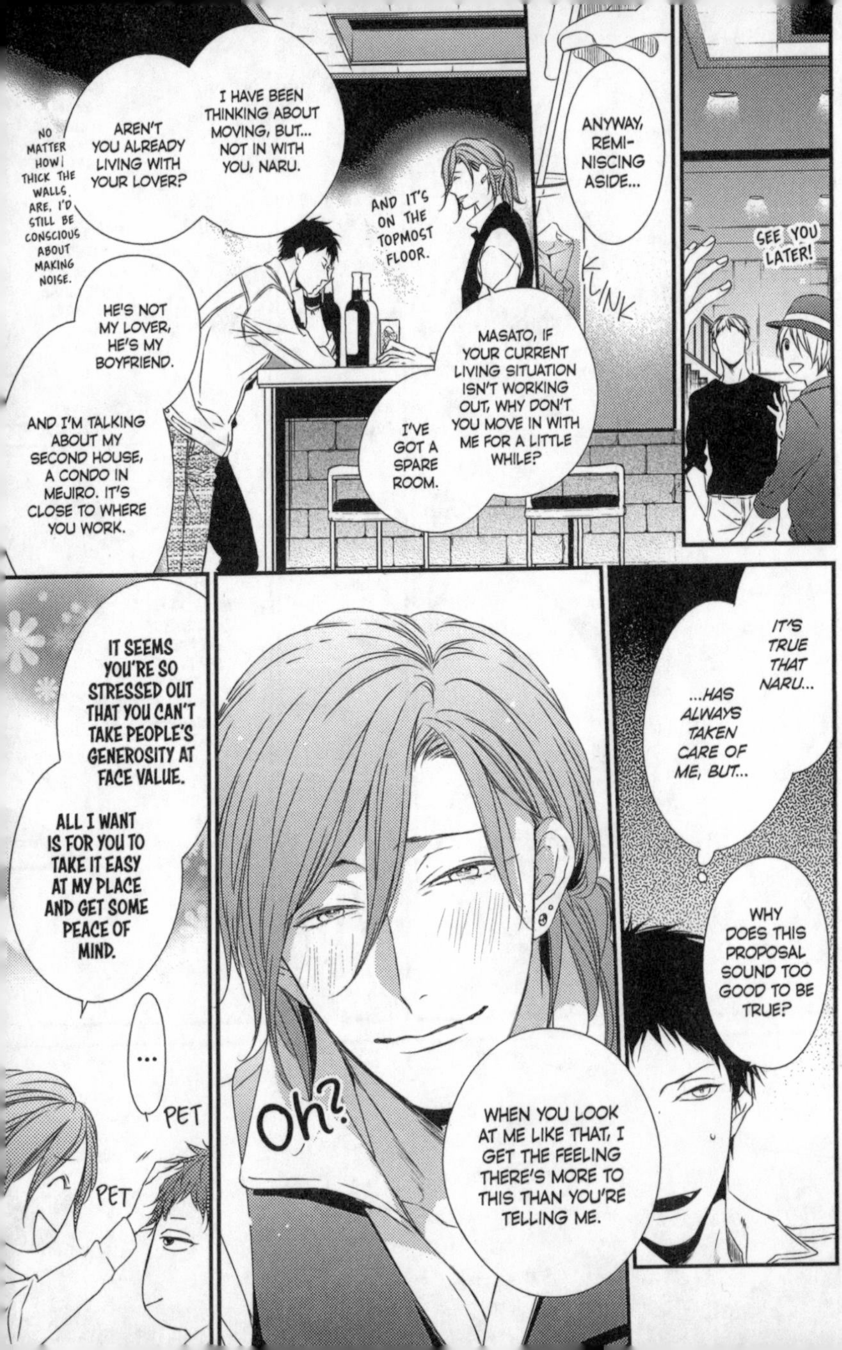
SEE YOU LATER!
ANYWAY, REMINISCING ASIDE...
KLINK
MASATO, IF YOUR CURRENT LIVING SITUATION ISN'T WORKING OUT, WHY DON'T YOU MOVE IN WITH ME FOR A LITTLE WHILE?
I'VE GOT A SPARE ROOM.
I HAVE BEEN THINKING ABOUT MOVING, BUT... NOT IN WITH YOU, NARU.
AREN'T YOU ALREADY LIVING WITH YOUR LOVER?
HE'S NOT MY LOVER, HE'S MY BOYFRIEND.
AND I'M TALKING ABOUT MY SECOND HOUSE, A CONDO IN MEJIRO. IT'S CLOSE TO WHERE YOU WORK.
AND IT'S ON THE TOPMOST FLOOR.
NO MATTER HOW THICK THE WALLS ARE, I'D STILL BE CONSCIOUS ABOUT MAKING NOISE.
IT'S TRUE THAT NARU...
...HAS ALWAYS TAKEN CARE OF ME, BUT...
WHY DOES THIS PROPOSAL SOUND TOO GOOD TO BE TRUE?
Oh?
WHEN YOU LOOK AT ME LIKE THAT, I GET THE FEELING THERE'S MORE TO THIS THAN YOU'RE TELLING ME.
IT SEEMS YOU'RE SO STRESSED OUT THAT YOU CAN'T TAKE PEOPLE'S GENEROSITY AT FACE VALUE.
ALL I WANT IS FOR YOU TO TAKE IT EASY AT MY PLACE AND GET SOME PEACE OF MIND.
...
PET
PET

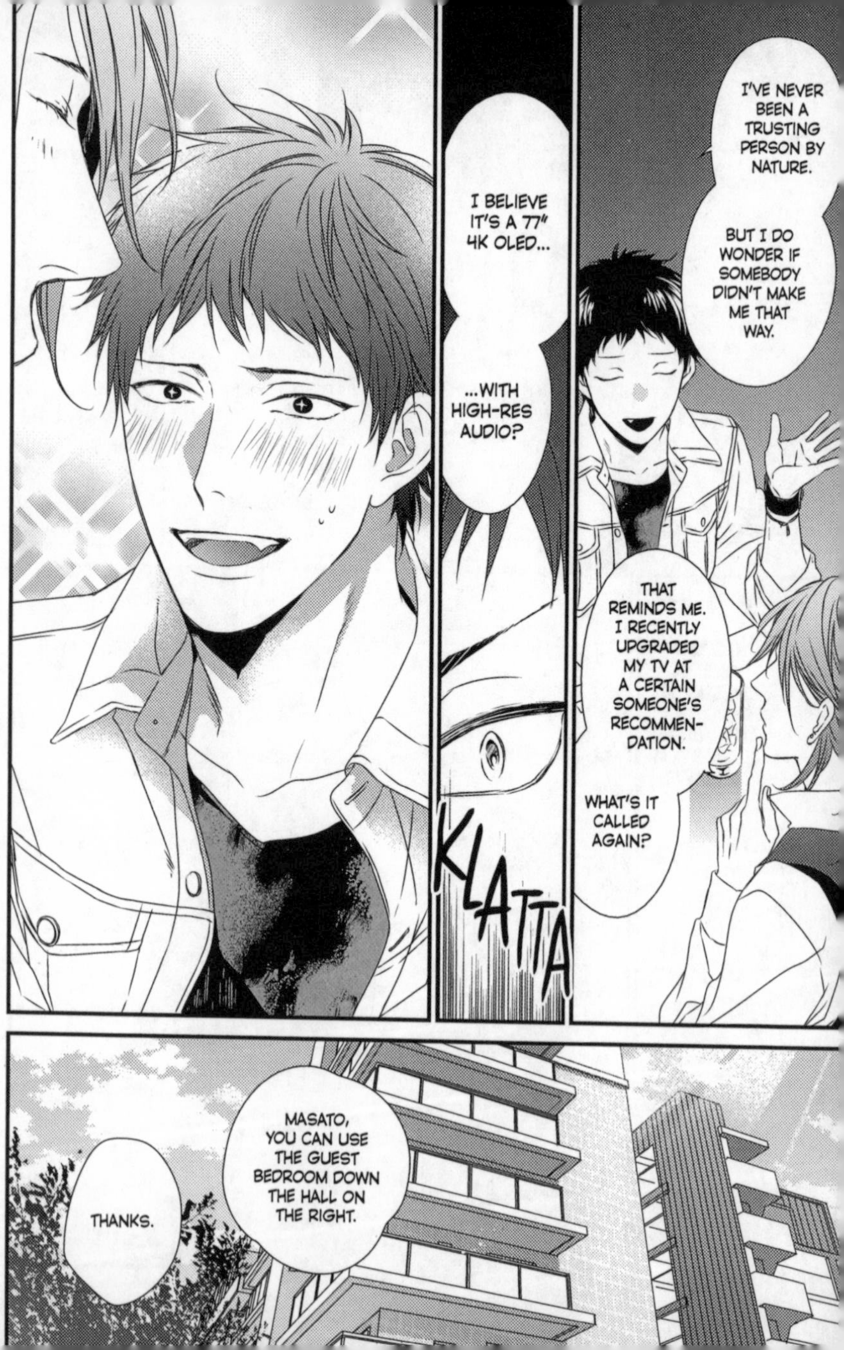
I'VE NEVER BEEN A TRUSTING PERSON BY NATURE.
BUT I DO WONDER IF SOMEBODY DIDN'T MAKE ME THAT WAY.
THAT REMINDS ME. I RECENTLY UPGRADED MY TV AT A CERTAIN SOMEONE'S RECOMMEN-DATION.
WHAT'S IT CALLED AGAIN?
KLATTA
I BELIEVE IT'S A 77" 4K OLED...
...WITH HIGH-RES AUDIO?
MASATO, YOU CAN USE THE GUEST BEDROOM DOWN THE HALL ON THE RIGHT.
THANKS.

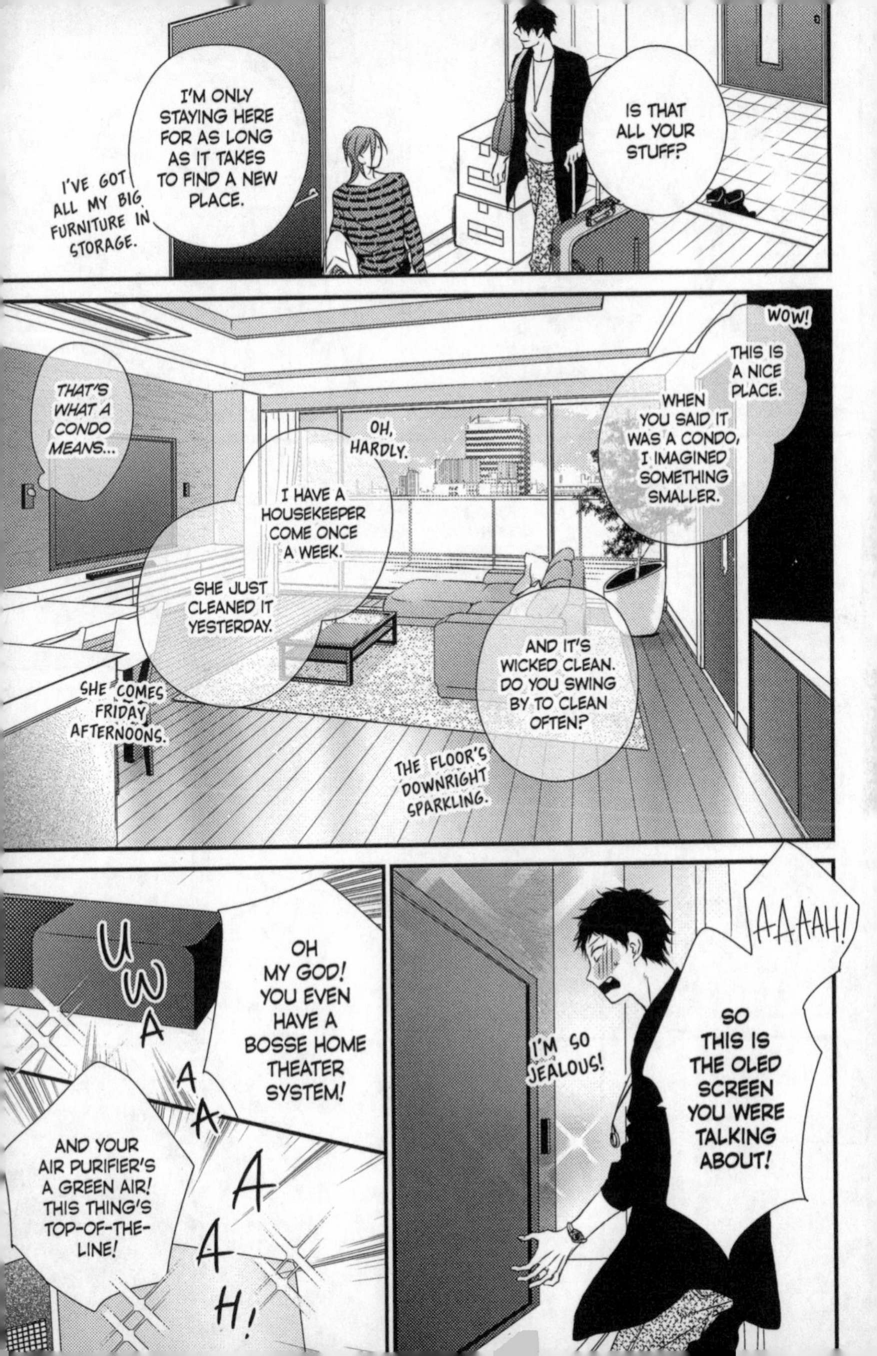
IS THAT ALL YOUR STUFF?
I'M ONLY STAYING HERE FOR AS LONG AS IT TAKES TO FIND A NEW PLACE.
I'VE GOT ALL MY BIG FURNITURE IN STORAGE.
WOW!
THIS IS A NICE PLACE.
WHEN YOU SAID IT WAS A CONDO, I IMAGINED SOMETHING SMALLER.
AND IT'S WICKED CLEAN. DO YOU SWING BY TO CLEAN OFTEN?
THE FLOOR'S DOWNRIGHT SPARKLING.
OH, HARDLY.
I HAVE A HOUSEKEEPER COME ONCE A WEEK.
SHE JUST CLEANED IT YESTERDAY.
THAT'S WHAT A CONDO MEANS...
SHE COMES FRIDAY AFTERNOONS.
AAAAH!
SO THIS IS THE OLED SCREEN YOU WERE TALKING ABOUT!
I'M SO JEALOUS!
UWAAAAAH!
OH MY GOD! YOU EVEN HAVE A BOSSE HOME THEATER SYSTEM!
AND YOUR AIR PURIFIER'S A GREEN AIR! THIS THING'S TOP-OF-THE-LINE!

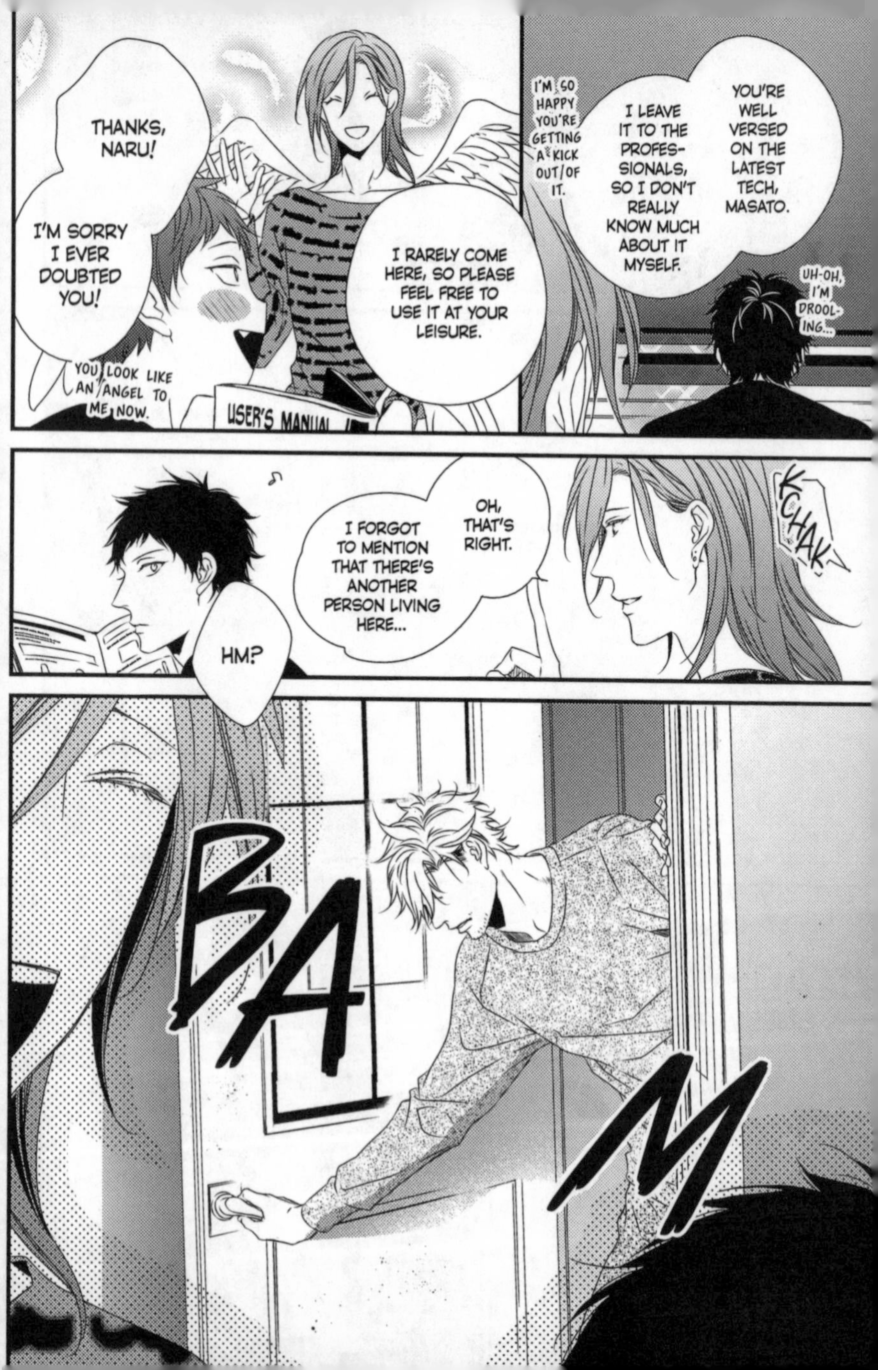
YOU'RE WELL VERSED ON THE LATEST TECH, MASATO.
I LEAVE IT TO THE PROFESSIONALS, SO I DON'T REALLY KNOW MUCH ABOUT IT MYSELF.
I'M SO HAPPY YOU'RE GETTING A KICK OUT OF IT.
UH-OH, I'M DROOLING...
I RARELY COME HERE, SO PLEASE FEEL FREE TO USE IT AT YOUR LEISURE.
THANKS, NARU!
I'M SORRY I EVER DOUBTED YOU!
YOU LOOK LIKE AN ANGEL TO ME NOW.
USER'S MANUAL
KCHAK
OH, THAT'S RIGHT.
I FORGOT TO MENTION THAT THERE'S ANOTHER PERSON LIVING HERE...
HM?
BAM

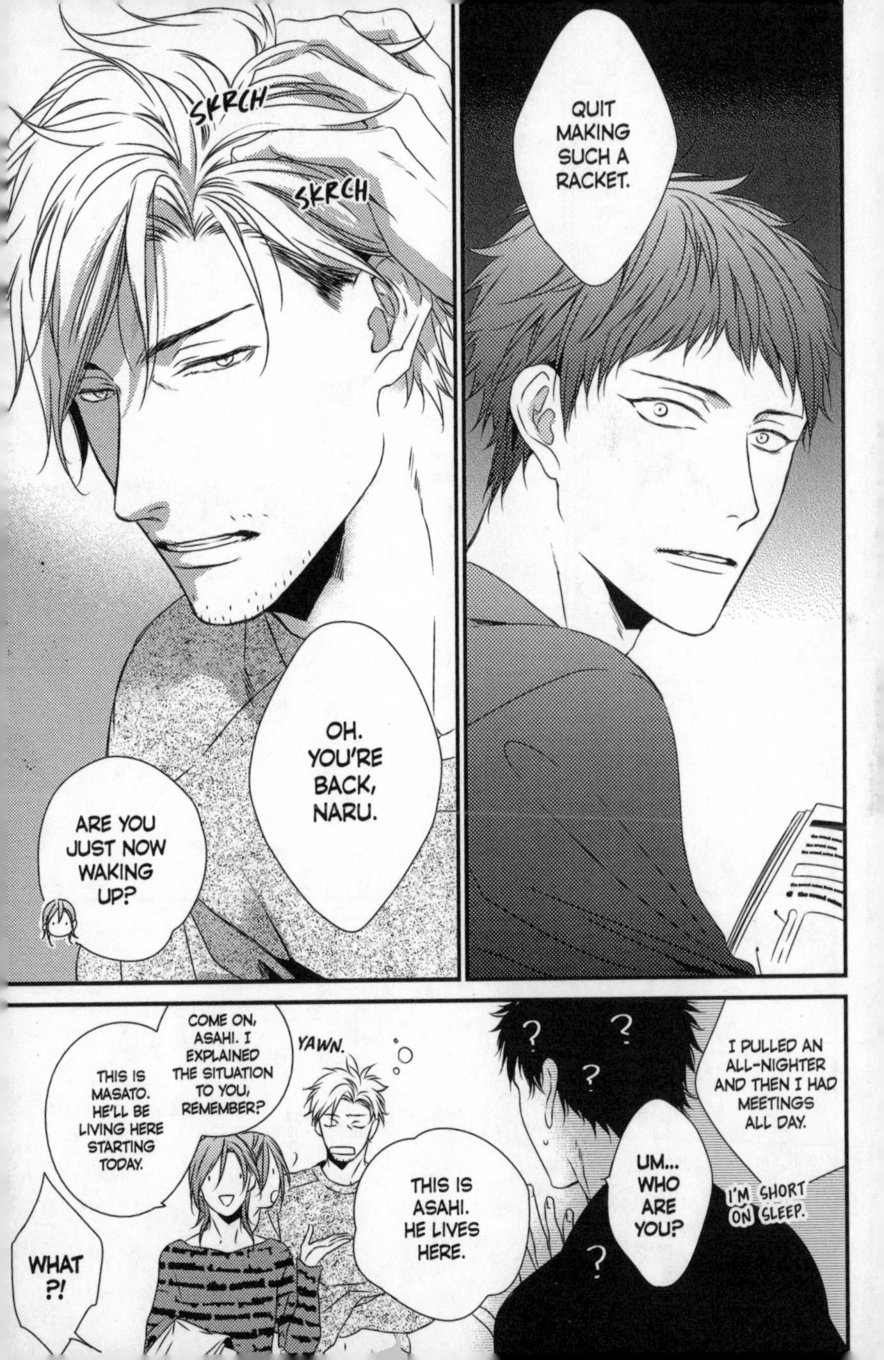
QUIT MAKING SUCH A RACKET.
SKRCH
SKRCH
OH. YOU'RE BACK, NARU.
ARE YOU JUST NOW WAKING UP?
I PULLED AN ALL-NIGHTER AND THEN I HAD MEETINGS ALL DAY.
I'M SHORT ON SLEEP.
UM... WHO ARE YOU?
THIS IS ASAHI. HE LIVES HERE.
YAWN.
COME ON, ASAHI. I EXPLAINED THE SITUATION TO YOU, REMEMBER?
THIS IS MASATO. HE'LL BE LIVING HERE STARTING TODAY.
WHAT?!

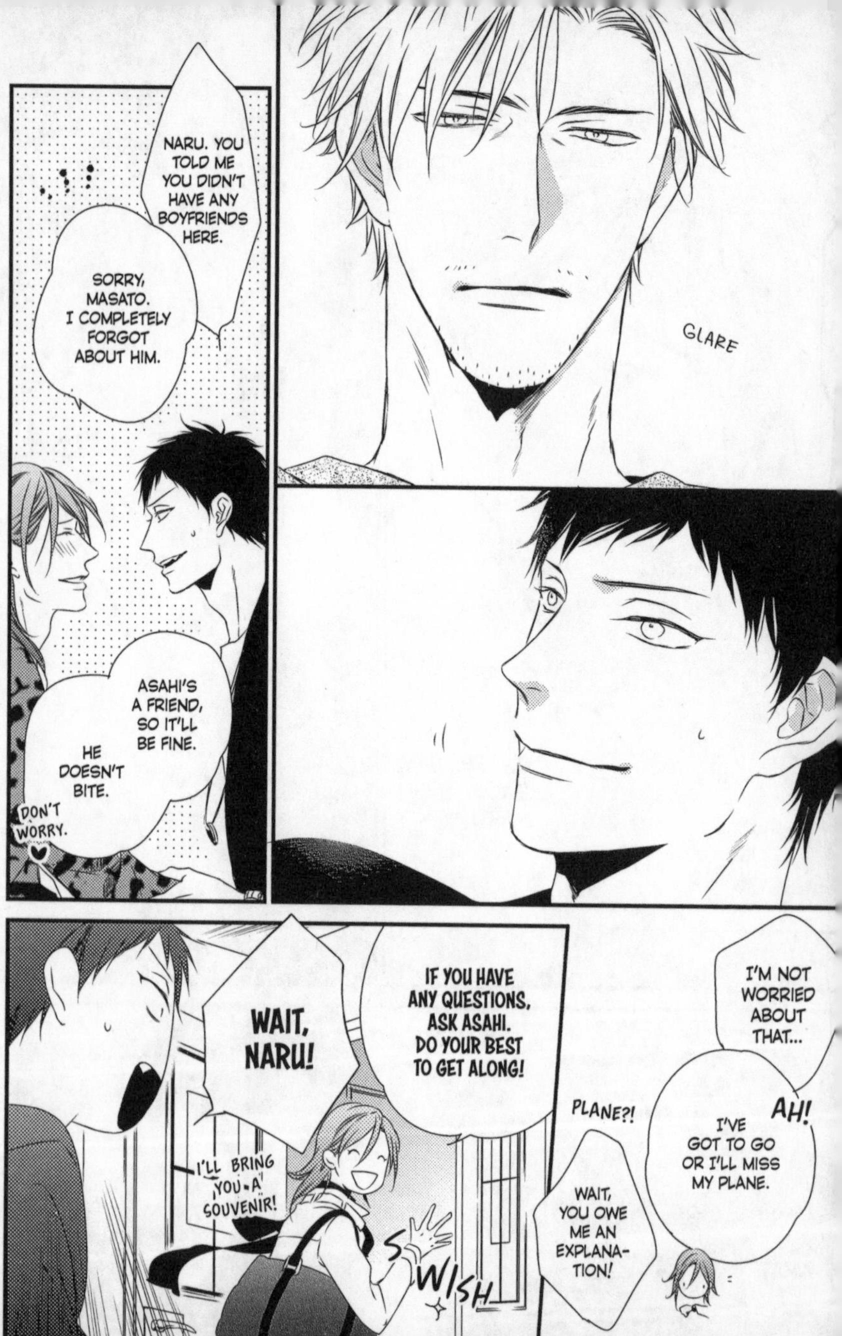
GLARE
NARU. YOU TOLD ME YOU DIDN'T HAVE ANY BOYFRIENDS HERE.
SORRY, MASATO. I COMPLETELY FORGOT ABOUT HIM.
ASAHI'S A FRIEND, SO IT'LL BE FINE.
HE DOESN'T BITE.
DON'T WORRY.
I'M NOT WORRIED ABOUT THAT...
AH!
I'VE GOT TO GO OR I'LL MISS MY PLANE.
PLANE?!
WAIT, YOU OWE ME AN EXPLANATION!
IF YOU HAVE ANY QUESTIONS, ASK ASAHI. DO YOUR BEST TO GET ALONG!
WAIT, NARU!
I'LL BRING YOU A SOUVENIR!
SWISH

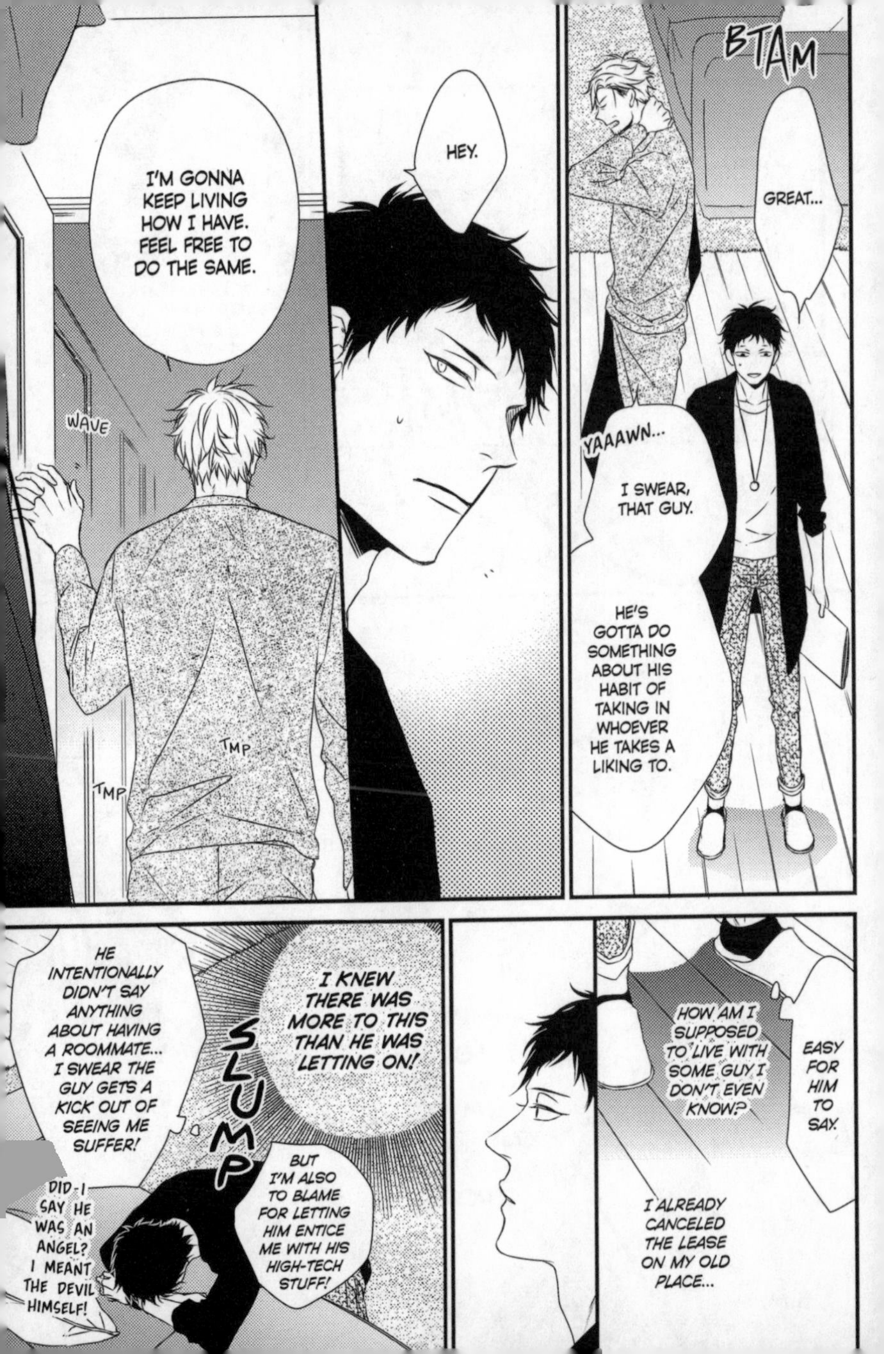
BTAM
GREAT...
YAAAWN...
I SWEAR, THAT GUY.
HE'S GOTTA DO SOMETHING ABOUT HIS HABIT OF TAKING IN WHOEVER HE TAKES A LIKING TO.
HEY.
I'M GONNA KEEP LIVING HOW I HAVE. FEEL FREE TO DO THE SAME.
WAVE
TMP
TMP
EASY FOR HIM TO SAY.
HOW AM I SUPPOSED TO LIVE WITH SOME GUY I DON'T EVEN KNOW?
I ALREADY CANCELED THE LEASE ON MY OLD PLACE...
I KNEW THERE WAS MORE TO THIS THAN HE WAS LETTING ON!
HE INTENTIONALLY DIDN'T SAY ANYTHING ABOUT HAVING A ROOMMATE... I SWEAR THE GUY GETS A KICK OUT OF SEEING ME SUFFER!
SLUMP
BUT I'M ALSO TO BLAME FOR LETTING HIM ENTICE ME WITH HIS HIGH-TECH STUFF!
DID I SAY HE WAS AN ANGEL? I MEANT THE DEVIL HIMSELF!

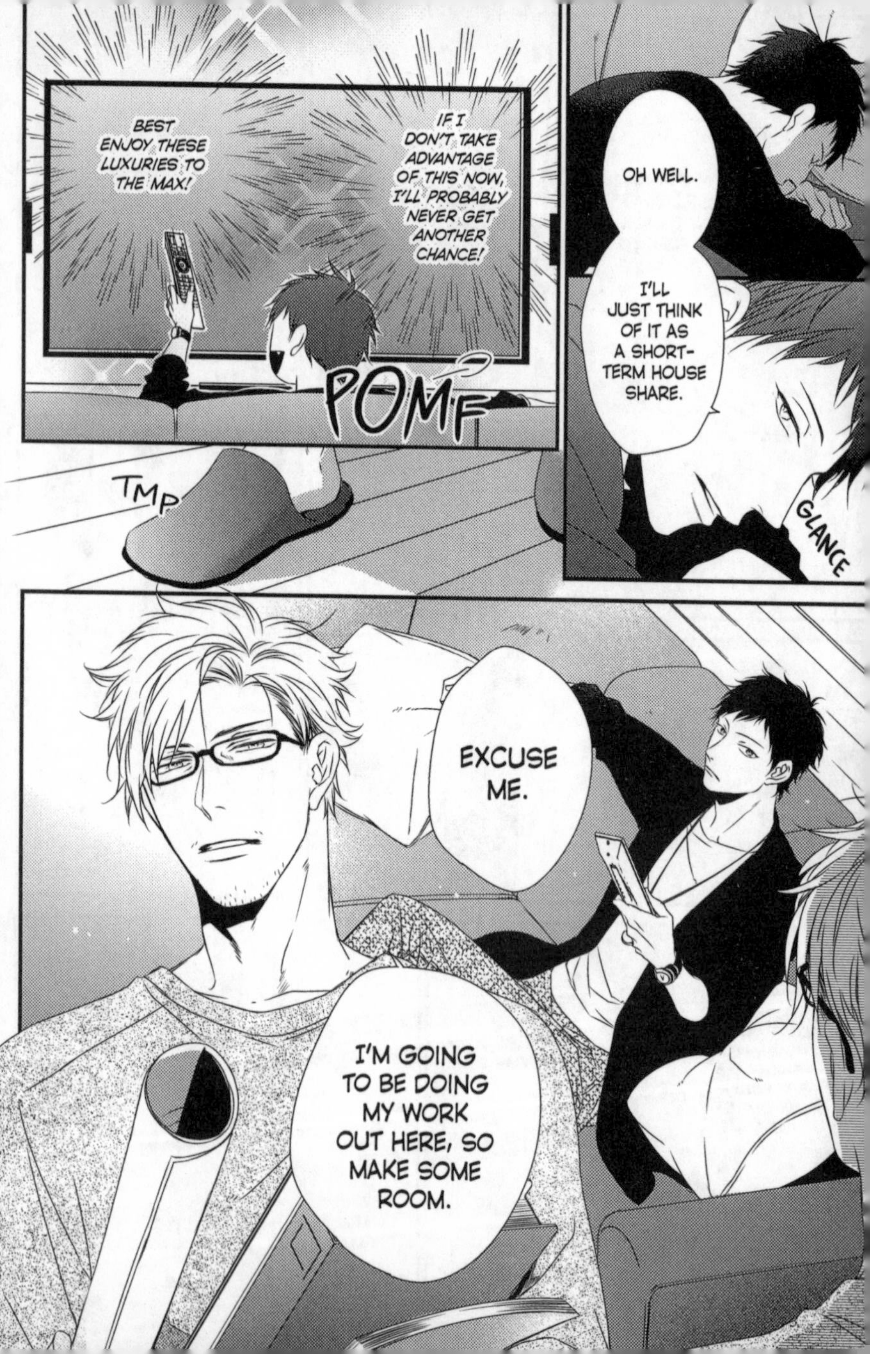
OH WELL.
I'LL JUST THINK OF IT AS A SHORT-TERM HOUSE SHARE.
GLANCE
IF I DON'T TAKE ADVANTAGE OF THIS NOW, I'LL PROBABLY NEVER GET ANOTHER CHANCE!
BEST ENJOY THESE LUXURIES TO THE MAX!
POMF
TMP
EXCUSE ME.
I'M GOING TO BE DOING MY WORK OUT HERE, SO MAKE SOME ROOM.

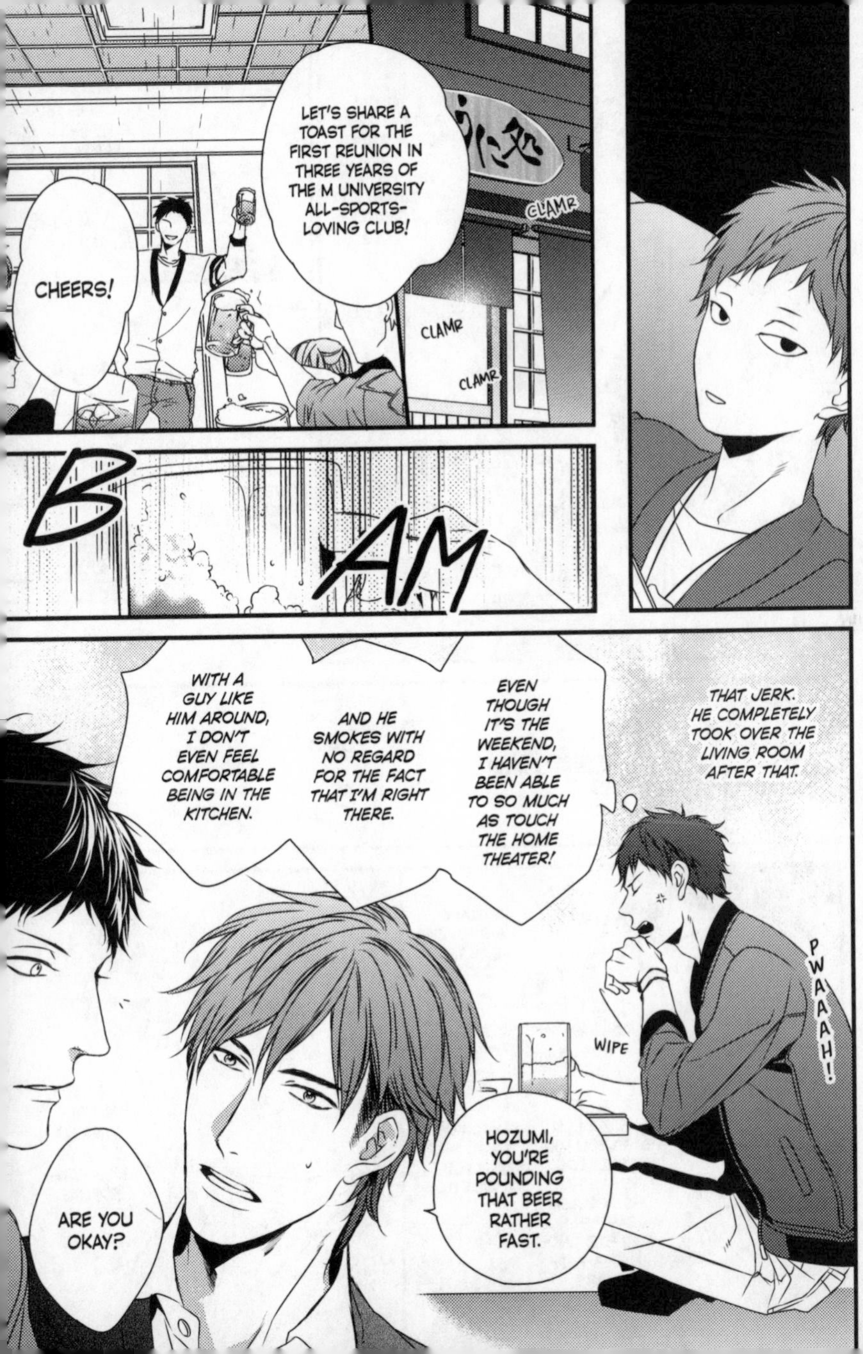
LET'S SHARE A TOAST FOR THE FIRST REUNION IN THREE YEARS OF THE M UNIVERSITY ALL-SPORTS-LOVING CLUB!
CLAMR
CLAMR
CLAMR
CHEERS!
BAM
THAT JERK. HE COMPLETELY TOOK OVER THE LIVING ROOM AFTER THAT.
EVEN THOUGH IT'S THE WEEKEND, I HAVEN'T BEEN ABLE TO SO MUCH AS TOUCH THE HOME THEATER!
AND HE SMOKES WITH NO REGARD FOR THE FACT THAT I'M RIGHT THERE.
WITH A GUY LIKE HIM AROUND, I DON'T EVEN FEEL COMFORTABLE BEING IN THE KITCHEN.
PWAAAH!
WIPE
HOZUMI, YOU'RE POUNDING THAT BEER RATHER FAST.
ARE YOU OKAY?

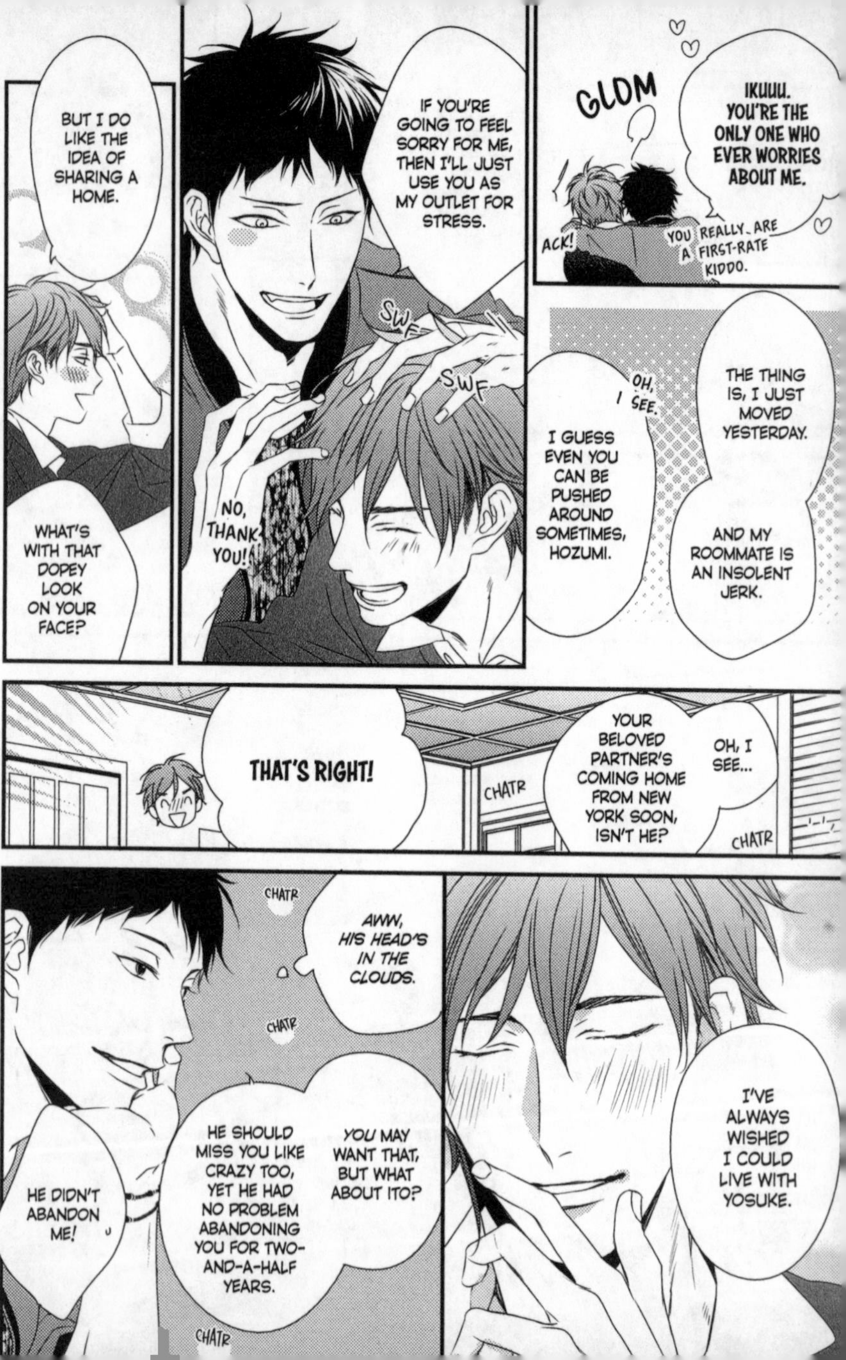
IKUUU. YOU'RE THE ONLY ONE WHO EVER WORRIES ABOUT ME.
GLOM
YOU REALLY ARE A FIRST-RATE KIDDO.
ACK!
THE THING IS, I JUST MOVED YESTERDAY.
AND MY ROOMMATE IS AN INSOLENT JERK.
OH, I SEE.
I GUESS EVEN YOU CAN BE PUSHED AROUND SOMETIMES, HOZUMI.
IF YOU'RE GOING TO FEEL SORRY FOR ME, THEN I'LL JUST USE YOU AS MY OUTLET FOR STRESS.
SWF
SWF
NO, THANK YOU!
BUT I DO LIKE THE IDEA OF SHARING A HOME.
WHAT'S WITH THAT DOPEY LOOK ON YOUR FACE?
OH, I SEE...
YOUR BELOVED PARTNER'S COMING HOME FROM NEW YORK SOON, ISN'T HE?
CHATR
CHATR
THAT'S RIGHT!
I'VE ALWAYS WISHED I COULD LIVE WITH YOSUKE.
CHATR
AWN, HIS HEAD'S IN THE CLOUDS.
CHATR
YOU MAY WANT THAT, BUT WHAT ABOUT ITO?
HE SHOULD MISS YOU LIKE CRAZY TOO, YET HE HAD NO PROBLEM ABANDONING YOU FOR TWO-AND-A-HALF YEARS.
HE DIDN'T ABANDON ME!
CHATR

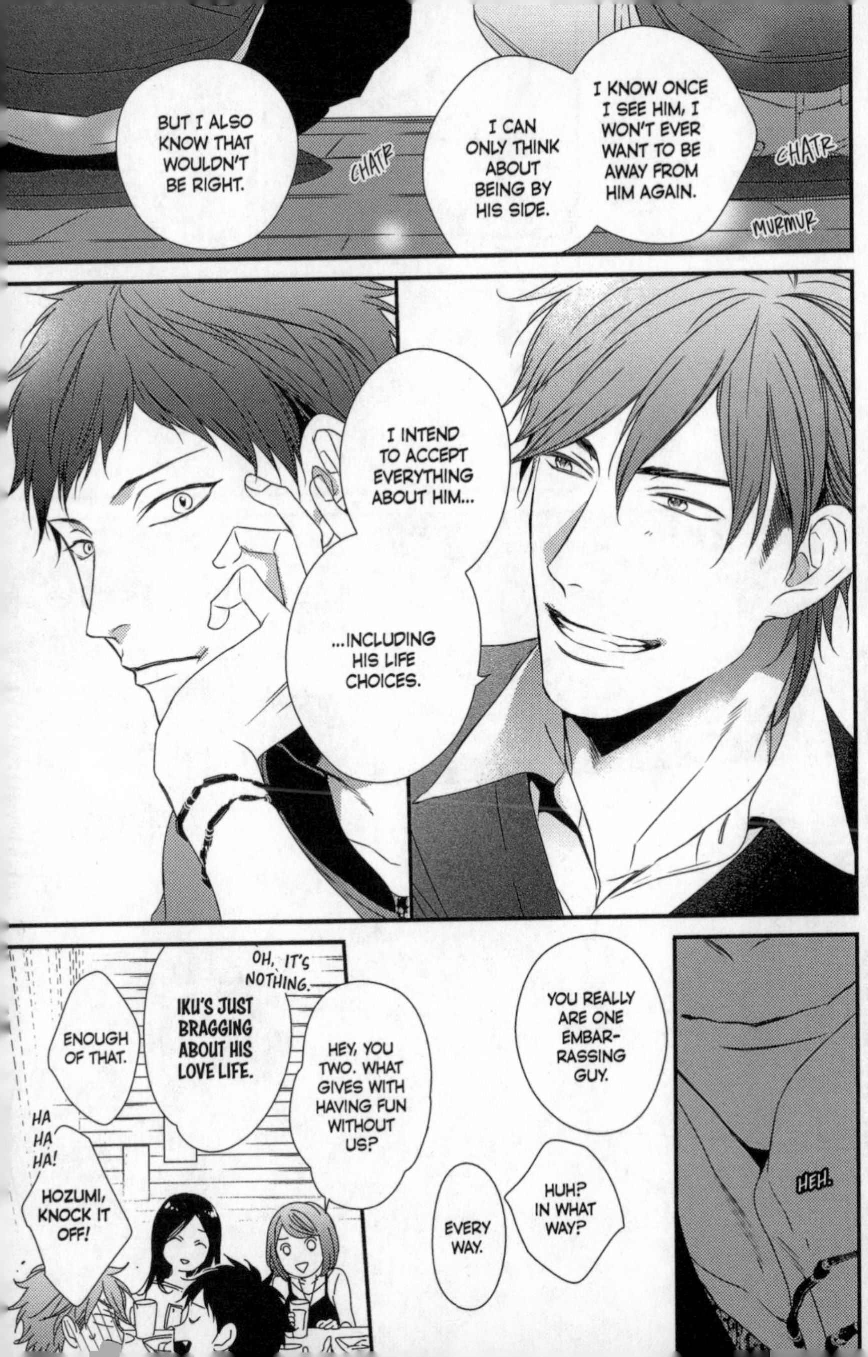
CHATR
I KNOW ONCE I SEE HIM, I WON'T EVER WANT TO BE AWAY FROM HIM AGAIN.
MURMUR
I CAN ONLY THINK ABOUT BEING BY HIS SIDE.
CHATR
BUT I ALSO KNOW THAT WOULDN'T BE RIGHT.
I INTEND TO ACCEPT EVERYTHING ABOUT HIM...
...INCLUDING HIS LIFE CHOICES.
HEH.
YOU REALLY ARE ONE EMBAR-RASSING GUY.
HUH? IN WHAT WAY?
EVERY WAY.
HEY, YOU TWO. WHAT GIVES WITH HAVING FUN WITHOUT US?
OH, IT'S NOTHING.
IKU'S JUST BRAGGING ABOUT HIS LOVE LIFE.
ENOUGH OF THAT.
HA HA HA!
HOZUMI, KNOCK IT OFF!

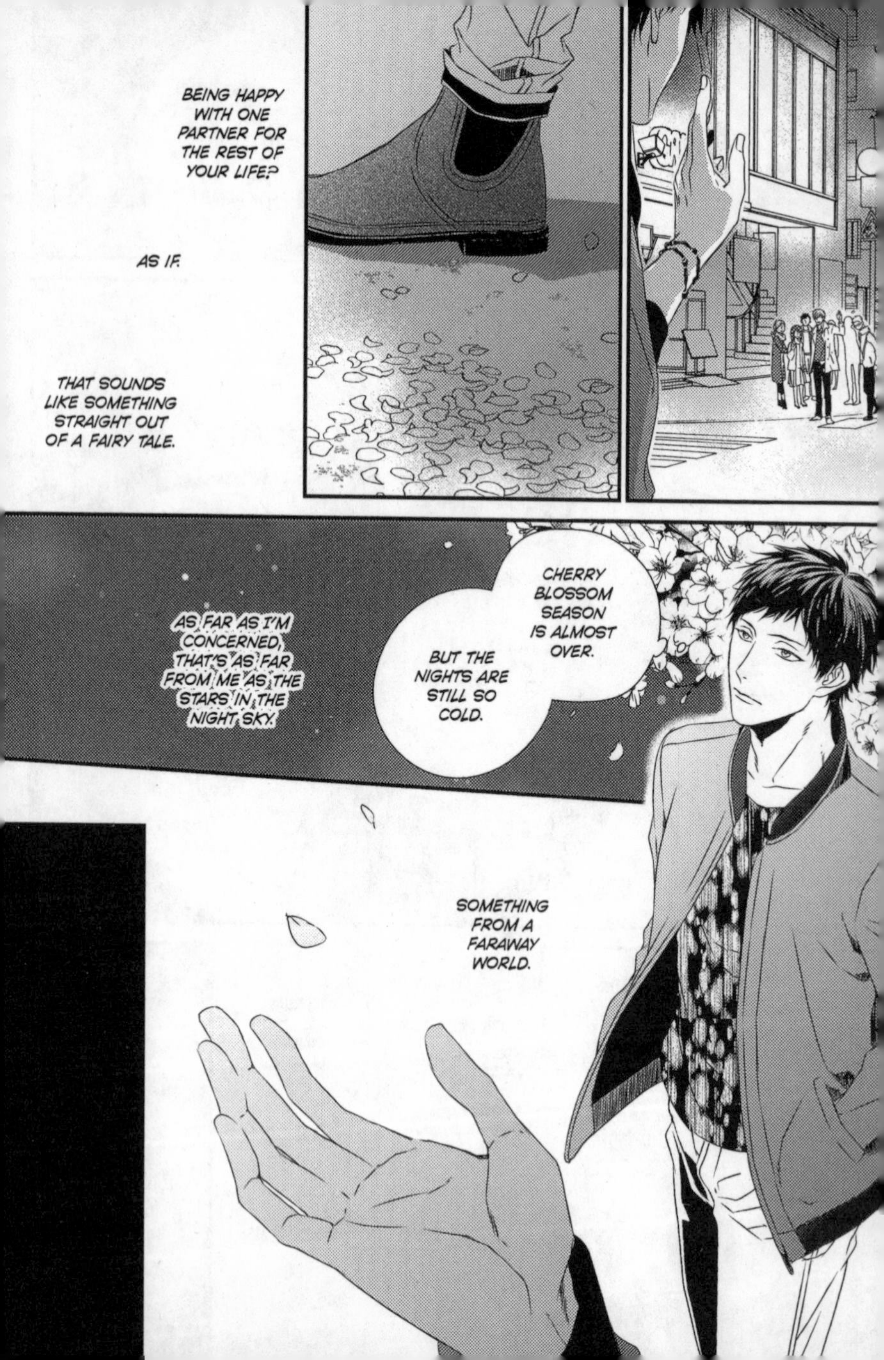
BEING HAPPY WITH ONE PARTNER FOR THE REST OF YOUR LIFE?
AS IF.
THAT SOUNDS LIKE SOMETHING STRAIGHT OUT OF A FAIRY TALE.
CHERRY BLOSSOM SEASON IS ALMOST OVER.
BUT THE NIGHTS ARE STILL SO COLD.
AS FAR AS I'M CONCERNED, THAT'S AS FAR FROM ME AS THE STARS IN THE NIGHT SKY.
SOMETHING FROM A FARAWAY WORLD.

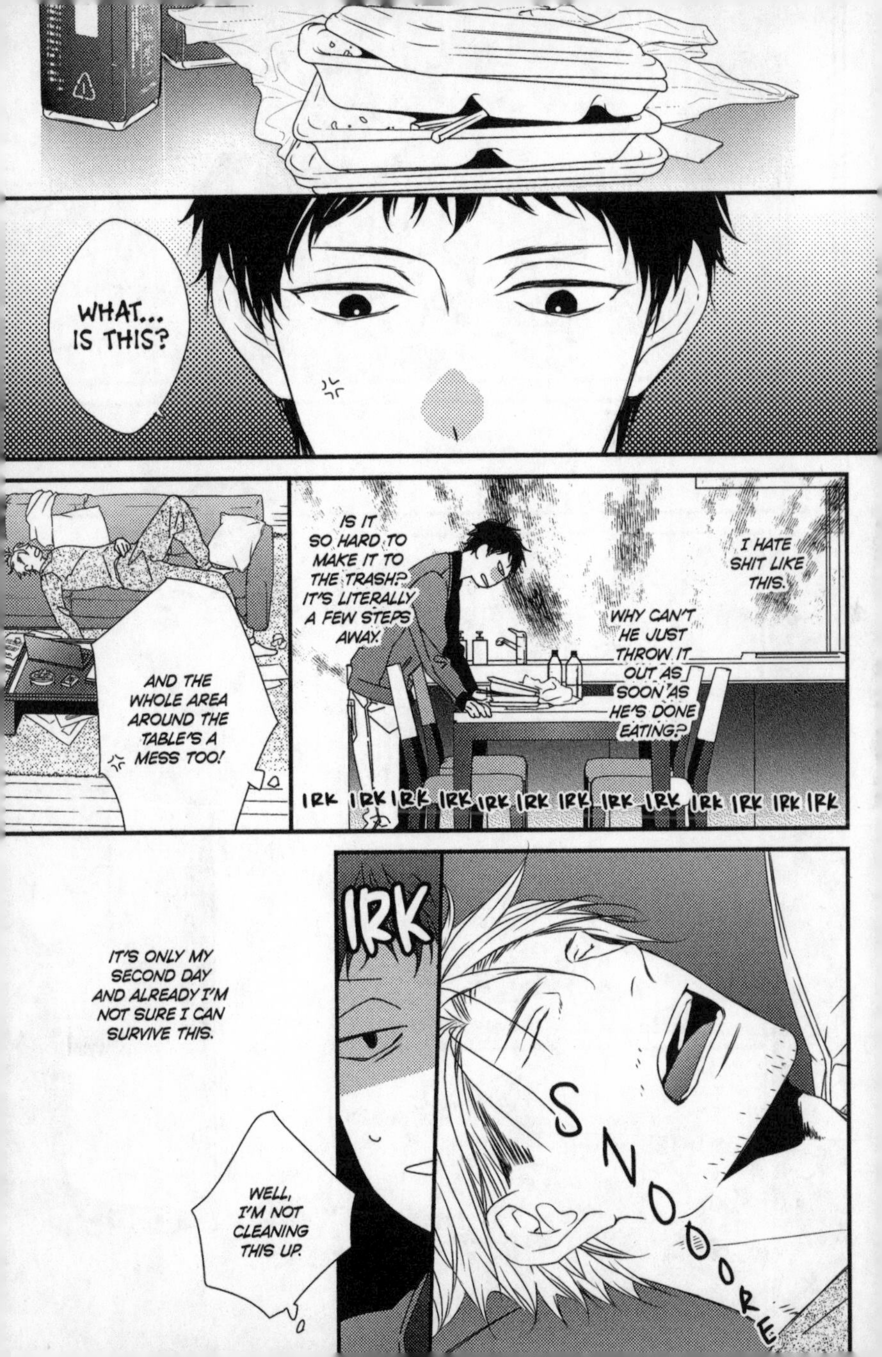
WHAT... IS THIS?
I HATE SHIT LIKE THIS.
WHY CAN'T HE JUST THROW IT OUT AS SOON AS HE'S DONE EATING?
IS IT SO HARD TO MAKE IT TO THE TRASH? IT'S LITERALLY A FEW STEPS AWAY.
IRK IRK IRK IRK IRK IRK IRK IRK IRK IRK IRK IRK IRK
AND THE WHOLE AREA AROUND THE TABLE'S A MESS TOO!
SNOOORE
IRK
IT'S ONLY MY SECOND DAY AND ALREADY I'M NOT SURE I CAN SURVIVE THIS.
WELL, I'M NOT CLEANING THIS UP.

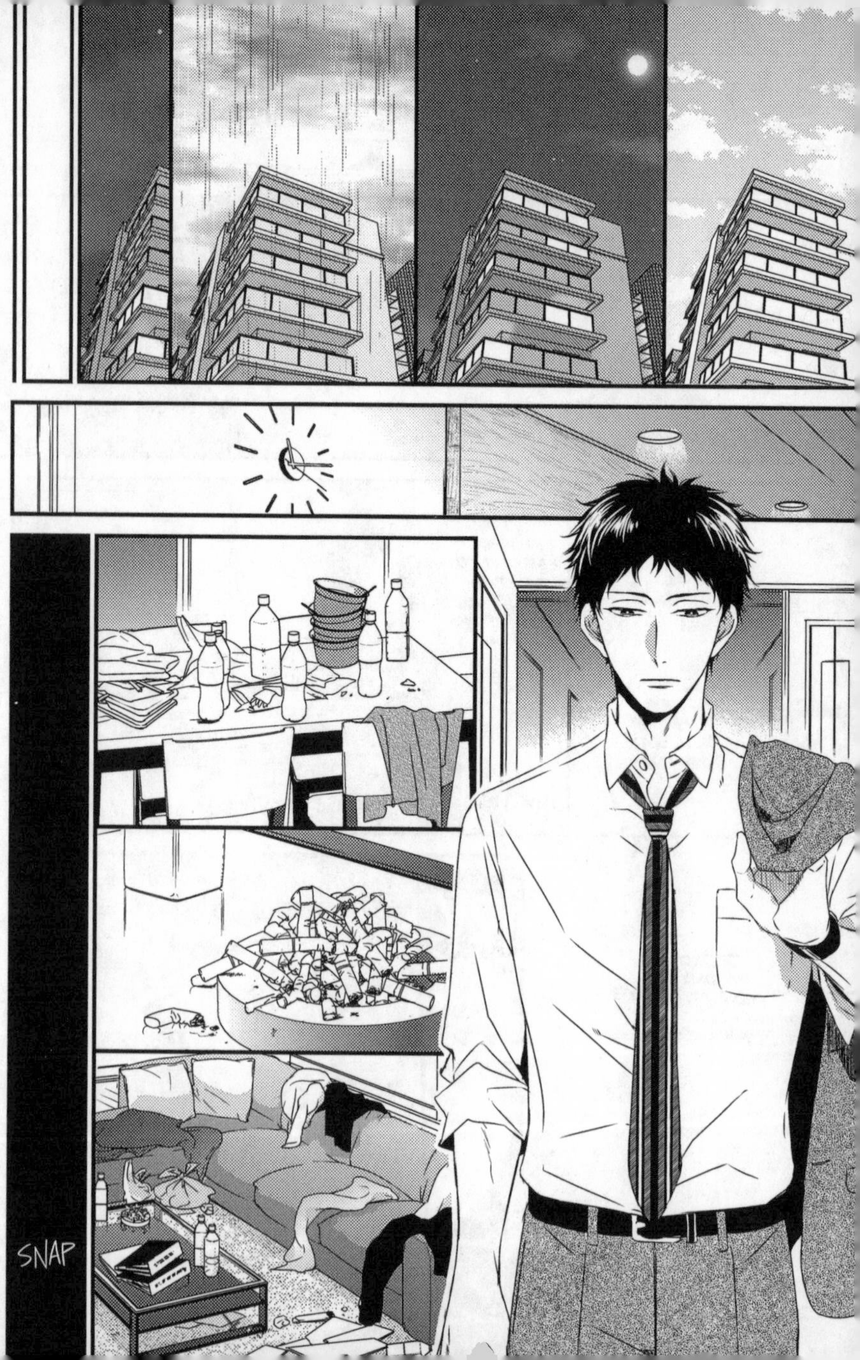
SNAP

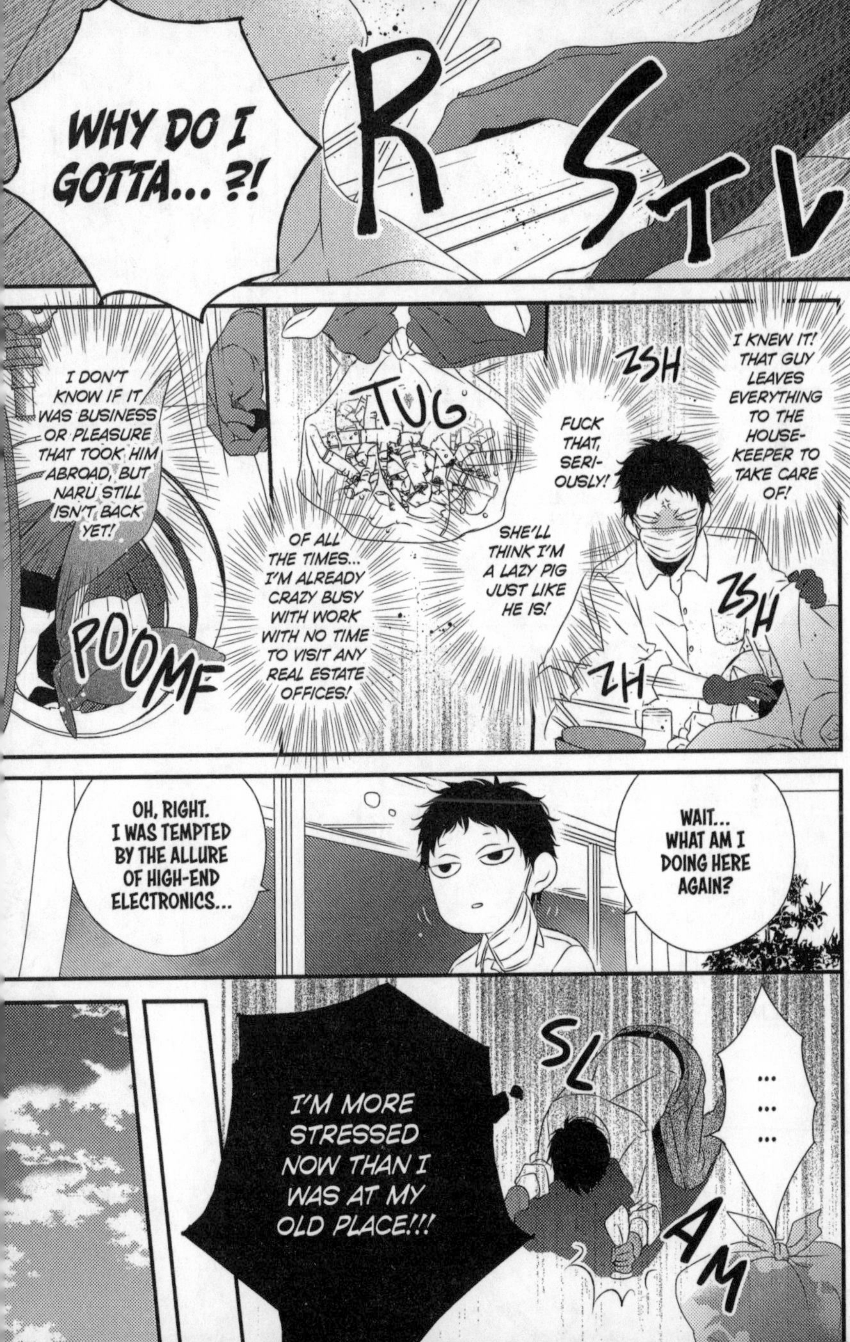
RSTL
WHY DO I GOTTA... ?!
I KNEW IT! THAT GUY LEAVES EVERYTHING TO THE HOUSE-KEEPER TO TAKE CARE OF!
ZSH
FUCK THAT, SERI-OUSLY!
SHE'LL THINK I'M A LAZY PIG JUST LIKE HE IS!
ZSH
ZH
TUG
OF ALL THE TIMES... I'M ALREADY CRAZY BUSY WITH WORK WITH NO TIME TO VISIT ANY REAL ESTATE OFFICES!
I DON'T KNOW IF IT WAS BUSINESS OR PLEASURE THAT TOOK HIM ABROAD, BUT NARU STILL ISN'T BACK YET!
POOMF
WAIT... WHAT AM I DOING HERE AGAIN?
OH, RIGHT. I WAS TEMPTED BY THE ALLURE OF HIGH-END ELECTRONICS...
... ...
SLAM
I'M MORE STRESSED NOW THAN I WAS AT MY OLD PLACE!!!

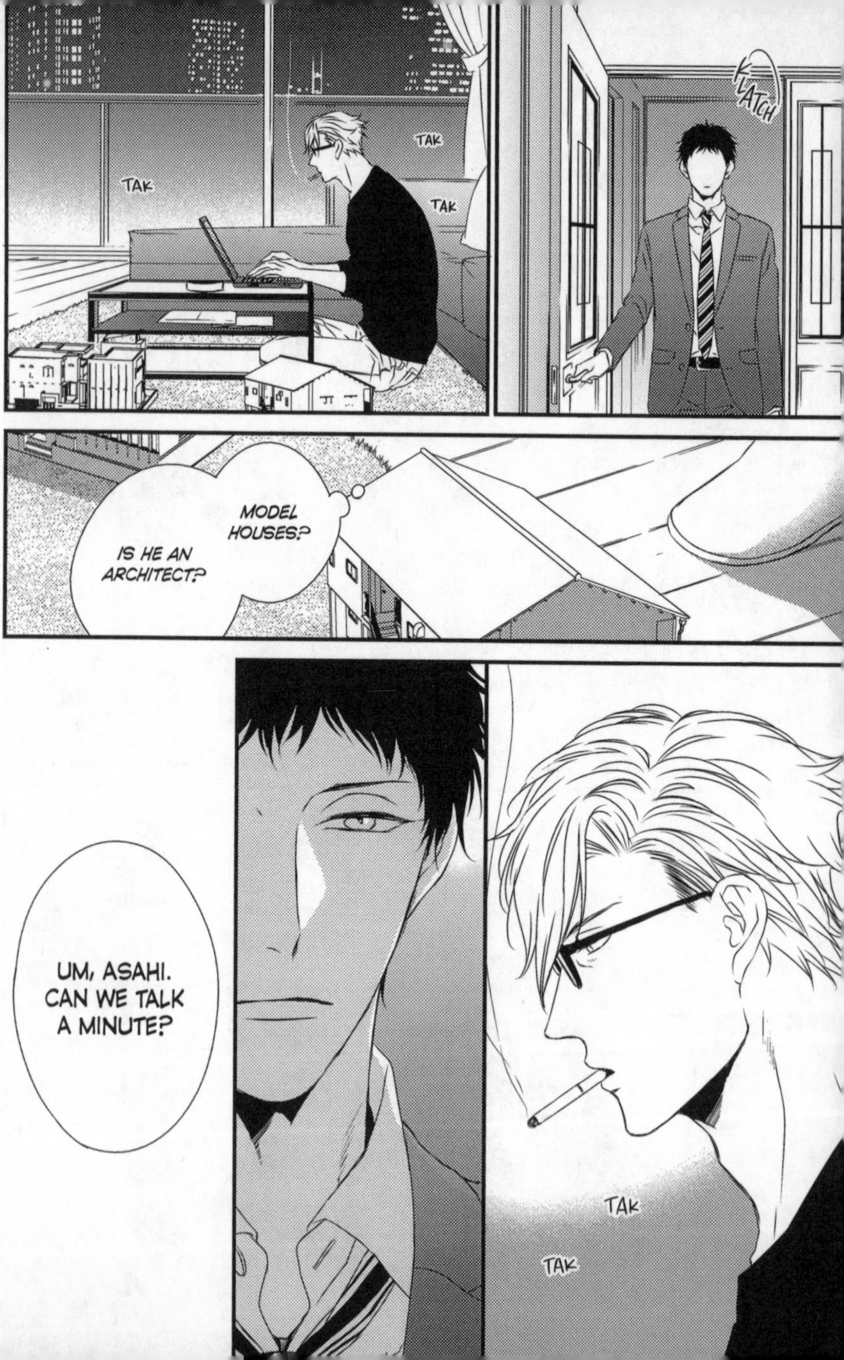
KLATCH
TAK
TAK
TAK
MODEL HOUSES?
IS HE AN ARCHITECT?
TAK
TAK
UM, ASAHI. CAN WE TALK A MINUTE?

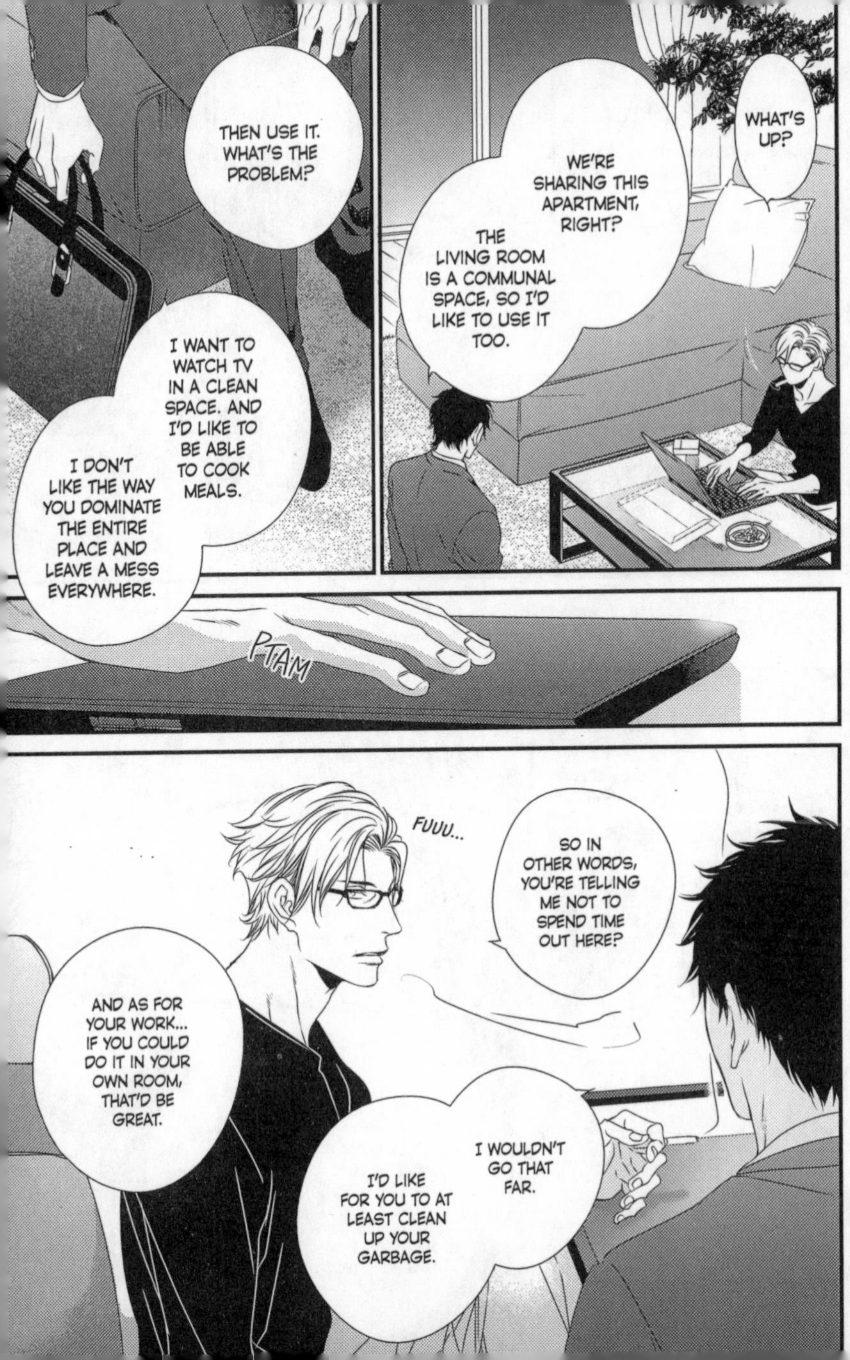
WHAT'S UP?
WE'RE SHARING THIS APARTMENT, RIGHT?
THE LIVING ROOM IS A COMMUNAL SPACE, SO I'D LIKE TO USE IT TOO.
THEN USE IT. WHAT'S THE PROBLEM?
I WANT TO WATCH TV IN A CLEAN SPACE. AND I'D LIKE TO BE ABLE TO COOK MEALS.
I DON'T LIKE THE WAY YOU DOMINATE THE ENTIRE PLACE AND LEAVE A MESS EVERYWHERE.
PTAM
FUUU...
...
SO IN OTHER WORDS, YOU'RE TELLING ME NOT TO SPEND TIME OUT HERE?
I WOULDN'T GO THAT FAR.
I'D LIKE FOR YOU TO AT LEAST CLEAN UP YOUR GARBAGE.
AND AS FOR YOUR WORK... IF YOU COULD DO IT IN YOUR OWN ROOM, THAT'D BE GREAT.

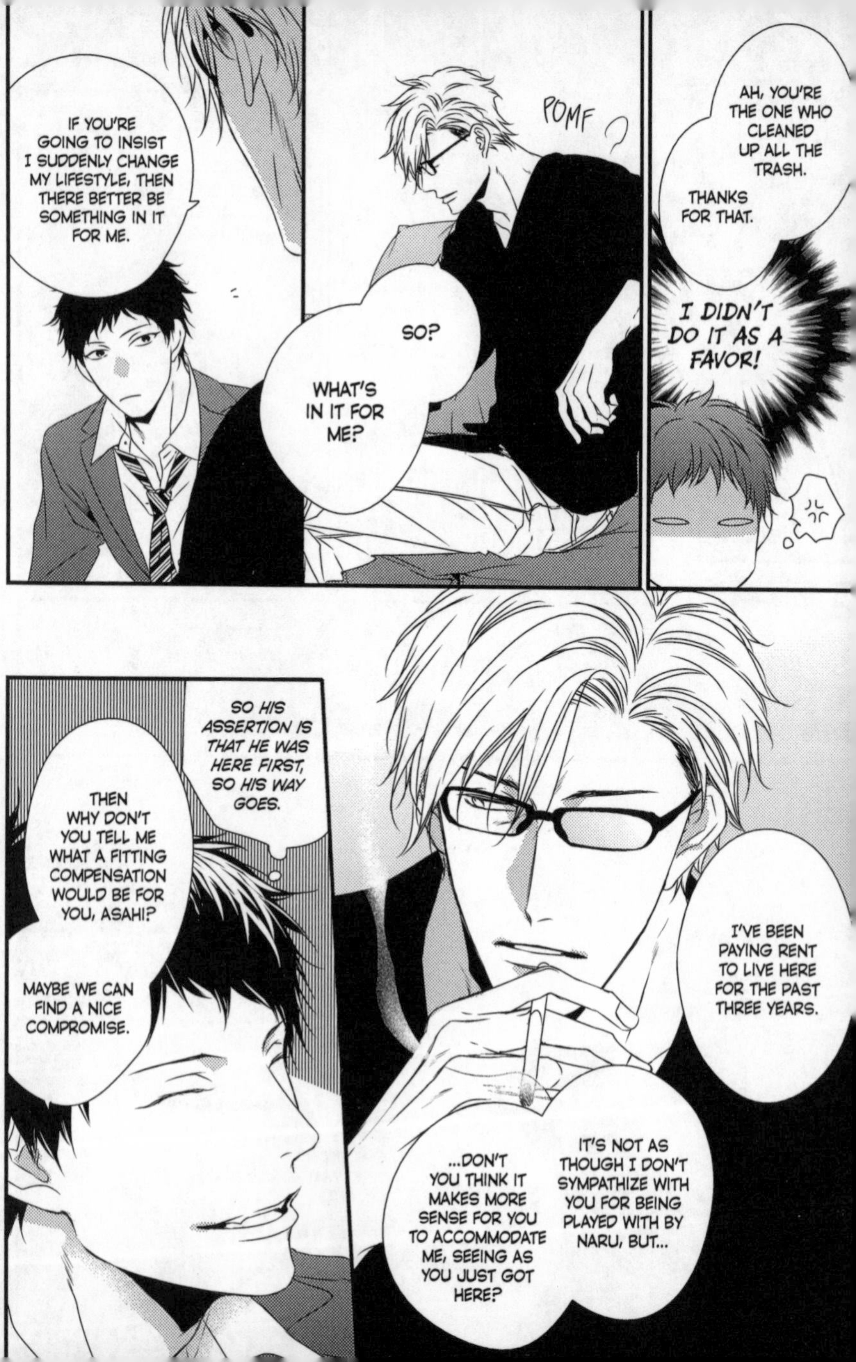
AH, YOU'RE THE ONE WHO CLEANED UP ALL THE TRASH.
THANKS FOR THAT.
I DIDN'T DO IT AS A FAVOR!
POMF
SO?
WHAT'S IN IT FOR ME?
IF YOU'RE GOING TO INSIST I SUDDENLY CHANGE MY LIFESTYLE, THEN THERE BETTER BE SOMETHING IN IT FOR ME.
I'VE BEEN PAYING RENT TO LIVE HERE FOR THE PAST THREE YEARS.
IT'S NOT AS THOUGH I DON'T SYMPATHIZE WITH YOU FOR BEING PLAYED WITH BY NARU, BUT...
...DON'T YOU THINK IT MAKES MORE SENSE FOR YOU TO ACCOMMODATE ME, SEEING AS YOU JUST GOT HERE?
SO HIS ASSERTION IS THAT HE WAS HERE FIRST, SO HIS WAY GOES.
THEN WHY DON'T YOU TELL ME WHAT A FITTING COMPENSATION WOULD BE FOR YOU, ASAHI?
MAYBE WE CAN FIND A NICE COMPROMISE.

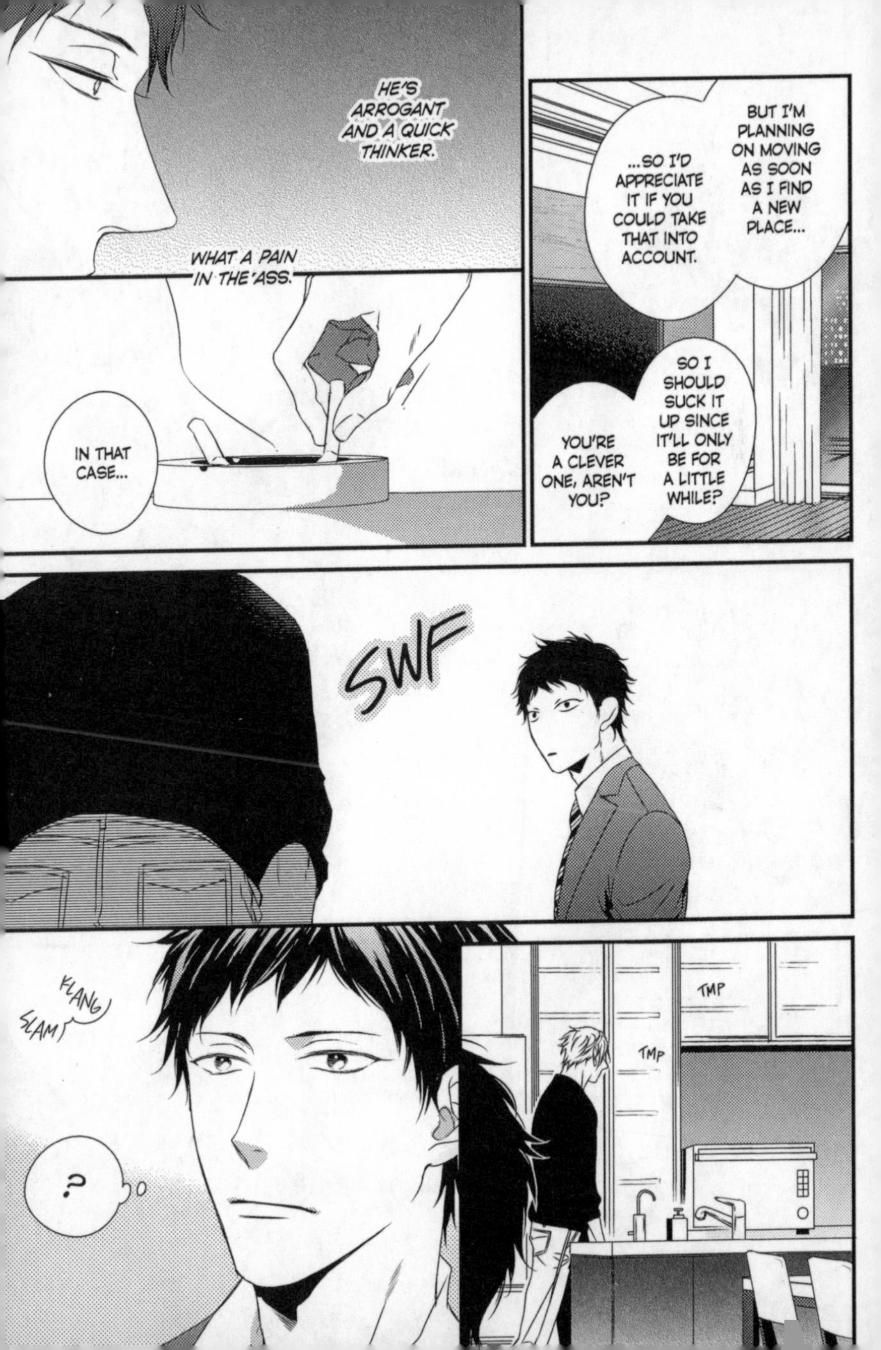
BUT I'M PLANNING ON MOVING AS SOON AS I FIND A NEW PLACE...
...SO I'D APPRECIATE IT IF YOU COULD TAKE THAT INTO ACCOUNT.
SO I SHOULD SUCK IT UP SINCE IT'LL ONLY BE FOR A LITTLE WHILE?
YOU'RE A CLEVER ONE, AREN'T YOU?
HE'S ARROGANT AND A QUICK THINKER.
WHAT A PAIN IN THE ASS.
IN THAT CASE...
SWF
TMP
TMP
KLANG
SLAM
?

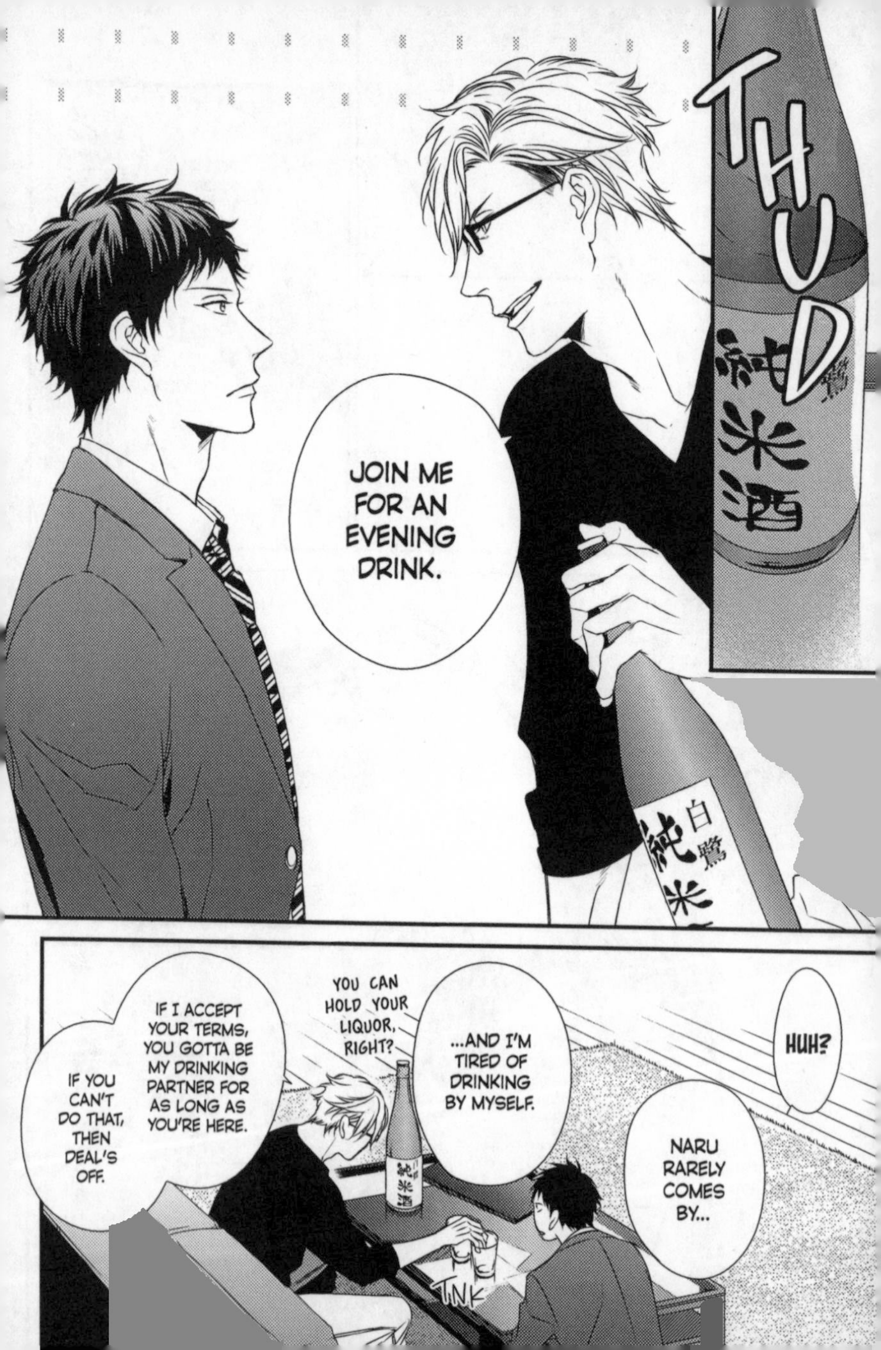
THUD
純米酒
JOIN ME FOR AN EVENING DRINK.
HUH?
NARU RARELY COMES BY...
...AND I'M TIRED OF DRINKING BY MYSELF.
YOU CAN HOLD YOUR LIQUOR, RIGHT?
IF I ACCEPT YOUR TERMS, YOU GOTTA BE MY DRINKING PARTNER FOR AS LONG AS YOU'RE HERE.
IF YOU CAN'T DO THAT, THEN DEAL'S OFF.
TNK

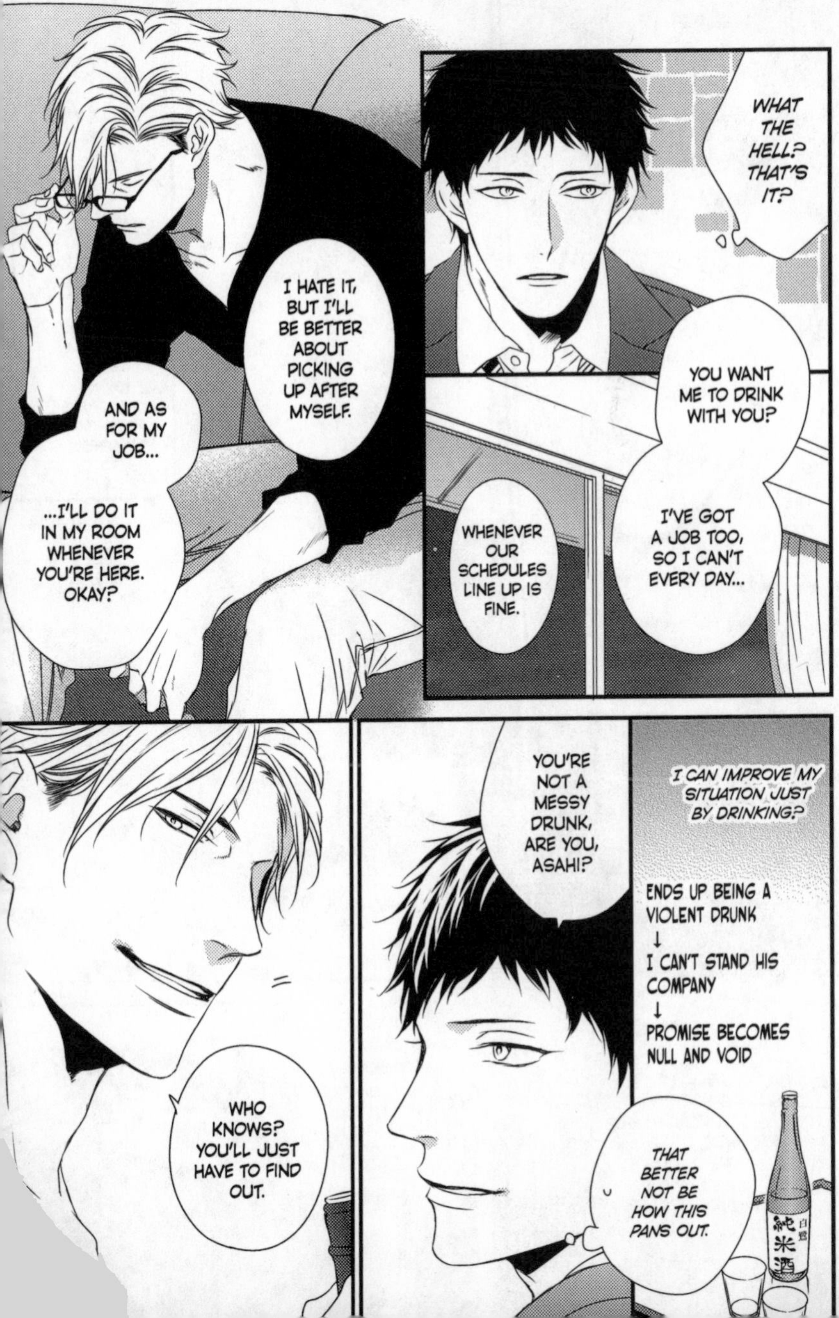
WHAT THE HELL? THAT'S IT?
YOU WANT ME TO DRINK WITH YOU?
I'VE GOT A JOB TOO, SO I CAN'T EVERY DAY...
WHENEVER OUR SCHEDULES LINE UP IS FINE.
I HATE IT, BUT I'LL BE BETTER ABOUT PICKING UP AFTER MYSELF.
AND AS FOR MY JOB...
...I'LL DO IT IN MY ROOM WHENEVER YOU'RE HERE. OKAY?
I CAN IMPROVE MY SITUATION JUST BY DRINKING?
YOU'RE NOT A MESSY DRUNK, ARE YOU, ASAHI?
ENDS UP BEING A VIOLENT DRUNK
↓
I CAN'T STAND HIS COMPANY
↓
PROMISE BECOMES NULL AND VOID
THAT BETTER NOT BE HOW THIS PANS OUT.
WHO KNOWS? YOU'LL JUST HAVE TO FIND OUT.

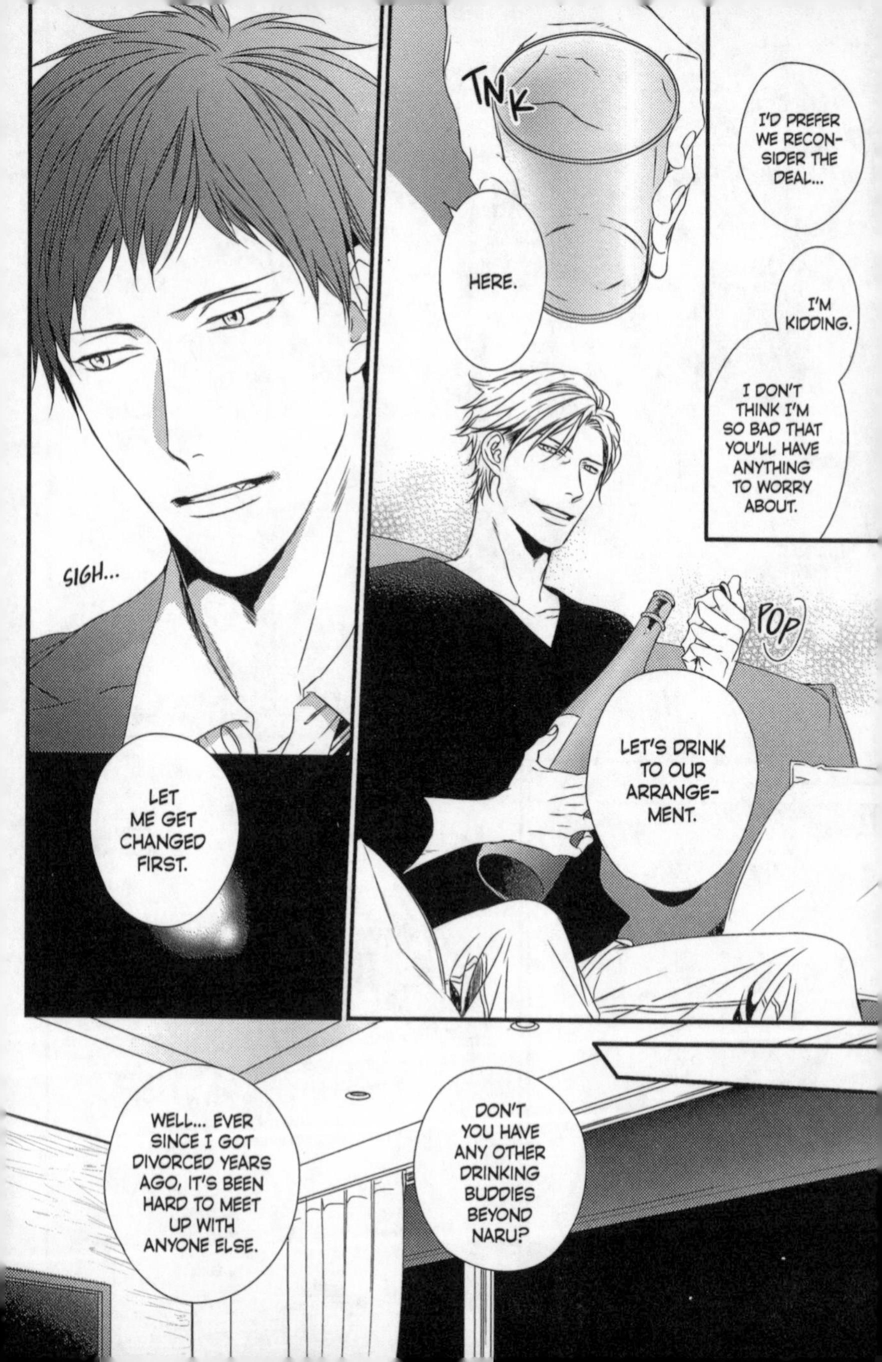
I'D PREFER WE RECONSIDER THE DEAL...
I'M KIDDING.
I DON'T THINK I'M SO BAD THAT YOU'LL HAVE ANYTHING TO WORRY ABOUT.
TNK
HERE.
POP
LET'S DRINK TO OUR ARRANGEMENT.
SIGH...
LET ME GET CHANGED FIRST.
DON'T YOU HAVE ANY OTHER DRINKING BUDDIES BEYOND NARU?
WELL... EVER SINCE I GOT DIVORCED YEARS AGO, IT'S BEEN HARD TO MEET UP WITH ANYONE ELSE.

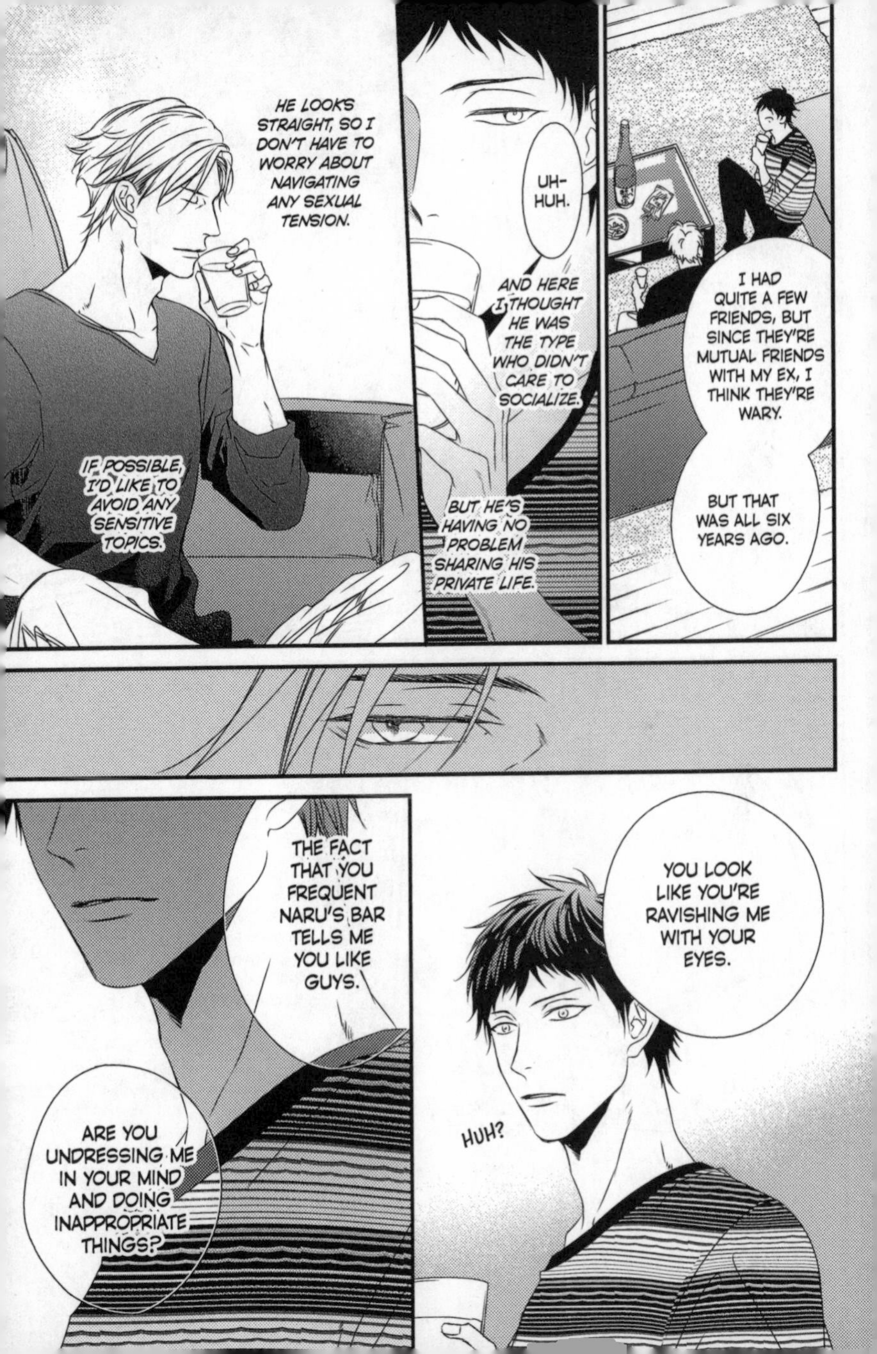
I HAD QUITE A FEW FRIENDS, BUT SINCE THEY'RE MUTUAL FRIENDS WITH MY EX, I THINK THEY'RE WARY.
BUT THAT WAS ALL SIX YEARS AGO.
UH-HUH.
AND HERE I THOUGHT HE WAS THE TYPE WHO DIDN'T CARE TO SOCIALIZE.
BUT HE'S HAVING NO PROBLEM SHARING HIS PRIVATE LIFE.
HE LOOKS STRAIGHT, SO I DON'T HAVE TO WORRY ABOUT NAVIGATING ANY SEXUAL TENSION.
IF POSSIBLE, I'D LIKE TO AVOID ANY SENSITIVE TOPICS.
YOU LOOK LIKE YOU'RE RAVISHING ME WITH YOUR EYES.
HUH?
THE FACT THAT YOU FREQUENT NARU'S BAR TELLS ME YOU LIKE GUYS.
ARE YOU UNDRESSING ME IN YOUR MIND AND DOING INAPPROPRIATE THINGS?

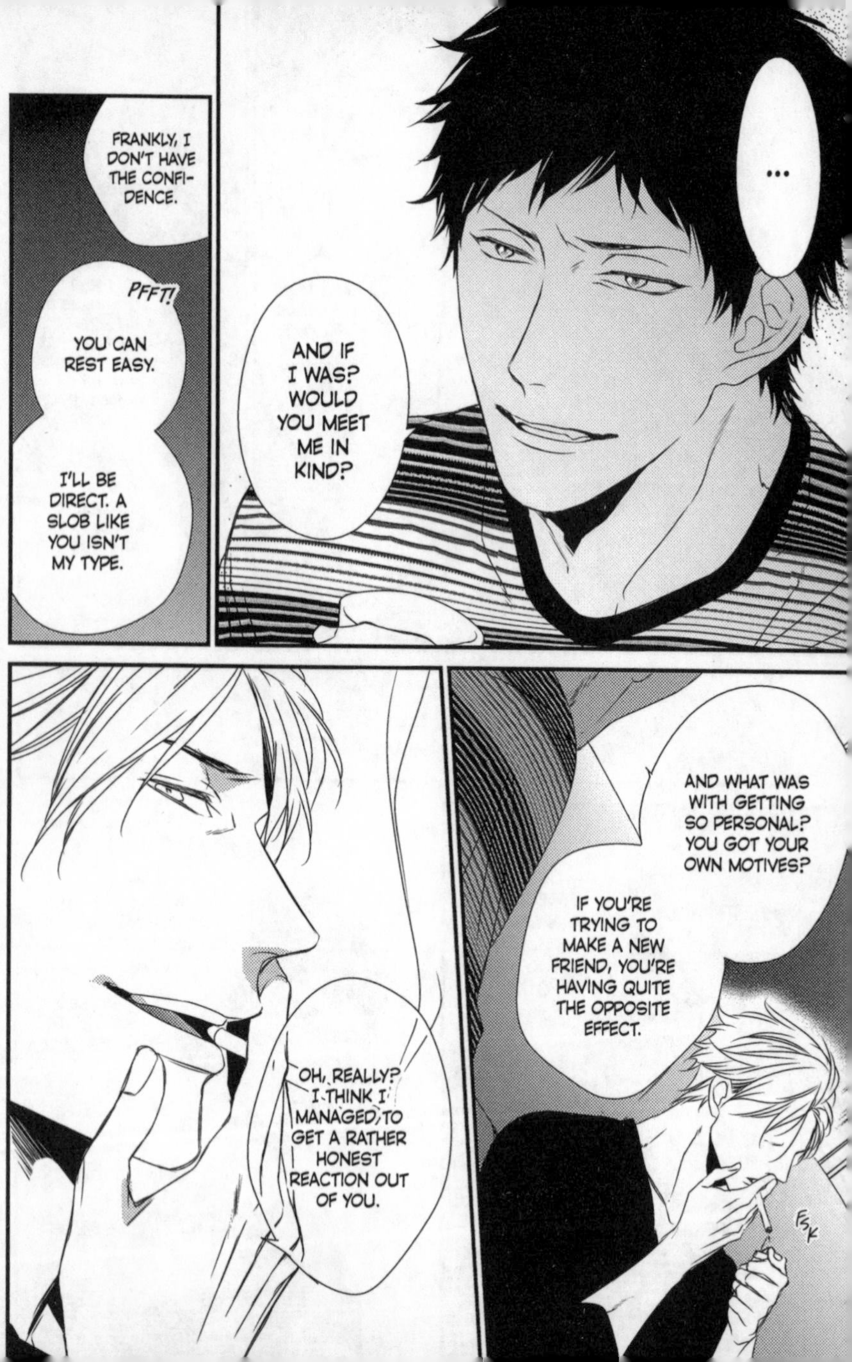
...
AND IF I WAS? WOULD YOU MEET ME IN KIND?
FRANKLY, I DON'T HAVE THE CONFI-DENCE.
PFFT!
YOU CAN REST EASY.
I'LL BE DIRECT. A SLOB LIKE YOU ISN'T MY TYPE.
AND WHAT WAS WITH GETTING SO PERSONAL? YOU GOT YOUR OWN MOTIVES?
IF YOU'RE TRYING TO MAKE A NEW FRIEND, YOU'RE HAVING QUITE THE OPPOSITE EFFECT.
FSK
OH, REALLY? I THINK I MANAGED TO GET A RATHER HONEST REACTION OUT OF YOU.

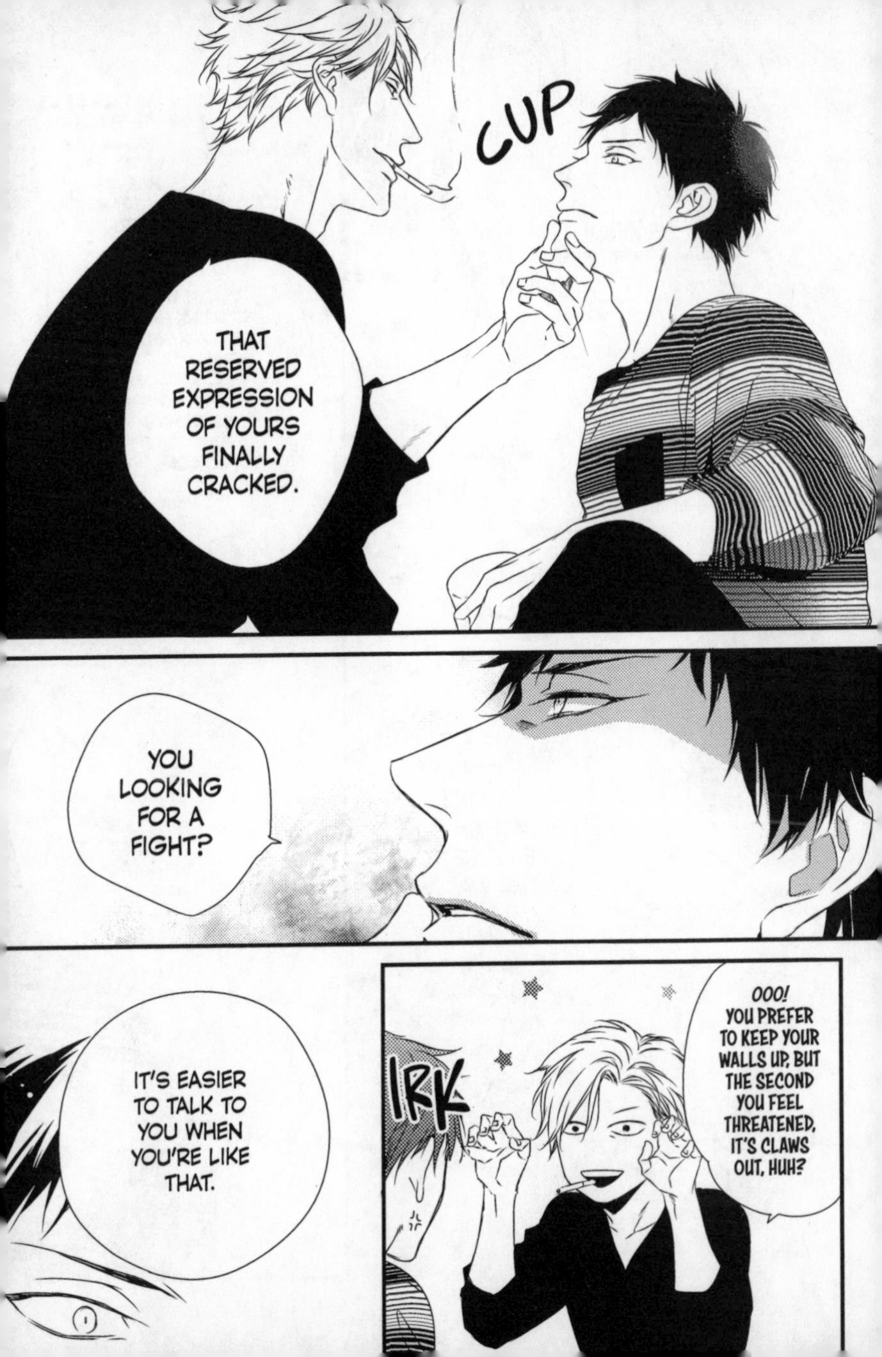
CUP
THAT RESERVED EXPRESSION OF YOURS FINALLY CRACKED.
YOU LOOKING FOR A FIGHT?
OOO! YOU PREFER TO KEEP YOUR WALLS UP, BUT THE SECOND YOU FEEL THREATENED, IT'S CLAWS OUT, HUH?
IRK
IT'S EASIER TO TALK TO YOU WHEN YOU'RE LIKE THAT.

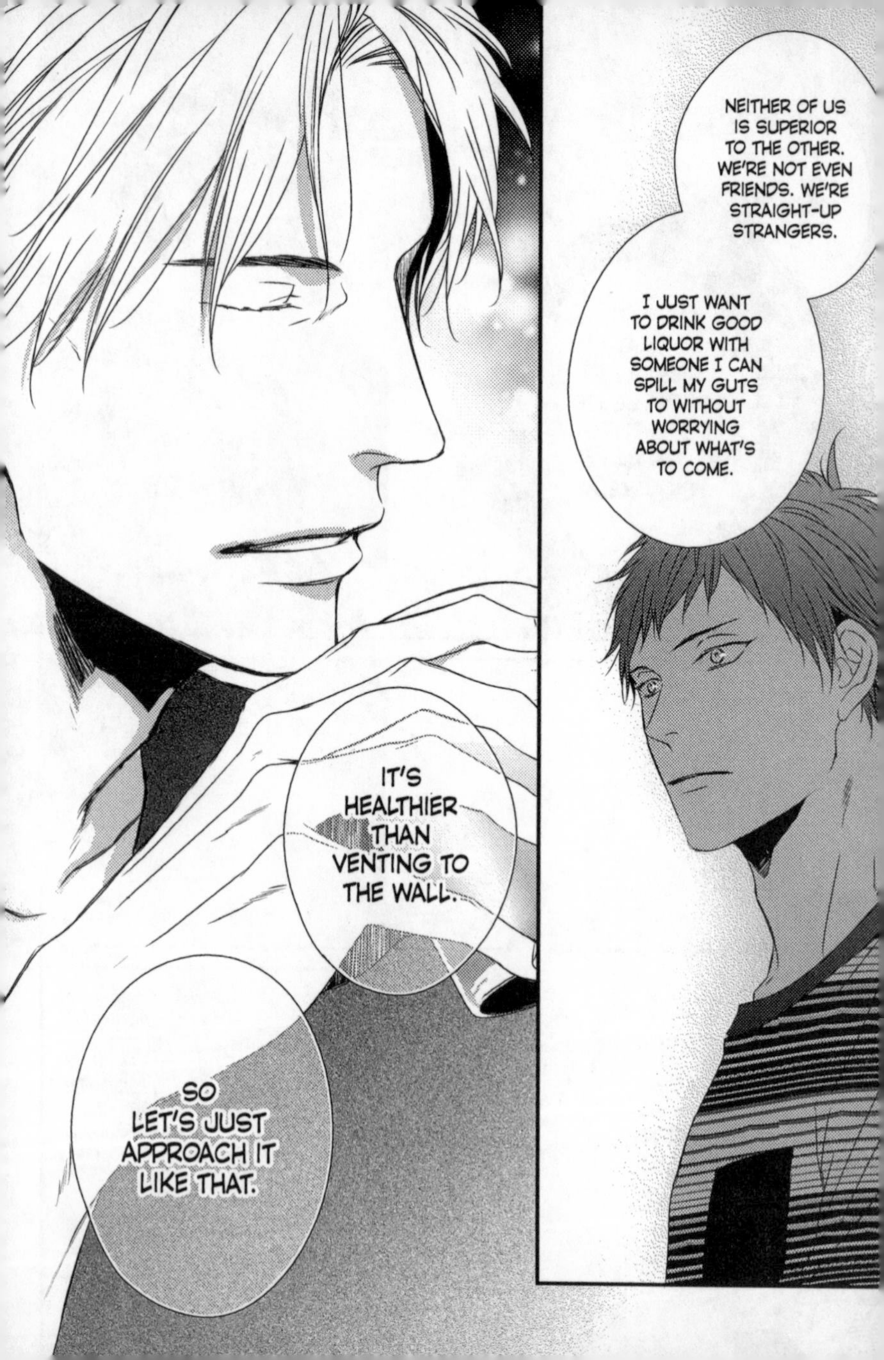
NEITHER OF US IS SUPERIOR TO THE OTHER. WE'RE NOT EVEN FRIENDS. WE'RE STRAIGHT-UP STRANGERS.
I JUST WANT TO DRINK GOOD LIQUOR WITH SOMEONE I CAN SPILL MY GUTS TO WITHOUT WORRYING ABOUT WHAT'S TO COME.
IT'S HEALTHIER THAN VENTING TO THE WALL.
SO LET'S JUST APPROACH IT LIKE THAT.

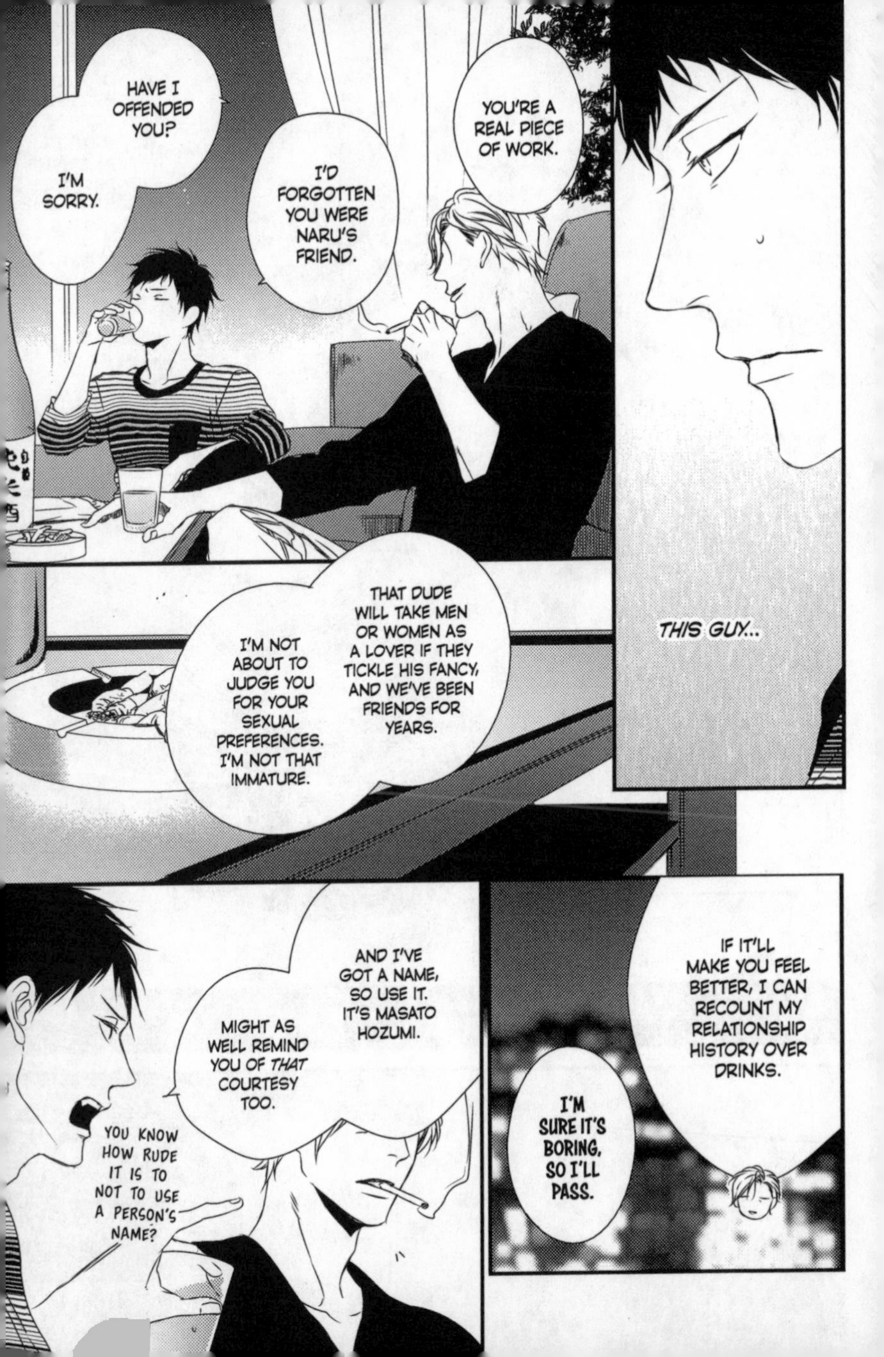
THIS GUY...
YOU'RE A REAL PIECE OF WORK.
I'D FORGOTTEN YOU WERE NARU'S FRIEND.
HAVE I OFFENDED YOU? I'M SORRY.
THAT DUDE WILL TAKE MEN OR WOMEN AS A LOVER IF THEY TICKLE HIS FANCY, AND WE'VE BEEN FRIENDS FOR YEARS.
I'M NOT ABOUT TO JUDGE YOU FOR YOUR SEXUAL PREFERENCES. I'M NOT THAT IMMATURE.
IF IT'LL MAKE YOU FEEL BETTER, I CAN RECOUNT MY RELATIONSHIP HISTORY OVER DRINKS.
I'M SURE IT'S BORING, SO I'LL PASS.
AND I'VE GOT A NAME, SO USE IT. IT'S MASATO HOZUMI.
MIGHT AS WELL REMIND YOU OF *THAT* COURTESY TOO.
YOU KNOW HOW RUDE IT IS TO NOT TO USE A PERSON'S NAME?

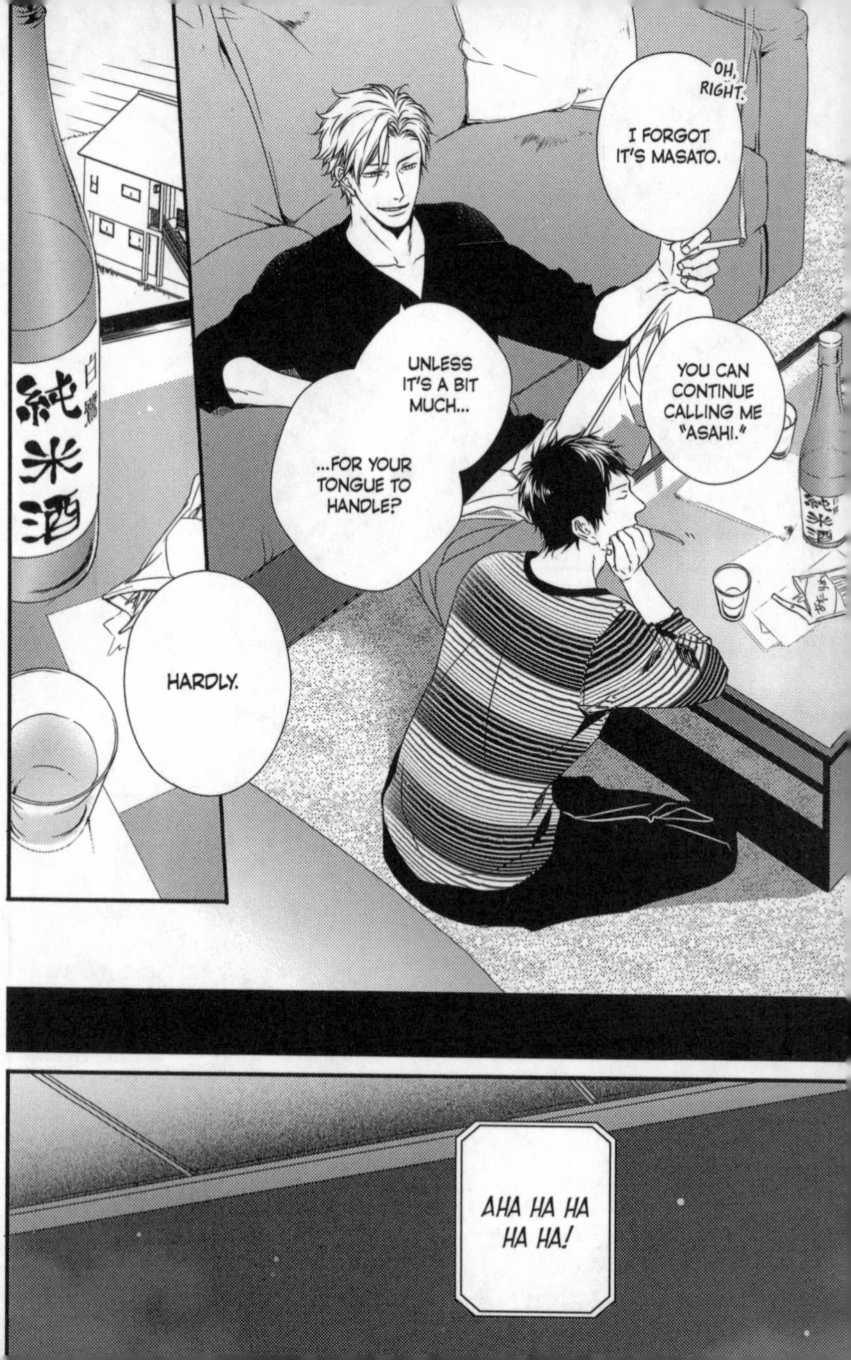
OH, RIGHT.
I FORGOT IT'S MASATO.
YOU CAN CONTINUE CALLING ME "ASAHI."
UNLESS IT'S A BIT MUCH...
...FOR YOUR TONGUE TO HANDLE?
純米酒
HARDLY.
AHA HA HA HA HA!

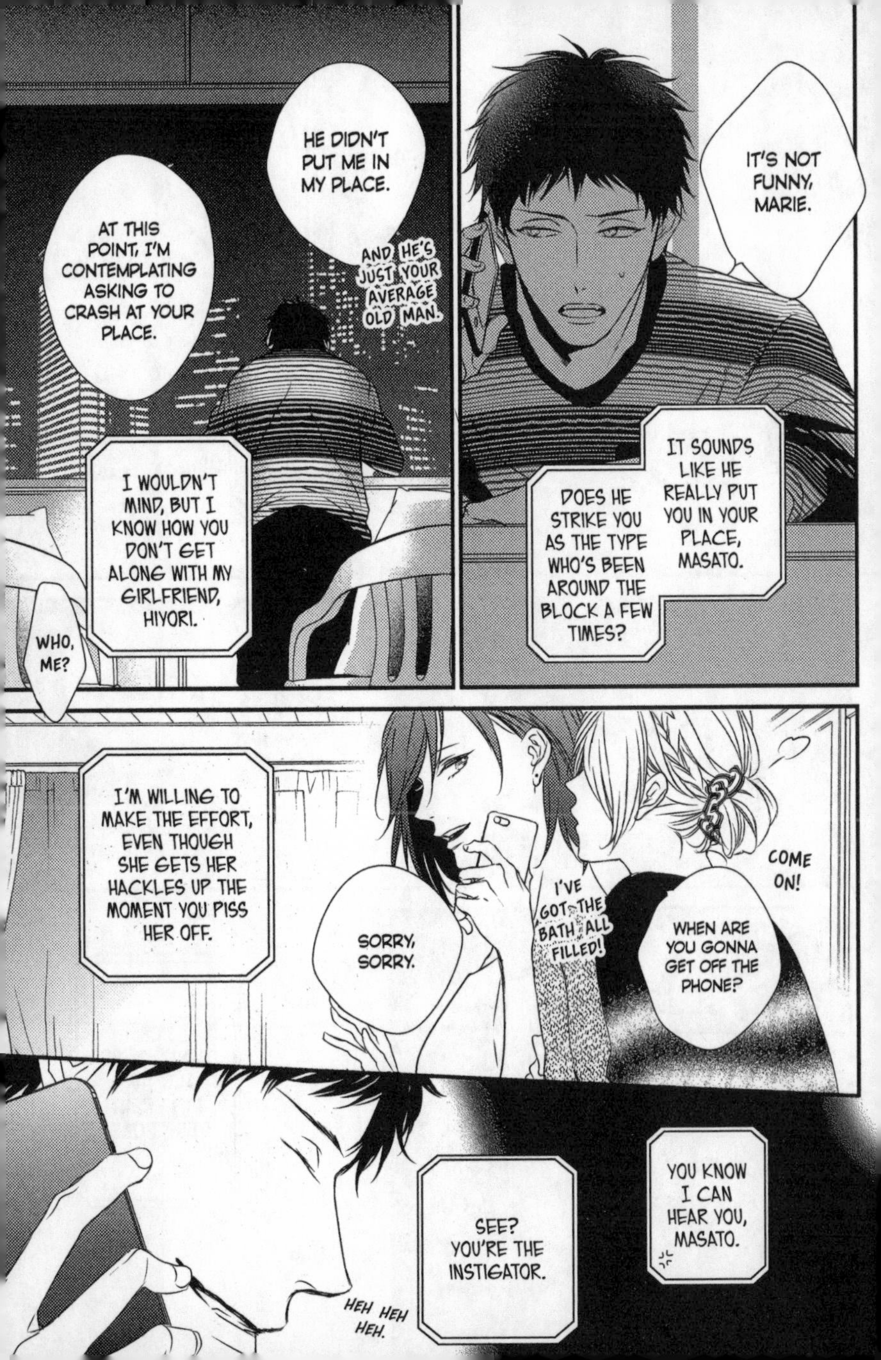
IT'S NOT FUNNY, MARIE.
IT SOUNDS LIKE HE REALLY PUT YOU IN YOUR PLACE, MASATO.
DOES HE STRIKE YOU AS THE TYPE WHO'S BEEN AROUND THE BLOCK A FEW TIMES?
HE DIDN'T PUT ME IN MY PLACE.
AND HE'S JUST YOUR AVERAGE OLD MAN.
AT THIS POINT, I'M CONTEMPLATING ASKING TO CRASH AT YOUR PLACE.
I WOULDN'T MIND, BUT I KNOW HOW YOU DON'T GET ALONG WITH MY GIRLFRIEND, HIYORI.
WHO, ME?
COME ON!
WHEN ARE YOU GONNA GET OFF THE PHONE?
I'VE GOT THE BATH ALL FILLED!
SORRY, SORRY.
I'M WILLING TO MAKE THE EFFORT, EVEN THOUGH SHE GETS HER HACKLES UP THE MOMENT YOU PISS HER OFF.
YOU KNOW I CAN HEAR YOU, MASATO.
SEE? YOU'RE THE INSTIGATOR.
HEH HEH HEH.

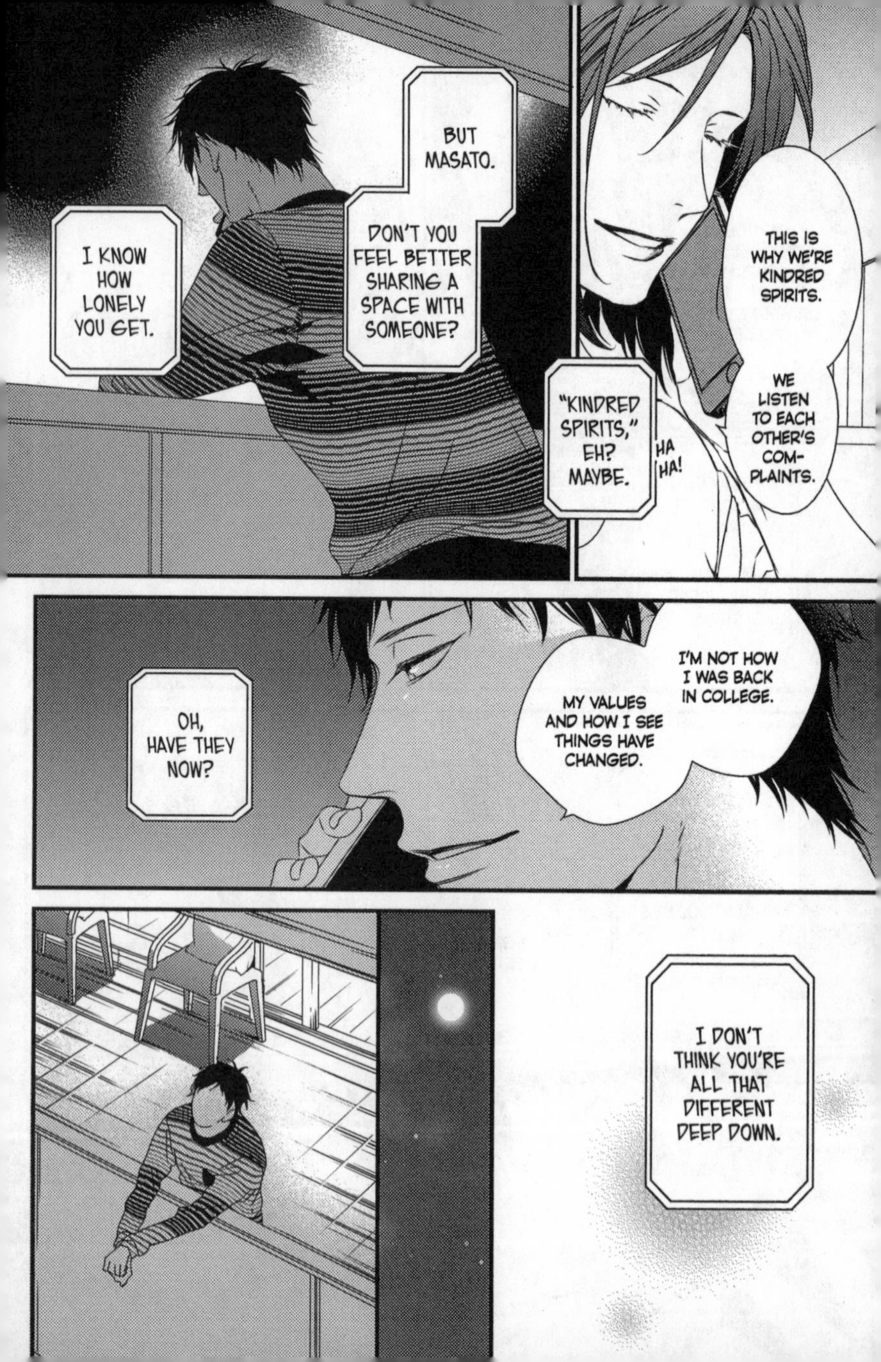
THIS IS WHY WE'RE KINDRED SPIRITS.
WE LISTEN TO EACH OTHER'S COM-PLAINTS.
HA HA!
"KINDRED SPIRITS," EH? MAYBE.
BUT MASATO.
DON'T YOU FEEL BETTER SHARING A SPACE WITH SOMEONE?
I KNOW HOW LONELY YOU GET.
I'M NOT HOW I WAS BACK IN COLLEGE.
MY VALUES AND HOW I SEE THINGS HAVE CHANGED.
OH, HAVE THEY NOW?
I DON'T THINK YOU'RE ALL THAT DIFFERENT DEEP DOWN.

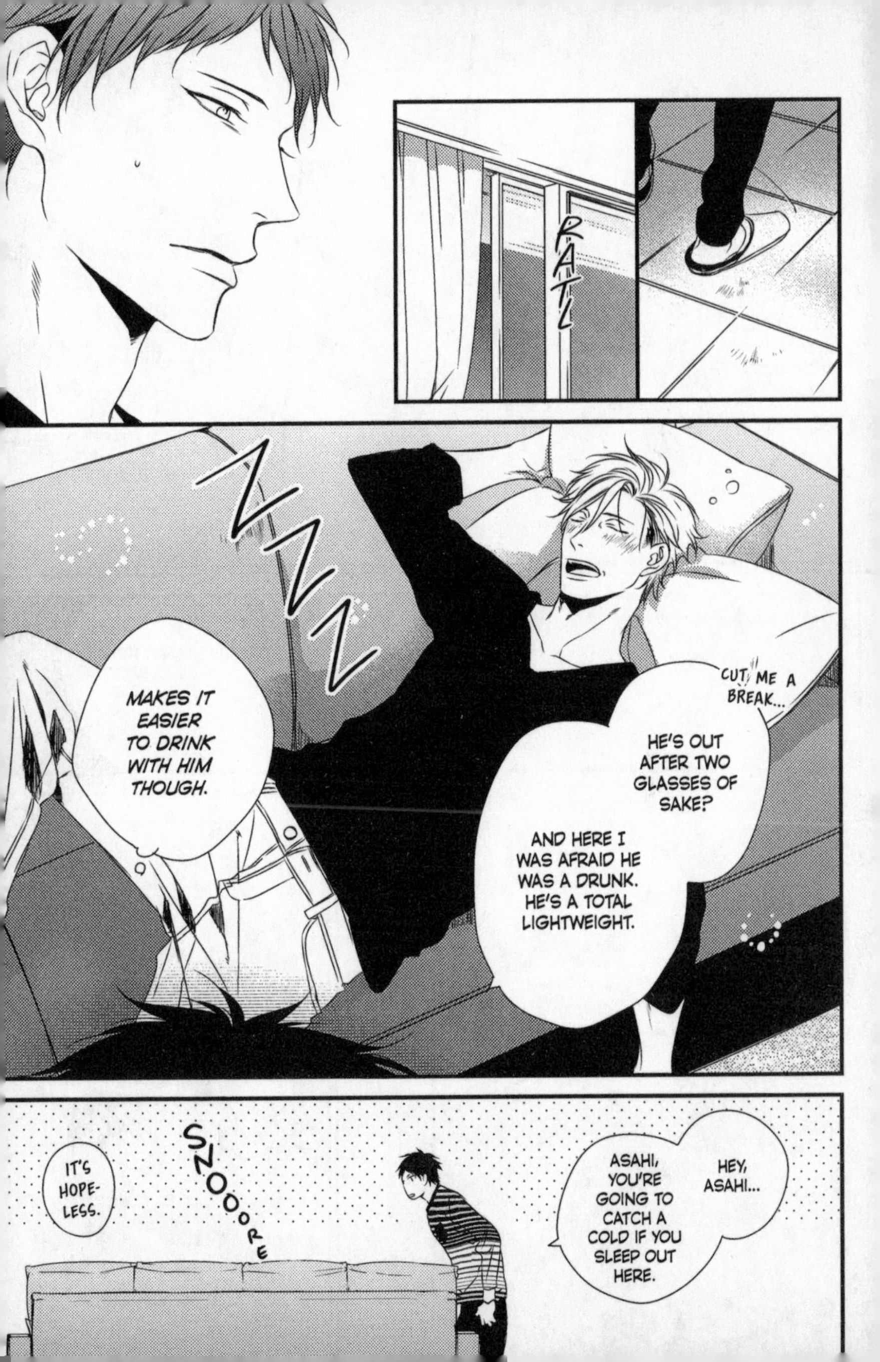
RATTL
CUT ME A BREAK...
HE'S OUT AFTER TWO GLASSES OF SAKE?
AND HERE I WAS AFRAID HE WAS A DRUNK. HE'S A TOTAL LIGHTWEIGHT.
ZZZ
MAKES IT EASIER TO DRINK WITH HIM THOUGH.
HEY, ASAHI...
ASAHI, YOU'RE GOING TO CATCH A COLD IF YOU SLEEP OUT HERE.
SNOOORE
IT'S HOPE-LESS.

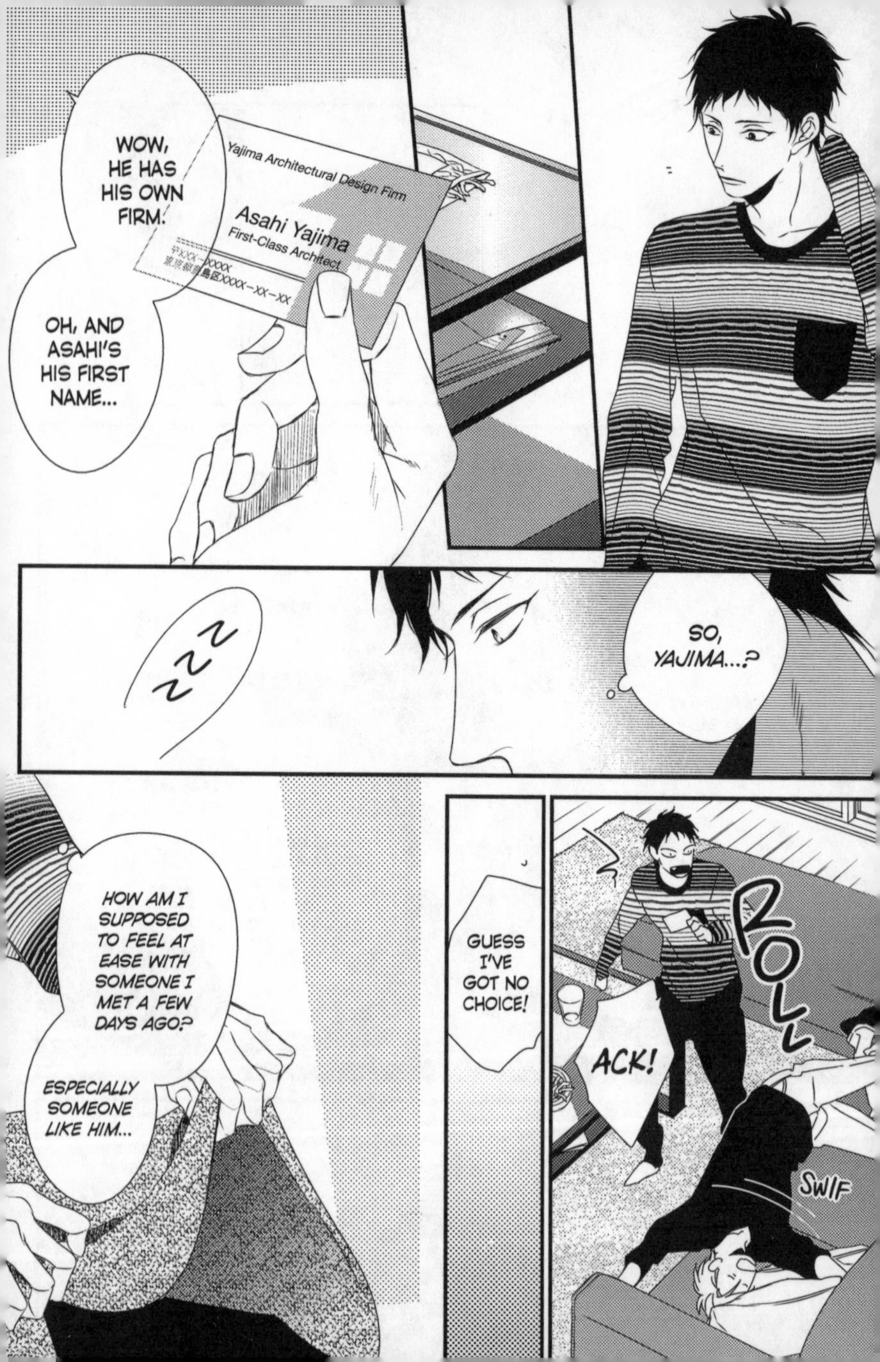
Yajima Architectural Design Firm
Asahi Yajima
First-Class Architect
WOW, HE HAS HIS OWN FIRM.
OH, AND ASAHI'S HIS FIRST NAME...
SO, YAJIMA...?
ZZZ
ROLL
ACK!
SWIF
GUESS I'VE GOT NO CHOICE!
HOW AM I SUPPOSED TO FEEL AT EASE WITH SOMEONE I MET A FEW DAYS AGO?
ESPECIALLY SOMEONE LIKE HIM...

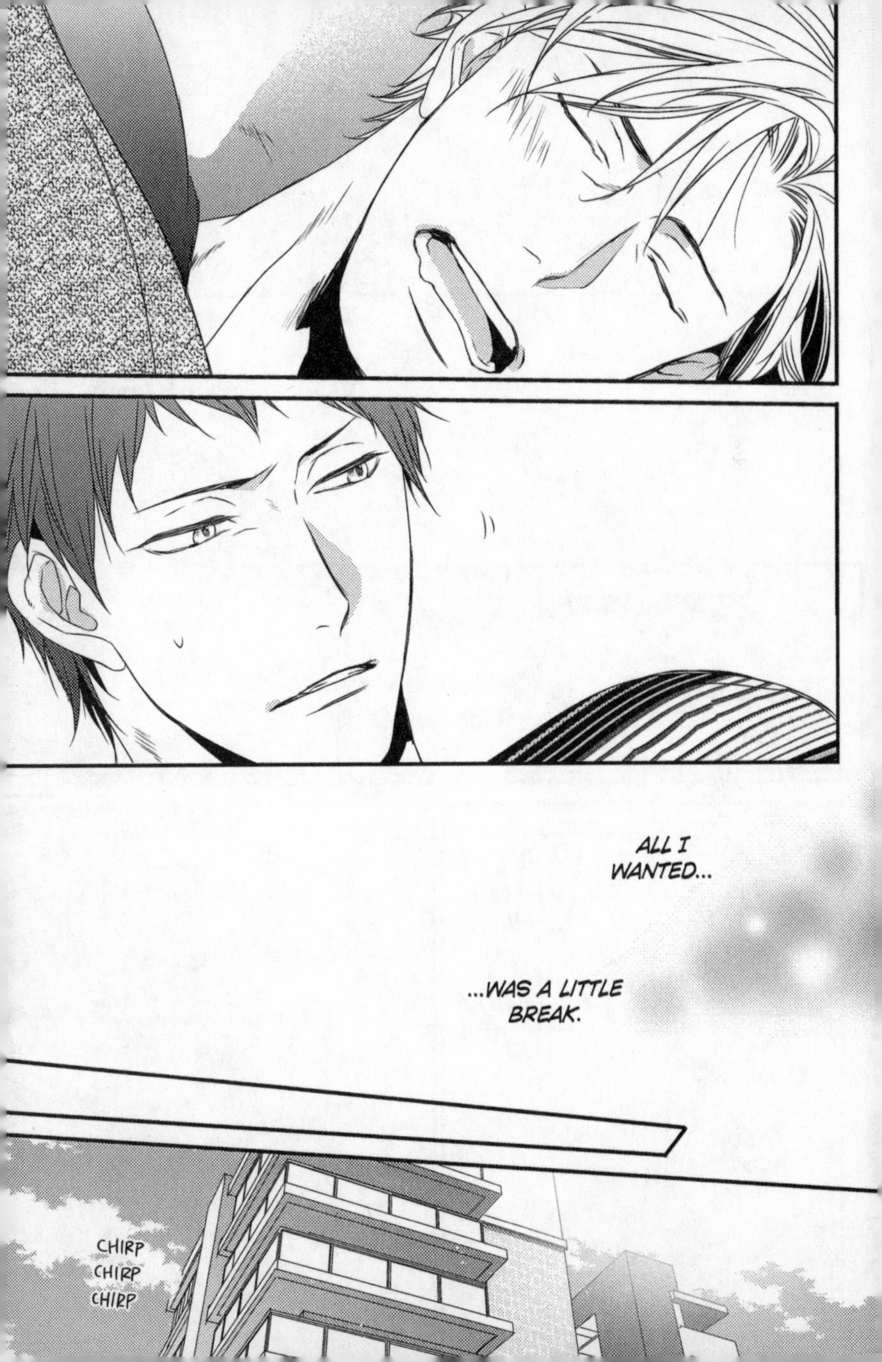
ALL I WANTED...
...WAS A LITTLE BREAK.
CHIRP CHIRP CHIRP

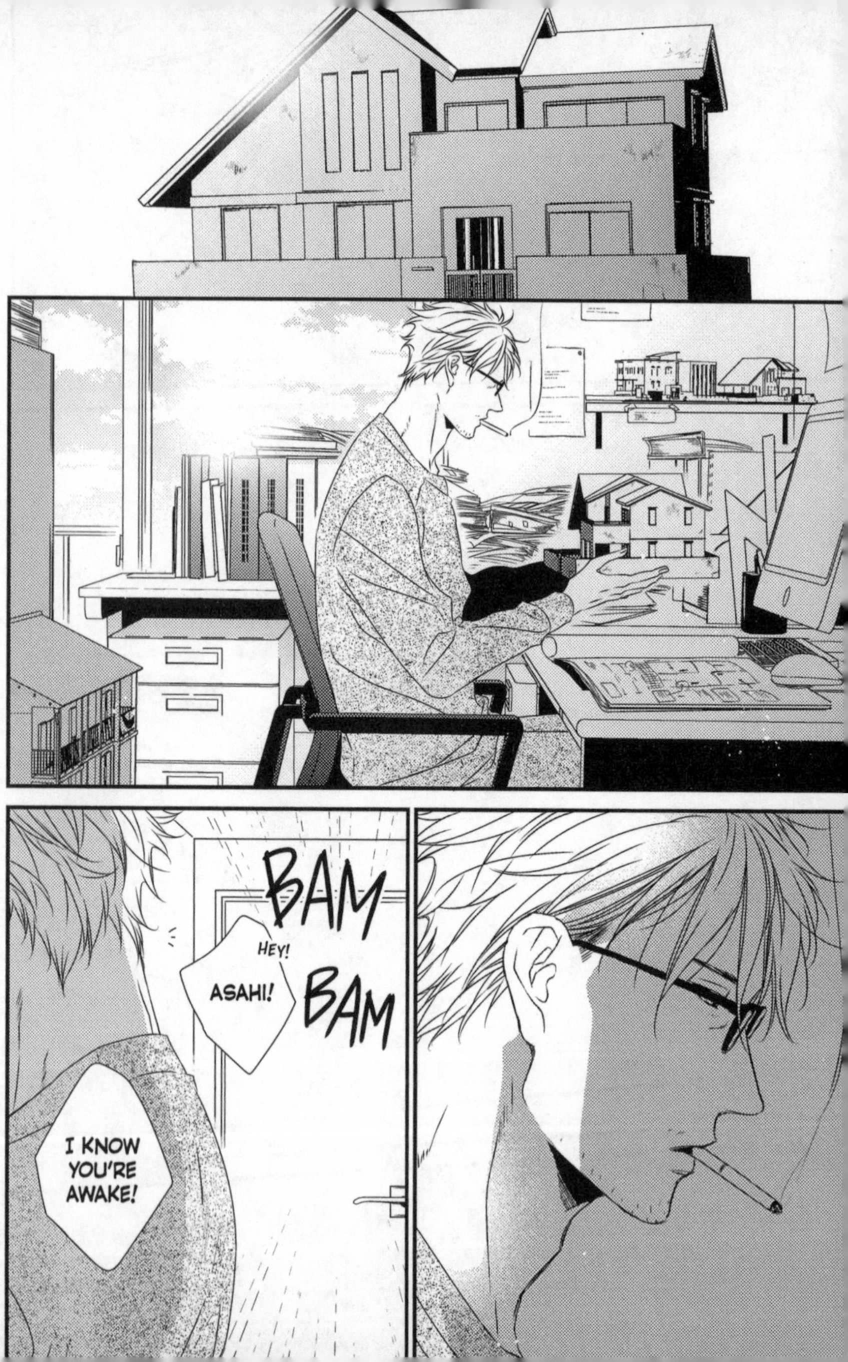
BAM
HEY! ASAHI!
BAM
I KNOW YOU'RE AWAKE!

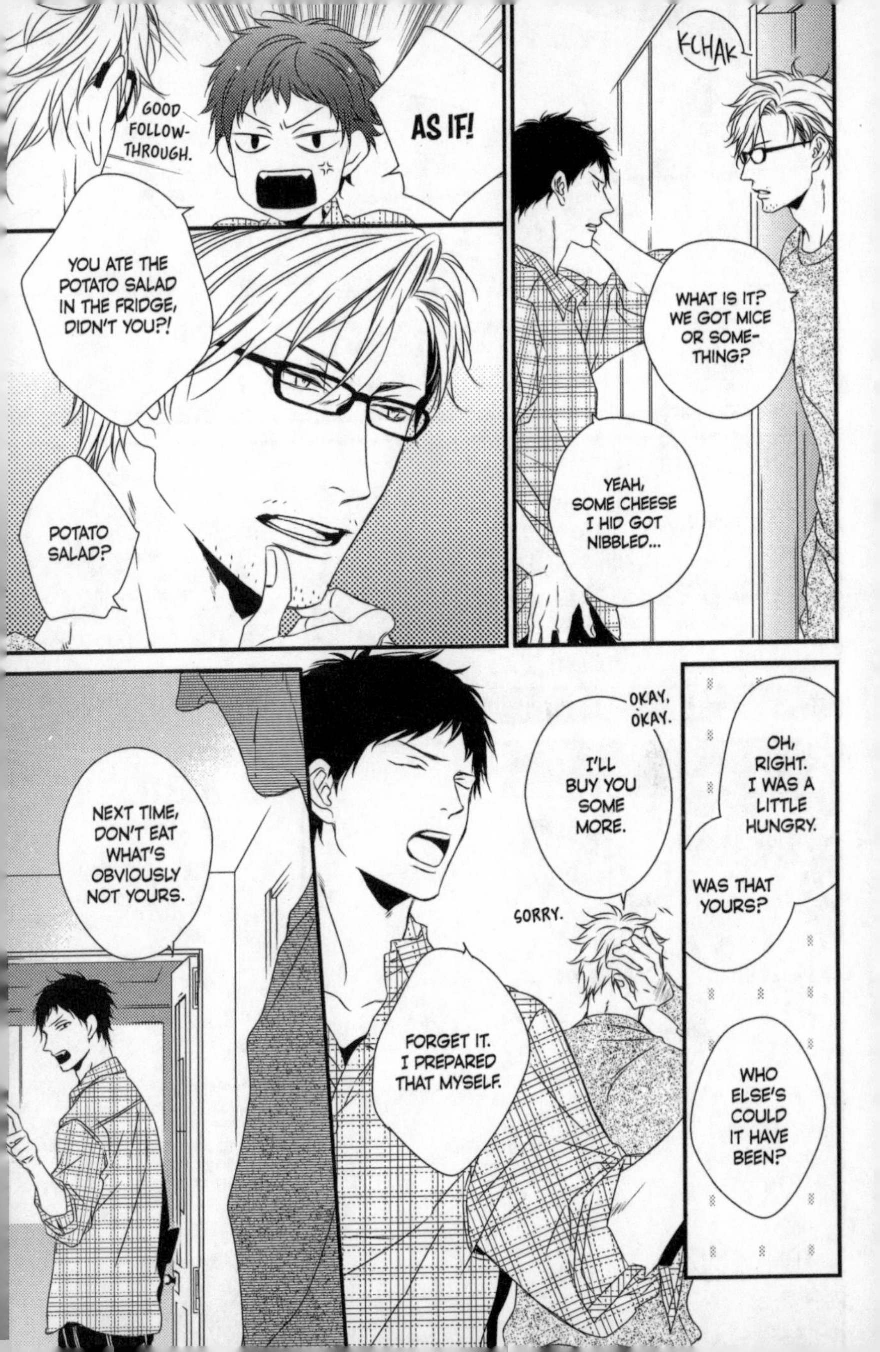
KCHAK
WHAT IS IT? WE GOT MICE OR SOME-THING?
YEAH, SOME CHEESE I HID GOT NIBBLED...
AS IF!
GOOD FOLLOW-THROUGH.
YOU ATE THE POTATO SALAD IN THE FRIDGE, DIDN'T YOU?!
POTATO SALAD?
OH, RIGHT. I WAS A LITTLE HUNGRY.
WAS THAT YOURS?
WHO ELSE'S COULD IT HAVE BEEN?
OKAY, OKAY.
I'LL BUY YOU SOME MORE.
SORRY.
FORGET IT. I PREPARED THAT MYSELF.
NEXT TIME, DON'T EAT WHAT'S OBVIOUSLY NOT YOURS.

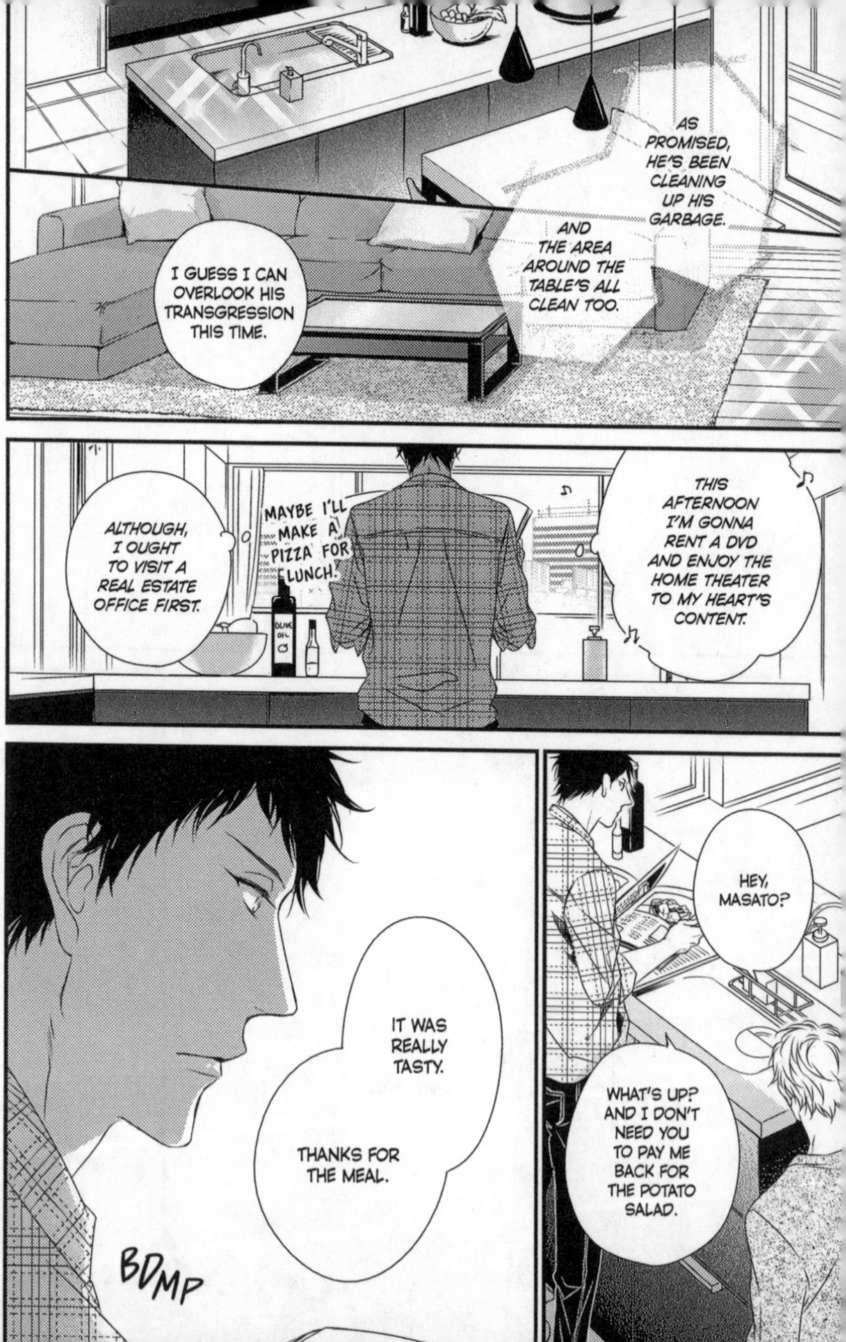
AS PROMISED, HE'S BEEN CLEANING UP HIS GARBAGE.
AND THE AREA AROUND THE TABLE'S ALL CLEAN TOO.
I GUESS I CAN OVERLOOK HIS TRANSGRESSION THIS TIME.
THIS AFTERNOON I'M GONNA RENT A DVD AND ENJOY THE HOME THEATER TO MY HEART'S CONTENT.
MAYBE I'LL MAKE A PIZZA FOR LUNCH!
ALTHOUGH, I OUGHT TO VISIT A REAL ESTATE OFFICE FIRST.
OLIVE OIL
HEY, MASATO?
WHAT'S UP? AND I DON'T NEED YOU TO PAY ME BACK FOR THE POTATO SALAD.
IT WAS REALLY TASTY.
THANKS FOR THE MEAL.
BDMP

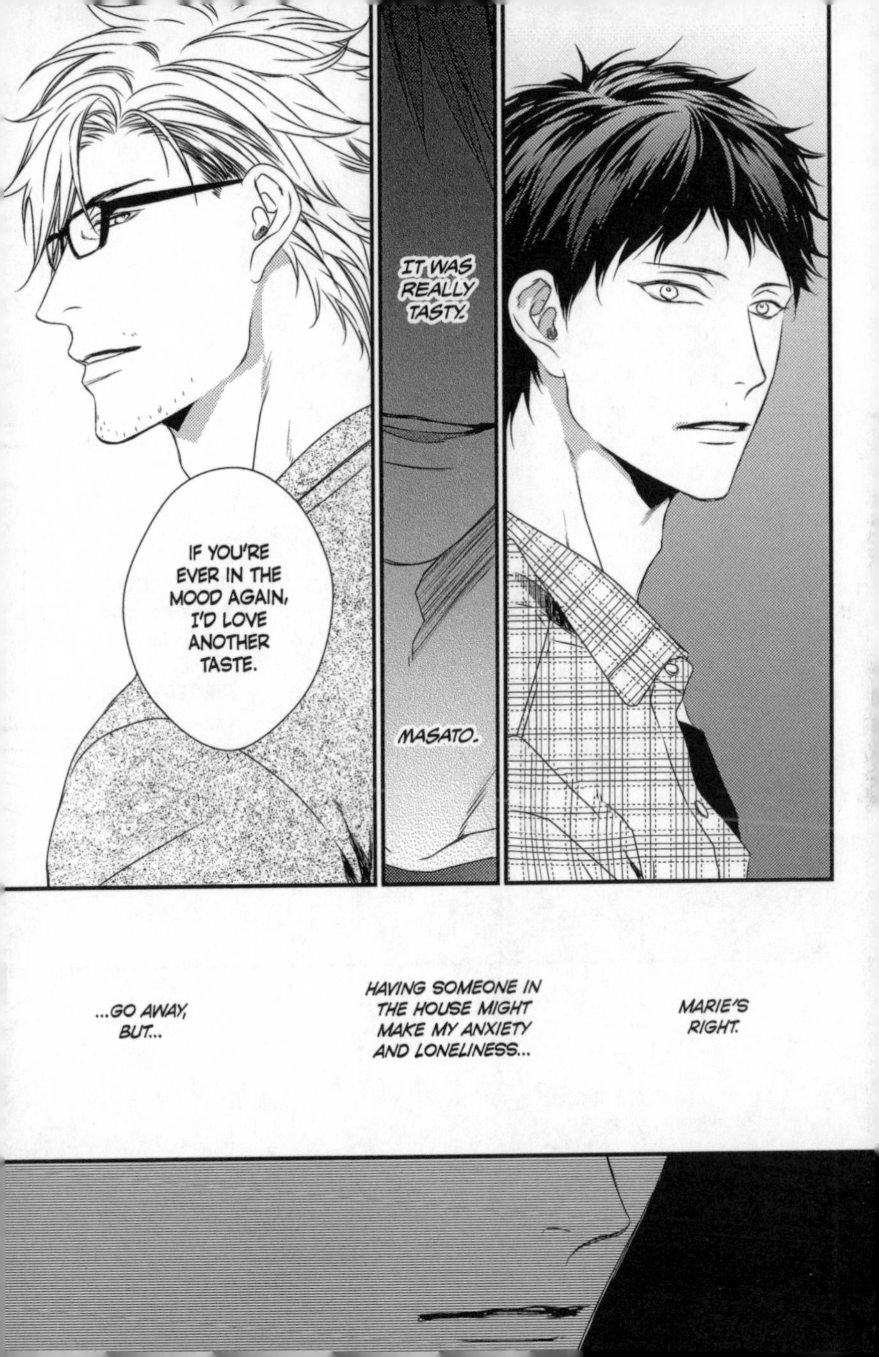
IT WAS REALLY TASTY.
MASATO.
IF YOU'RE EVER IN THE MOOD AGAIN, I'D LOVE ANOTHER TASTE.
MARIE'S RIGHT.
HAVING SOMEONE IN THE HOUSE MIGHT MAKE MY ANXIETY AND LONELINESS...
...GO AWAY, BUT...

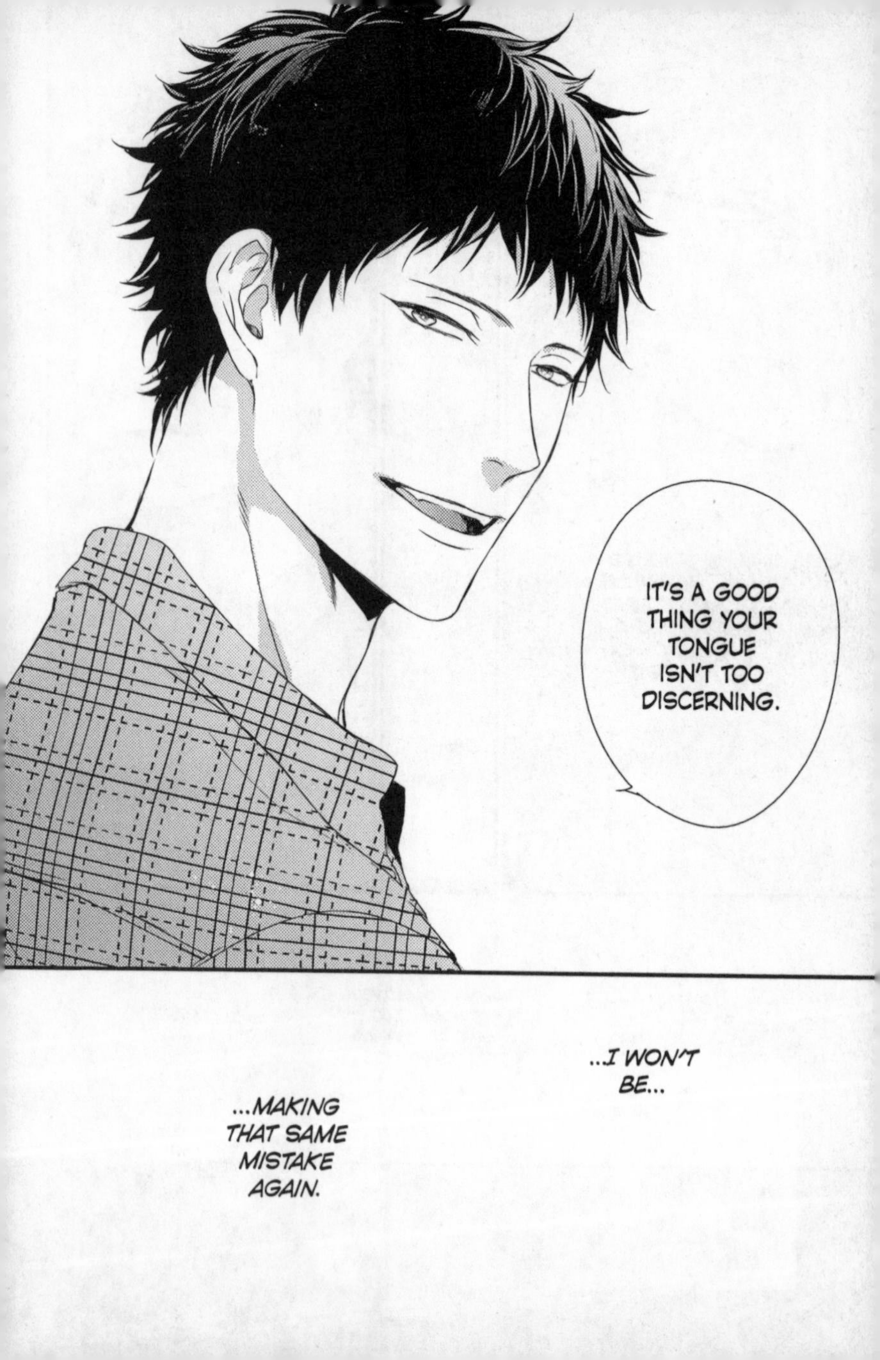
IT'S A GOOD THING YOUR TONGUE ISN'T TOO DISCERNING.
...I WON'T BE...
...MAKING THAT SAME MISTAKE AGAIN.

LOVE NEST

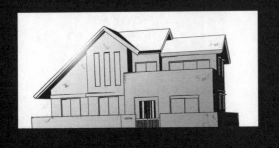

THE CORRELATION BETWEEN ONE'S USUAL SPOT ON THE SOFA AND EMOTIONAL DISTANCE ①

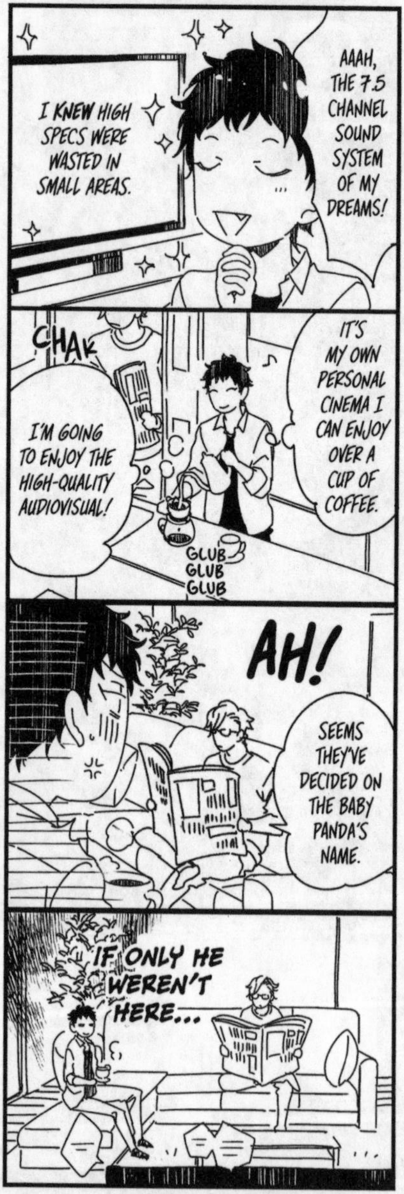
AAAH, THE 7.5 CHANNEL SOUND SYSTEM OF MY DREAMS!
I KNEW HIGH SPECS WERE WASTED IN SMALL AREAS.
IT'S MY OWN PERSONAL CINEMA I CAN ENJOY OVER A CUP OF COFFEE.
CHAK
I'M GOING TO ENJOY THE HIGH-QUALITY AUDIOVISUAL!
GLUB GLUB GLUB
AH!
SEEMS THEY'VE DECIDED ON THE BABY PANDA'S NAME.
IF ONLY HE WEREN'T HERE...

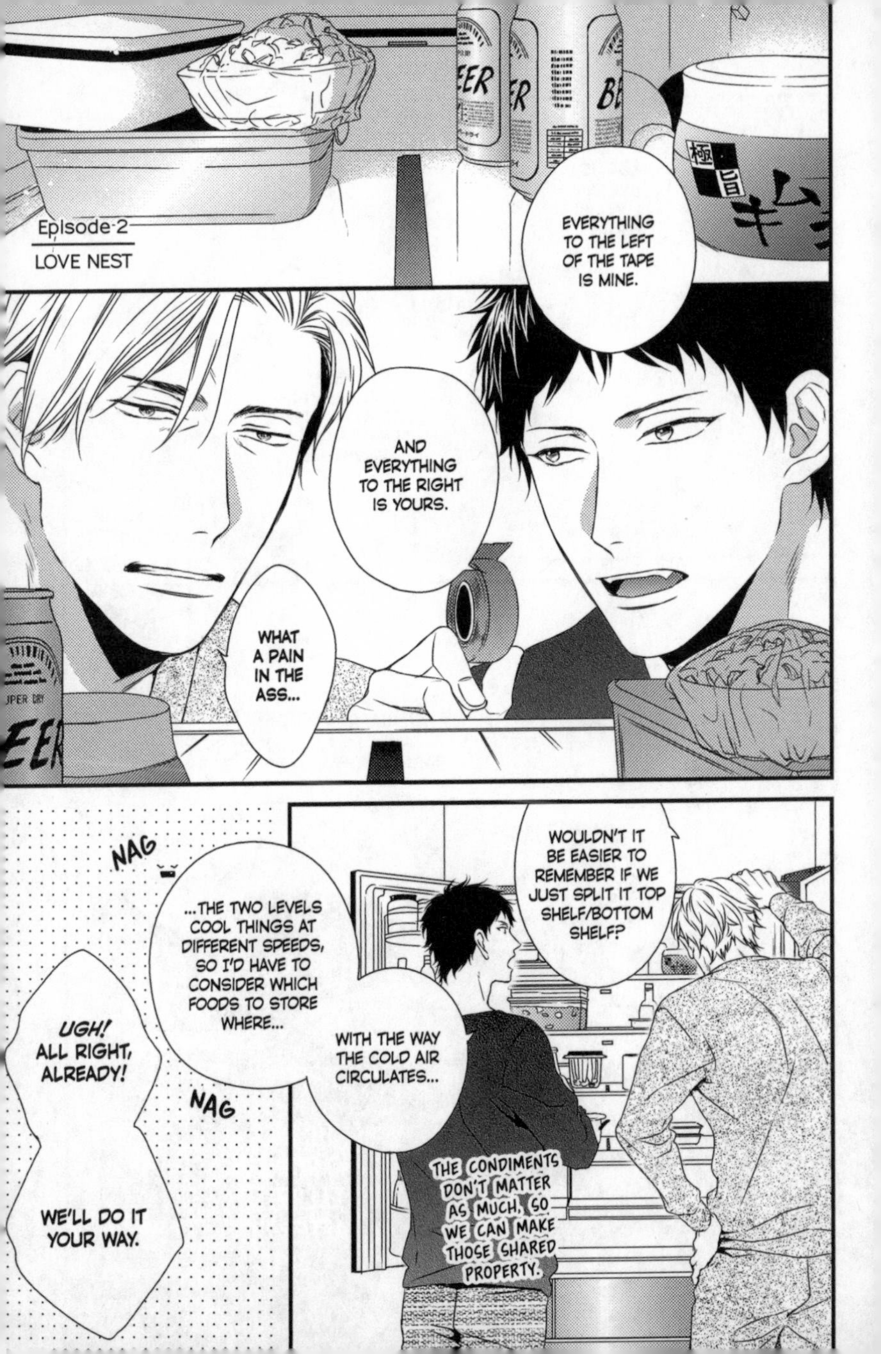
Episode 2
LOVE NEST
EVERYTHING TO THE LEFT OF THE TAPE IS MINE.
AND EVERYTHING TO THE RIGHT IS YOURS.
WHAT A PAIN IN THE ASS...
WOULDN'T IT BE EASIER TO REMEMBER IF WE JUST SPLIT IT TOP SHELF/BOTTOM SHELF?
WITH THE WAY THE COLD AIR CIRCULATES...
...THE TWO LEVELS COOL THINGS AT DIFFERENT SPEEDS, SO I'D HAVE TO CONSIDER WHICH FOODS TO STORE WHERE...
THE CONDIMENTS DON'T MATTER AS MUCH, SO WE CAN MAKE THOSE SHARED PROPERTY.
NAG
NAG
UGH! ALL RIGHT, ALREADY!
WE'LL DO IT YOUR WAY.

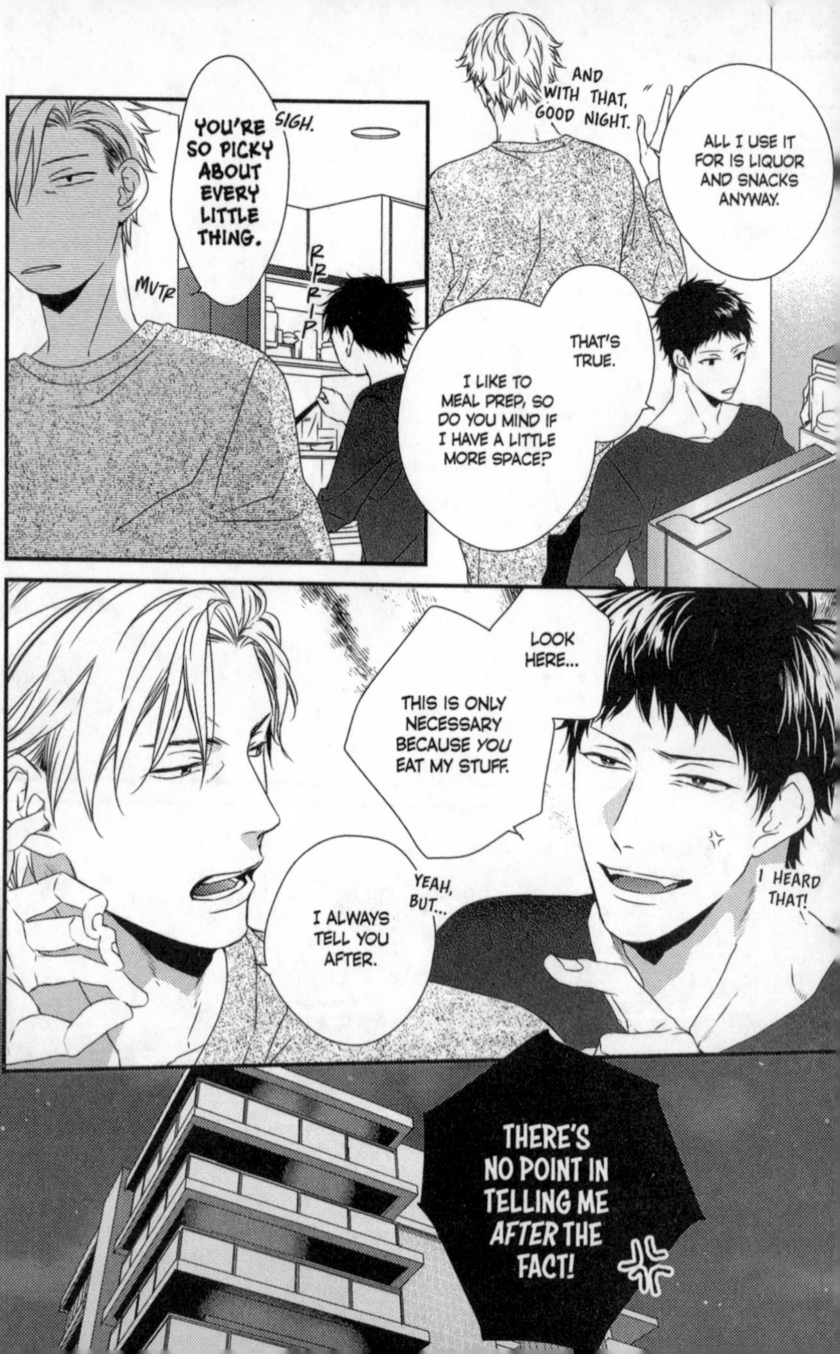
ALL I USE IT FOR IS LIQUOR AND SNACKS ANYWAY.
AND WITH THAT, GOOD NIGHT.
THAT'S TRUE.
I LIKE TO MEAL PREP, SO DO YOU MIND IF I HAVE A LITTLE MORE SPACE?
SIGH.
YOU'RE SO PICKY ABOUT EVERY LITTLE THING.
RRRIP
MUTR
LOOK HERE...
THIS IS ONLY NECESSARY BECAUSE *YOU* EAT MY STUFF.
I HEARD THAT!
YEAH, BUT...
I ALWAYS TELL YOU AFTER.
THERE'S NO POINT IN TELLING ME *AFTER* THE FACT!

Episode 2

LOVE NEST

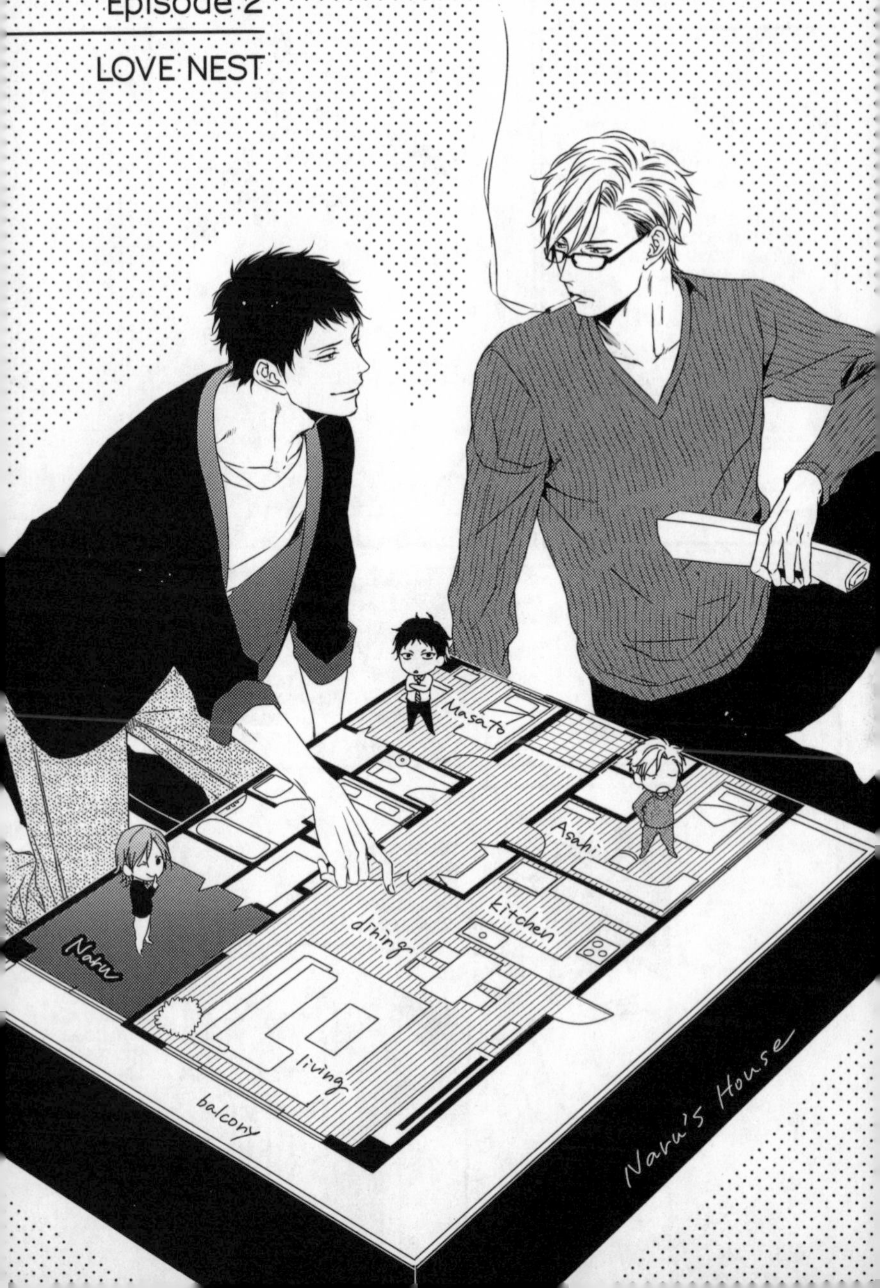
Masato
Asahi
Naru
kitchen
dining
living
balcony
Naru's House

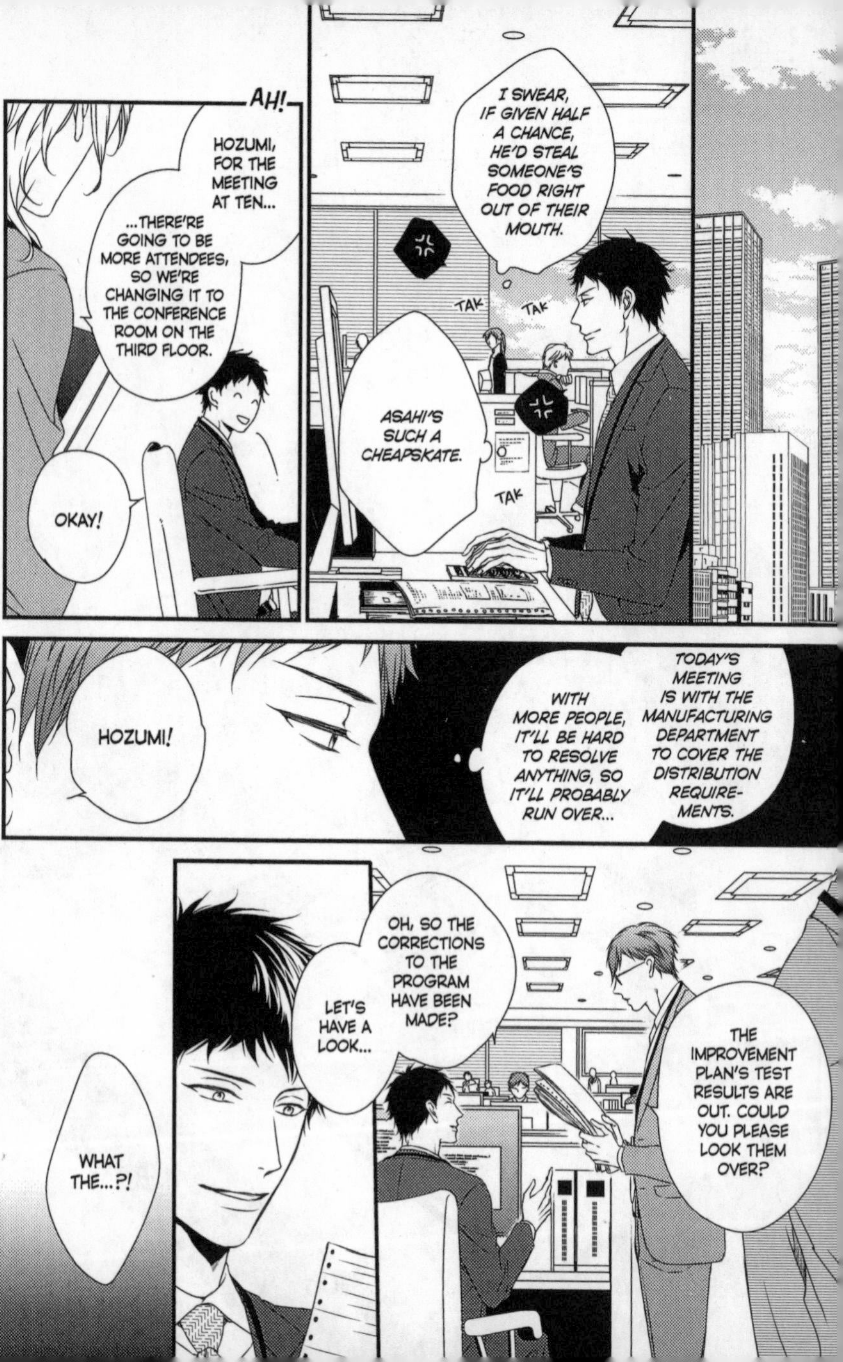
I SWEAR, IF GIVEN HALF A CHANCE, HE'D STEAL SOMEONE'S FOOD RIGHT OUT OF THEIR MOUTH.
TAK
TAK
ASAHI'S SUCH A CHEAPSKATE.
TAK
AH!
HOZUMI, FOR THE MEETING AT TEN...
...THERE'RE GOING TO BE MORE ATTENDEES, SO WE'RE CHANGING IT TO THE CONFERENCE ROOM ON THE THIRD FLOOR.
OKAY!
TODAY'S MEETING IS WITH THE MANUFACTURING DEPARTMENT TO COVER THE DISTRIBUTION REQUIRE-MENTS.
WITH MORE PEOPLE, IT'LL BE HARD TO RESOLVE ANYTHING, SO IT'LL PROBABLY RUN OVER...
HOZUMI!
THE IMPROVEMENT PLAN'S TEST RESULTS ARE OUT. COULD YOU PLEASE LOOK THEM OVER?
OH, SO THE CORRECTIONS TO THE PROGRAM HAVE BEEN MADE?
LET'S HAVE A LOOK...
WHAT THE...?!

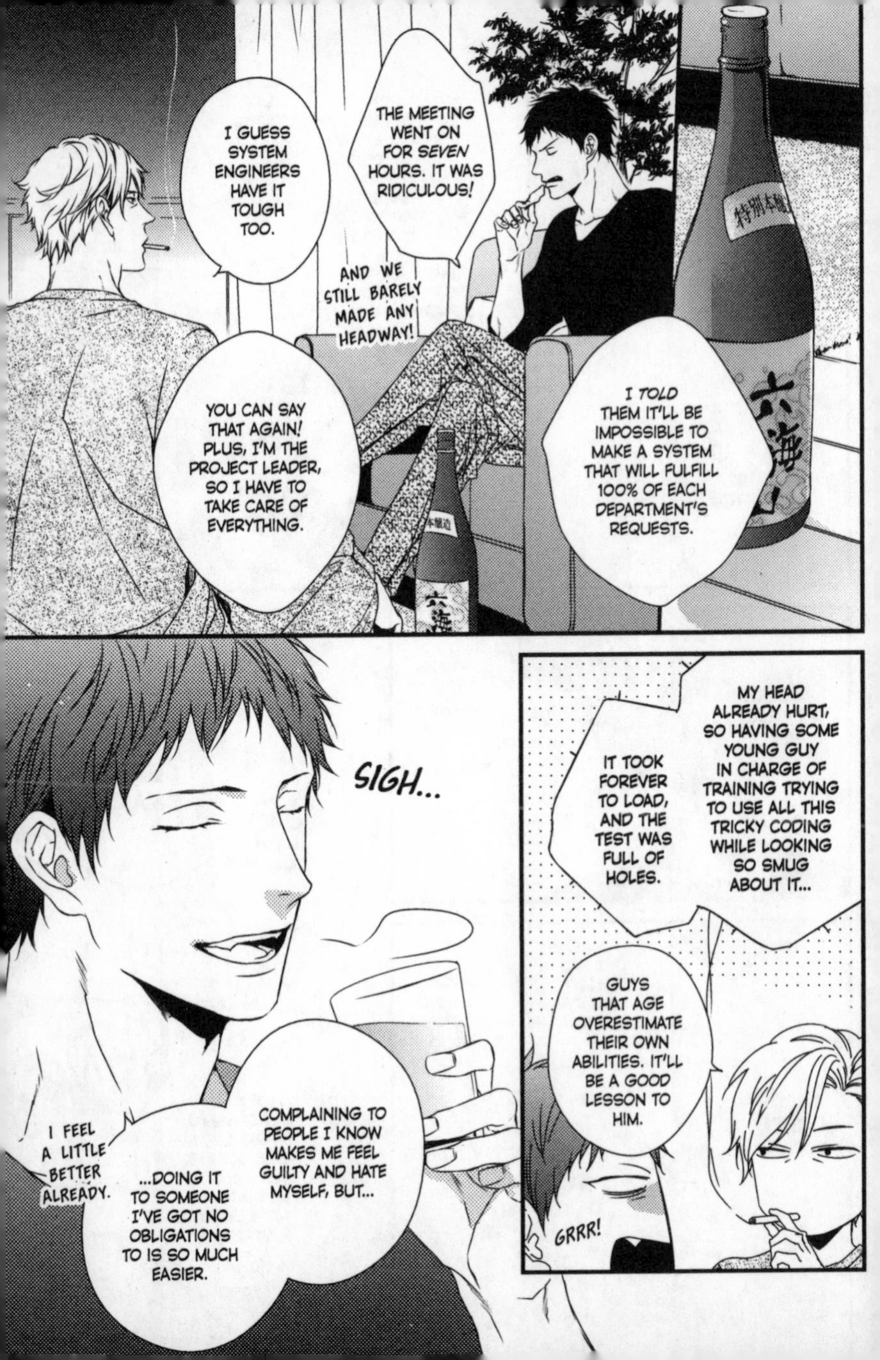
THE MEETING WENT ON FOR SEVEN HOURS. IT WAS RIDICULOUS!
AND WE STILL BARELY MADE ANY HEADWAY!
I GUESS SYSTEM ENGINEERS HAVE IT TOUGH TOO.
YOU CAN SAY THAT AGAIN! PLUS, I'M THE PROJECT LEADER, SO I HAVE TO TAKE CARE OF EVERYTHING.
I TOLD THEM IT'LL BE IMPOSSIBLE TO MAKE A SYSTEM THAT WILL FULFILL 100% OF EACH DEPARTMENT'S REQUESTS.
MY HEAD ALREADY HURT, SO HAVING SOME YOUNG GUY IN CHARGE OF TRAINING TRYING TO USE ALL THIS TRICKY CODING WHILE LOOKING SO SMUG ABOUT IT...
IT TOOK FOREVER TO LOAD, AND THE TEST WAS FULL OF HOLES.
GUYS THAT AGE OVERESTIMATE THEIR OWN ABILITIES. IT'LL BE A GOOD LESSON TO HIM.
GRRR!
SIGH...
COMPLAINING TO PEOPLE I KNOW MAKES ME FEEL GUILTY AND HATE MYSELF, BUT...
...DOING IT TO SOMEONE I'VE GOT NO OBLIGATIONS TO IS SO MUCH EASIER.
I FEEL A LITTLE BETTER ALREADY.

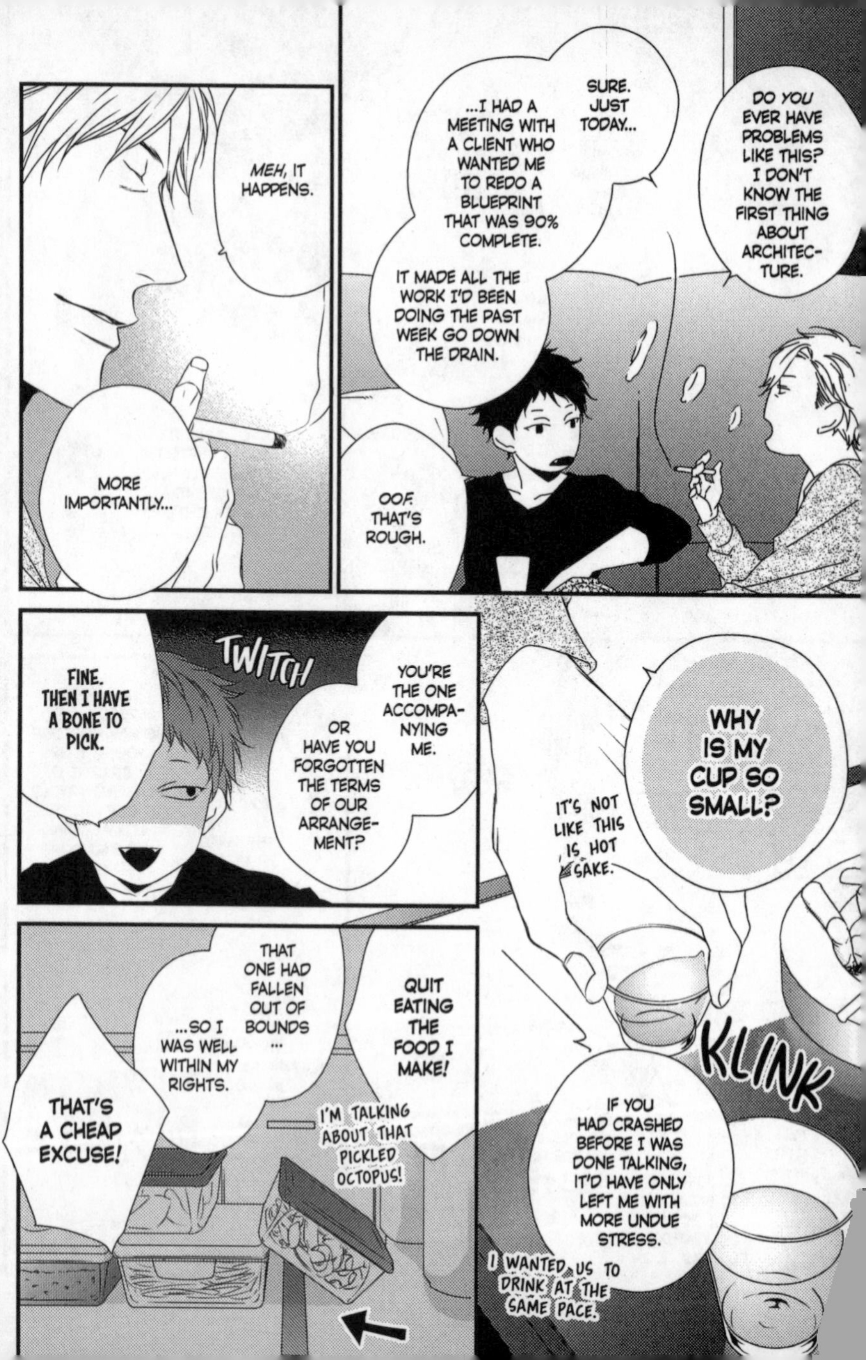
DO YOU EVER HAVE PROBLEMS LIKE THIS? I DON'T KNOW THE FIRST THING ABOUT ARCHITEC-TURE.
SURE. JUST TODAY...
...I HAD A MEETING WITH A CLIENT WHO WANTED ME TO REDO A BLUEPRINT THAT WAS 90% COMPLETE.
IT MADE ALL THE WORK I'D BEEN DOING THE PAST WEEK GO DOWN THE DRAIN.
OOF. THAT'S ROUGH.
MEH, IT HAPPENS.
MORE IMPORTANTLY...
WHY IS MY CUP SO SMALL?
IT'S NOT LIKE THIS IS HOT SAKE.
KLINK
IF YOU HAD CRASHED BEFORE I WAS DONE TALKING, IT'D HAVE ONLY LEFT ME WITH MORE UNDUE STRESS.
I WANTED US TO DRINK AT THE SAME PACE.
YOU'RE THE ONE ACCOMPA-NYING ME.
OR HAVE YOU FORGOTTEN THE TERMS OF OUR ARRANGE-MENT?
TWITCH
FINE. THEN I HAVE A BONE TO PICK.
QUIT EATING THE FOOD I MAKE!
I'M TALKING ABOUT THAT PICKLED OCTOPUS!
THAT ONE HAD FALLEN OUT OF BOUNDS...
...SO I WAS WELL WITHIN MY RIGHTS.
THAT'S A CHEAP EXCUSE!

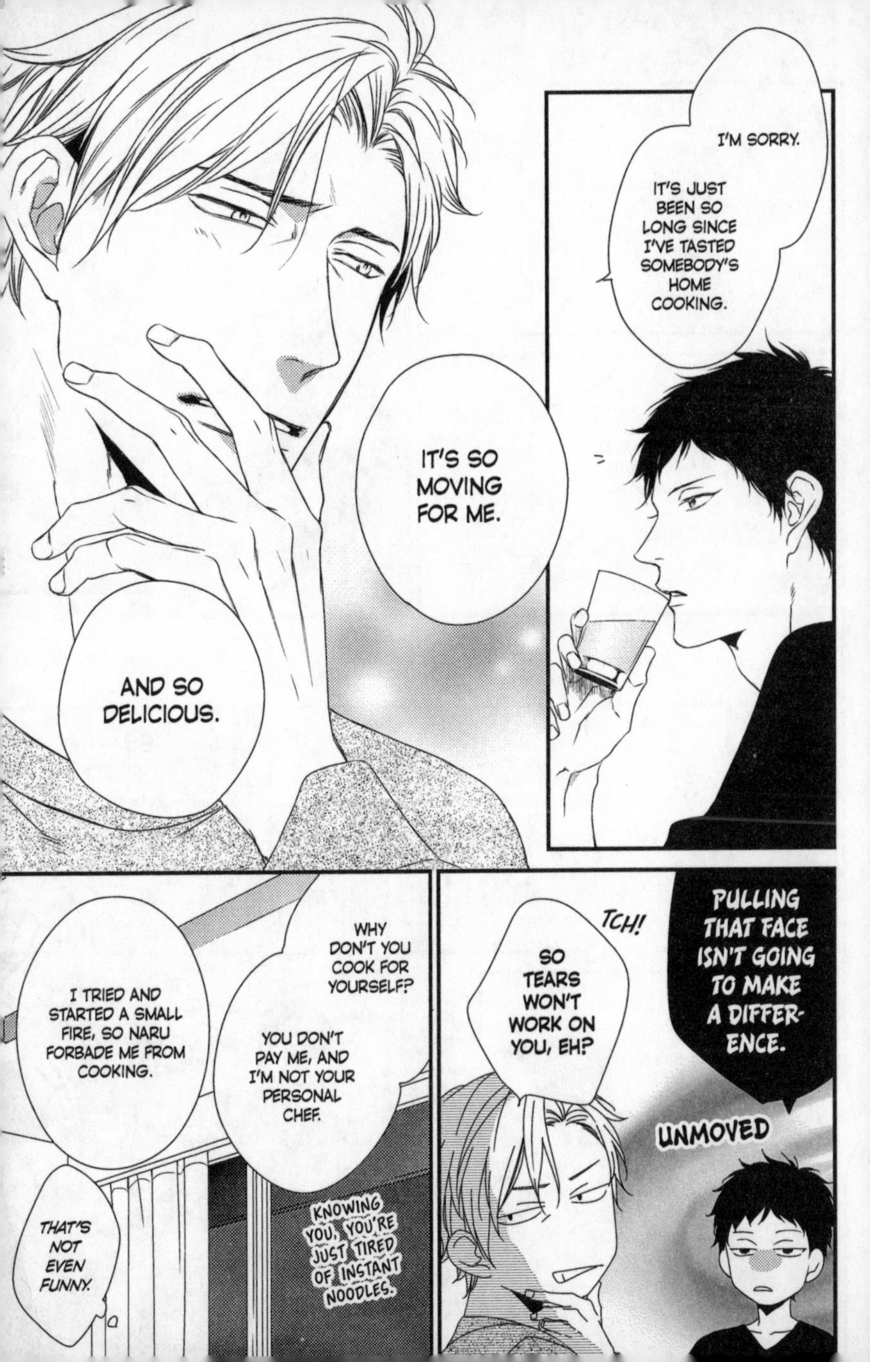
I'M SORRY.
IT'S JUST BEEN SO LONG SINCE I'VE TASTED SOMEBODY'S HOME COOKING.
IT'S SO MOVING FOR ME.
AND SO DELICIOUS.
PULLING THAT FACE ISN'T GOING TO MAKE A DIFFERENCE.
TCH!
SO TEARS WON'T WORK ON YOU, EH?
UNMOVED
WHY DON'T YOU COOK FOR YOURSELF?
YOU DON'T PAY ME, AND I'M NOT YOUR PERSONAL CHEF.
I TRIED AND STARTED A SMALL FIRE, SO NARU FORBADE ME FROM COOKING.
KNOWING YOU, YOU'RE JUST TIRED OF INSTANT NOODLES.
THAT'S NOT EVEN FUNNY.

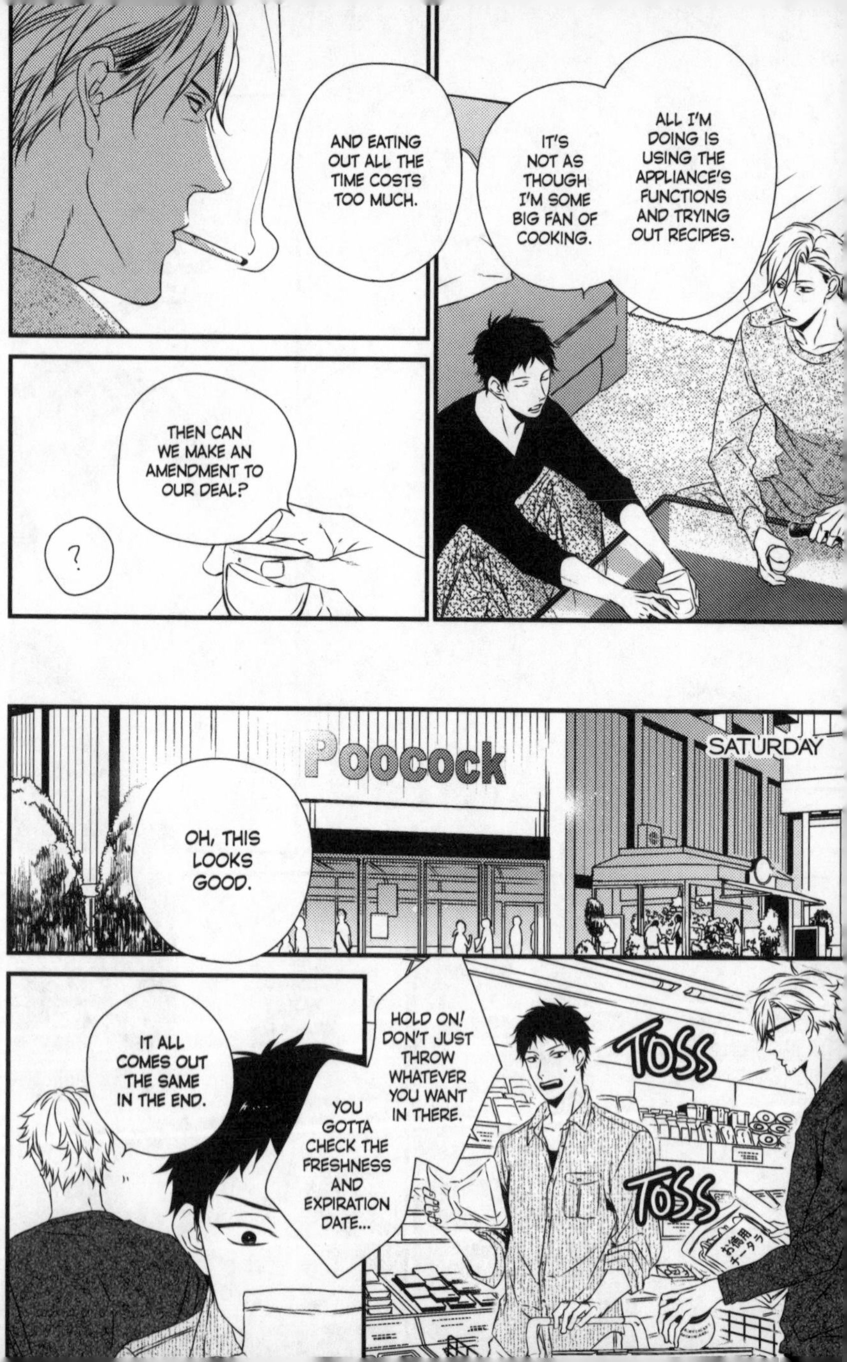
ALL I'M DOING IS USING THE APPLIANCE'S FUNCTIONS AND TRYING OUT RECIPES.
IT'S NOT AS THOUGH I'M SOME BIG FAN OF COOKING.
AND EATING OUT ALL THE TIME COSTS TOO MUCH.
THEN CAN WE MAKE AN AMENDMENT TO OUR DEAL?
?
SATURDAY
Poocock
OH, THIS LOOKS GOOD.
TOSS
TOSS
お徳用
チータラ
HOLD ON! DON'T JUST THROW WHATEVER YOU WANT IN THERE.
YOU GOTTA CHECK THE FRESHNESS AND EXPIRATION DATE...
IT ALL COMES OUT THE SAME IN THE END.

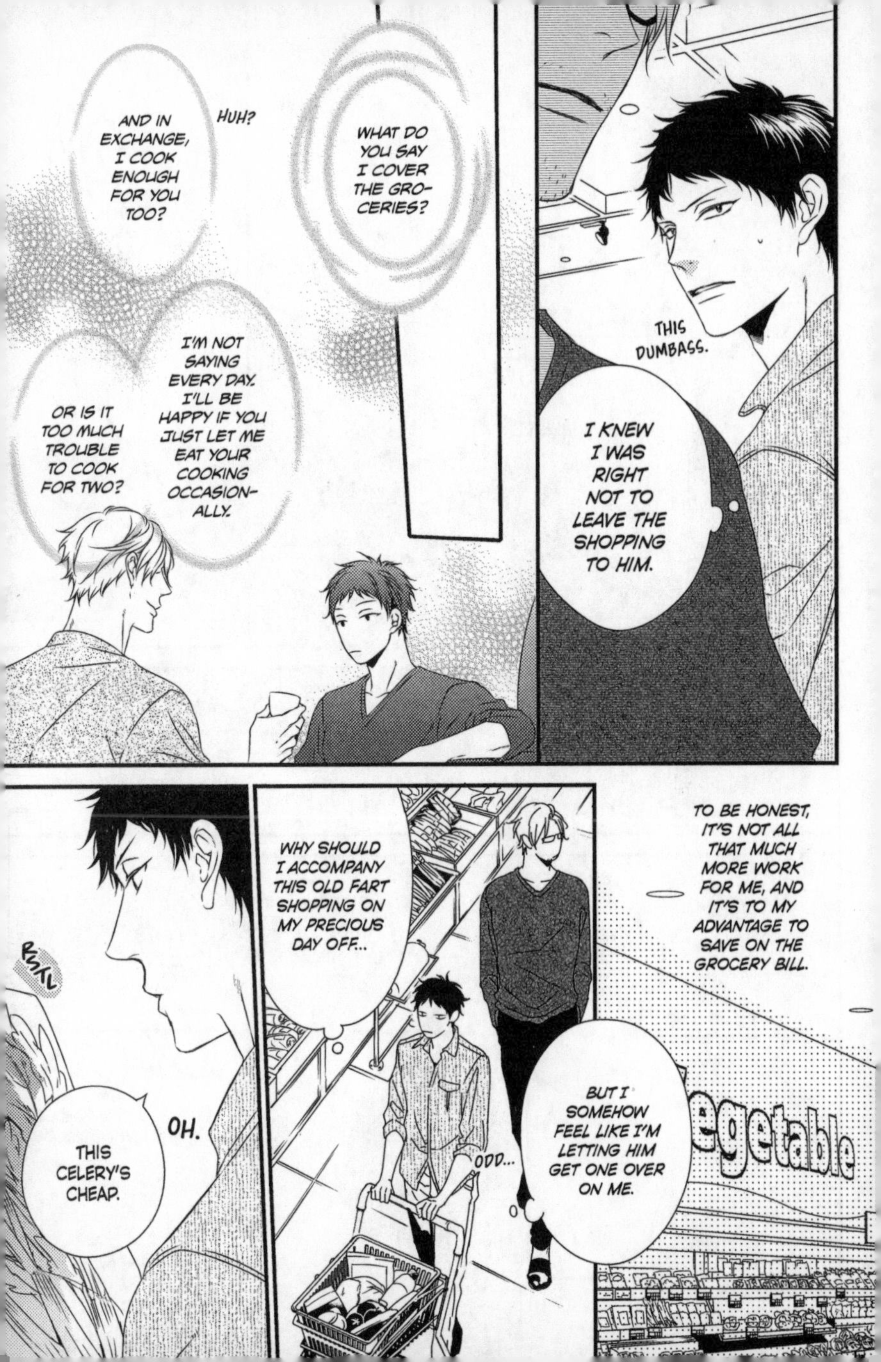
THIS DUMBASS.
I KNEW I WAS RIGHT NOT TO LEAVE THE SHOPPING TO HIM.
WHAT DO YOU SAY I COVER THE GRO-CERIES?
HUH?
AND IN EXCHANGE, I COOK ENOUGH FOR YOU TOO?
I'M NOT SAYING EVERY DAY. I'LL BE HAPPY IF YOU JUST LET ME EAT YOUR COOKING OCCASION-ALLY.
OR IS IT TOO MUCH TROUBLE TO COOK FOR TWO?
TO BE HONEST, IT'S NOT ALL THAT MUCH MORE WORK FOR ME, AND IT'S TO MY ADVANTAGE TO SAVE ON THE GROCERY BILL.
BUT I SOMEHOW FEEL LIKE I'M LETTING HIM GET ONE OVER ON ME.
egetable
WHY SHOULD I ACCOMPANY THIS OLD FART SHOPPING ON MY PRECIOUS DAY OFF...
ODD...
RSSTL
OH.
THIS CELERY'S CHEAP.

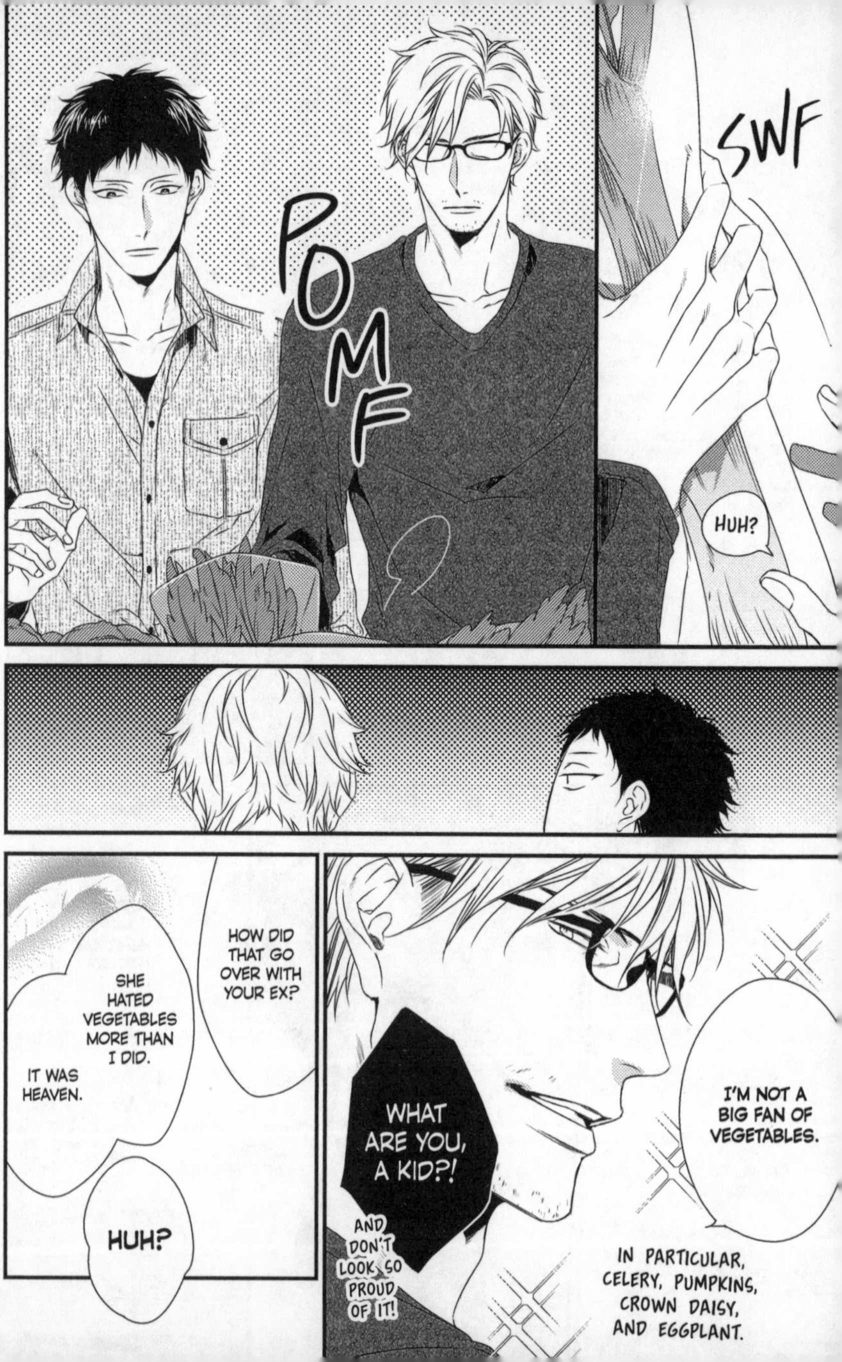
SWF
HUH?
POMF
I'M NOT A BIG FAN OF VEGETABLES.
IN PARTICULAR, CELERY, PUMPKINS, CROWN DAISY, AND EGGPLANT.
WHAT ARE YOU, A KID?!
AND DON'T LOOK SO PROUD OF IT!
HOW DID THAT GO OVER WITH YOUR EX?
SHE HATED VEGETABLES MORE THAN I DID.
IT WAS HEAVEN.
HUH?

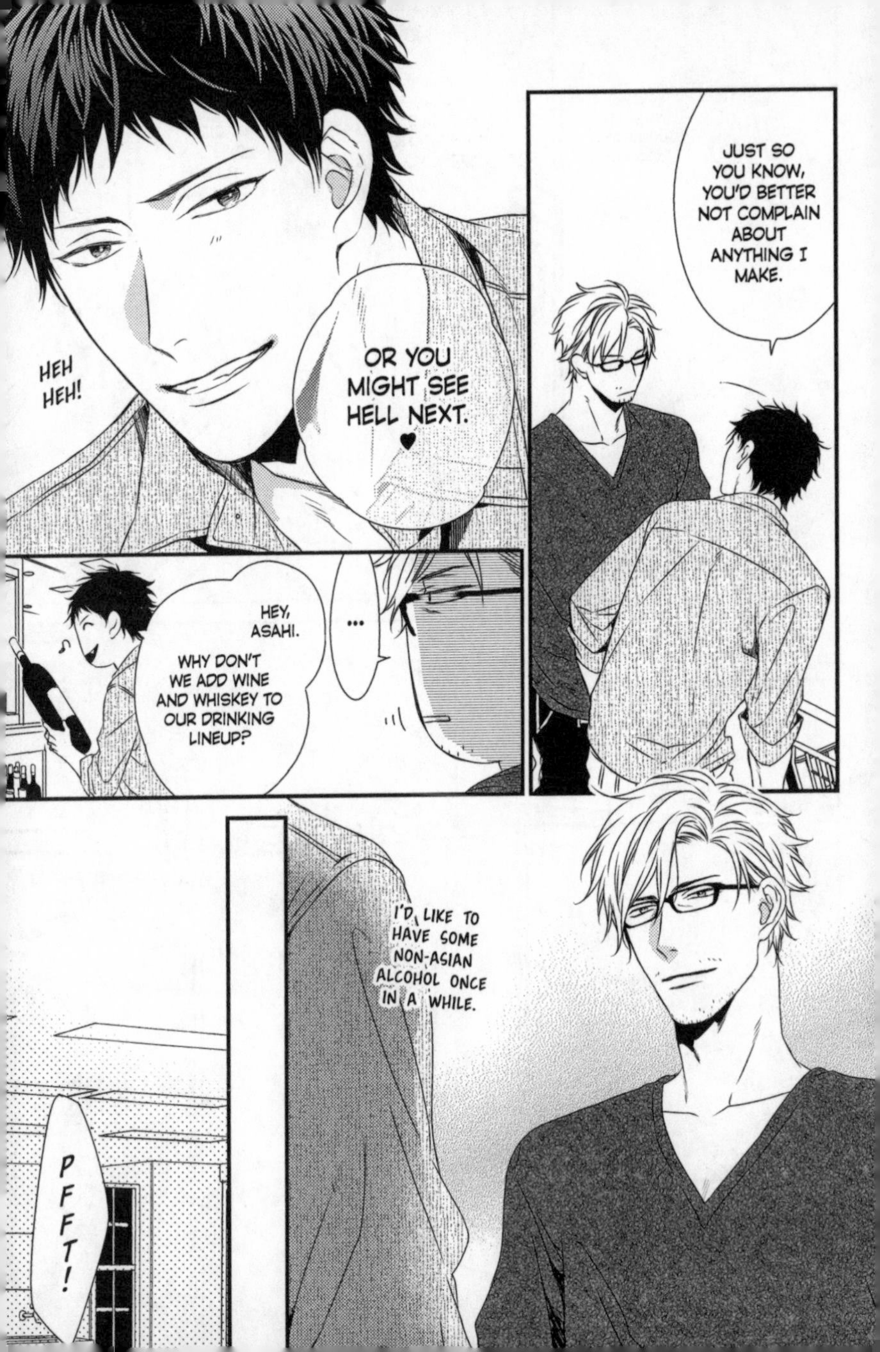
JUST SO YOU KNOW, YOU'D BETTER NOT COMPLAIN ABOUT ANYTHING I MAKE.
OR YOU MIGHT SEE HELL NEXT. ♥
HEH HEH!
...
HEY, ASAHI.
WHY DON'T WE ADD WINE AND WHISKEY TO OUR DRINKING LINEUP?
I'D LIKE TO HAVE SOME NON-ASIAN ALCOHOL ONCE IN A WHILE.
PFFT!

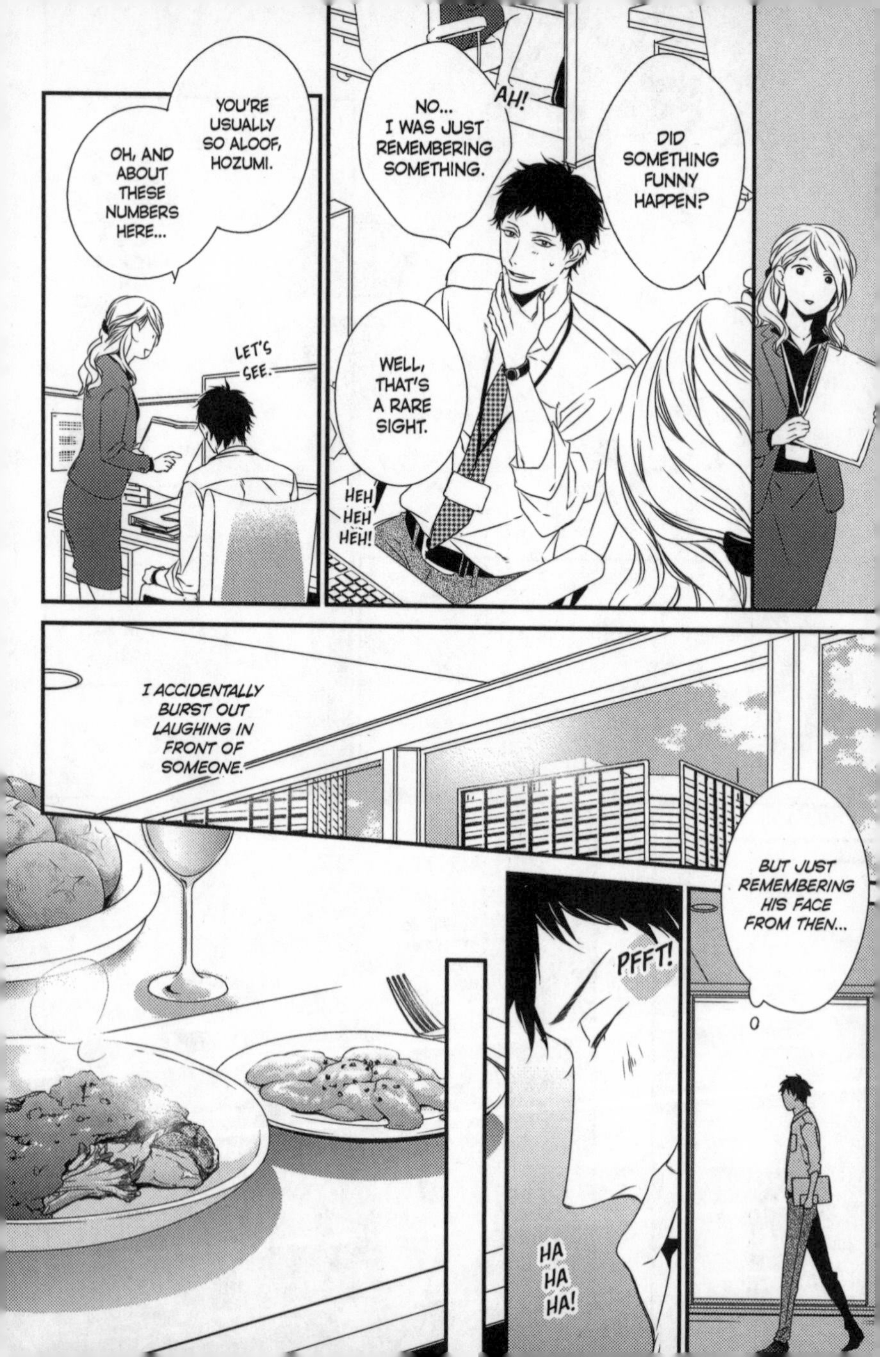

DID SOMETHING FUNNY HAPPEN?
AH!
NO... I WAS JUST REMEMBERING SOMETHING.
WELL, THAT'S A RARE SIGHT.
HEH HEH HEH!
YOU'RE USUALLY SO ALOOF, HOZUMI.
OH, AND ABOUT THESE NUMBERS HERE...
LET'S SEE.
I ACCIDENTALLY BURST OUT LAUGHING IN FRONT OF SOMEONE.
BUT JUST REMEMBERING HIS FACE FROM THEN...
PFFT!
HA HA HA!

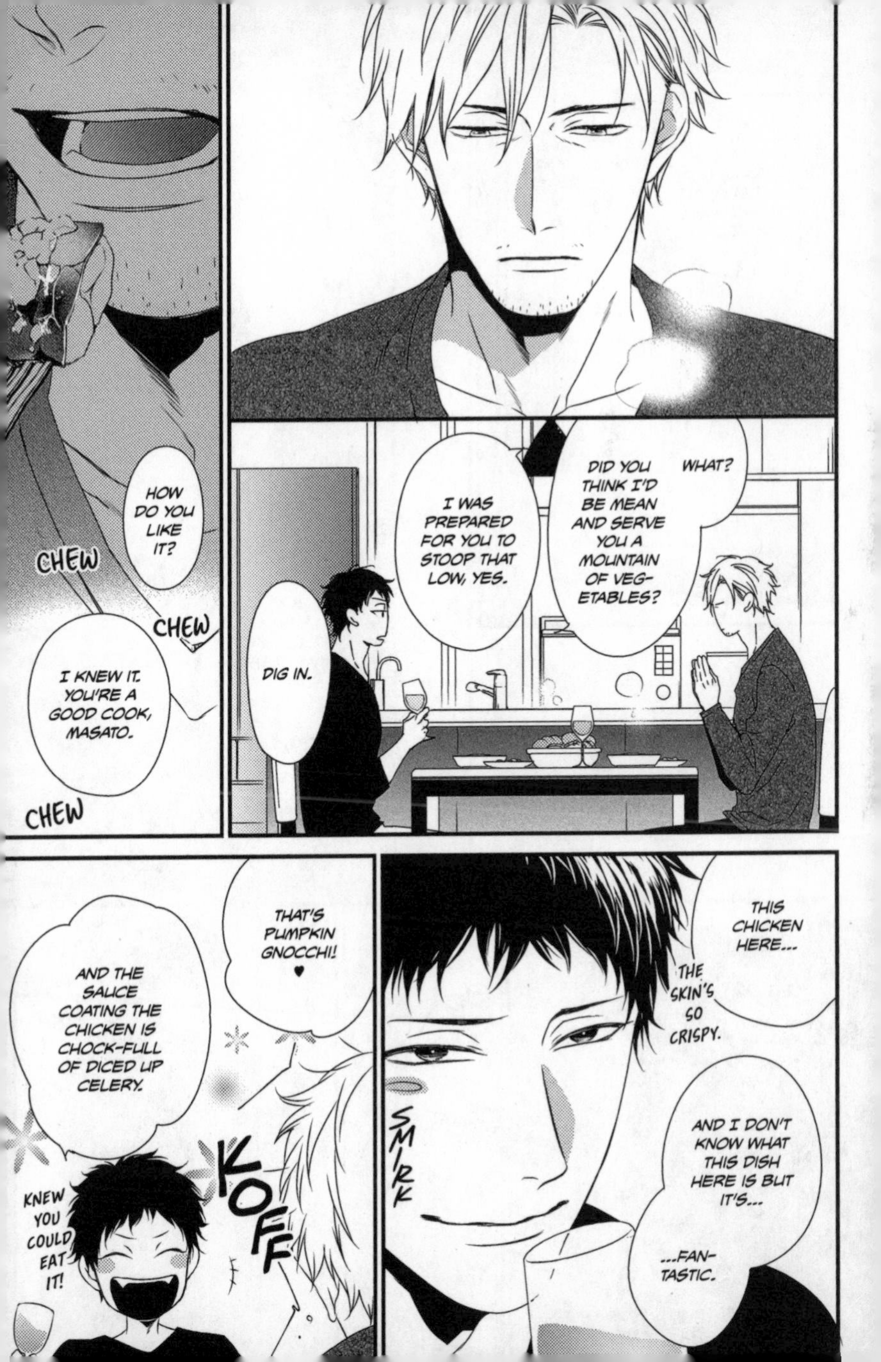
WHAT?
DID YOU THINK I'D BE MEAN AND SERVE YOU A MOUNTAIN OF VEG-ETABLES?
I WAS PREPARED FOR YOU TO STOOP THAT LOW, YES.
DIG IN.
HOW DO YOU LIKE IT?
CHEW
CHEW
I KNEW IT. YOU'RE A GOOD COOK, MASATO.
CHEW
THIS CHICKEN HERE...
THE SKIN'S SO CRISPY.
SMIRK
AND I DON'T KNOW WHAT THIS DISH HERE IS BUT IT'S...
...FAN-TASTIC.
THAT'S PUMPKIN GNOCCHI! ♥
AND THE SAUCE COATING THE CHICKEN IS CHOCK-FULL OF DICED UP CELERY.
KOFF
KNEW YOU COULD EAT IT!

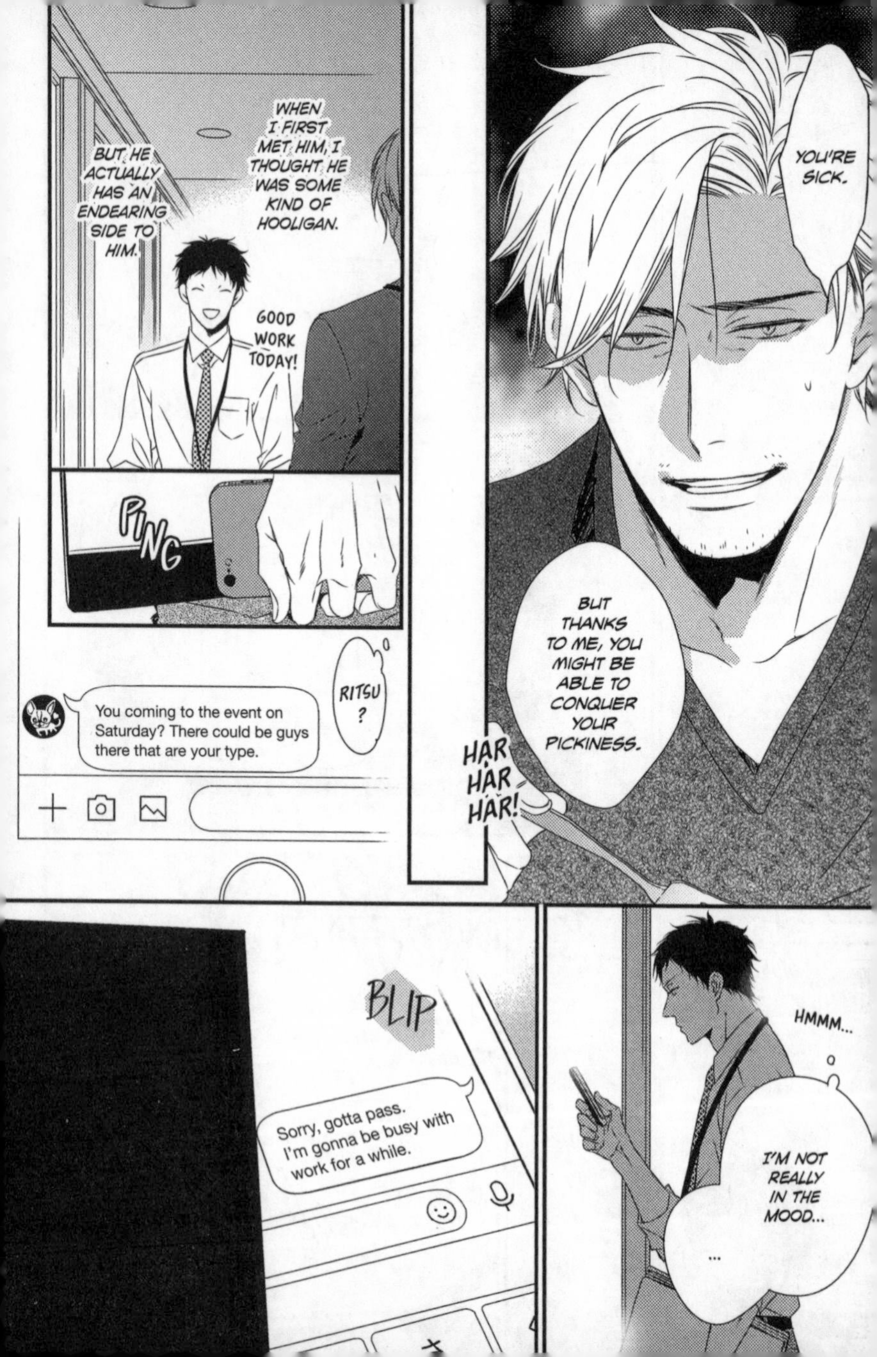
YOU'RE SICK.
BUT THANKS TO ME, YOU MIGHT BE ABLE TO CONQUER YOUR PICKINESS.
HAR HAR HAR!
WHEN I FIRST MET HIM, I THOUGHT HE WAS SOME KIND OF HOOLIGAN.
BUT HE ACTUALLY HAS AN ENDEARING SIDE TO HIM.
GOOD WORK TODAY!
PING
RITSU?
You coming to the event on Saturday? There could be guys there that are your type.
HMMM...
I'M NOT REALLY IN THE MOOD...
...
BLIP
Sorry, gotta pass. I'm gonna be busy with work for a while.

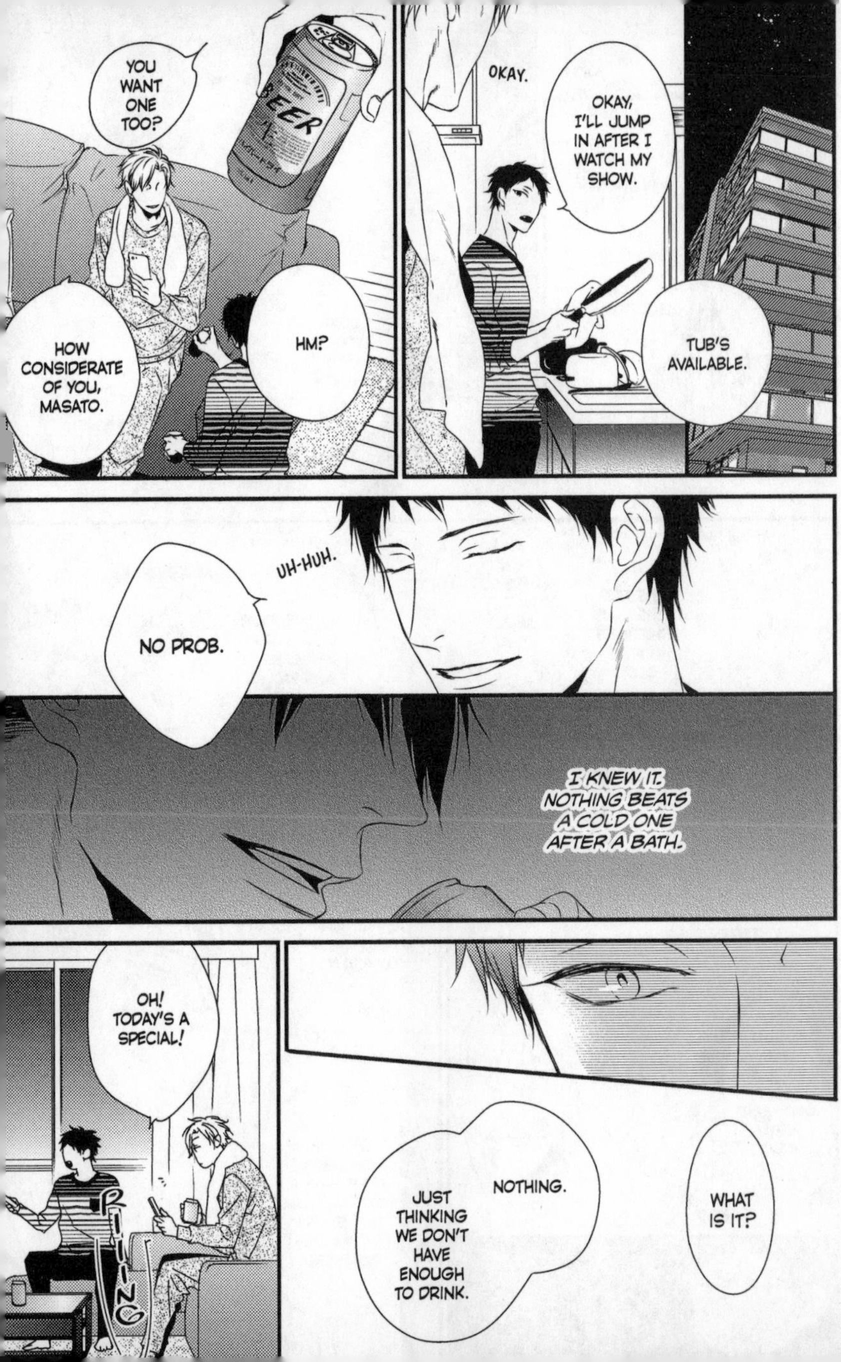
TUB'S AVAILABLE.
OKAY, I'LL JUMP IN AFTER I WATCH MY SHOW.
OKAY.
YOU WANT ONE TOO?
HM?
HOW CONSIDERATE OF YOU, MASATO.
UH-HUH.
NO PROB.
I KNEW IT. NOTHING BEATS A COLD ONE AFTER A BATH.
WHAT IS IT?
NOTHING.
JUST THINKING WE DON'T HAVE ENOUGH TO DRINK.
OH! TODAY'S A SPECIAL!
RIIING

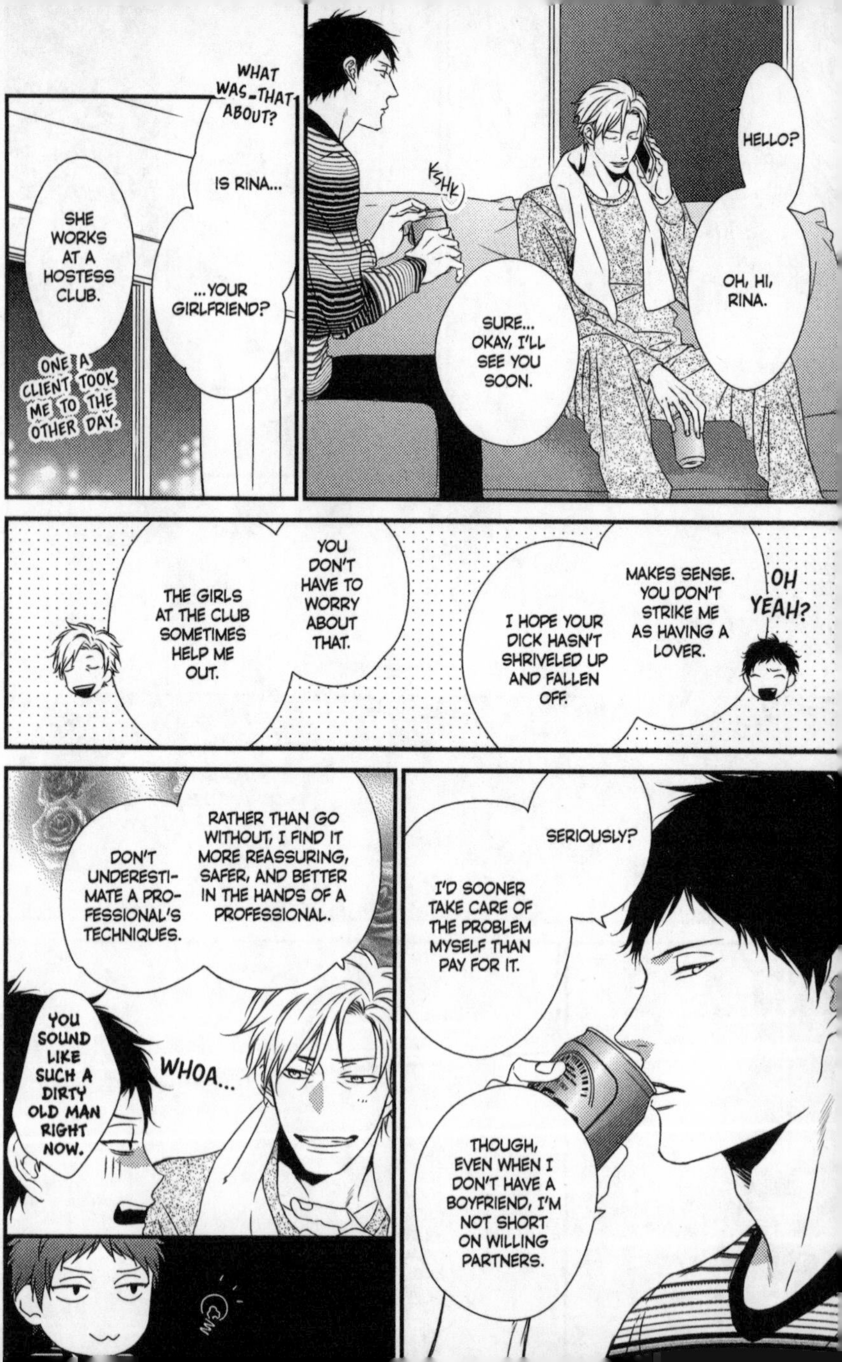
HELLO?
OH, HI, RINA.
KSHK
SURE... OKAY, I'LL SEE YOU SOON.
WHAT WAS-THAT ABOUT?
IS RINA...
...YOUR GIRLFRIEND?
SHE WORKS AT A HOSTESS CLUB.
ONE A CLIENT TOOK ME TO THE OTHER DAY.
OH YEAH?
MAKES SENSE. YOU DON'T STRIKE ME AS HAVING A LOVER.
I HOPE YOUR DICK HASN'T SHRIVELED UP AND FALLEN OFF.
YOU DON'T HAVE TO WORRY ABOUT THAT.
THE GIRLS AT THE CLUB SOMETIMES HELP ME OUT.
SERIOUSLY?
I'D SOONER TAKE CARE OF THE PROBLEM MYSELF THAN PAY FOR IT.
THOUGH, EVEN WHEN I DON'T HAVE A BOYFRIEND, I'M NOT SHORT ON WILLING PARTNERS.
RATHER THAN GO WITHOUT, I FIND IT MORE REASSURING, SAFER, AND BETTER IN THE HANDS OF A PROFESSIONAL.
DON'T UNDERESTI-MATE A PRO-FESSIONAL'S TECHNIQUES.
WHOA...
YOU SOUND LIKE SUCH A DIRTY OLD MAN RIGHT NOW.

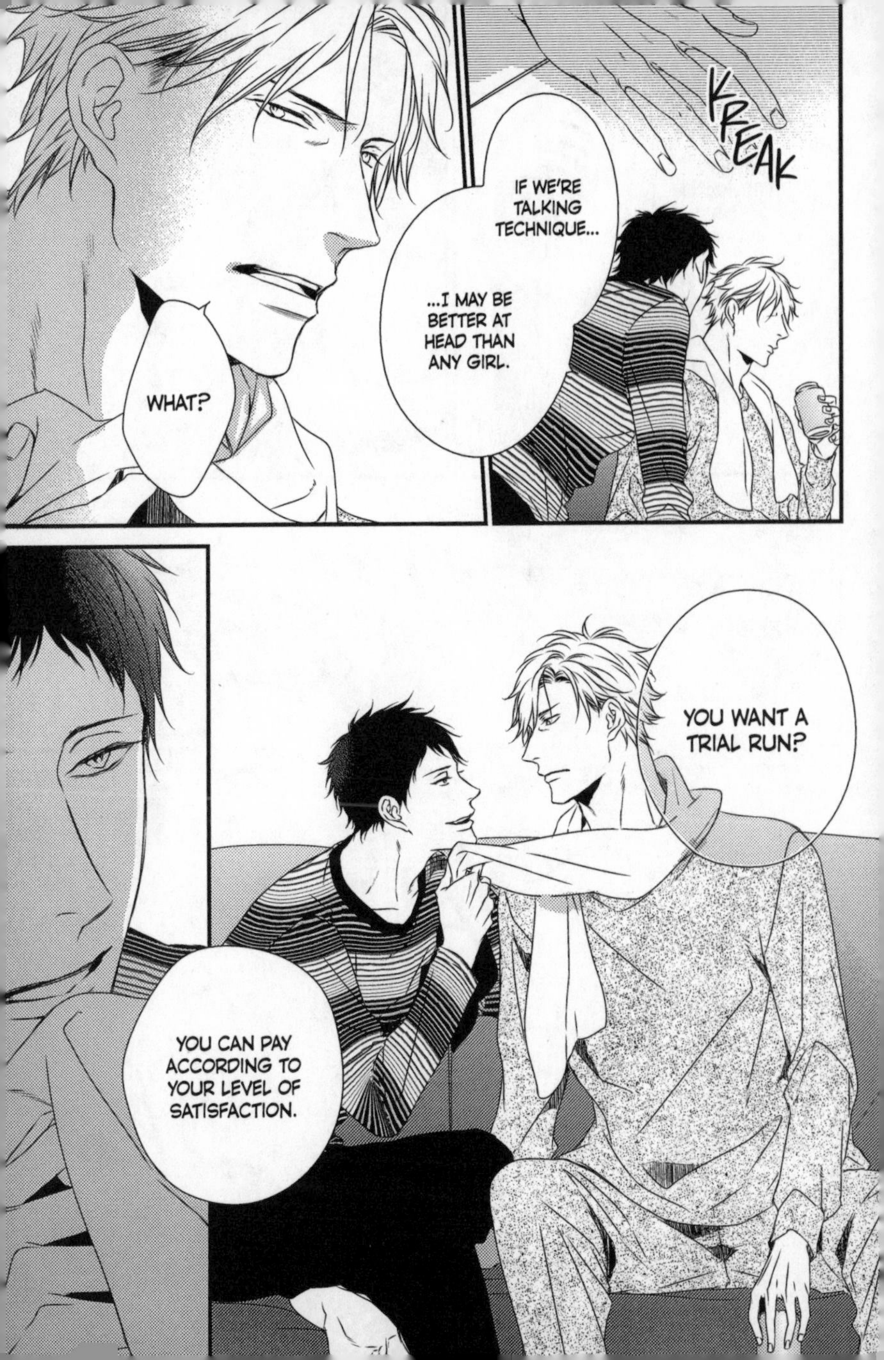
KREAK
IF WE'RE TALKING TECHNIQUE...
...I MAY BE BETTER AT HEAD THAN ANY GIRL.
WHAT?
YOU WANT A TRIAL RUN?
YOU CAN PAY ACCORDING TO YOUR LEVEL OF SATISFACTION.

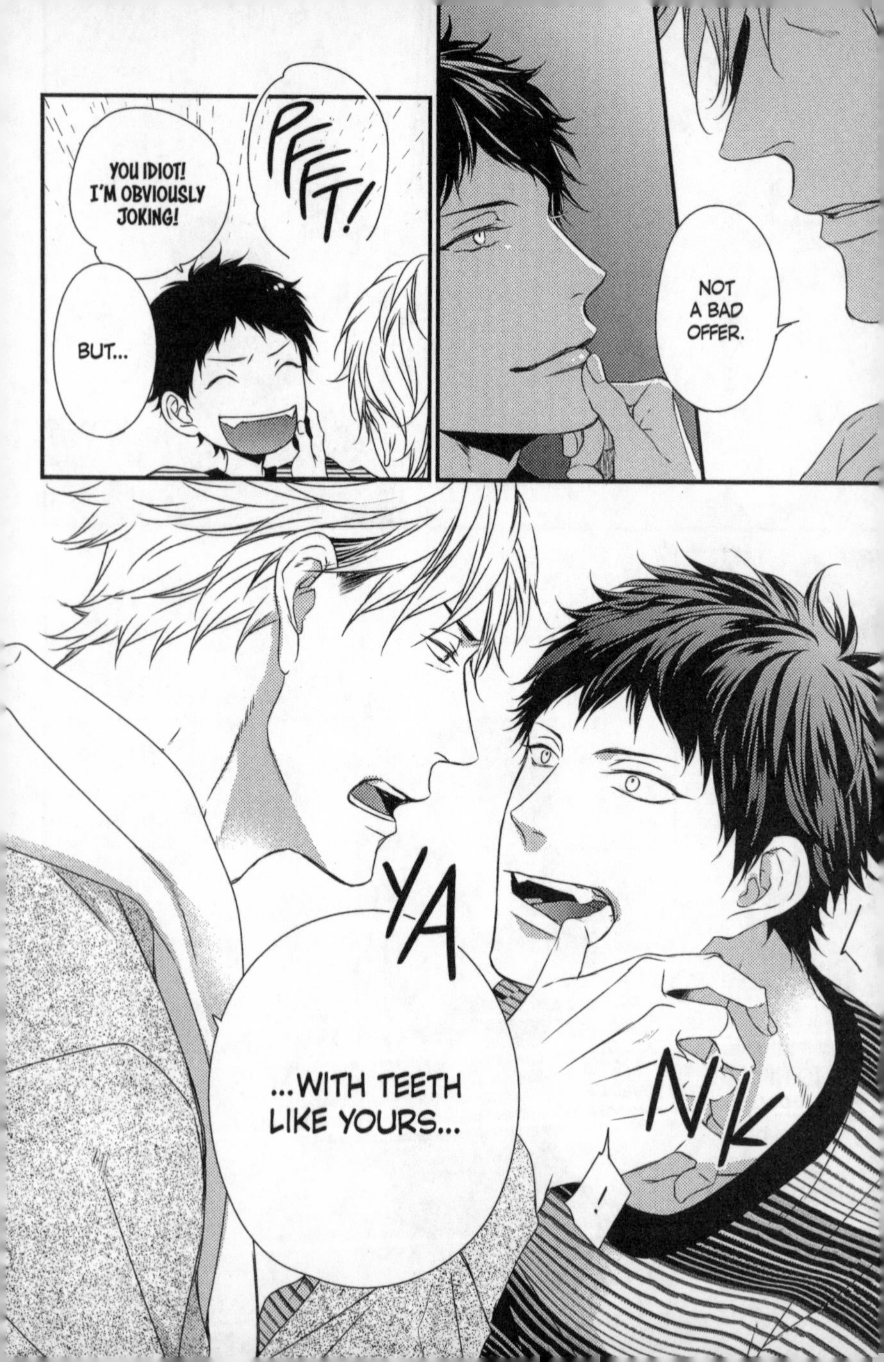
NOT A BAD OFFER.
PFFT!
YOU IDIOT! I'M OBVIOUSLY JOKING!
BUT...
YANK
...WITH TEETH LIKE YOURS...
!

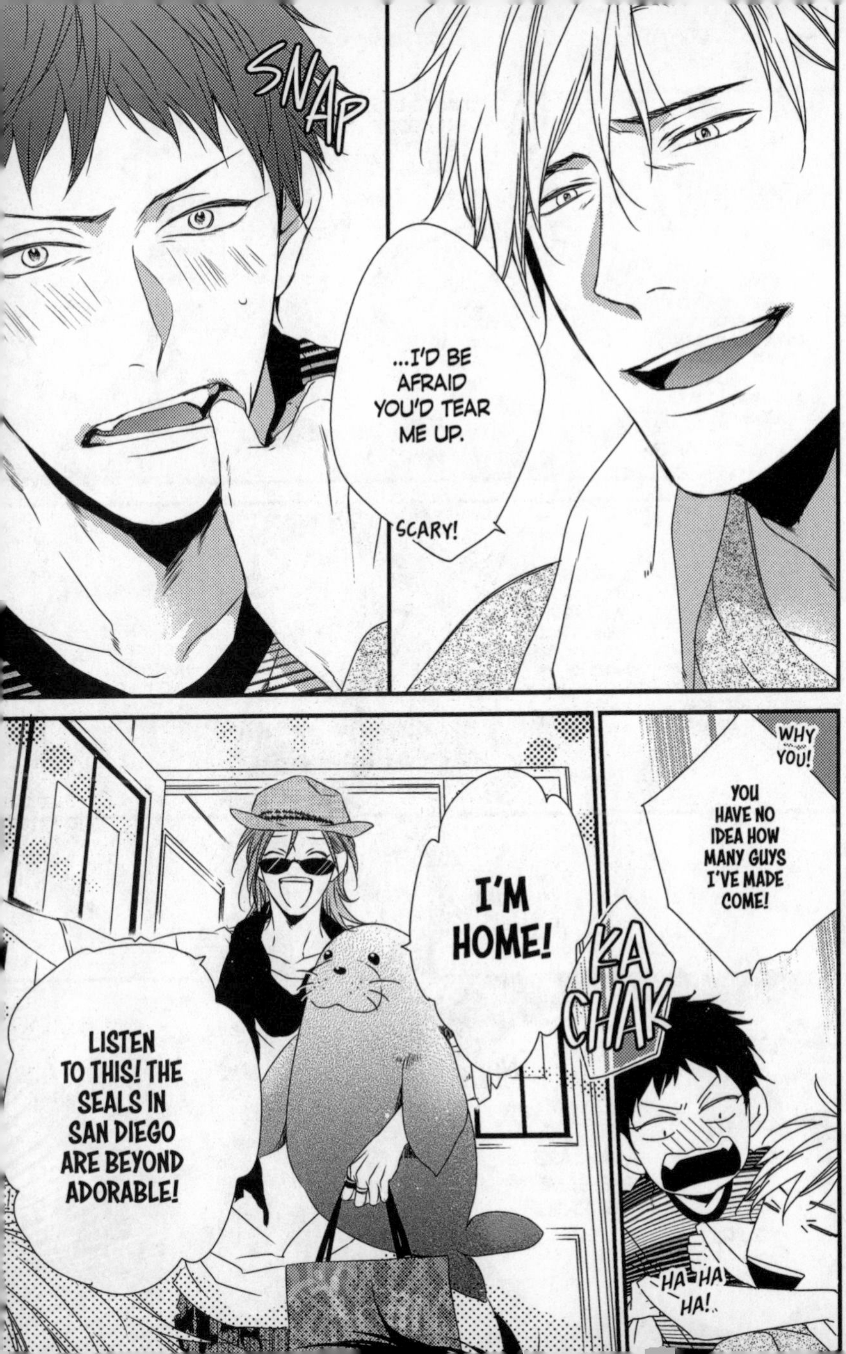
...I'D BE AFRAID YOU'D TEAR ME UP.
SCARY!
SNAP
WHY YOU!
YOU HAVE NO IDEA HOW MANY GUYS I'VE MADE COME!
HA HA HA!
KA CHAK
I'M HOME!
LISTEN TO THIS! THE SEALS IN SAN DIEGO ARE BEYOND ADORABLE!

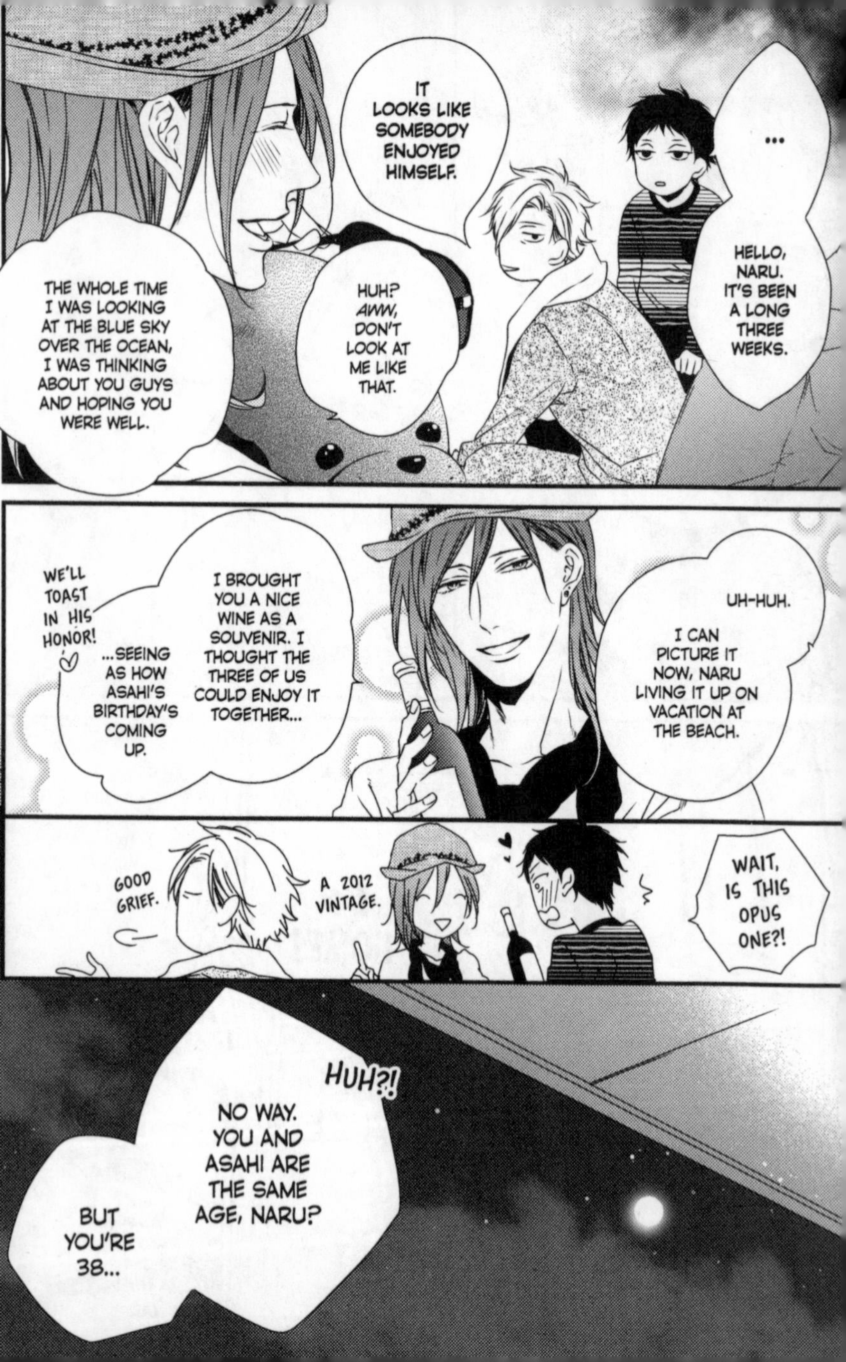
...
HELLO, NARU. IT'S BEEN A LONG THREE WEEKS.
IT LOOKS LIKE SOMEBODY ENJOYED HIMSELF.
HUH? AWW, DON'T LOOK AT ME LIKE THAT.
THE WHOLE TIME I WAS LOOKING AT THE BLUE SKY OVER THE OCEAN, I WAS THINKING ABOUT YOU GUYS AND HOPING YOU WERE WELL.
UH-HUH.
I CAN PICTURE IT NOW, NARU LIVING IT UP ON VACATION AT THE BEACH.
I BROUGHT YOU A NICE WINE AS A SOUVENIR. I THOUGHT THE THREE OF US COULD ENJOY IT TOGETHER...
...SEEING AS HOW ASAHI'S BIRTHDAY'S COMING UP.
WE'LL TOAST IN HIS HONOR!
WAIT, IS THIS OPUS ONE?!
A 2012 VINTAGE.
GOOD GRIEF.
HUH?!
NO WAY. YOU AND ASAHI ARE THE SAME AGE, NARU?
BUT YOU'RE 38...

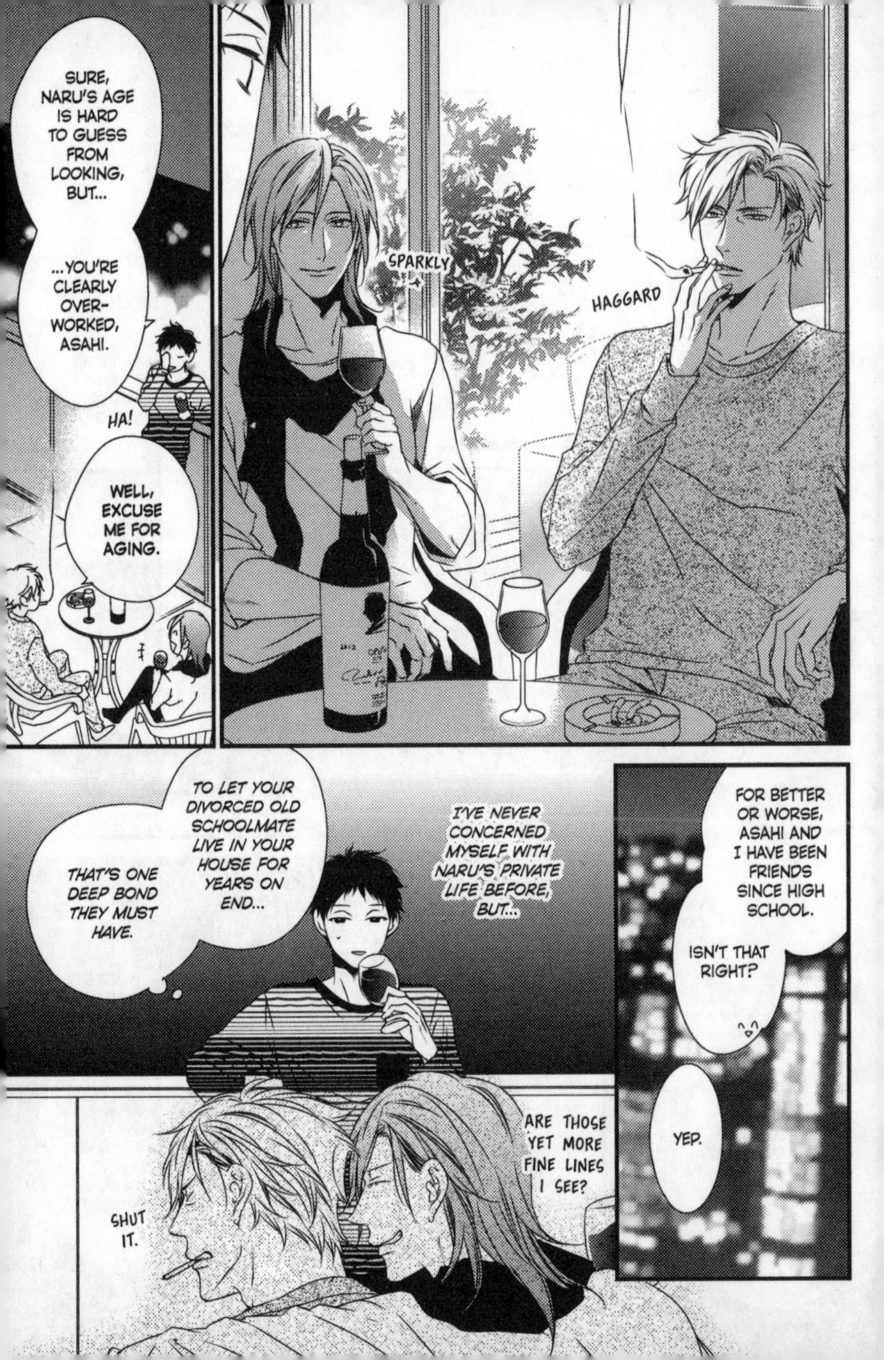
SPARKLY
HAGGARD
SURE, NARU'S AGE IS HARD TO GUESS FROM LOOKING, BUT...
...YOU'RE CLEARLY OVER-WORKED, ASAHI.
HA!
WELL, EXCUSE ME FOR AGING.
FOR BETTER OR WORSE, ASAHI AND I HAVE BEEN FRIENDS SINCE HIGH SCHOOL.
ISN'T THAT RIGHT?
YEP.
I'VE NEVER CONCERNED MYSELF WITH NARU'S PRIVATE LIFE BEFORE, BUT...
TO LET YOUR DIVORCED OLD SCHOOLMATE LIVE IN YOUR HOUSE FOR YEARS ON END...
THAT'S ONE DEEP BOND THEY MUST HAVE.
ARE THOSE YET MORE FINE LINES I SEE?
SHUT IT.

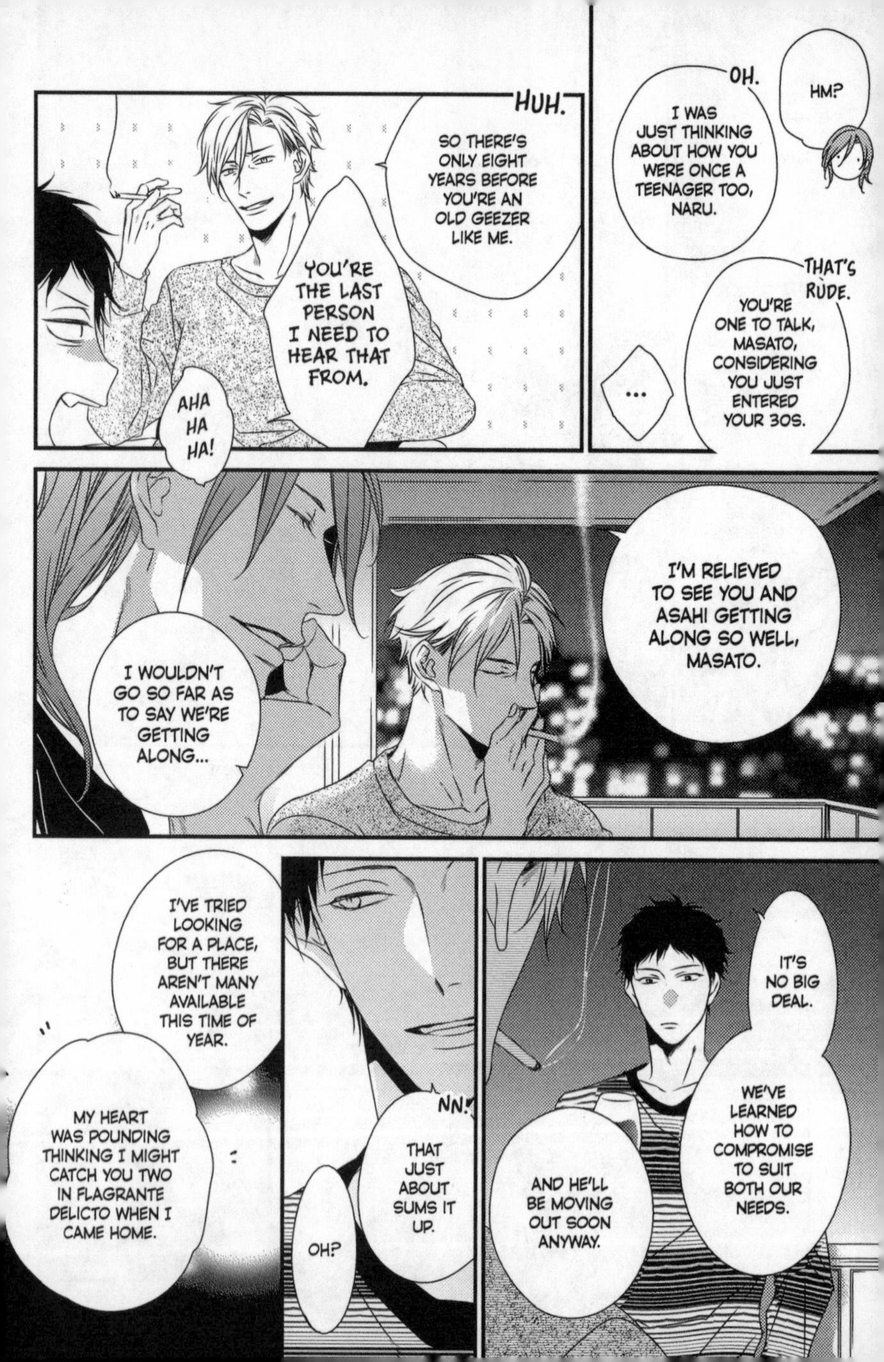
HM?
OH.
I WAS JUST THINKING ABOUT HOW YOU WERE ONCE A TEENAGER TOO, NARU.
THAT'S RUDE.
YOU'RE ONE TO TALK, MASATO, CONSIDERING YOU JUST ENTERED YOUR 30S.
...
HUH.
SO THERE'S ONLY EIGHT YEARS BEFORE YOU'RE AN OLD GEEZER LIKE ME.
YOU'RE THE LAST PERSON I NEED TO HEAR THAT FROM.
AHA HA HA!
I'M RELIEVED TO SEE YOU AND ASAHI GETTING ALONG SO WELL, MASATO.
I WOULDN'T GO SO FAR AS TO SAY WE'RE GETTING ALONG...
IT'S NO BIG DEAL.
WE'VE LEARNED HOW TO COMPROMISE TO SUIT BOTH OUR NEEDS.
AND HE'LL BE MOVING OUT SOON ANYWAY.
I'VE TRIED LOOKING FOR A PLACE, BUT THERE AREN'T MANY AVAILABLE THIS TIME OF YEAR.
NN!
THAT JUST ABOUT SUMS IT UP.
OH?
MY HEART WAS POUNDING THINKING I MIGHT CATCH YOU TWO IN FLAGRANTE DELICTO WHEN I CAME HOME.

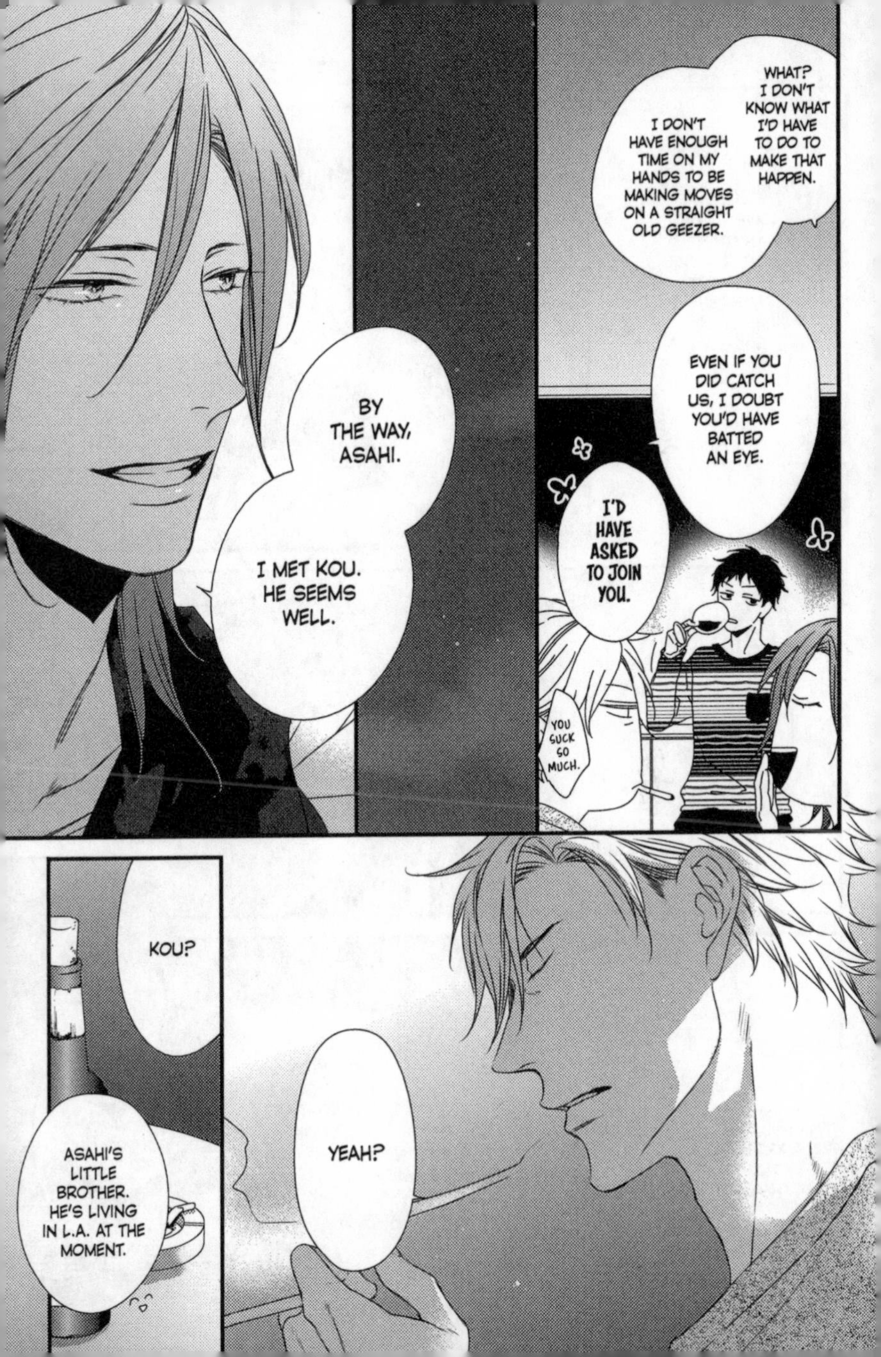
WHAT? I DON'T KNOW WHAT I'D HAVE TO DO TO MAKE THAT HAPPEN.
I DON'T HAVE ENOUGH TIME ON MY HANDS TO BE MAKING MOVES ON A STRAIGHT OLD GEEZER.
EVEN IF YOU DID CATCH US, I DOUBT YOU'D HAVE BATTED AN EYE.
I'D HAVE ASKED TO JOIN YOU.
YOU SUCK SO MUCH.
BY THE WAY, ASAHI.
I MET KOU. HE SEEMS WELL.
KOU?
YEAH?
ASAHI'S LITTLE BROTHER. HE'S LIVING IN L.A. AT THE MOMENT.

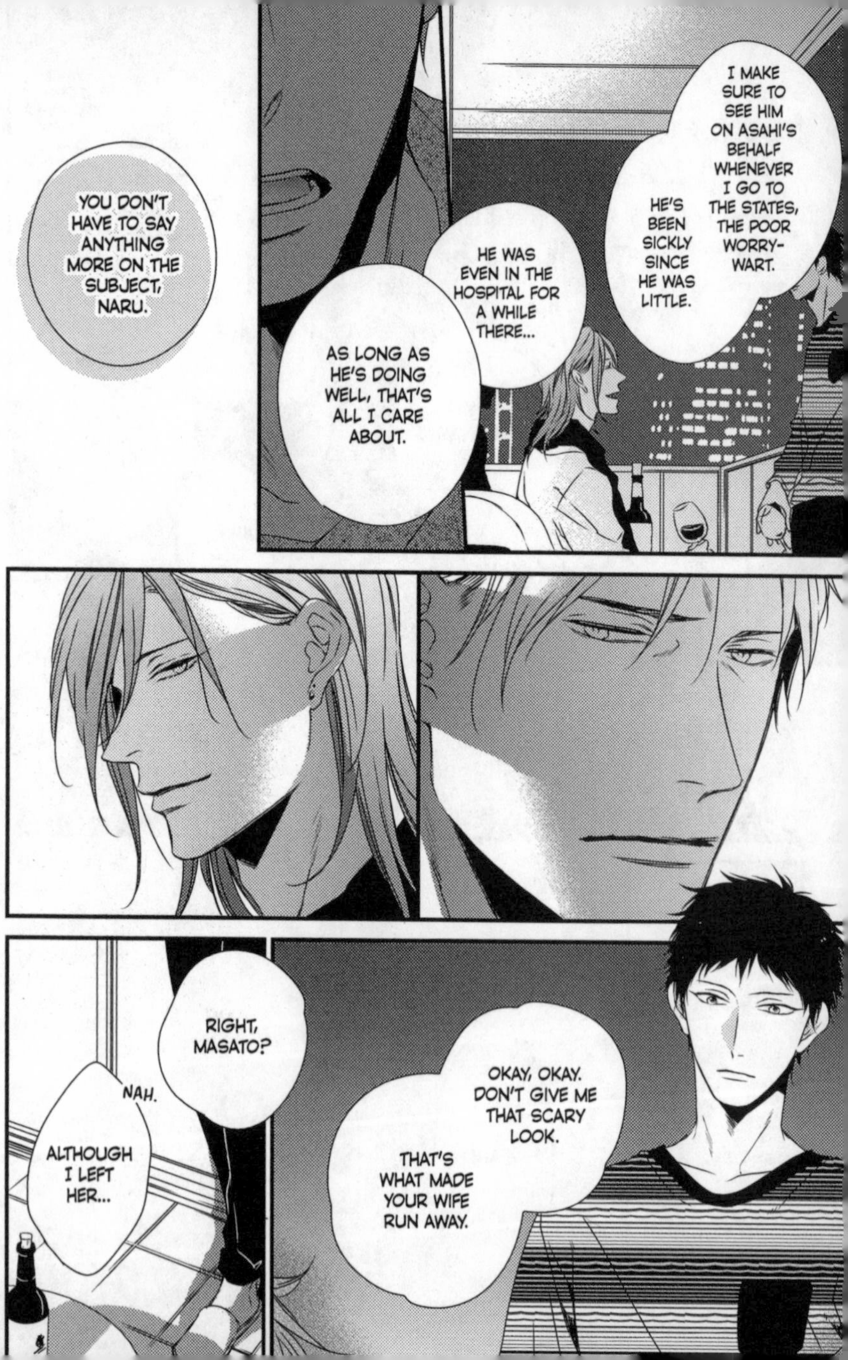
I MAKE SURE TO SEE HIM ON ASAHI'S BEHALF WHENEVER I GO TO THE STATES, THE POOR WORRY-WART.
HE'S BEEN SICKLY SINCE HE WAS LITTLE.
HE WAS EVEN IN THE HOSPITAL FOR A WHILE THERE...
AS LONG AS HE'S DOING WELL, THAT'S ALL I CARE ABOUT.
YOU DON'T HAVE TO SAY ANYTHING MORE ON THE SUBJECT, NARU.
OKAY, OKAY. DON'T GIVE ME THAT SCARY LOOK.
THAT'S WHAT MADE YOUR WIFE RUN AWAY.
RIGHT, MASATO?
NAH.
ALTHOUGH I LEFT HER...

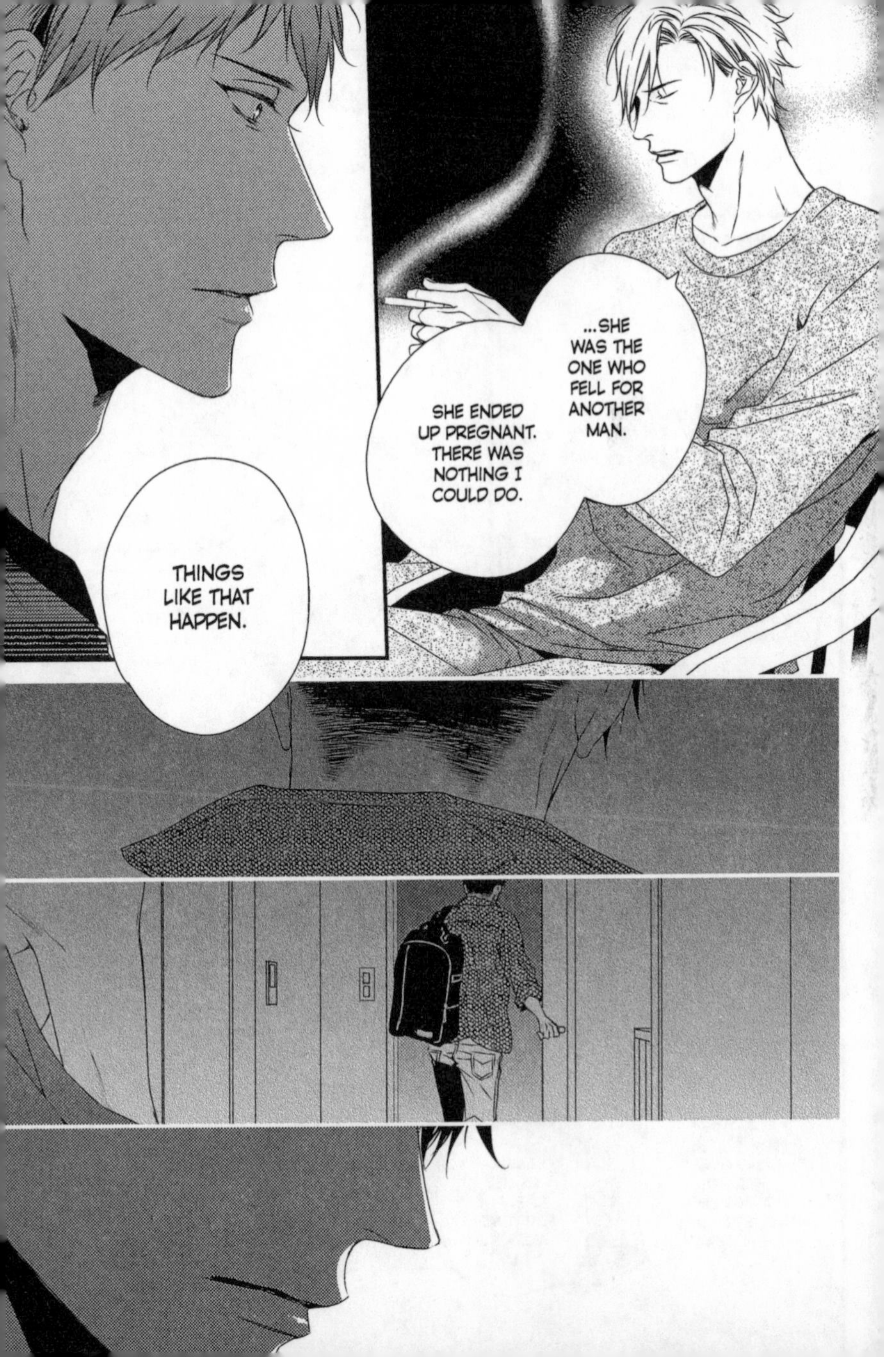
...SHE WAS THE ONE WHO FELL FOR ANOTHER MAN.
SHE ENDED UP PREGNANT. THERE WAS NOTHING I COULD DO.
THINGS LIKE THAT HAPPEN.

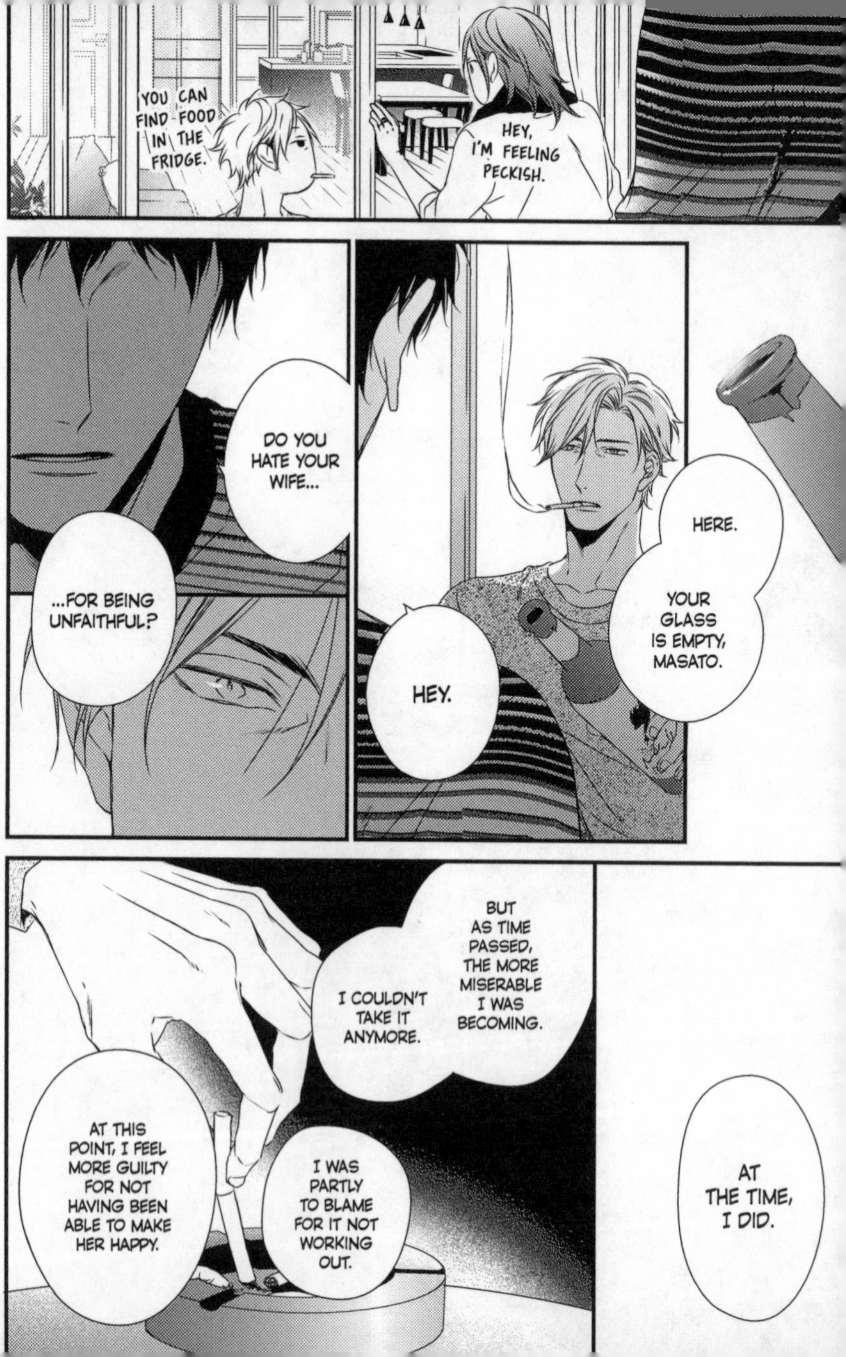
HEY, I'M FEELING PECKISH.
YOU CAN FIND FOOD IN THE FRIDGE.
HERE.
YOUR GLASS IS EMPTY, MASATO.
HEY.
DO YOU HATE YOUR WIFE...
...FOR BEING UNFAITHFUL?
AT THE TIME, I DID.
BUT AS TIME PASSED, THE MORE MISERABLE I WAS BECOMING.
I COULDN'T TAKE IT ANYMORE.
I WAS PARTLY TO BLAME FOR IT NOT WORKING OUT.
AT THIS POINT, I FEEL MORE GUILTY FOR NOT HAVING BEEN ABLE TO MAKE HER HAPPY.

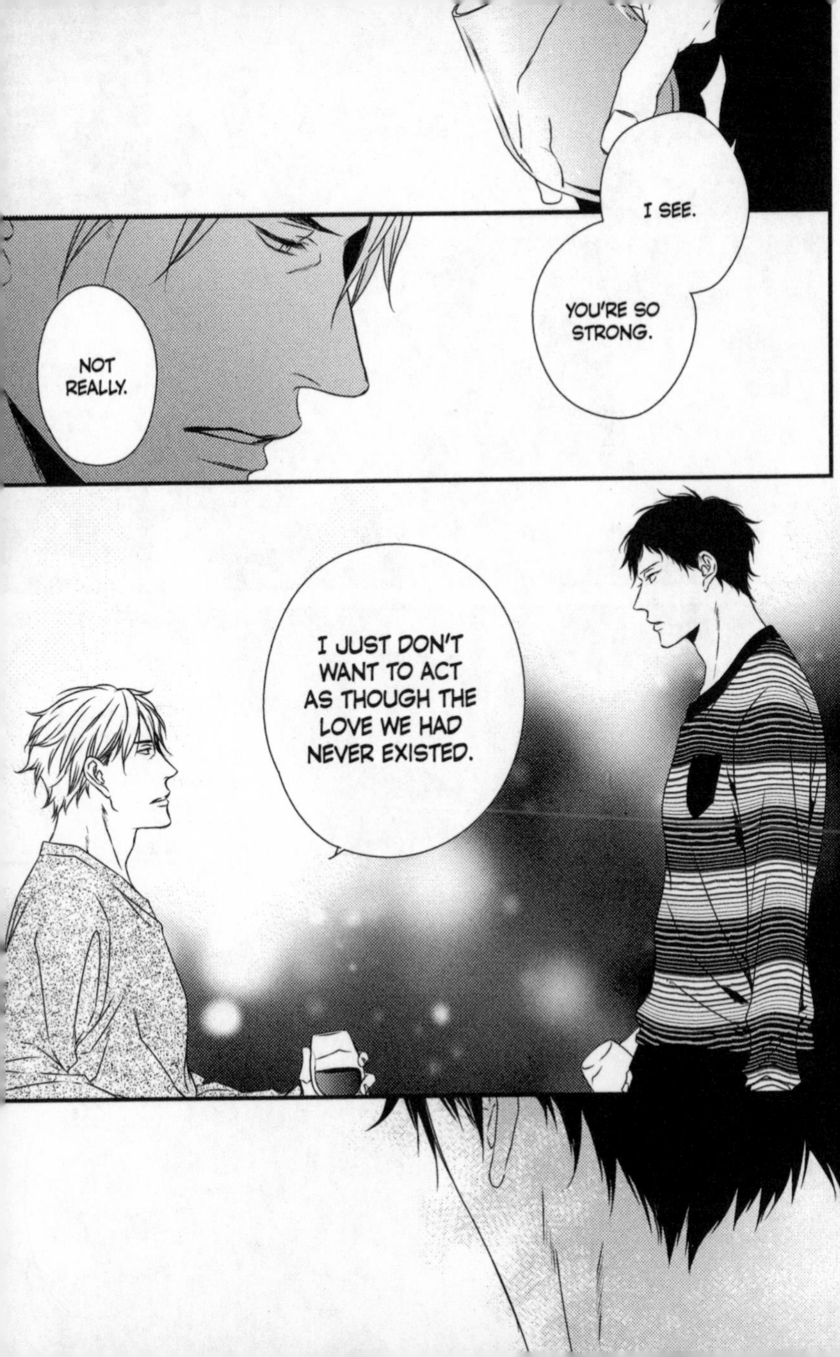
I SEE.
YOU'RE SO STRONG.
NOT REALLY.
I JUST DON'T WANT TO ACT AS THOUGH THE LOVE WE HAD NEVER EXISTED.

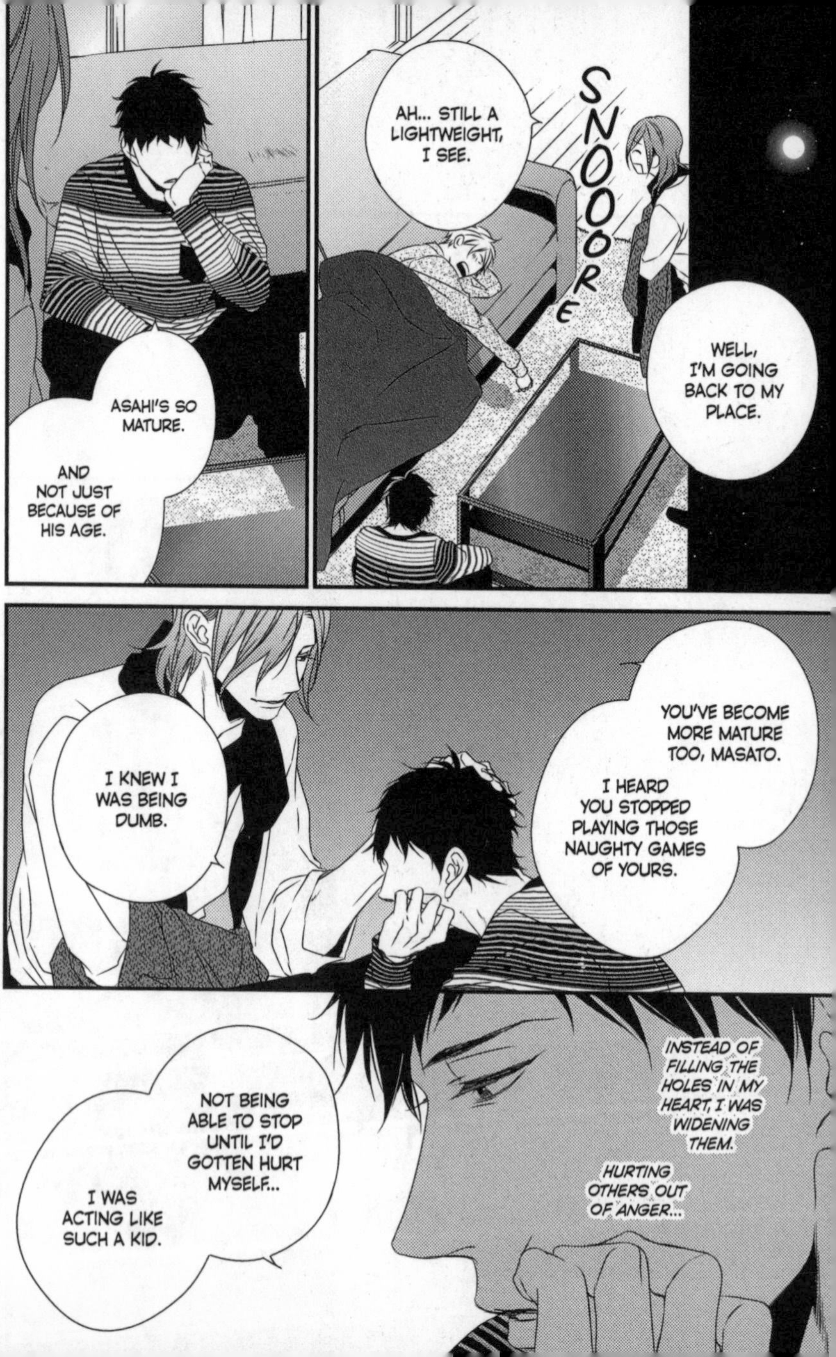
SNOOORE
AH... STILL A LIGHTWEIGHT, I SEE.
WELL, I'M GOING BACK TO MY PLACE.
ASAHI'S SO MATURE.
AND NOT JUST BECAUSE OF HIS AGE.
YOU'VE BECOME MORE MATURE TOO, MASATO.
I HEARD YOU STOPPED PLAYING THOSE NAUGHTY GAMES OF YOURS.
I KNEW I WAS BEING DUMB.
INSTEAD OF FILLING THE HOLES IN MY HEART, I WAS WIDENING THEM.
HURTING OTHERS OUT OF ANGER...
NOT BEING ABLE TO STOP UNTIL I'D GOTTEN HURT MYSELF...
I WAS ACTING LIKE SUCH A KID.

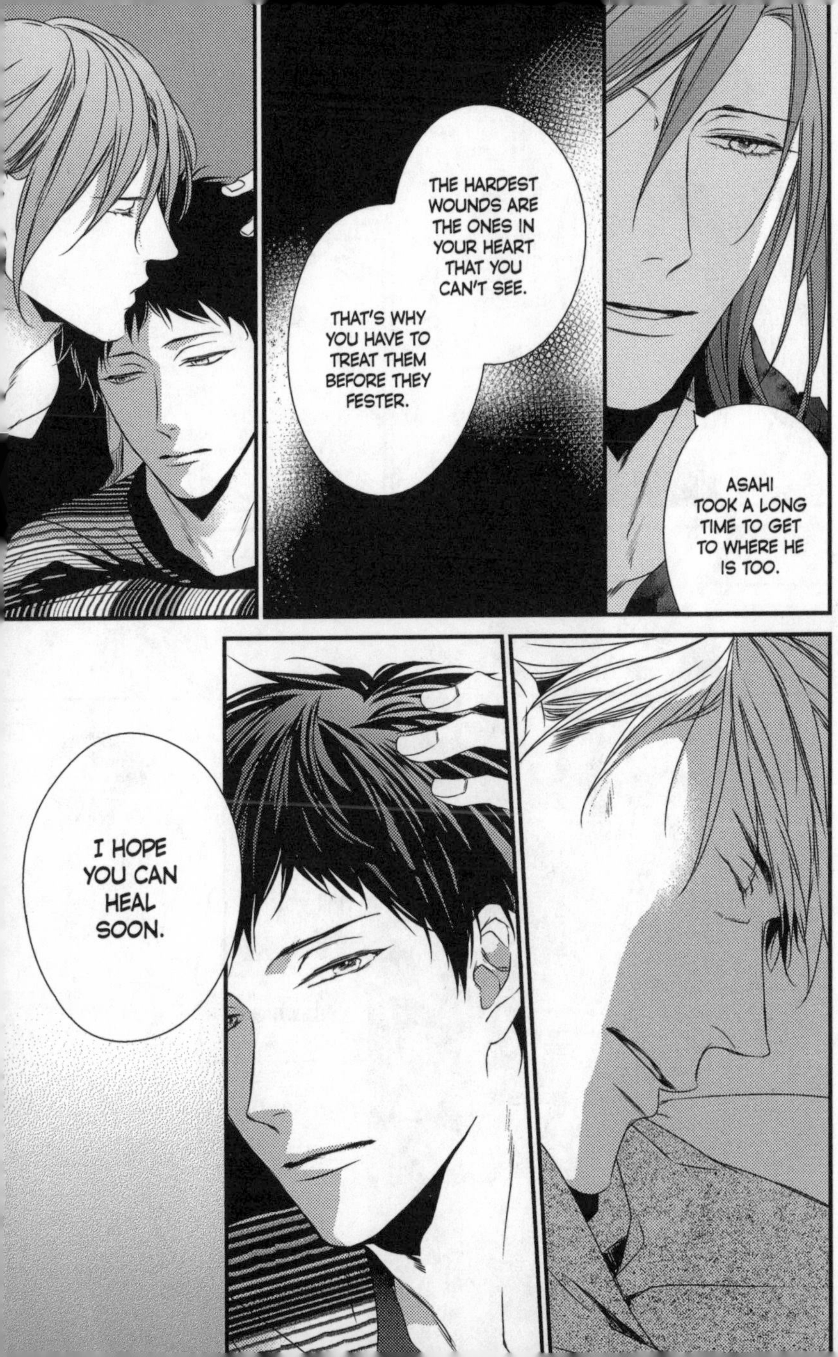
ASAHI TOOK A LONG TIME TO GET TO WHERE HE IS TOO.
THE HARDEST WOUNDS ARE THE ONES IN YOUR HEART THAT YOU CAN'T SEE.
THAT'S WHY YOU HAVE TO TREAT THEM BEFORE THEY FESTER.
I HOPE YOU CAN HEAL SOON.

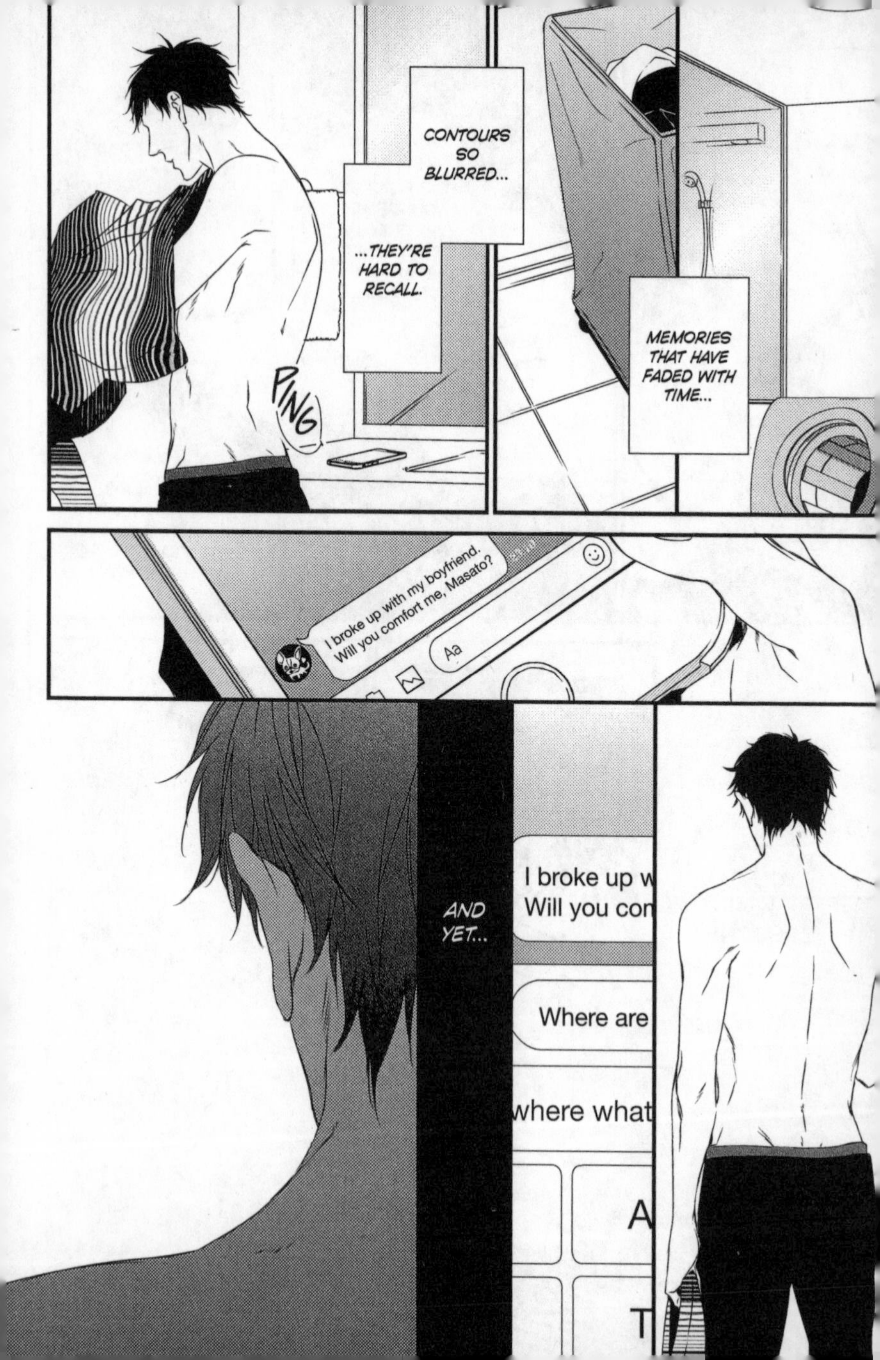
MEMORIES THAT HAVE FADED WITH TIME...
CONTOURS SO BLURRED...
...THEY'RE HARD TO RECALL.
PING
I broke up with my boyfriend. Will you comfort me, Masato?
Aa
I broke up w
Will you com
Where are
where what
A
T
AND YET...

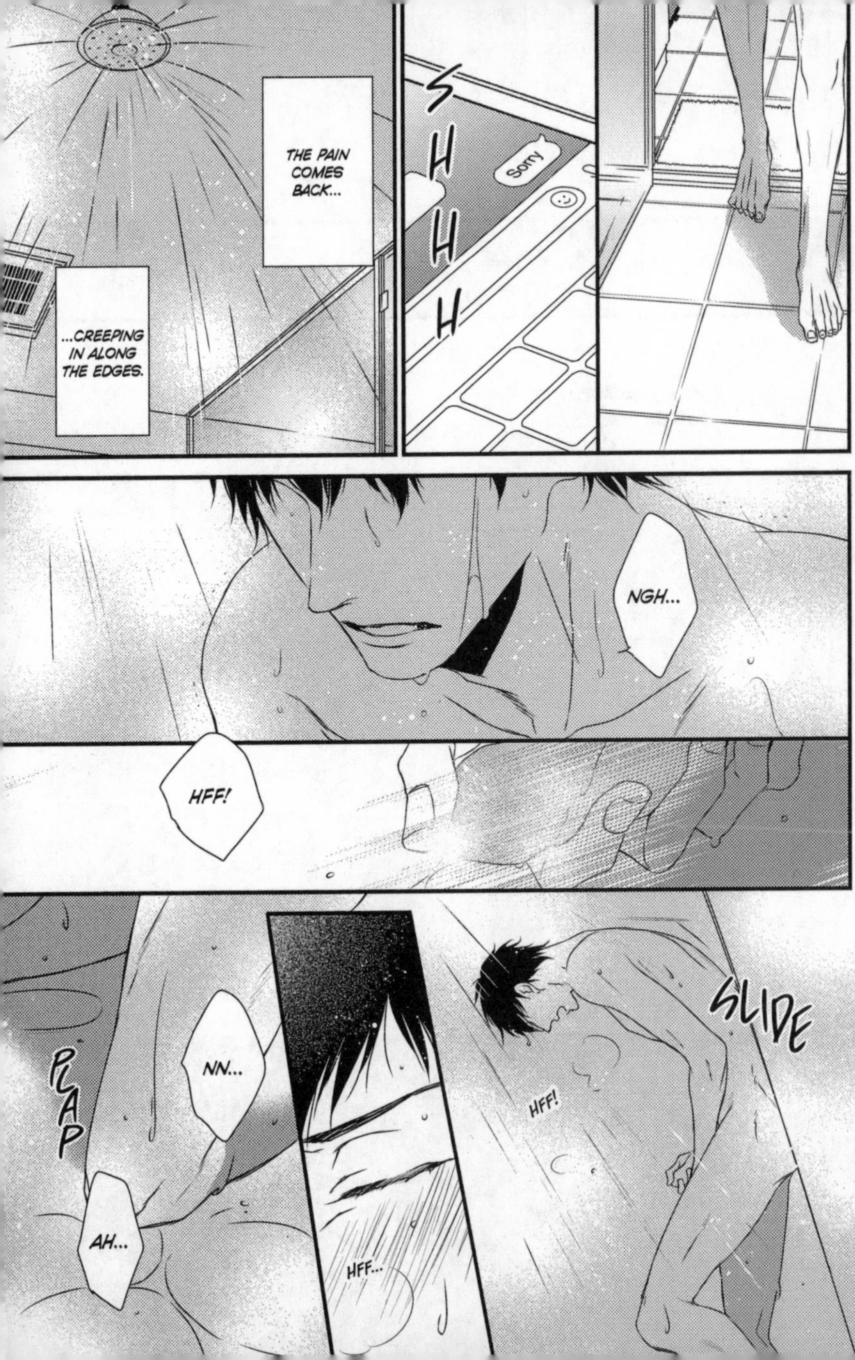
SHHHH
Sorry
THE PAIN COMES BACK...
...CREEPING IN ALONG THE EDGES.
NGH...
HFF!
SLIDE
HFF!
HFF...
NN...
PLAP
AH...

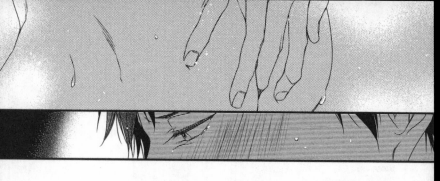

PLEASE.

...DISAPPEAR FROM
INSIDE ME...

JUST...

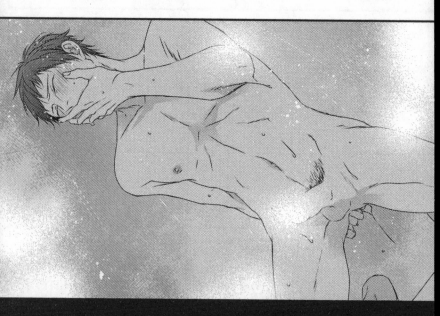

...KAZUOMI.

LOVE NEST

THE CORRELATION BETWEEN ONE'S USUAL SPOT ON THE SOFA AND EMOTIONAL DISTANCE ②

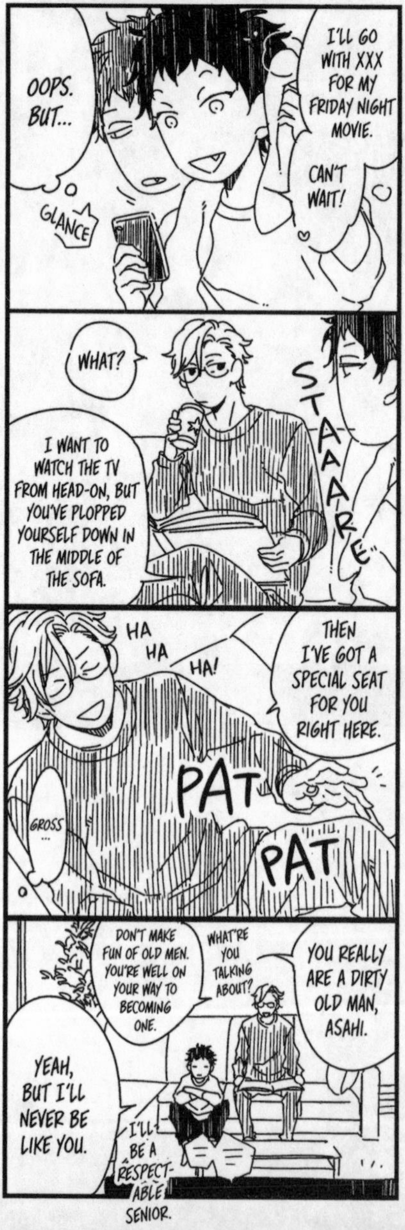
I'LL GO WITH XXX FOR MY FRIDAY NIGHT MOVIE.
CAN'T WAIT!
OOPS. BUT...
GLANCE
STAAAARE
WHAT?
I WANT TO WATCH THE TV FROM HEAD-ON, BUT YOU'VE PLOPPED YOURSELF DOWN IN THE MIDDLE OF THE SOFA.
THEN I'VE GOT A SPECIAL SEAT FOR YOU RIGHT HERE.
HA HA HA!
PAT
PAT
GROSS...
YOU REALLY ARE A DIRTY OLD MAN, ASAHI.
WHAT'RE YOU TALKING ABOUT?
DON'T MAKE FUN OF OLD MEN. YOU'RE WELL ON YOUR WAY TO BECOMING ONE.
YEAH, BUT I'LL NEVER BE LIKE YOU.
I'LL BE A RESPECTABLE SENIOR.

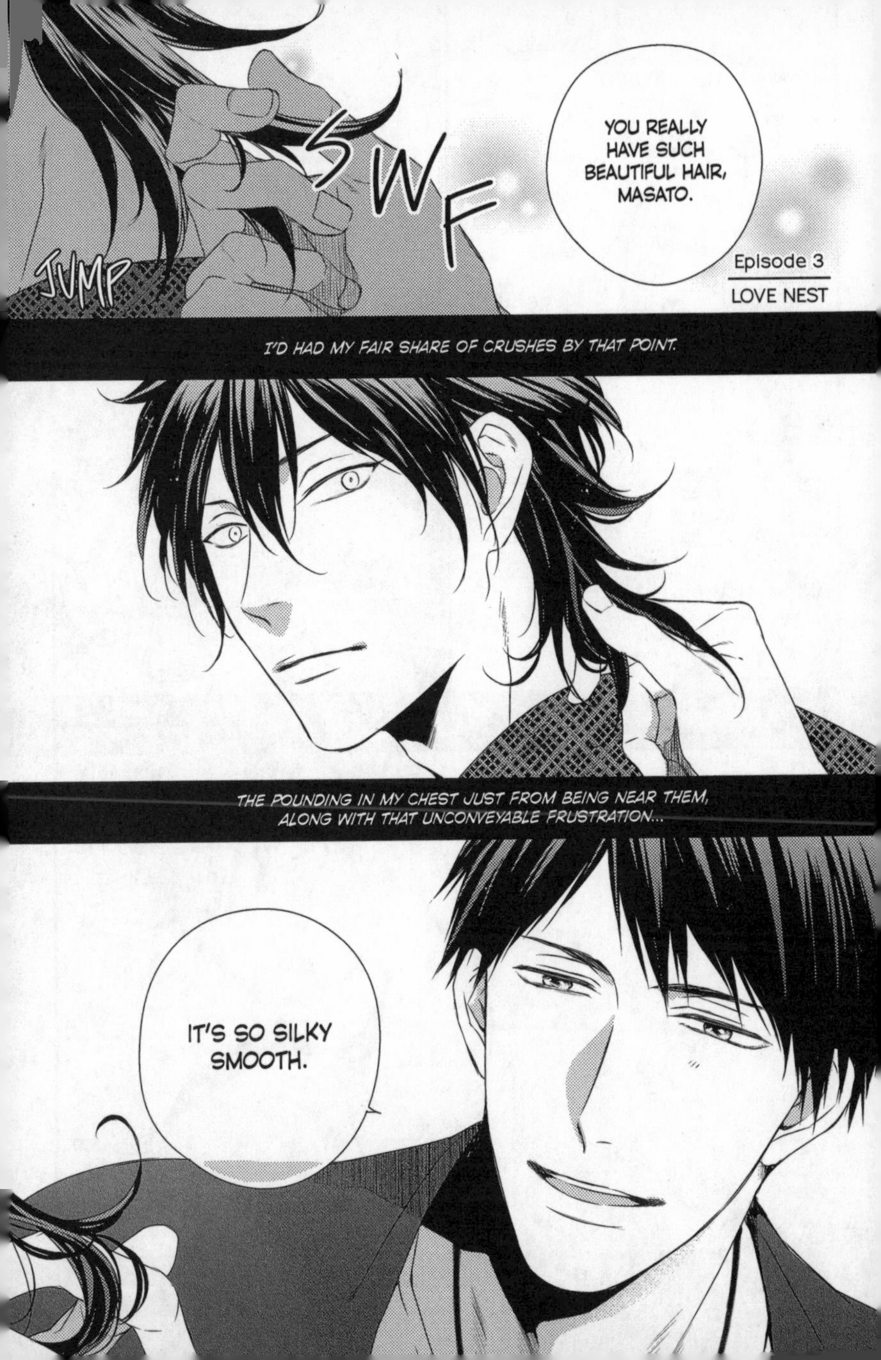
Episode 3
LOVE NEST
YOU REALLY HAVE SUCH BEAUTIFUL HAIR, MASATO.
SWF
JUMP
I'D HAD MY FAIR SHARE OF CRUSHES BY THAT POINT.
THE POUNDING IN MY CHEST JUST FROM BEING NEAR THEM, ALONG WITH THAT UNCONVEYABLE FRUSTRATION...
IT'S SO SILKY SMOOTH.

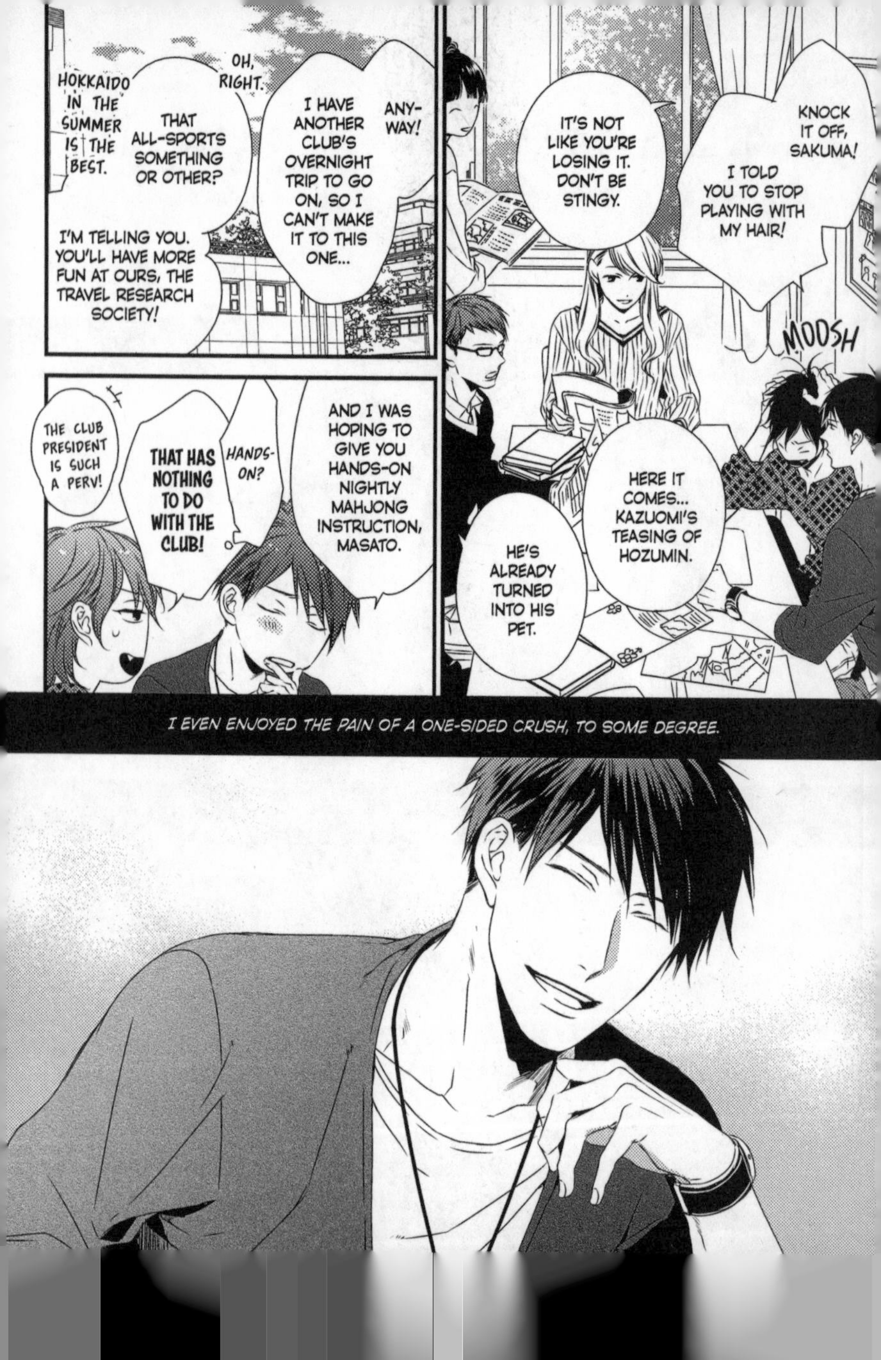
KNOCK IT OFF, SAKUMA!
I TOLD YOU TO STOP PLAYING WITH MY HAIR!
MOOSH
IT'S NOT LIKE YOU'RE LOSING IT. DON'T BE STINGY.
HERE IT COMES... KAZUOMI'S TEASING OF HOZUMIN.
HE'S ALREADY TURNED INTO HIS PET.
ANY-WAY!
I HAVE ANOTHER CLUB'S OVERNIGHT TRIP TO GO ON, SO I CAN'T MAKE IT TO THIS ONE...
OH, RIGHT.
THAT ALL-SPORTS SOMETHING OR OTHER?
HOKKAIDO IN THE SUMMER IS THE BEST.
I'M TELLING YOU. YOU'LL HAVE MORE FUN AT OURS, THE TRAVEL RESEARCH SOCIETY!
AND I WAS HOPING TO GIVE YOU HANDS-ON NIGHTLY MAHJONG INSTRUCTION, MASATO.
HANDS-ON?
THAT HAS NOTHING TO DO WITH THE CLUB!
THE CLUB PRESIDENT IS SUCH A PERV!
I EVEN ENJOYED THE PAIN OF A ONE-SIDED CRUSH, TO SOME DEGREE.

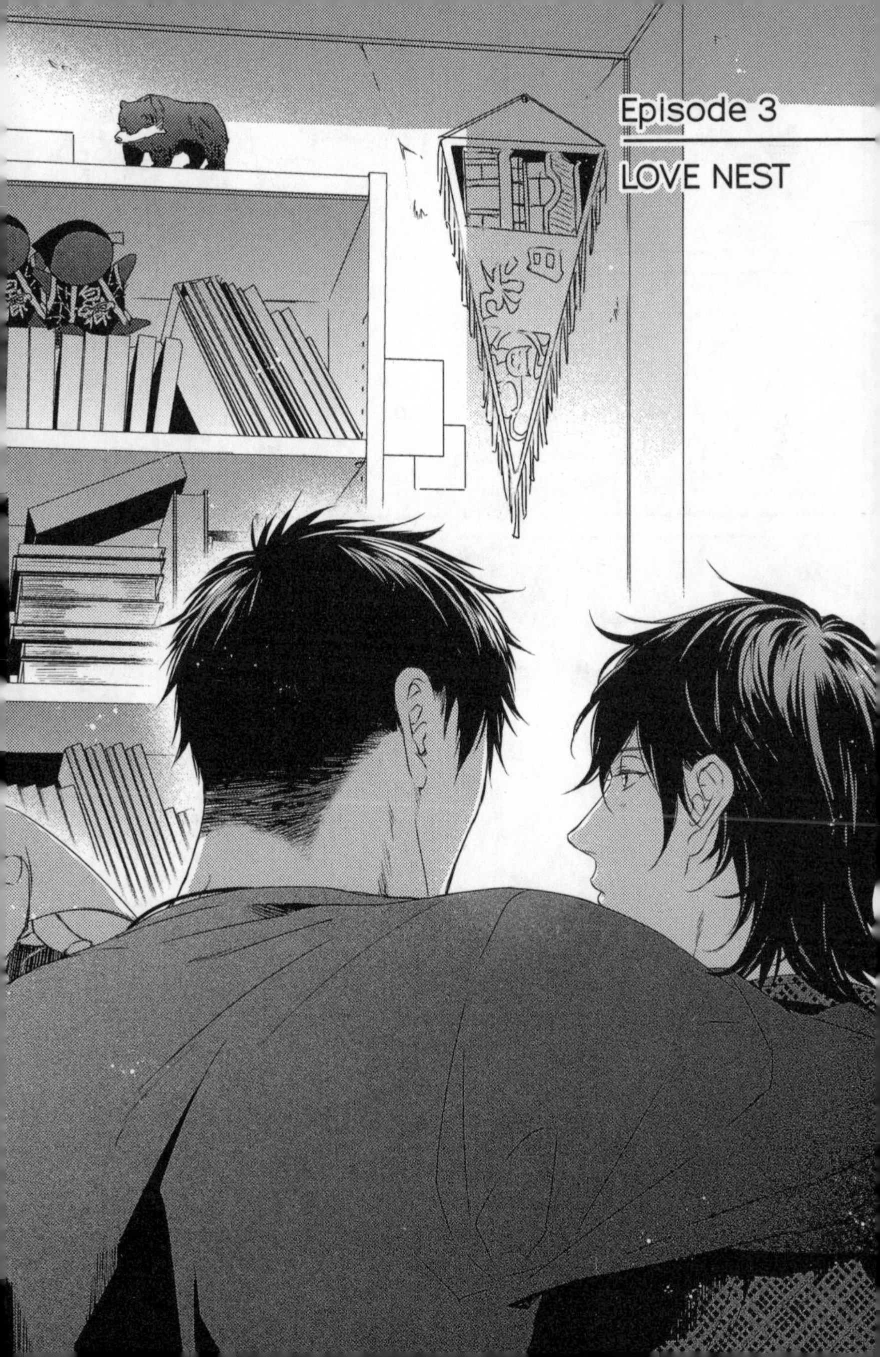
Episode 3
LOVE NEST

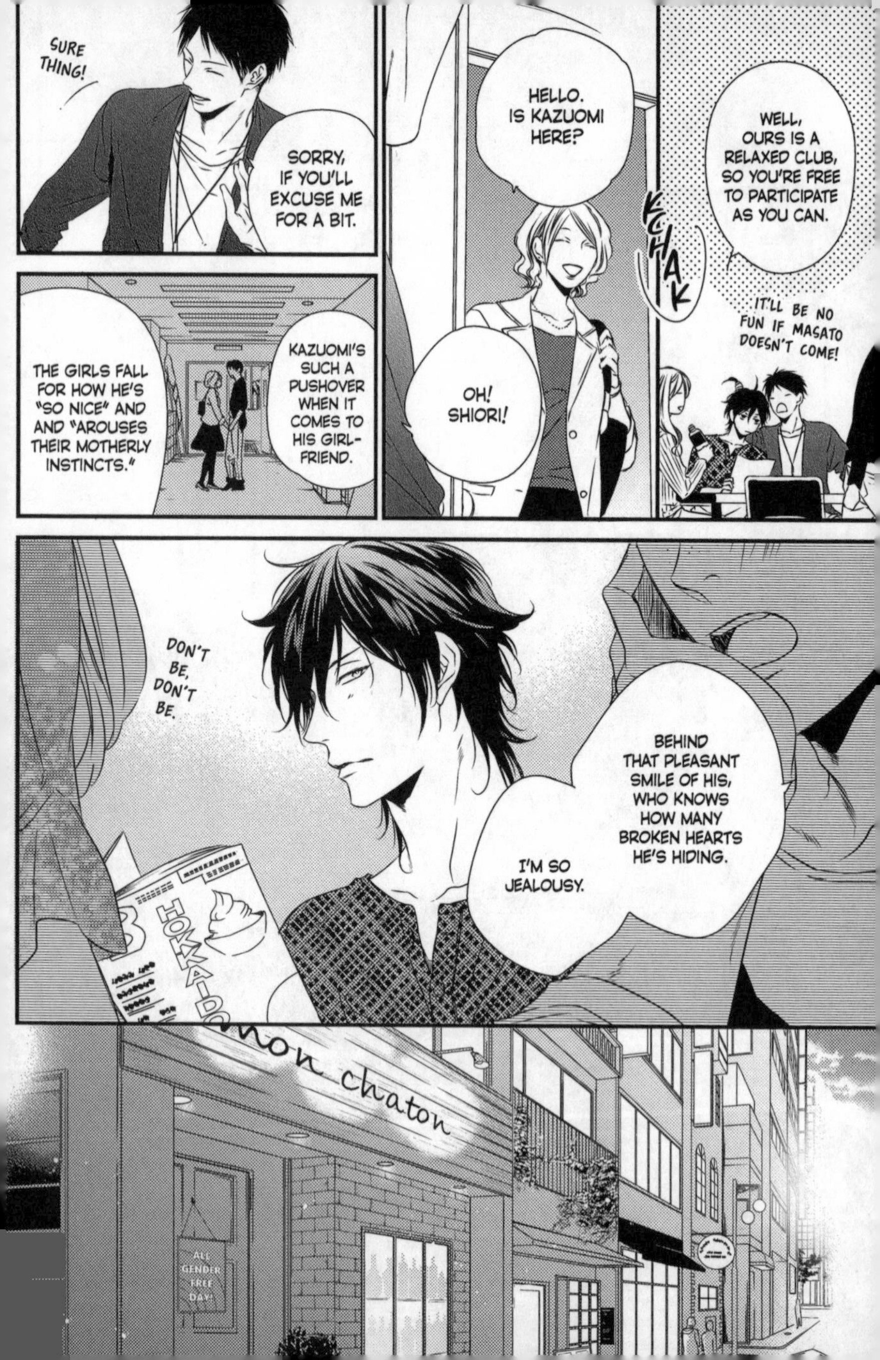
WELL, OURS IS A RELAXED CLUB, SO YOU'RE FREE TO PARTICIPATE AS YOU CAN.
KCHAK
IT'LL BE NO FUN IF MASATO DOESN'T COME!
HELLO. IS KAZUOMI HERE?
OH! SHIORI!
SORRY, IF YOU'LL EXCUSE ME FOR A BIT.
SURE THING!
KAZUOMI'S SUCH A PUSHOVER WHEN IT COMES TO HIS GIRLFRIEND.
THE GIRLS FALL FOR HOW HE'S "SO NICE" AND AND "AROUSES THEIR MOTHERLY INSTINCTS."
BEHIND THAT PLEASANT SMILE OF HIS, WHO KNOWS HOW MANY BROKEN HEARTS HE'S HIDING.
I'M SO JEALOUSY.
DON'T BE, DON'T BE.
mon chaton
ALL GENDER FREE DAY!

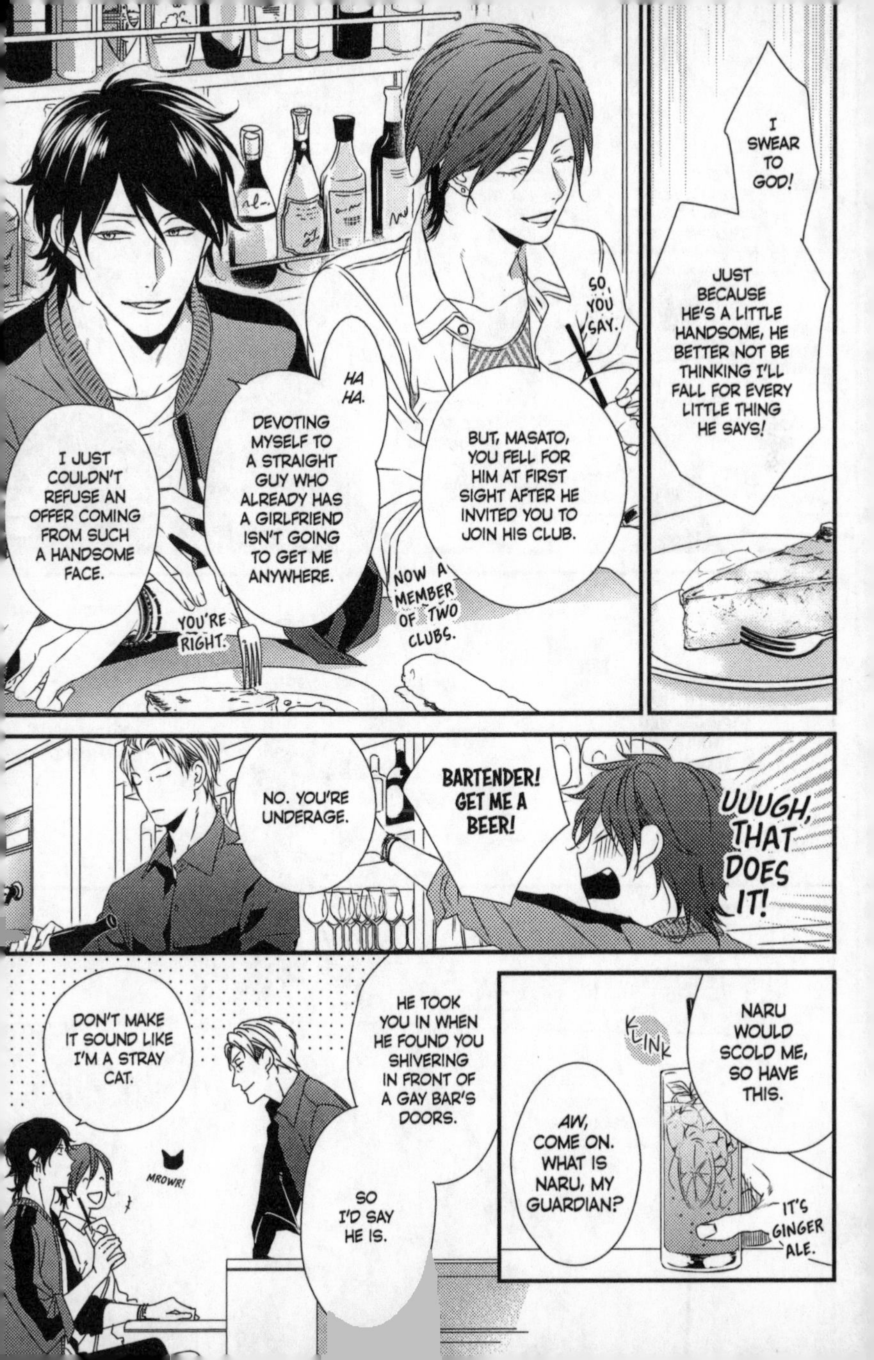
I SWEAR TO GOD!
JUST BECAUSE HE'S A LITTLE HANDSOME, HE BETTER NOT BE THINKING I'LL FALL FOR EVERY LITTLE THING HE SAYS!
SO, YOU SAY.
BUT, MASATO, YOU FELL FOR HIM AT FIRST SIGHT AFTER HE INVITED YOU TO JOIN HIS CLUB.
NOW A MEMBER OF TWO CLUBS.
HA HA.
DEVOTING MYSELF TO A STRAIGHT GUY WHO ALREADY HAS A GIRLFRIEND ISN'T GOING TO GET ME ANYWHERE.
YOU'RE RIGHT.
I JUST COULDN'T REFUSE AN OFFER COMING FROM SUCH A HANDSOME FACE.
UUUGH, THAT DOES IT!
BARTENDER! GET ME A BEER!
NO. YOU'RE UNDERAGE.
NARU WOULD SCOLD ME, SO HAVE THIS.
KLINK
AW, COME ON. WHAT IS NARU, MY GUARDIAN?
IT'S GINGER ALE.
HE TOOK YOU IN WHEN HE FOUND YOU SHIVERING IN FRONT OF A GAY BAR'S DOORS.
SO I'D SAY HE IS.
DON'T MAKE IT SOUND LIKE I'M A STRAY CAT.
MROWR!

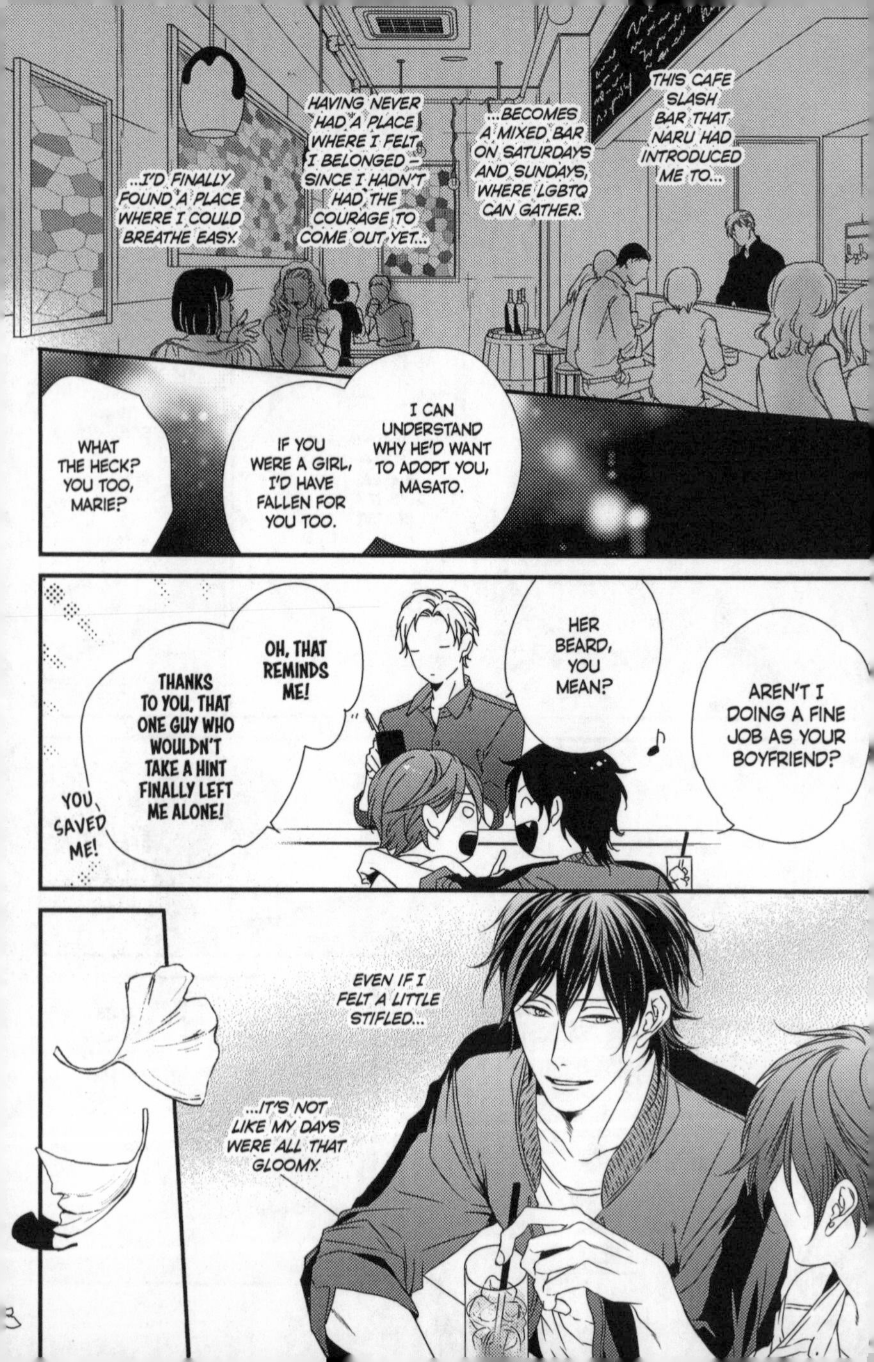
THIS CAFE SLASH BAR THAT NARU HAD INTRODUCED ME TO...
...BECOMES A MIXED BAR ON SATURDAYS AND SUNDAYS, WHERE LGBTQ CAN GATHER.
HAVING NEVER HAD A PLACE WHERE I FELT I BELONGED — SINCE I HADN'T HAD THE COURAGE TO COME OUT YET...
...I'D FINALLY FOUND A PLACE WHERE I COULD BREATHE EASY.
I CAN UNDERSTAND WHY HE'D WANT TO ADOPT YOU, MASATO.
IF YOU WERE A GIRL, I'D HAVE FALLEN FOR YOU TOO.
WHAT THE HECK? YOU TOO, MARIE?
AREN'T I DOING A FINE JOB AS YOUR BOYFRIEND?
HER BEARD, YOU MEAN?
OH, THAT REMINDS ME!
THANKS TO YOU, THAT ONE GUY WHO WOULDN'T TAKE A HINT FINALLY LEFT ME ALONE!
YOU SAVED ME!
EVEN IF I FELT A LITTLE STIFLED...
...IT'S NOT LIKE MY DAYS WERE ALL THAT GLOOMY.

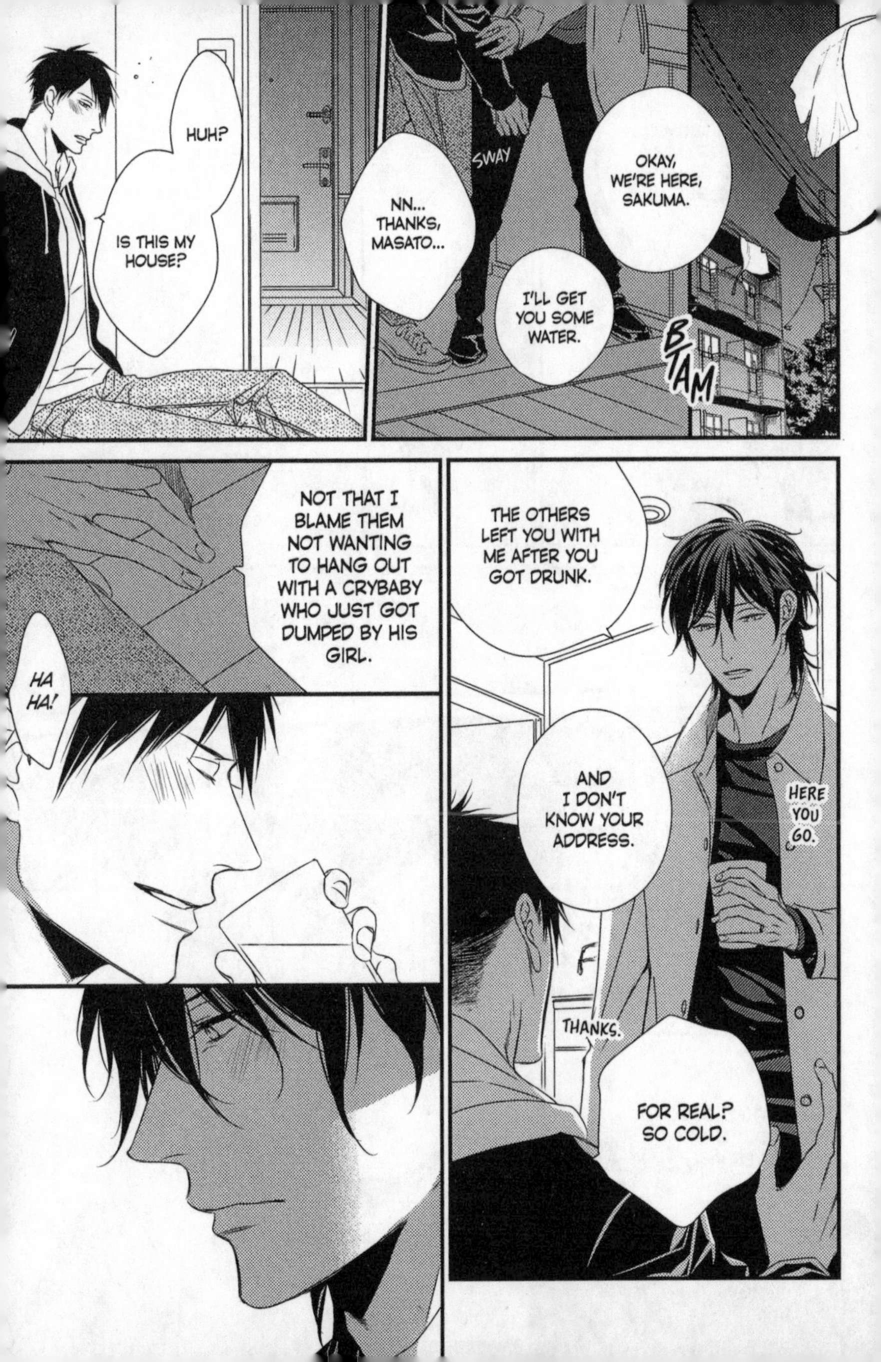
OKAY, WE'RE HERE, SAKUMA.
BTAM
I'LL GET YOU SOME WATER.
SWAY
NN... THANKS, MASATO...
HUH?
IS THIS MY HOUSE?
THE OTHERS LEFT YOU WITH ME AFTER YOU GOT DRUNK.
HERE YOU GO.
AND I DON'T KNOW YOUR ADDRESS.
F
THANKS.
FOR REAL? SO COLD.
NOT THAT I BLAME THEM NOT WANTING TO HANG OUT WITH A CRYBABY WHO JUST GOT DUMPED BY HIS GIRL.
HA HA!

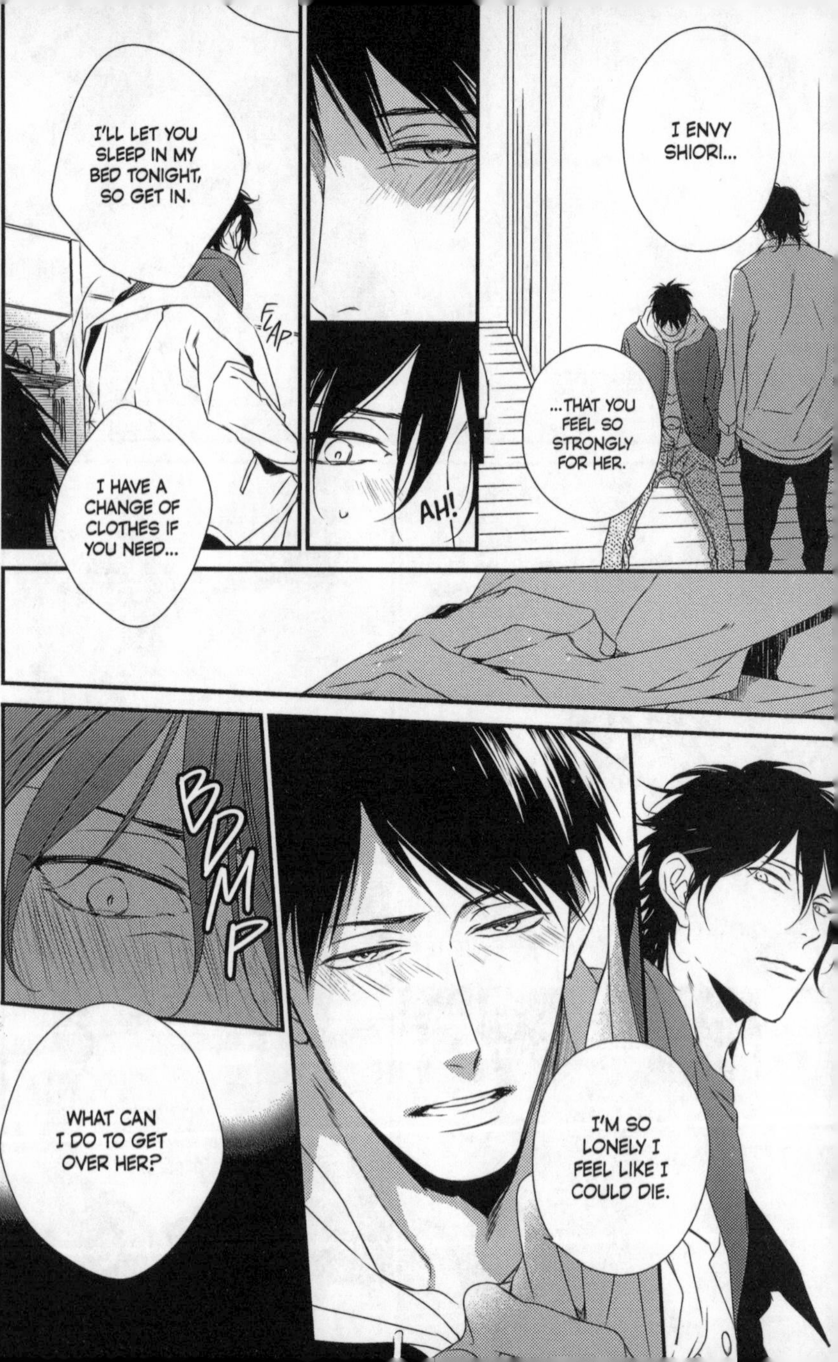
I ENVY SHIORI...
...THAT YOU FEEL SO STRONGLY FOR HER.
AH!
I'LL LET YOU SLEEP IN MY BED TONIGHT, SO GET IN.
FLAP
I HAVE A CHANGE OF CLOTHES IF YOU NEED...
I'M SO LONELY I FEEL LIKE I COULD DIE.
BDMP
WHAT CAN I DO TO GET OVER HER?

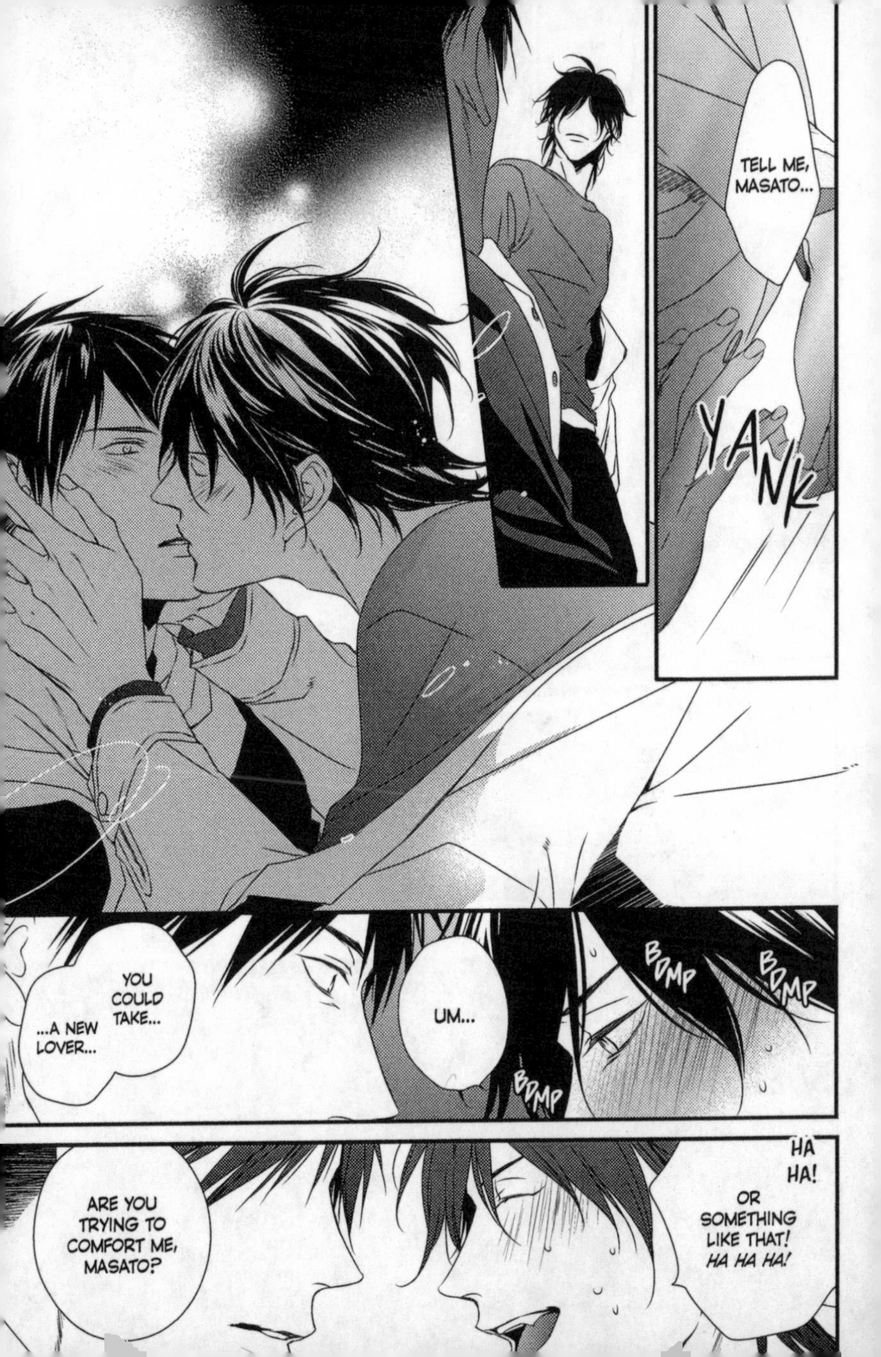
TELL ME, MASATO...
YANK
BOMP
BOMP
BOMP
UM...
YOU COULD TAKE...
...A NEW LOVER...
HA HA!
OR SOMETHING LIKE THAT! *HA HA HA!*
ARE YOU TRYING TO COMFORT ME, MASATO?

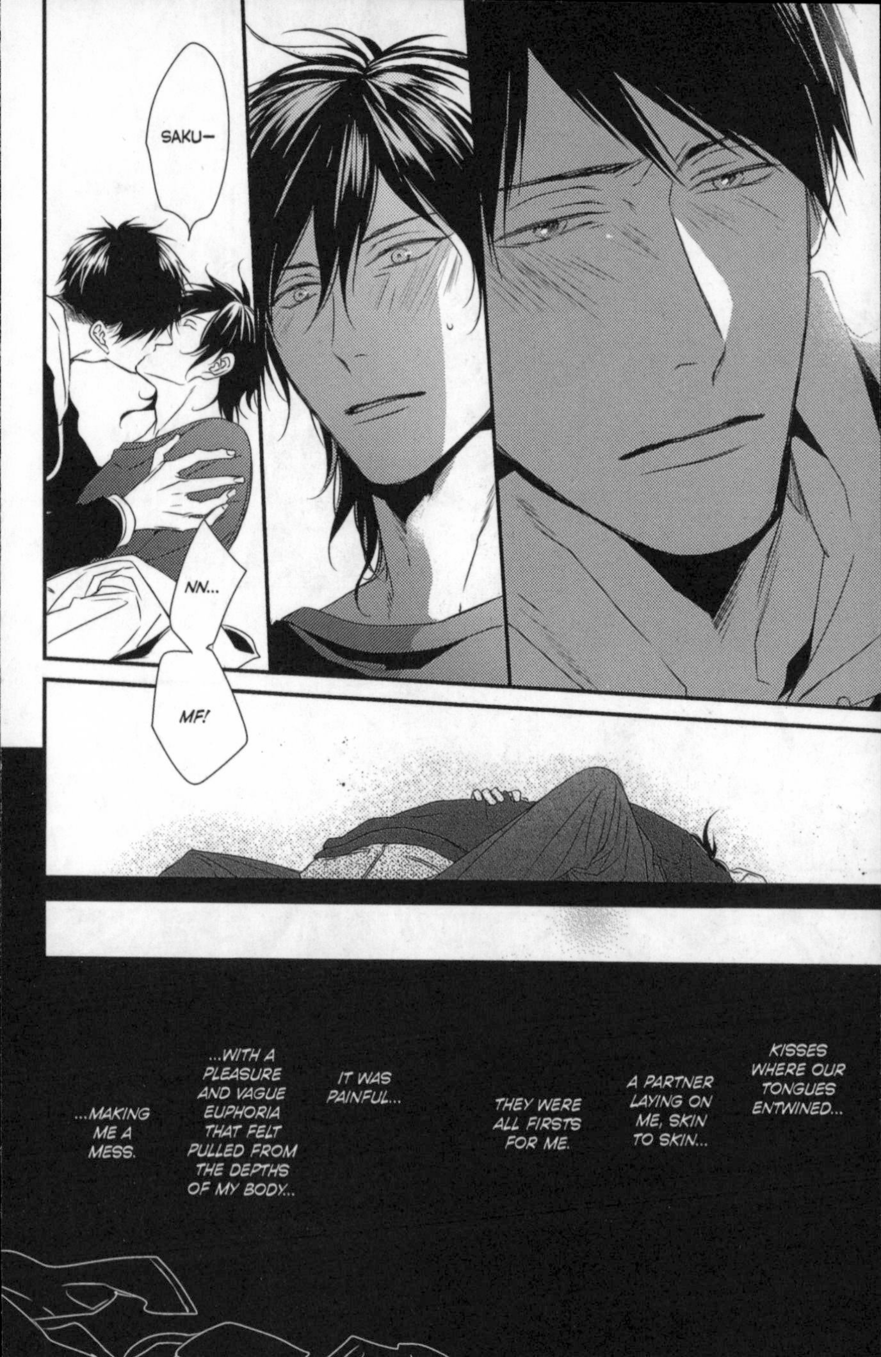
SAKU—
NN...
MF!
KISSES WHERE OUR TONGUES ENTWINED...
A PARTNER LAYING ON ME, SKIN TO SKIN...
THEY WERE ALL FIRSTS FOR ME.
IT WAS PAINFUL...
...WITH A PLEASURE AND VAGUE EUPHORIA THAT FELT PULLED FROM THE DEPTHS OF MY BODY...
...MAKING ME A MESS.

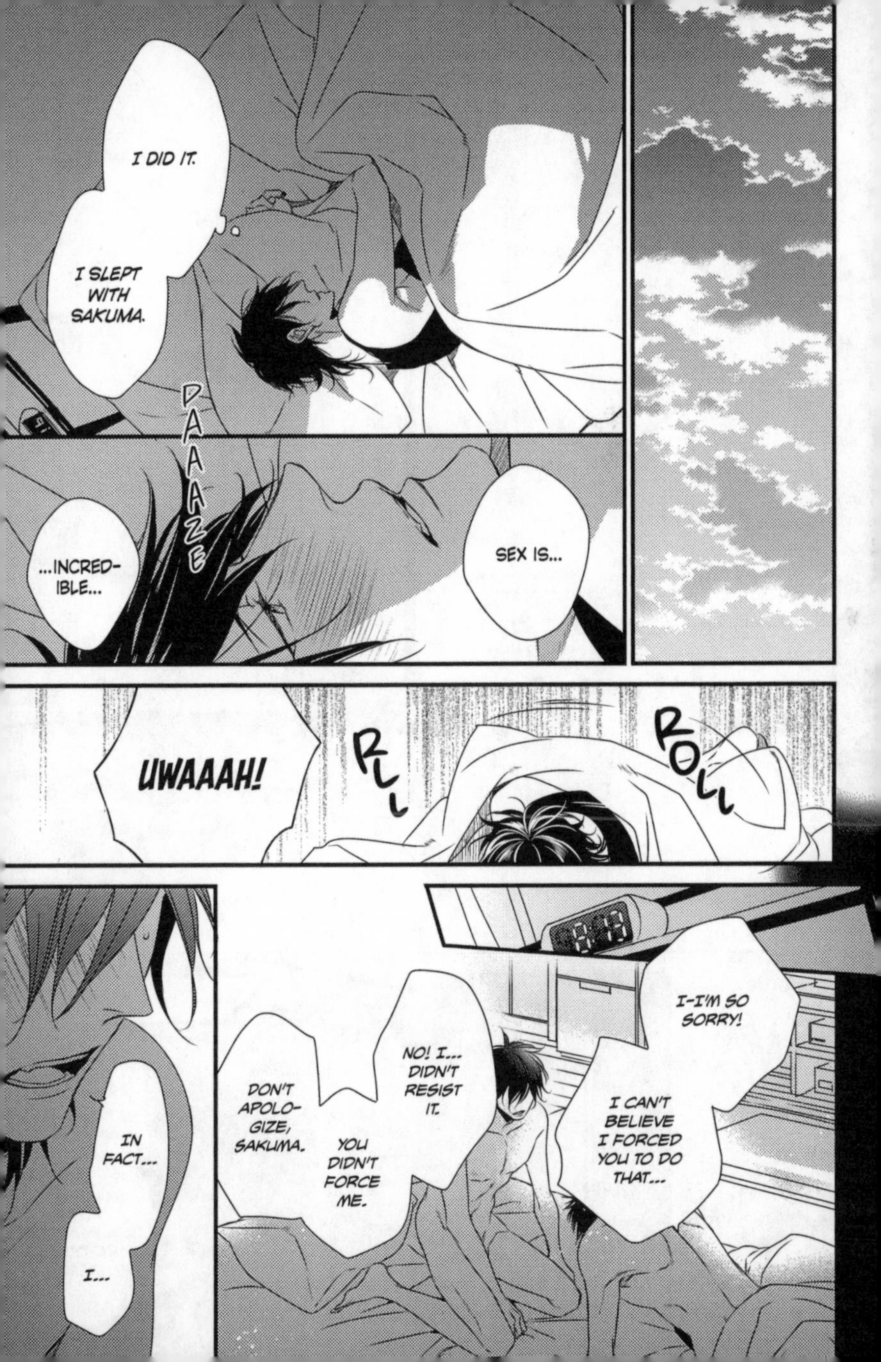
I DID IT.
I SLEPT WITH SAKUMA.
SEX IS...
DAAAAZE
...INCRED-IBLE...
ROLL
RLL
UWAAAH!
I-I'M SO SORRY!
I CAN'T BELIEVE I FORCED YOU TO DO THAT...
NO! I... DIDN'T RESIST IT.
DON'T APOLO-GIZE, SAKUMA.
YOU DIDN'T FORCE ME.
IN FACT...
I...

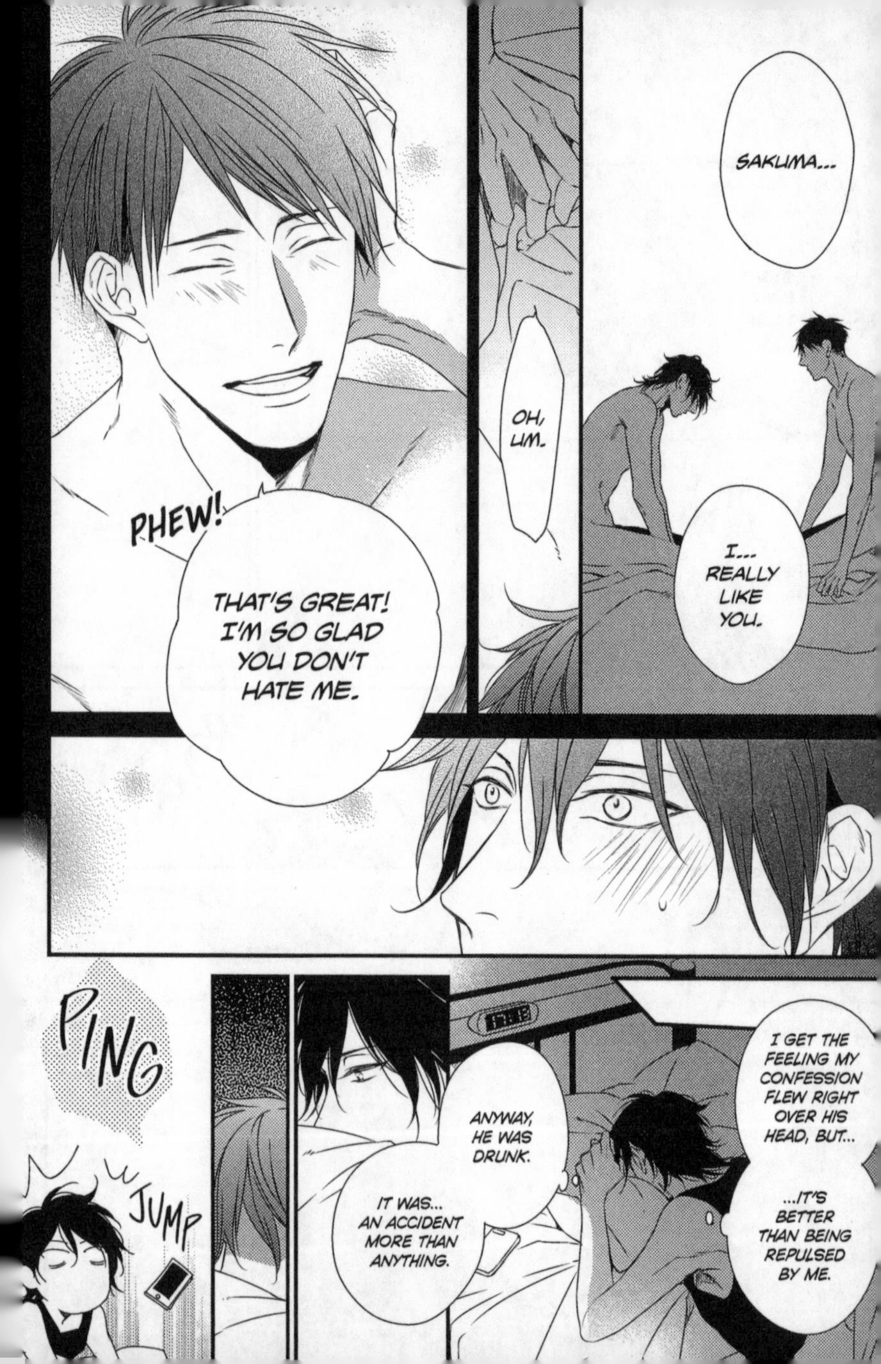
SAKUMA...
I... REALLY LIKE YOU.
OH, UM.
PHEW!
THAT'S GREAT! I'M SO GLAD YOU DON'T HATE ME.
I GET THE FEELING MY CONFESSION FLEW RIGHT OVER HIS HEAD, BUT...
...IT'S BETTER THAN BEING REPULSED BY ME.
ANYWAY, HE WAS DRUNK.
IT WAS... AN ACCIDENT MORE THAN ANYTHING.
PING
JUMP

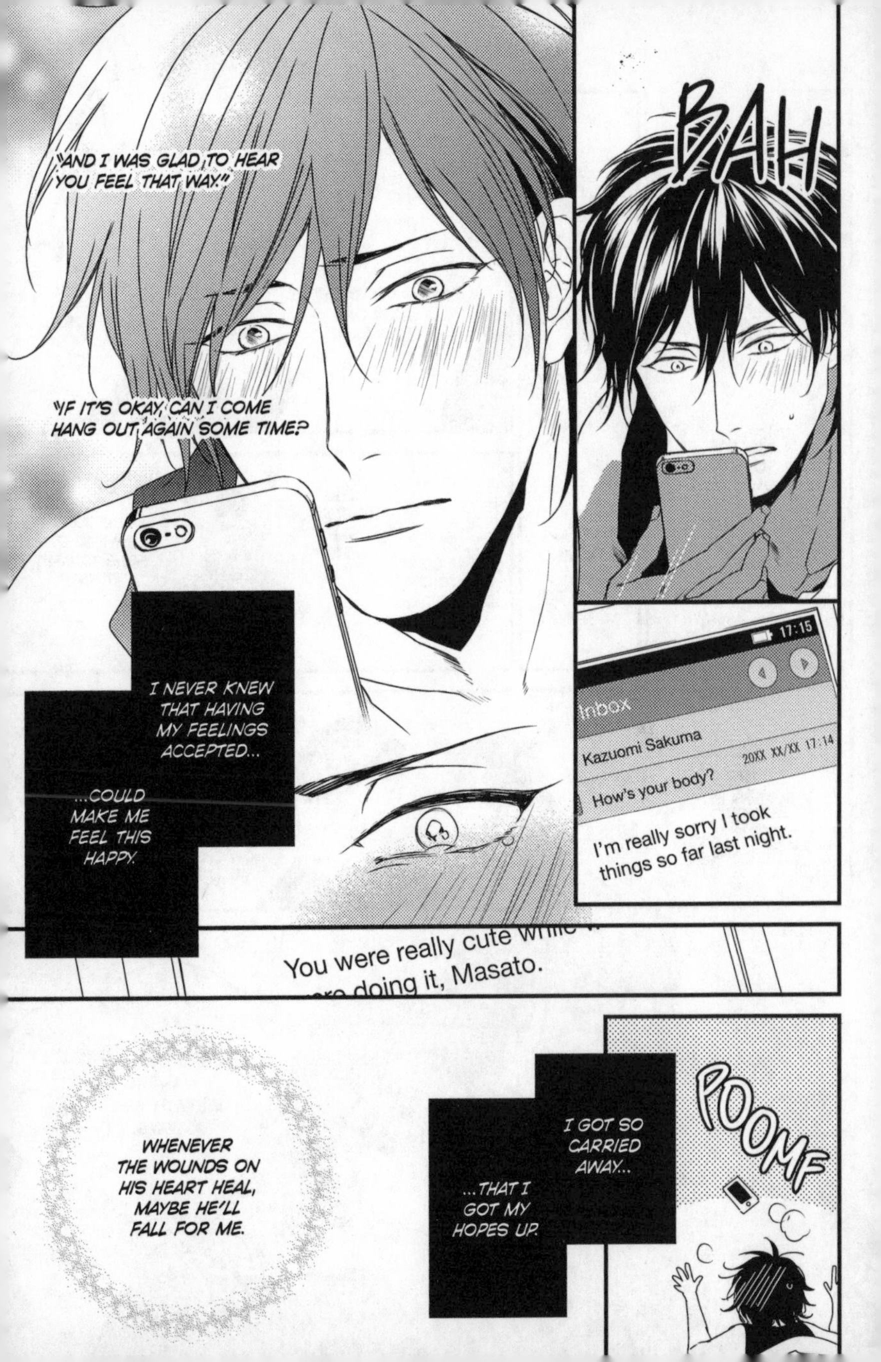
BAH
Inbox
17:15
Kazuomi Sakuma
20XX XX/XX 17:14
How's your body?
I'm really sorry I took things so far last night.
"And I was glad to hear you feel that way."
"If it's okay, can I come hang out again some time?"
I never knew that having my feelings accepted...
...could make me feel this happy.
You were really cute while
doing it, Masato.
POOMF
I got so carried away...
...that I got my hopes up.
Whenever the wounds on his heart heal, maybe he'll fall for me.

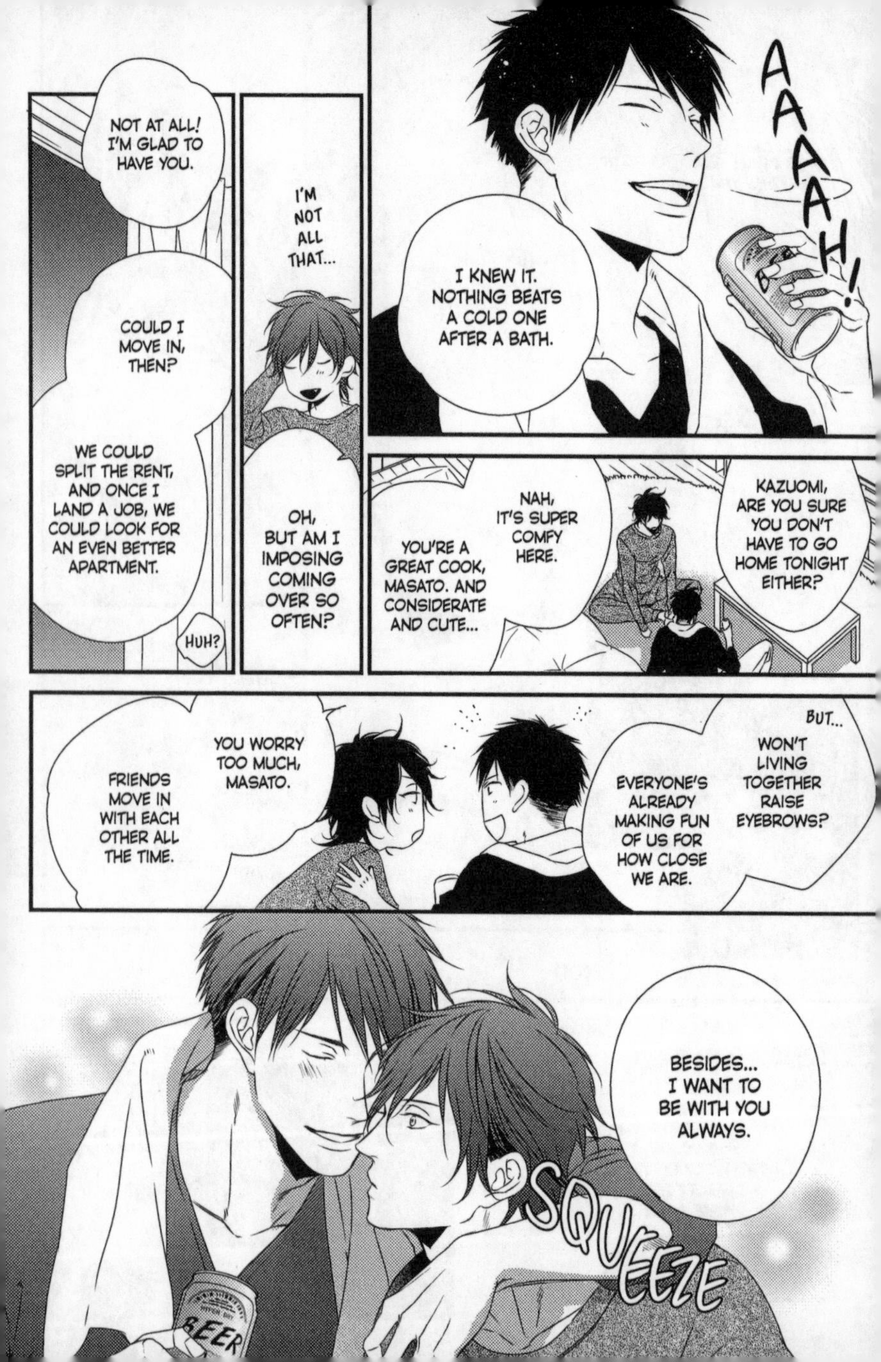
AAAAAH!
I KNEW IT. NOTHING BEATS A COLD ONE AFTER A BATH.
KAZUOMI, ARE YOU SURE YOU DON'T HAVE TO GO HOME TONIGHT EITHER?
NAH, IT'S SUPER COMFY HERE.
YOU'RE A GREAT COOK, MASATO. AND CONSIDERATE AND CUTE...
I'M NOT ALL THAT...
OH, BUT AM I IMPOSING COMING OVER SO OFTEN?
NOT AT ALL! I'M GLAD TO HAVE YOU.
COULD I MOVE IN, THEN?
HUH?
WE COULD SPLIT THE RENT, AND ONCE I LAND A JOB, WE COULD LOOK FOR AN EVEN BETTER APARTMENT.
BUT...
WON'T LIVING TOGETHER RAISE EYEBROWS?
EVERYONE'S ALREADY MAKING FUN OF US FOR HOW CLOSE WE ARE.
YOU WORRY TOO MUCH, MASATO.
FRIENDS MOVE IN WITH EACH OTHER ALL THE TIME.
BESIDES... I WANT TO BE WITH YOU ALWAYS.
SQUEEZE
BEER

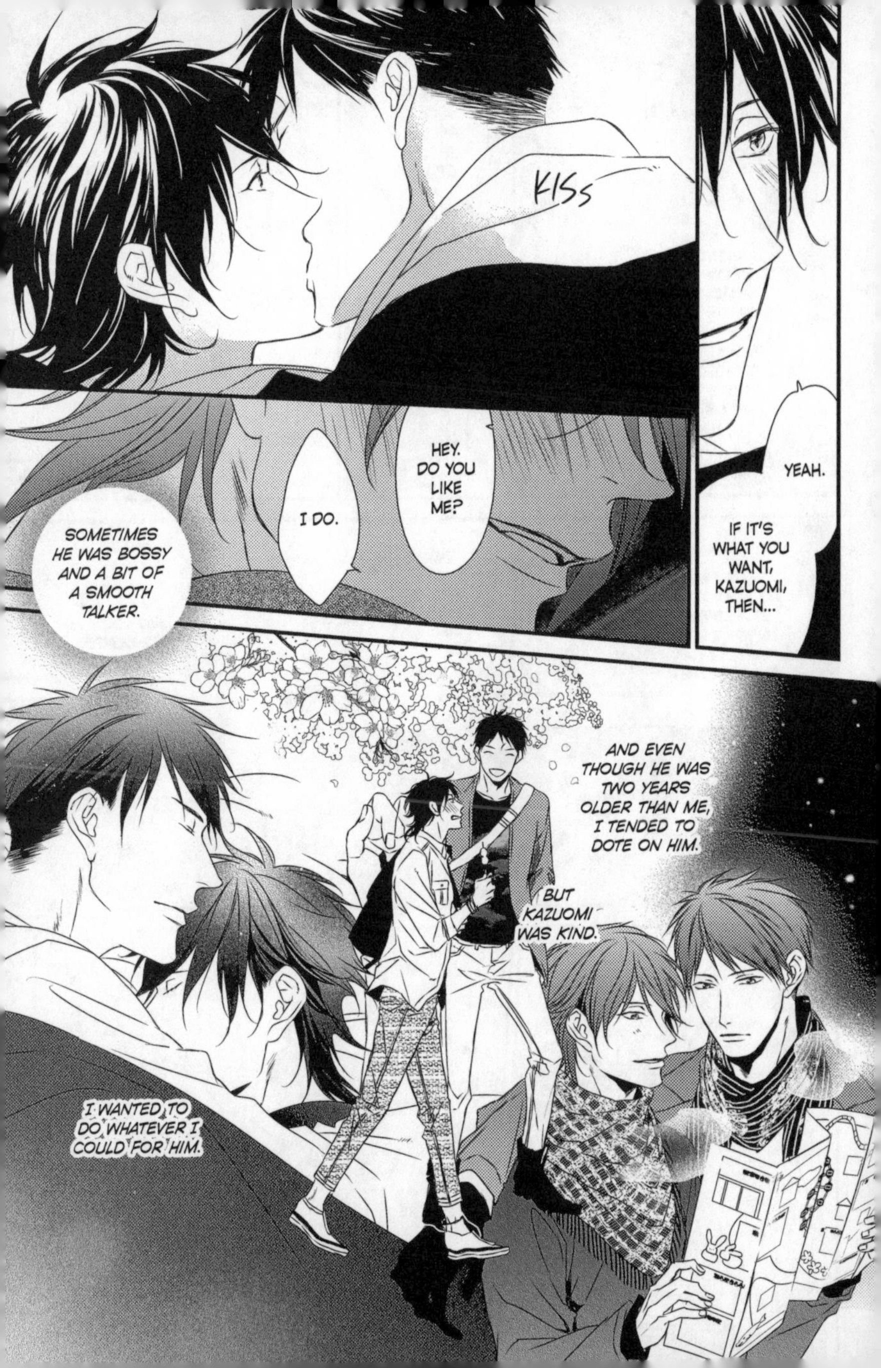
YEAH.
IF IT'S WHAT YOU WANT, KAZUOMI, THEN...
KISS
HEY. DO YOU LIKE ME?
I DO.
SOMETIMES HE WAS BOSSY AND A BIT OF A SMOOTH TALKER.
AND EVEN THOUGH HE WAS TWO YEARS OLDER THAN ME, I TENDED TO DOTE ON HIM.
BUT KAZUOMI WAS KIND.
I WANTED TO DO WHATEVER I COULD FOR HIM.

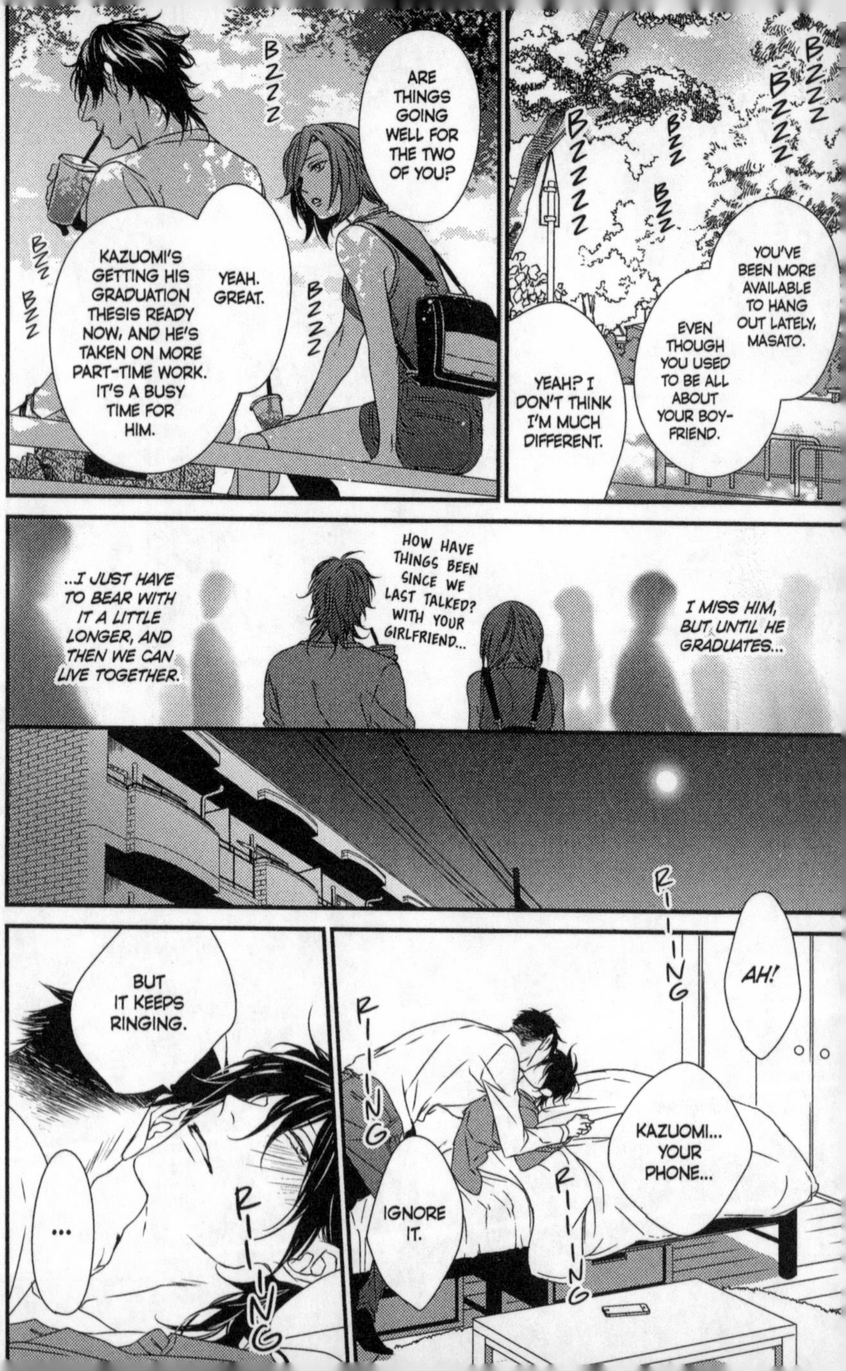
BZZZ
BZZZZ
BZZZZZ
BZZ
BZZ
YOU'VE BEEN MORE AVAILABLE TO HANG OUT LATELY, MASATO.
EVEN THOUGH YOU USED TO BE ALL ABOUT YOUR BOY-FRIEND.
YEAH? I DON'T THINK I'M MUCH DIFFERENT.
BZZZ
ARE THINGS GOING WELL FOR THE TWO OF YOU?
BZZZ
YEAH. GREAT.
KAZUOMI'S GETTING HIS GRADUATION THESIS READY NOW, AND HE'S TAKEN ON MORE PART-TIME WORK. IT'S A BUSY TIME FOR HIM.
BZZ
BZZ
I MISS HIM, BUT UNTIL HE GRADUATES...
HOW HAVE THINGS BEEN SINCE WE LAST TALKED? WITH YOUR GIRLFRIEND...
...I JUST HAVE TO BEAR WITH IT A LITTLE LONGER, AND THEN WE CAN LIVE TOGETHER.
RIIING
AH!
KAZUOMI... YOUR PHONE...
RIIING
IGNORE IT.
RIIING
BUT IT KEEPS RINGING.
...
RIIING

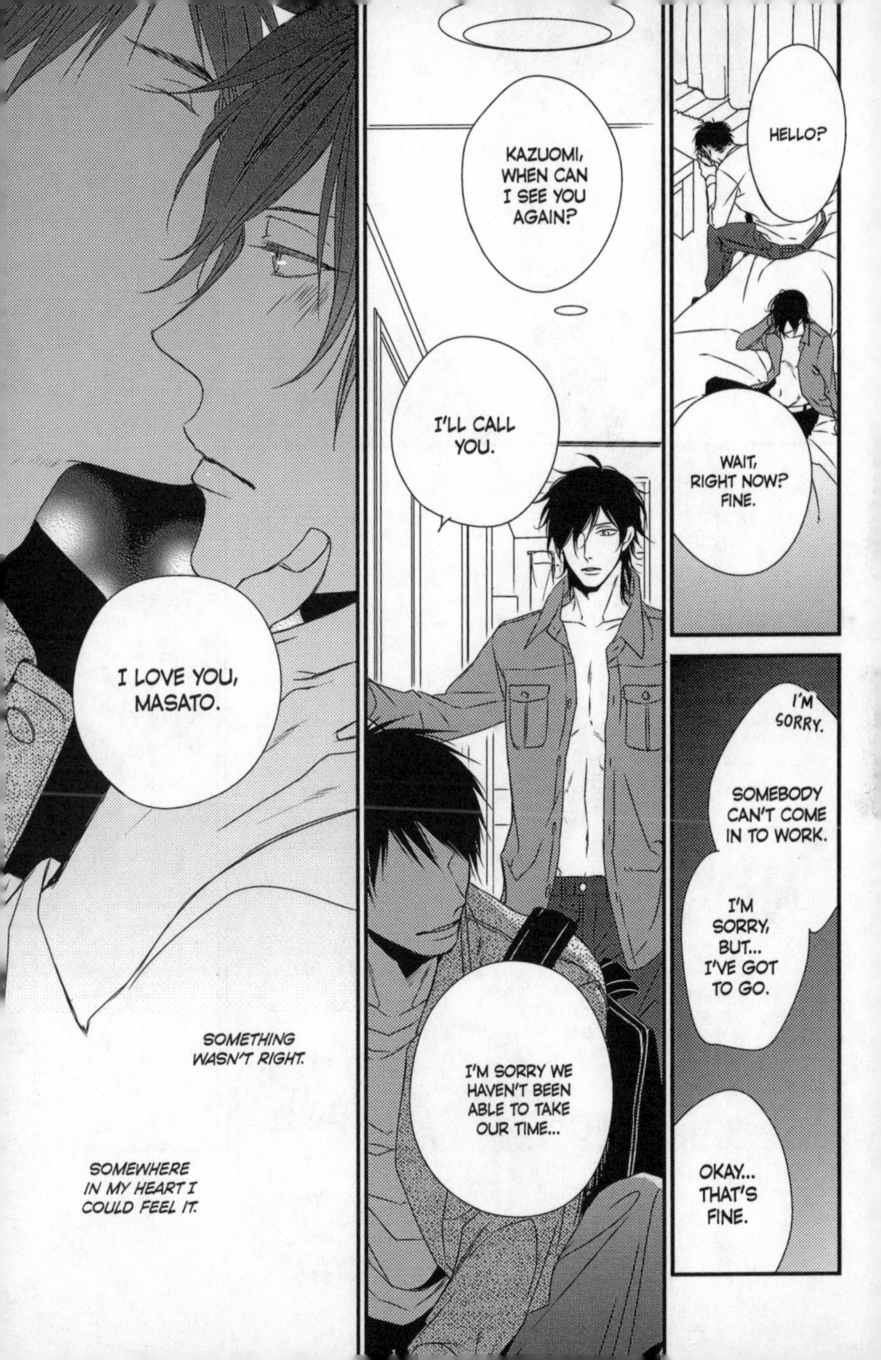
HELLO?
WAIT, RIGHT NOW? FINE.
I'M SORRY.
SOMEBODY CAN'T COME IN TO WORK.
I'M SORRY, BUT... I'VE GOT TO GO.
OKAY... THAT'S FINE.
KAZUOMI, WHEN CAN I SEE YOU AGAIN?
I'LL CALL YOU.
I'M SORRY WE HAVEN'T BEEN ABLE TO TAKE OUR TIME...
I LOVE YOU, MASATO.
SOMETHING WASN'T RIGHT.
SOMEWHERE IN MY HEART I COULD FEEL IT.

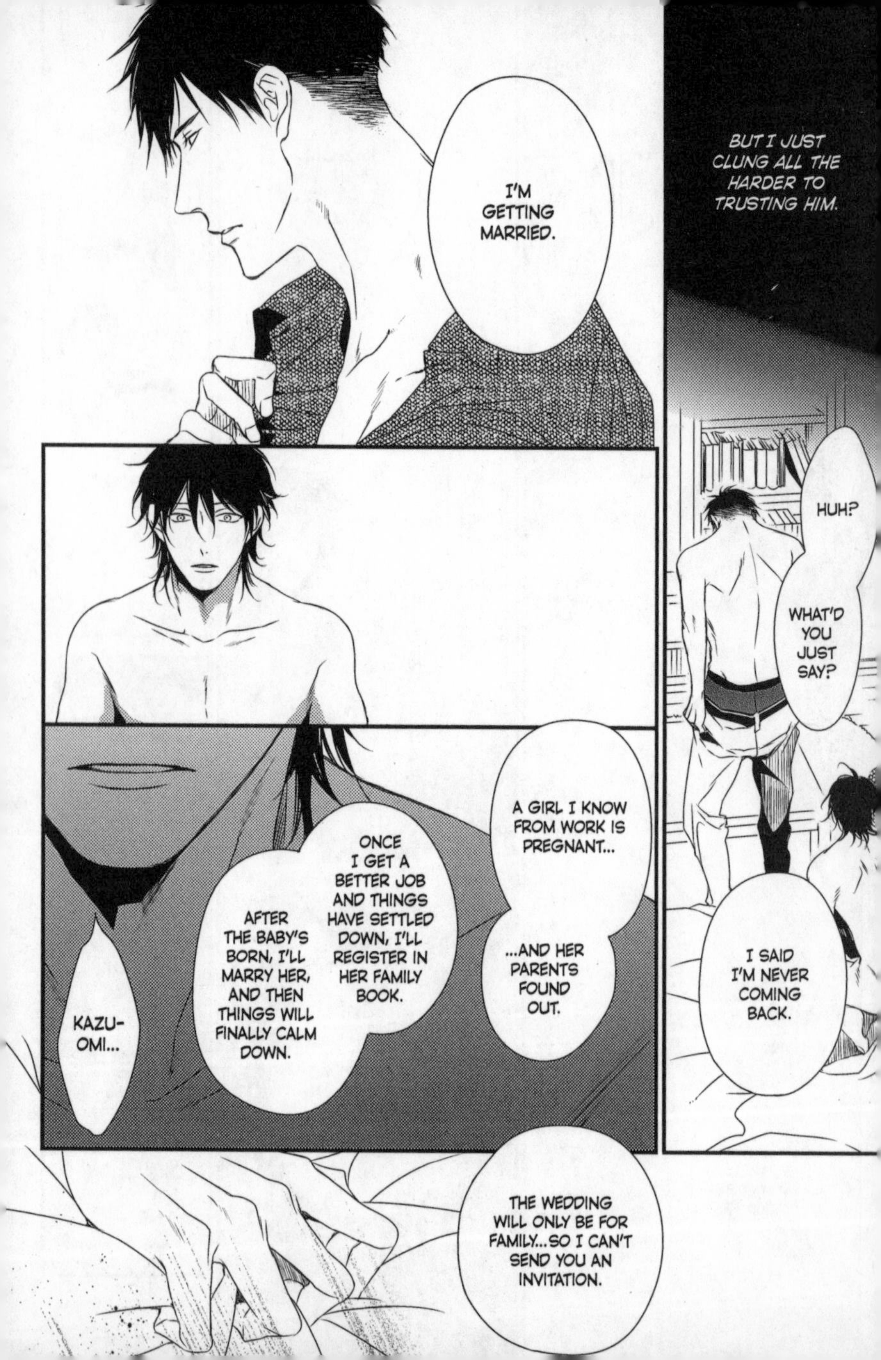
BUT I JUST CLUNG ALL THE HARDER TO TRUSTING HIM.
HUH?
WHAT'D YOU JUST SAY?
I SAID I'M NEVER COMING BACK.
I'M GETTING MARRIED.
A GIRL I KNOW FROM WORK IS PREGNANT...
...AND HER PARENTS FOUND OUT.
ONCE I GET A BETTER JOB AND THINGS HAVE SETTLED DOWN, I'LL REGISTER IN HER FAMILY BOOK.
AFTER THE BABY'S BORN, I'LL MARRY HER, AND THEN THINGS WILL FINALLY CALM DOWN.
KAZU-OMI...
THE WEDDING WILL ONLY BE FOR FAMILY...SO I CAN'T SEND YOU AN INVITATION.

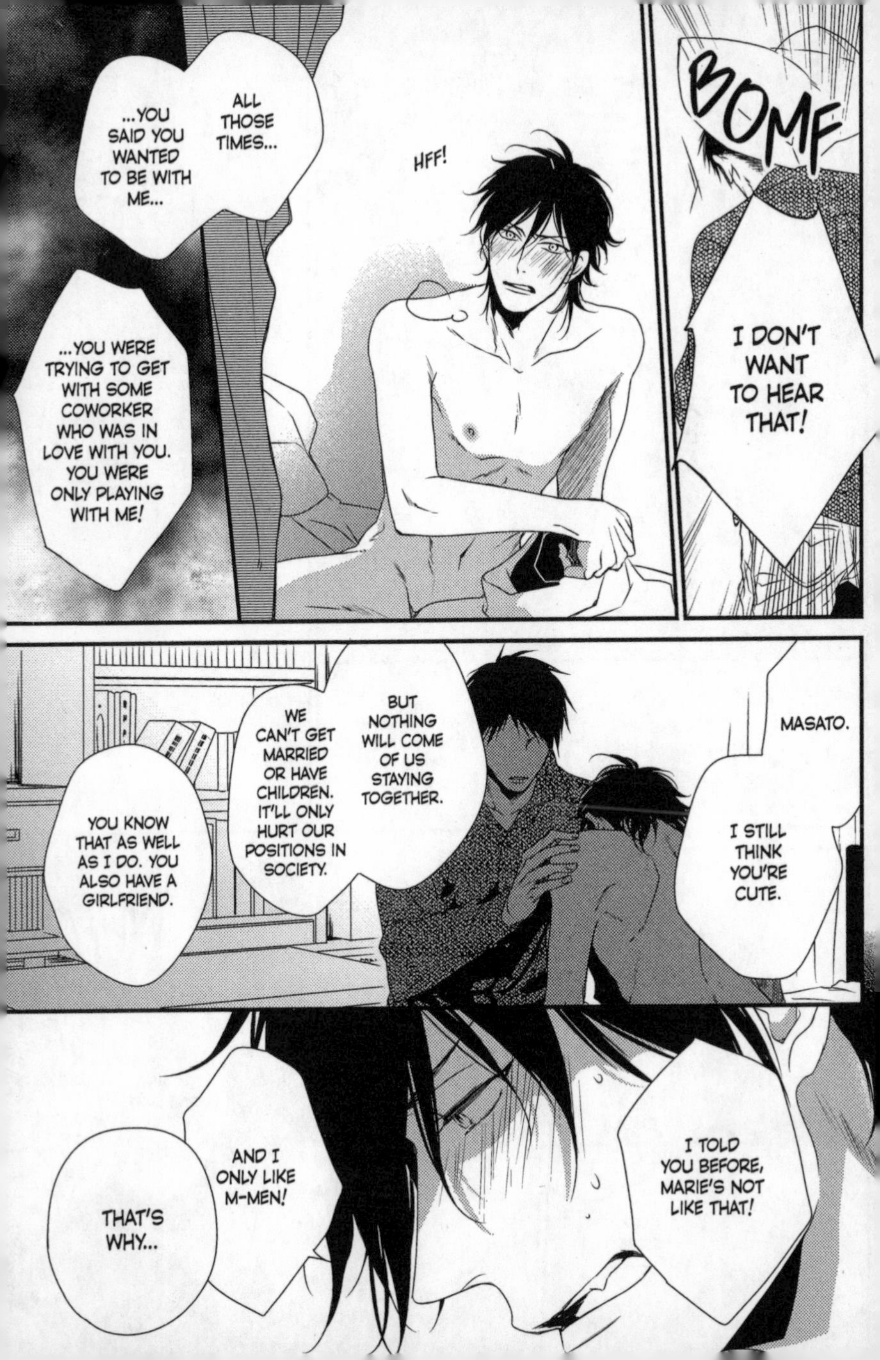
BOMF
I DON'T WANT TO HEAR THAT!
HFF!
ALL THOSE TIMES...
...YOU SAID YOU WANTED TO BE WITH ME...
...YOU WERE TRYING TO GET WITH SOME COWORKER WHO WAS IN LOVE WITH YOU. YOU WERE ONLY PLAYING WITH ME!
MASATO.
I STILL THINK YOU'RE CUTE.
BUT NOTHING WILL COME OF US STAYING TOGETHER.
WE CAN'T GET MARRIED OR HAVE CHILDREN. IT'LL ONLY HURT OUR POSITIONS IN SOCIETY.
YOU KNOW THAT AS WELL AS I DO. YOU ALSO HAVE A GIRLFRIEND.
I TOLD YOU BEFORE, MARIE'S NOT LIKE THAT!
AND I ONLY LIKE M-MEN!
THAT'S WHY...

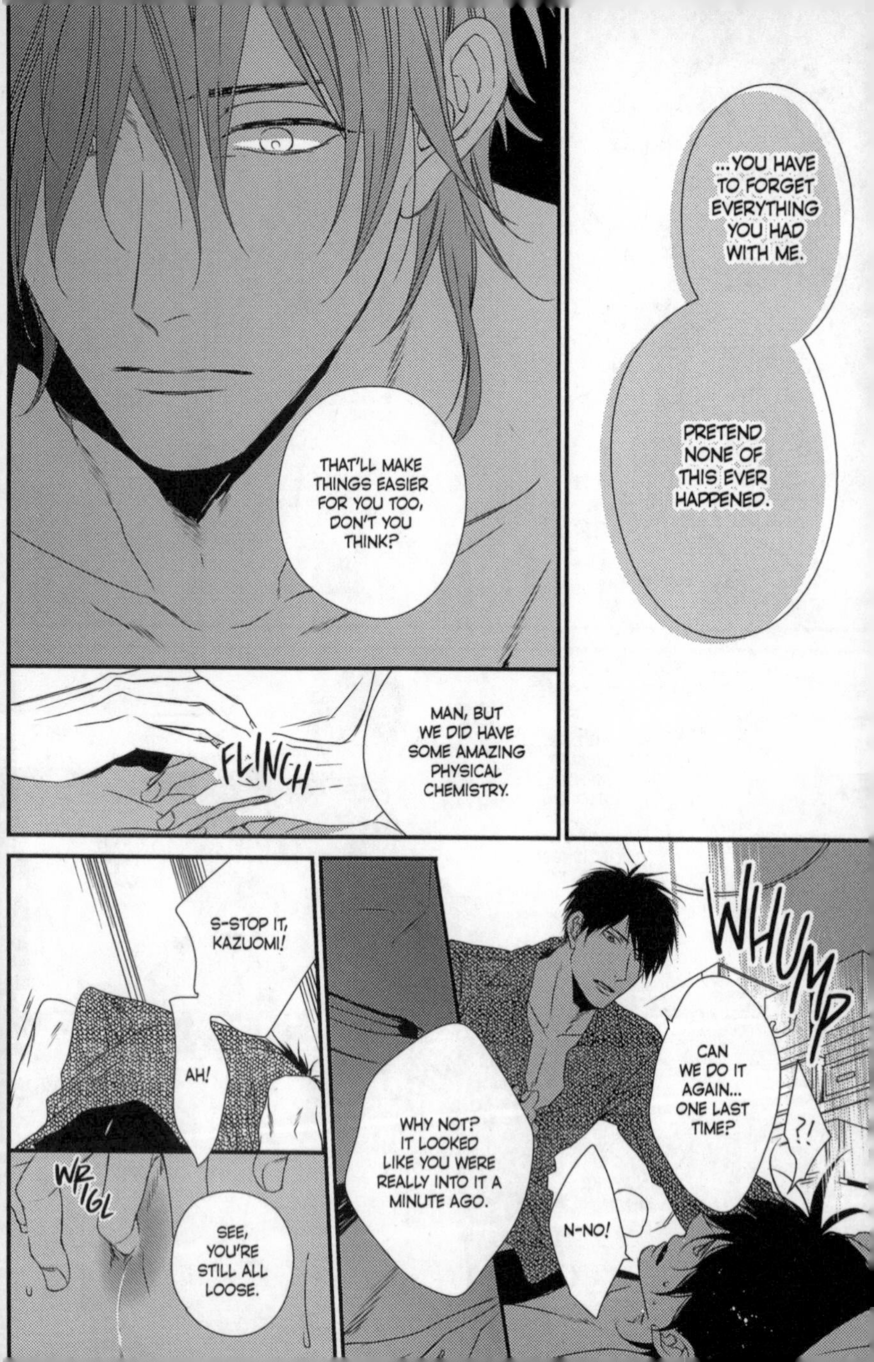
...YOU HAVE TO FORGET EVERYTHING YOU HAD WITH ME.
PRETEND NONE OF THIS EVER HAPPENED.
THAT'LL MAKE THINGS EASIER FOR YOU TOO, DON'T YOU THINK?
MAN, BUT WE DID HAVE SOME AMAZING PHYSICAL CHEMISTRY.
FLINCH
WHUMP
?!
CAN WE DO IT AGAIN... ONE LAST TIME?
N-NO!
WHY NOT? IT LOOKED LIKE YOU WERE REALLY INTO IT A MINUTE AGO.
S-STOP IT, KAZUOMI!
AH!
WRIGL
SEE, YOU'RE STILL ALL LOOSE.

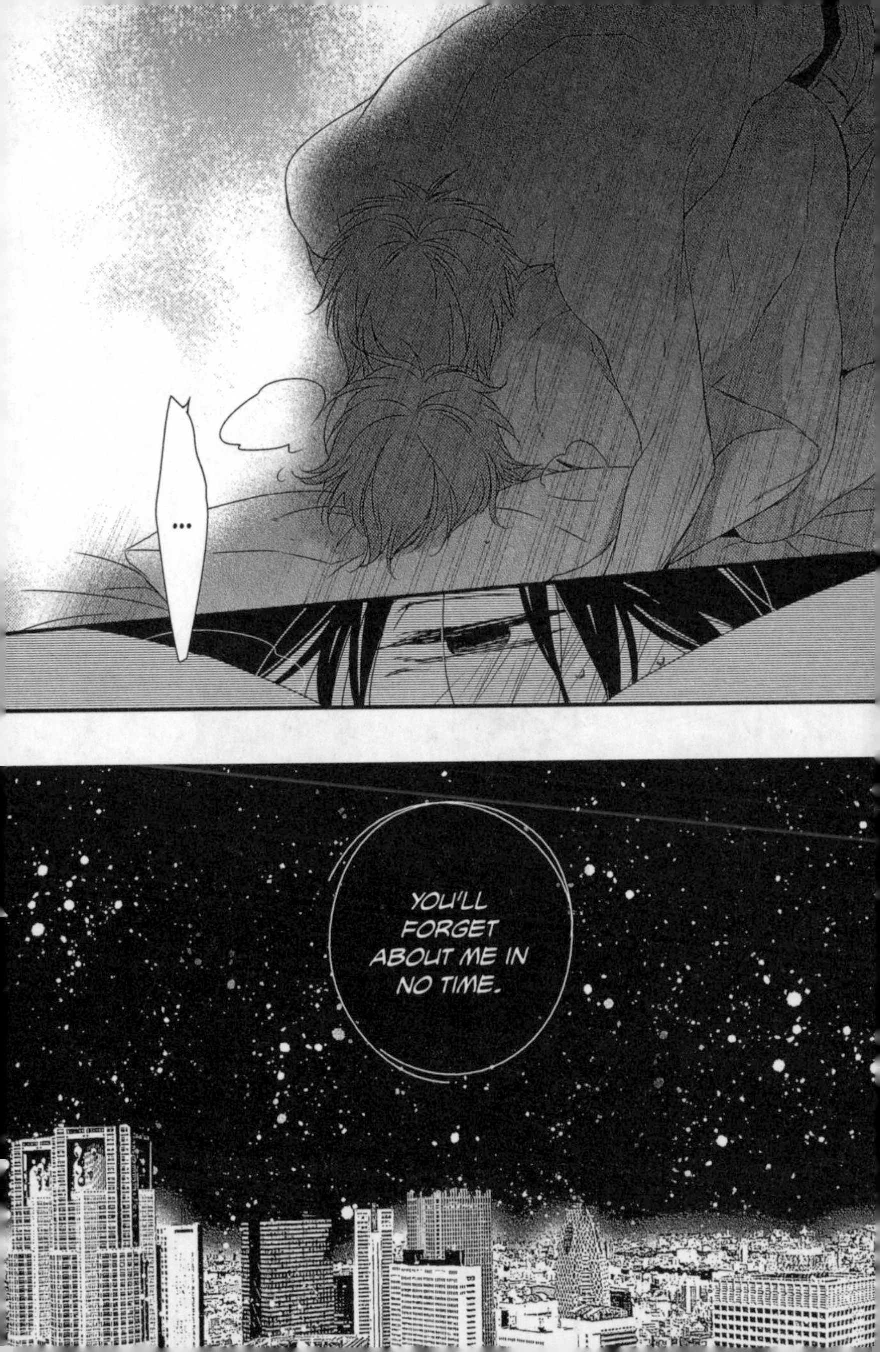
...
YOU'LL FORGET ABOUT ME IN NO TIME.

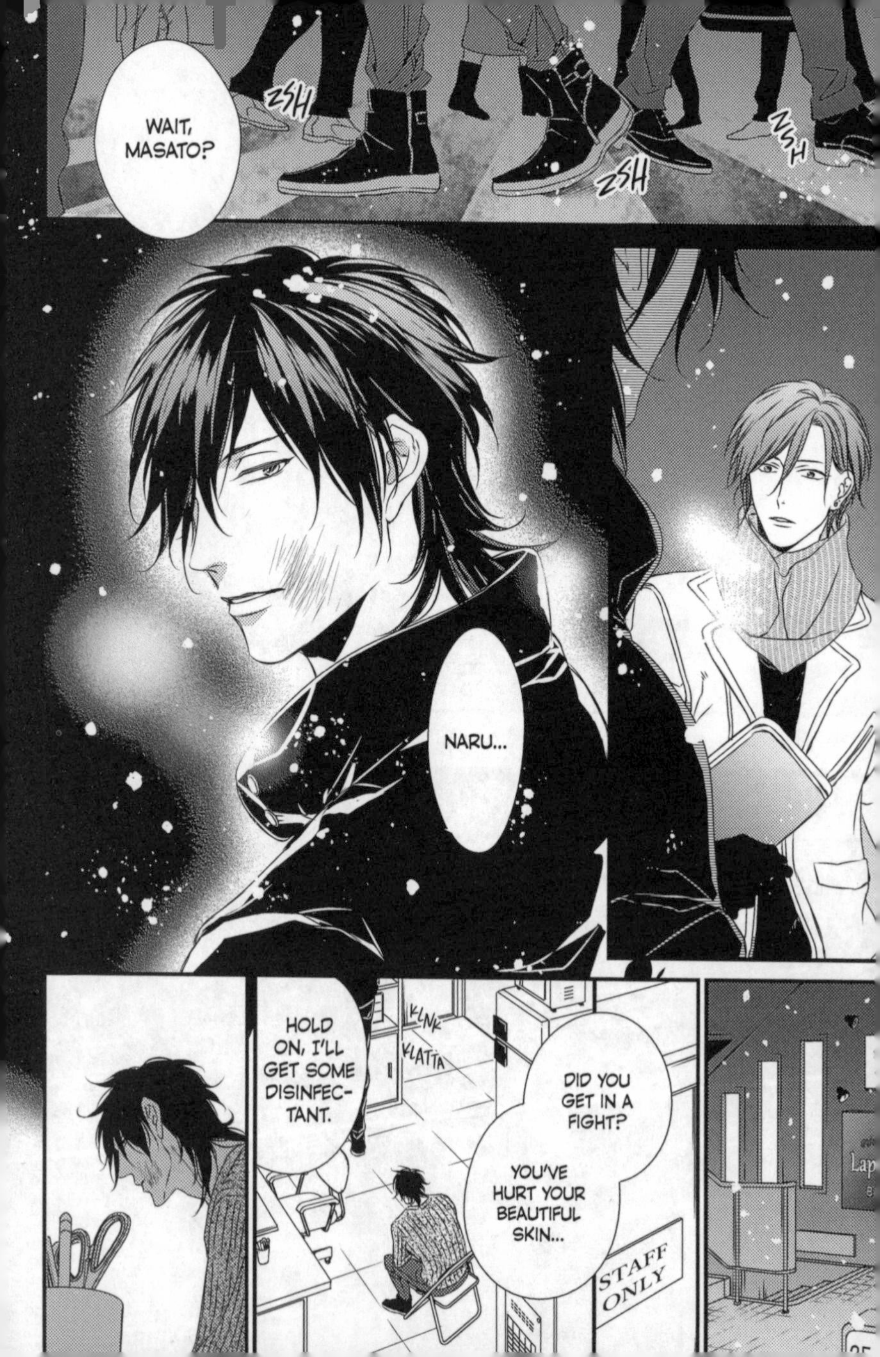
ZSH
ZSH
ZSH
WAIT, MASATO?
NARU...
DID YOU GET IN A FIGHT?
YOU'VE HURT YOUR BEAUTIFUL SKIN...
STAFF ONLY
KLNK
KLATTA
HOLD ON, I'LL GET SOME DISINFEC-TANT.

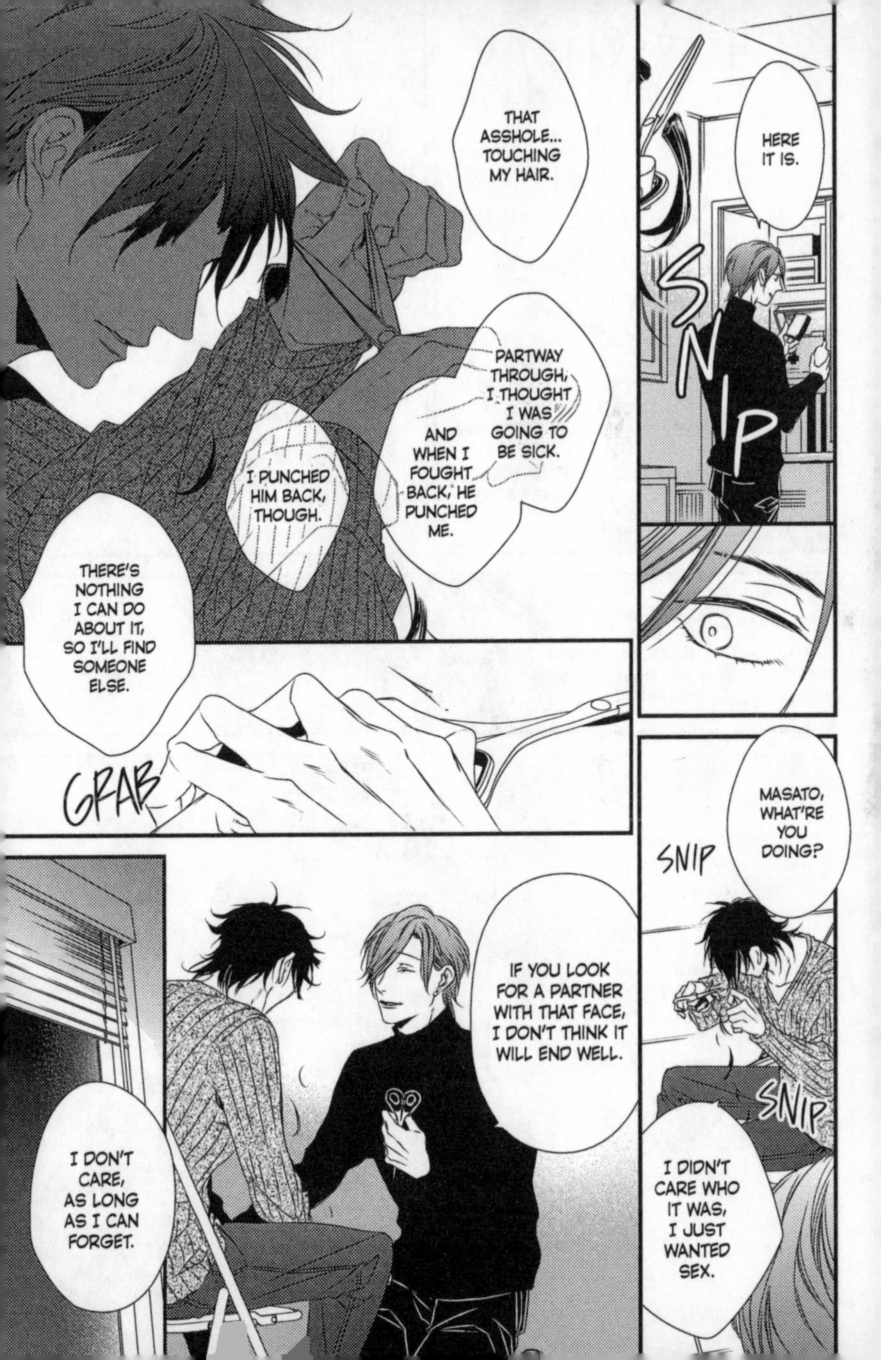
HERE IT IS.
SNIP
THAT ASSHOLE... TOUCHING MY HAIR.
PARTWAY THROUGH, I THOUGHT I WAS GOING TO BE SICK.
AND WHEN I FOUGHT BACK, HE PUNCHED ME.
I PUNCHED HIM BACK, THOUGH.
THERE'S NOTHING I CAN DO ABOUT IT, SO I'LL FIND SOMEONE ELSE.
GRAB
MASATO, WHAT'RE YOU DOING?
SNIP
SNIP
I DIDN'T CARE WHO IT WAS, I JUST WANTED SEX.
IF YOU LOOK FOR A PARTNER WITH THAT FACE, I DON'T THINK IT WILL END WELL.
I DON'T CARE, AS LONG AS I CAN FORGET.

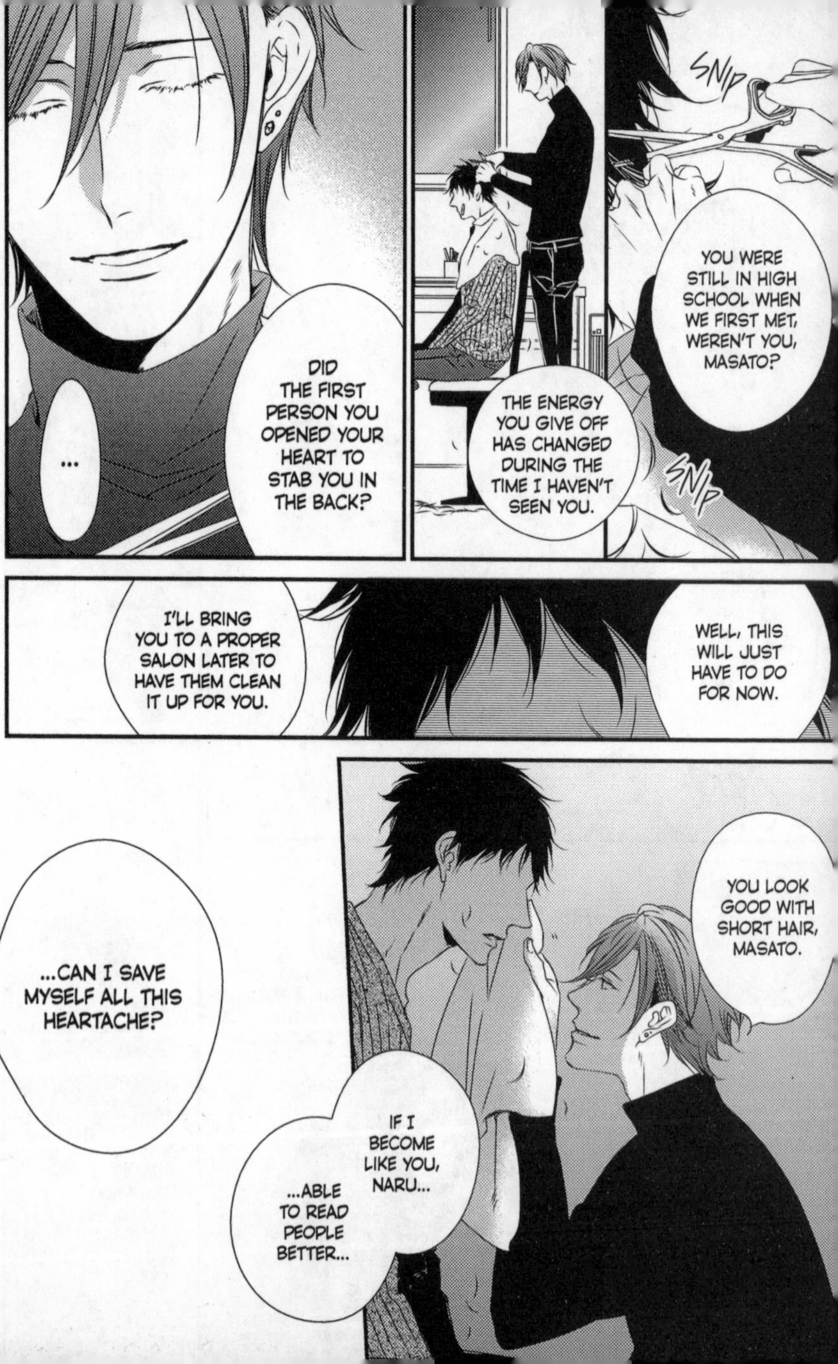
SNIP
YOU WERE STILL IN HIGH SCHOOL WHEN WE FIRST MET, WEREN'T YOU, MASATO?
SNIP
THE ENERGY YOU GIVE OFF HAS CHANGED DURING THE TIME I HAVEN'T SEEN YOU.
DID THE FIRST PERSON YOU OPENED YOUR HEART TO STAB YOU IN THE BACK?
...
WELL, THIS WILL JUST HAVE TO DO FOR NOW.
I'LL BRING YOU TO A PROPER SALON LATER TO HAVE THEM CLEAN IT UP FOR YOU.
YOU LOOK GOOD WITH SHORT HAIR, MASATO.
IF I BECOME LIKE YOU, NARU...
...ABLE TO READ PEOPLE BETTER...
...CAN I SAVE MYSELF ALL THIS HEARTACHE?

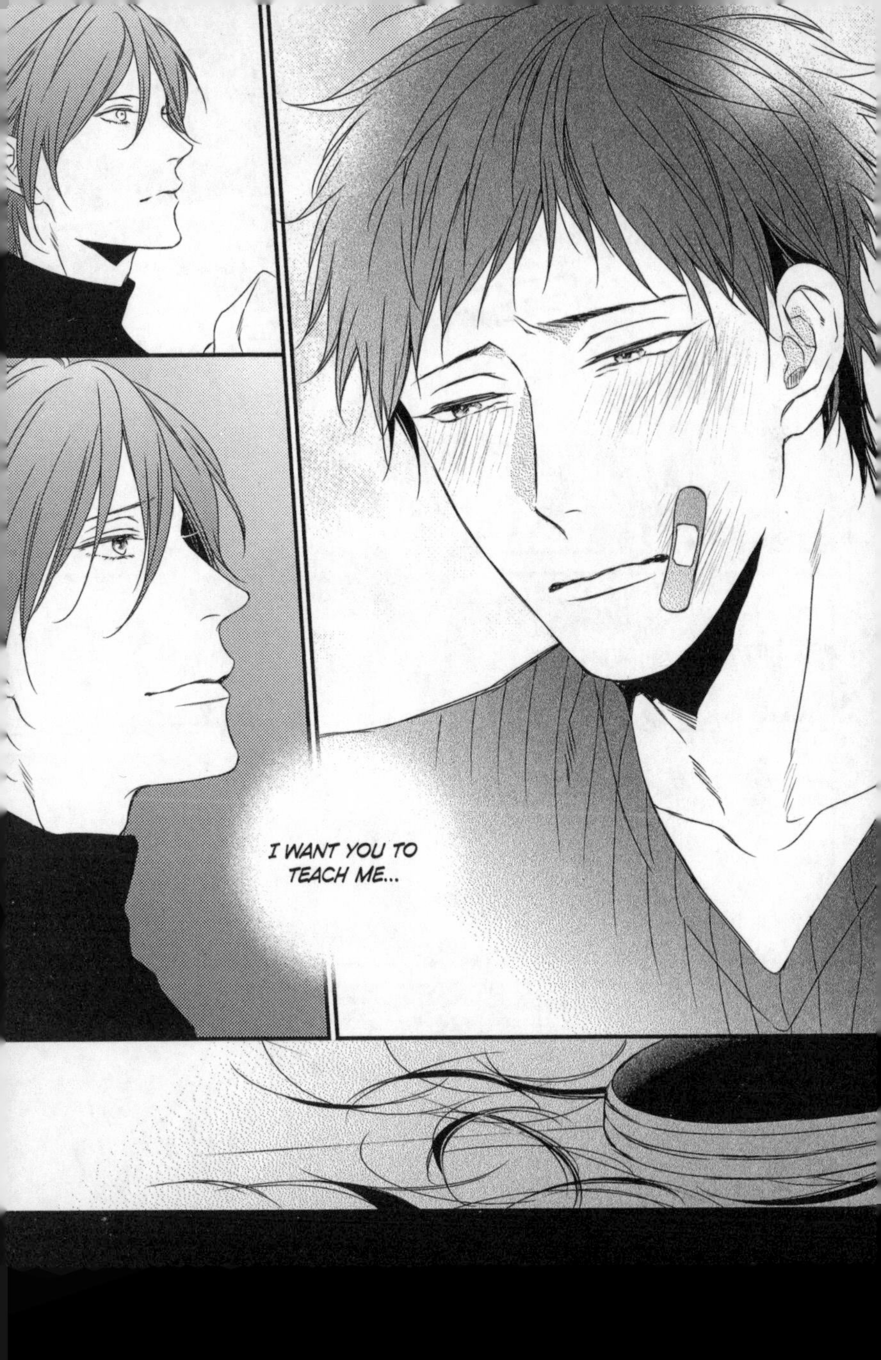
I WANT YOU TO
TEACH ME...

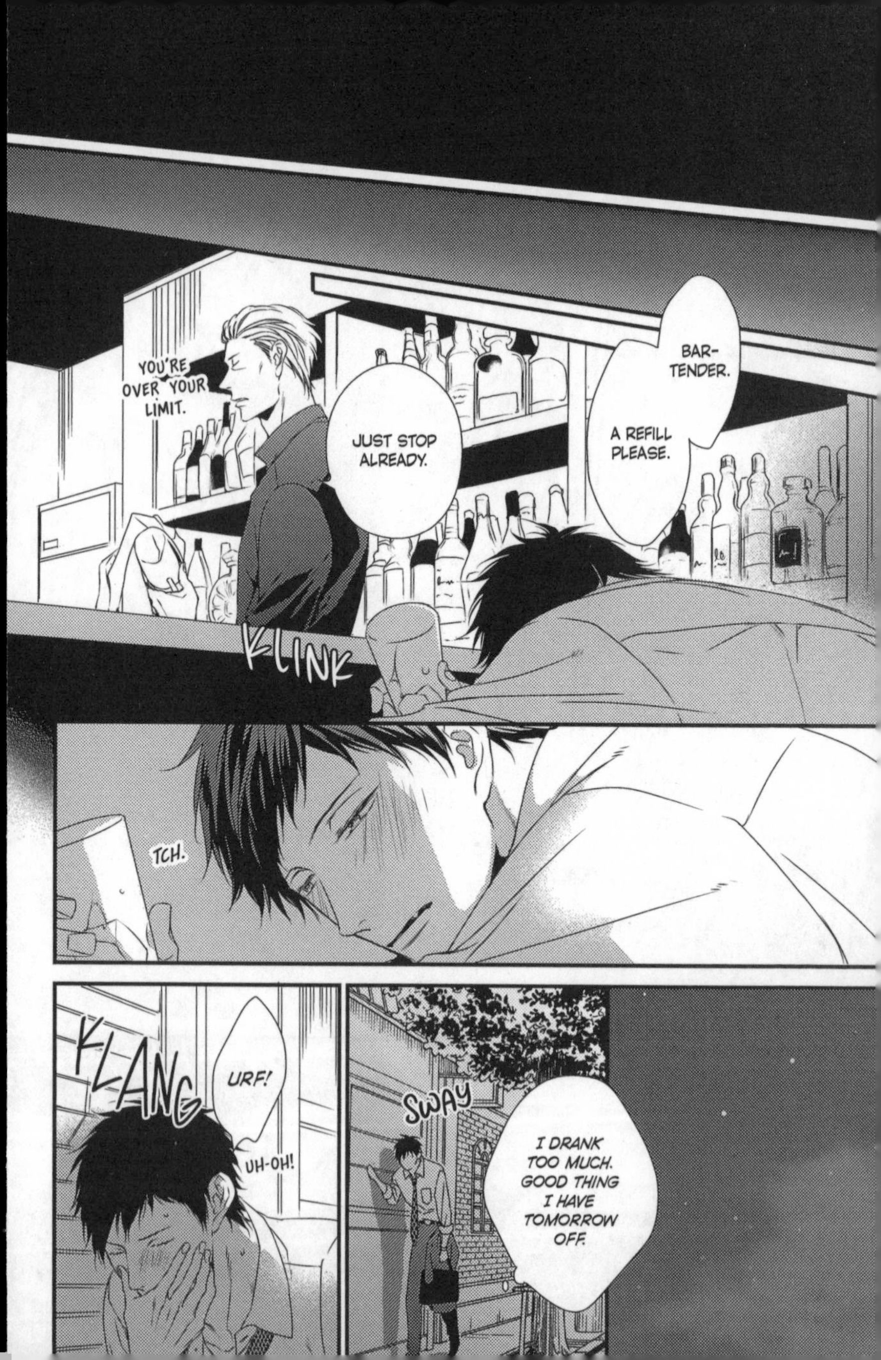
BAR-TENDER.
A REFILL PLEASE.
JUST STOP ALREADY.
YOU'RE OVER YOUR LIMIT.
KLINK
TCH.
SWAY
I DRANK TOO MUCH. GOOD THING I HAVE TOMORROW OFF.
KLANG
URF!
UH-OH!

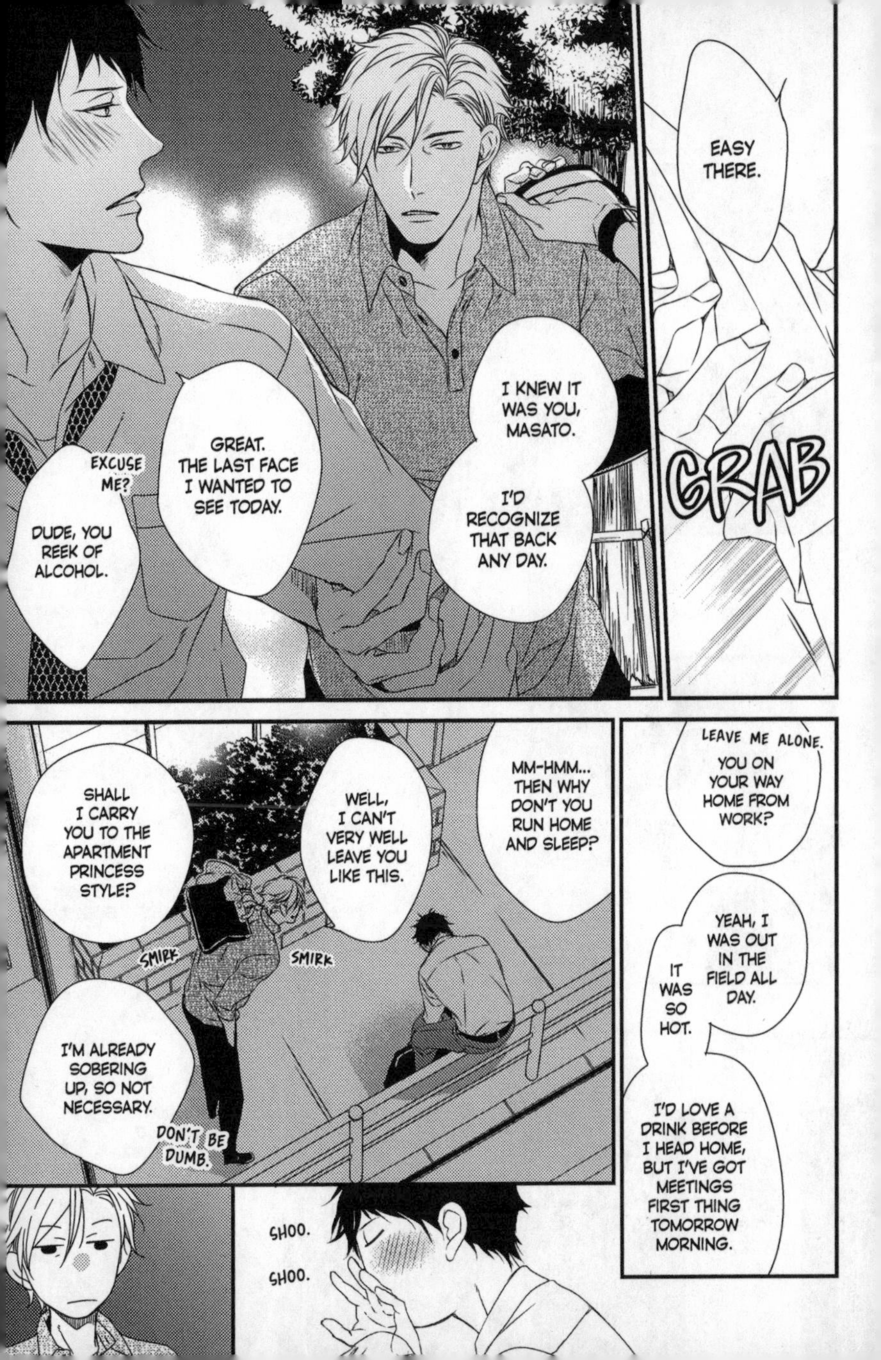
GRAB
EASY THERE.
I KNEW IT WAS YOU, MASATO.
I'D RECOGNIZE THAT BACK ANY DAY.
GREAT. THE LAST FACE I WANTED TO SEE TODAY.
EXCUSE ME?
DUDE, YOU REEK OF ALCOHOL.
LEAVE ME ALONE.
YOU ON YOUR WAY HOME FROM WORK?
YEAH, I WAS OUT IN THE FIELD ALL DAY.
IT WAS SO HOT.
I'D LOVE A DRINK BEFORE I HEAD HOME, BUT I'VE GOT MEETINGS FIRST THING TOMORROW MORNING.
MM-HMM... THEN WHY DON'T YOU RUN HOME AND SLEEP?
WELL, I CAN'T VERY WELL LEAVE YOU LIKE THIS.
SHALL I CARRY YOU TO THE APARTMENT PRINCESS STYLE?
SMIRK
SMIRK
I'M ALREADY SOBERING UP, SO NOT NECESSARY.
DON'T BE DUMB.
SHOO.
SHOO.

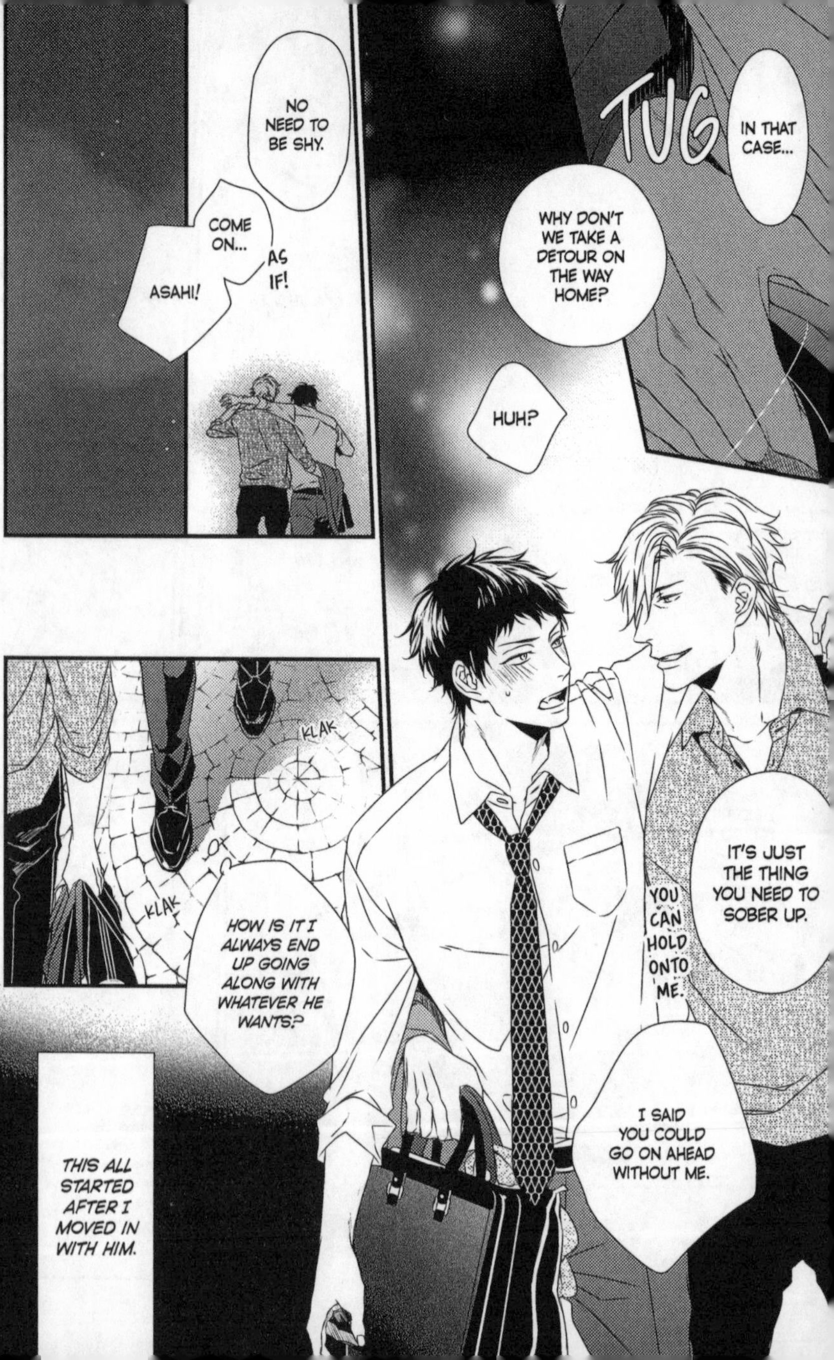
TUG
IN THAT CASE...
WHY DON'T WE TAKE A DETOUR ON THE WAY HOME?
HUH?
IT'S JUST THE THING YOU NEED TO SOBER UP.
YOU CAN HOLD ONTO ME.
I SAID YOU COULD GO ON AHEAD WITHOUT ME.
NO NEED TO BE SHY.
COME ON...
AS IF!
ASAHI!
KLAK
KLAK
HOW IS IT I ALWAYS END UP GOING ALONG WITH WHATEVER HE WANTS?
THIS ALL STARTED AFTER I MOVED IN WITH HIM.

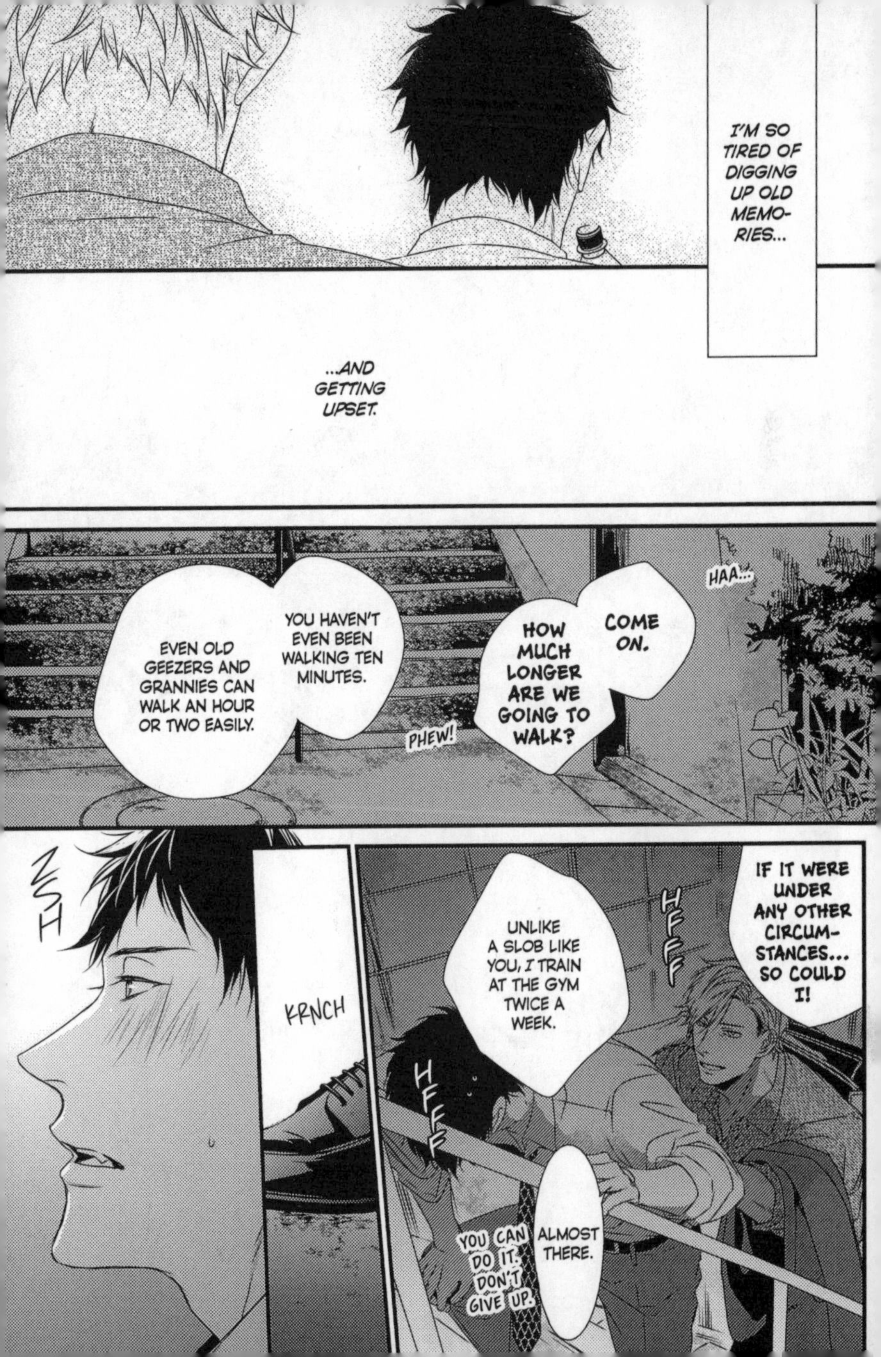
I'M SO TIRED OF DIGGING UP OLD MEMORIES...
...AND GETTING UPSET.
HAA...
COME ON.
HOW MUCH LONGER ARE WE GOING TO WALK?
PHEW!
YOU HAVEN'T EVEN BEEN WALKING TEN MINUTES.
EVEN OLD GEEZERS AND GRANNIES CAN WALK AN HOUR OR TWO EASILY.
IF IT WERE UNDER ANY OTHER CIRCUMSTANCES... SO COULD I!
HFFF
UNLIKE A SLOB LIKE YOU, I TRAIN AT THE GYM TWICE A WEEK.
HFFF
ALMOST THERE.
YOU CAN DO IT. DON'T GIVE UP.
KRNCH
ZSH

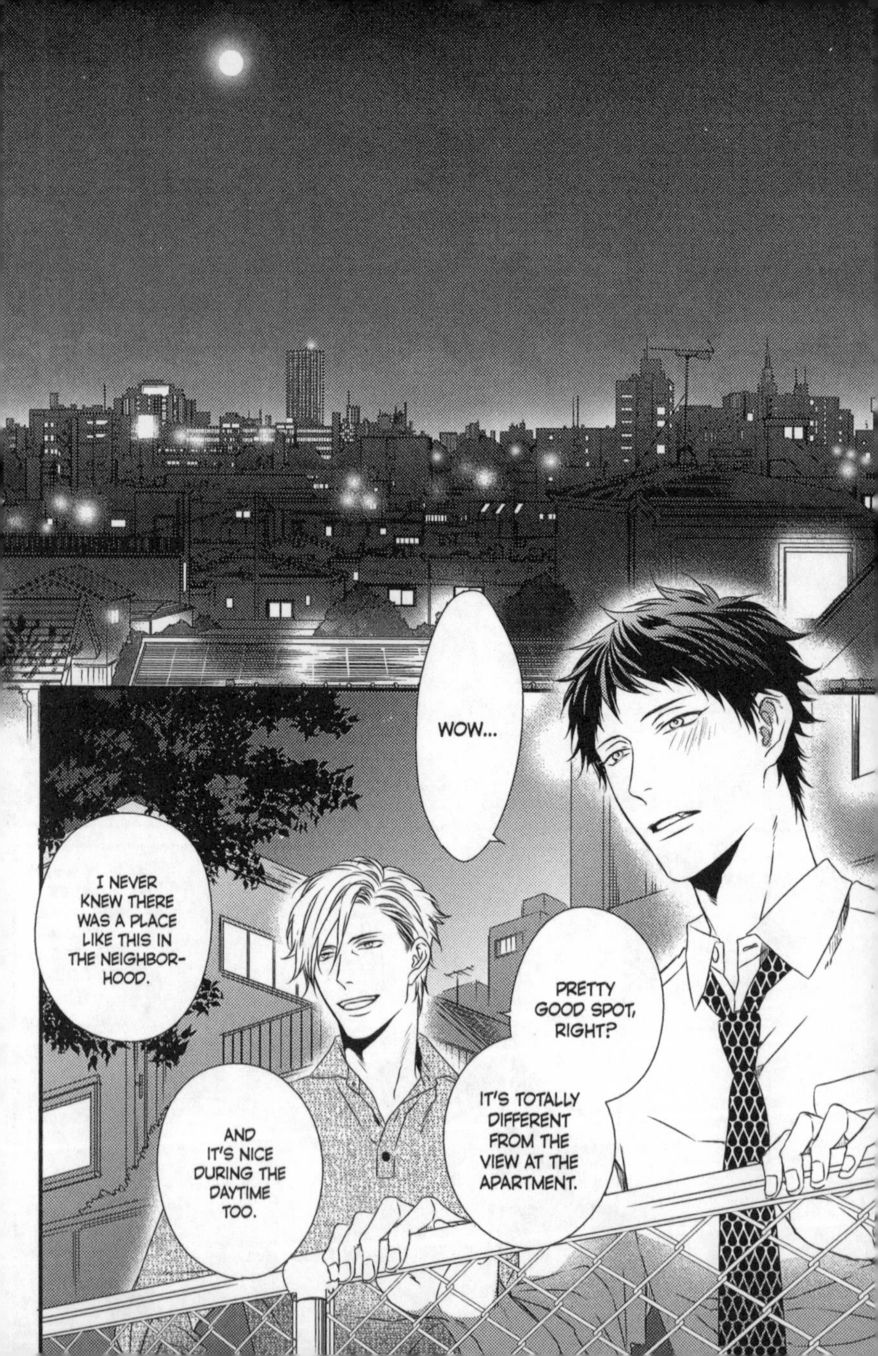
WOW...
PRETTY GOOD SPOT, RIGHT?
IT'S TOTALLY DIFFERENT FROM THE VIEW AT THE APARTMENT.
I NEVER KNEW THERE WAS A PLACE LIKE THIS IN THE NEIGHBOR-HOOD.
AND IT'S NICE DURING THE DAYTIME TOO.

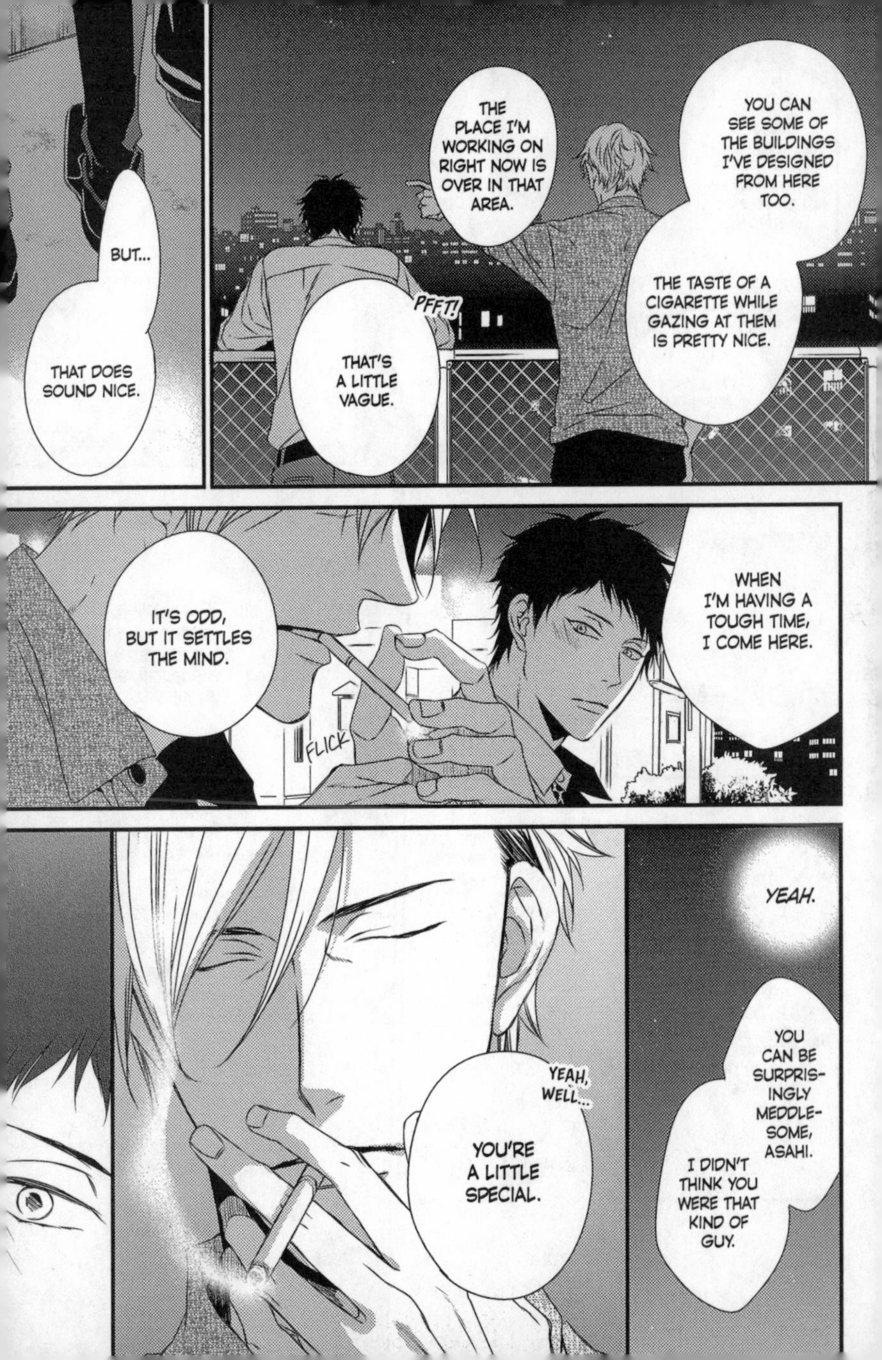
YOU CAN SEE SOME OF THE BUILDINGS I'VE DESIGNED FROM HERE TOO.
THE PLACE I'M WORKING ON RIGHT NOW IS OVER IN THAT AREA.
THE TASTE OF A CIGARETTE WHILE GAZING AT THEM IS PRETTY NICE.
PFFT!
THAT'S A LITTLE VAGUE.
BUT...
THAT DOES SOUND NICE.
WHEN I'M HAVING A TOUGH TIME, I COME HERE.
IT'S ODD, BUT IT SETTLES THE MIND.
FLICK
YEAH.
YOU CAN BE SURPRIS-INGLY MEDDLE-SOME, ASAHI.
I DIDN'T THINK YOU WERE THAT KIND OF GUY.
YEAH, WELL...
YOU'RE A LITTLE SPECIAL.

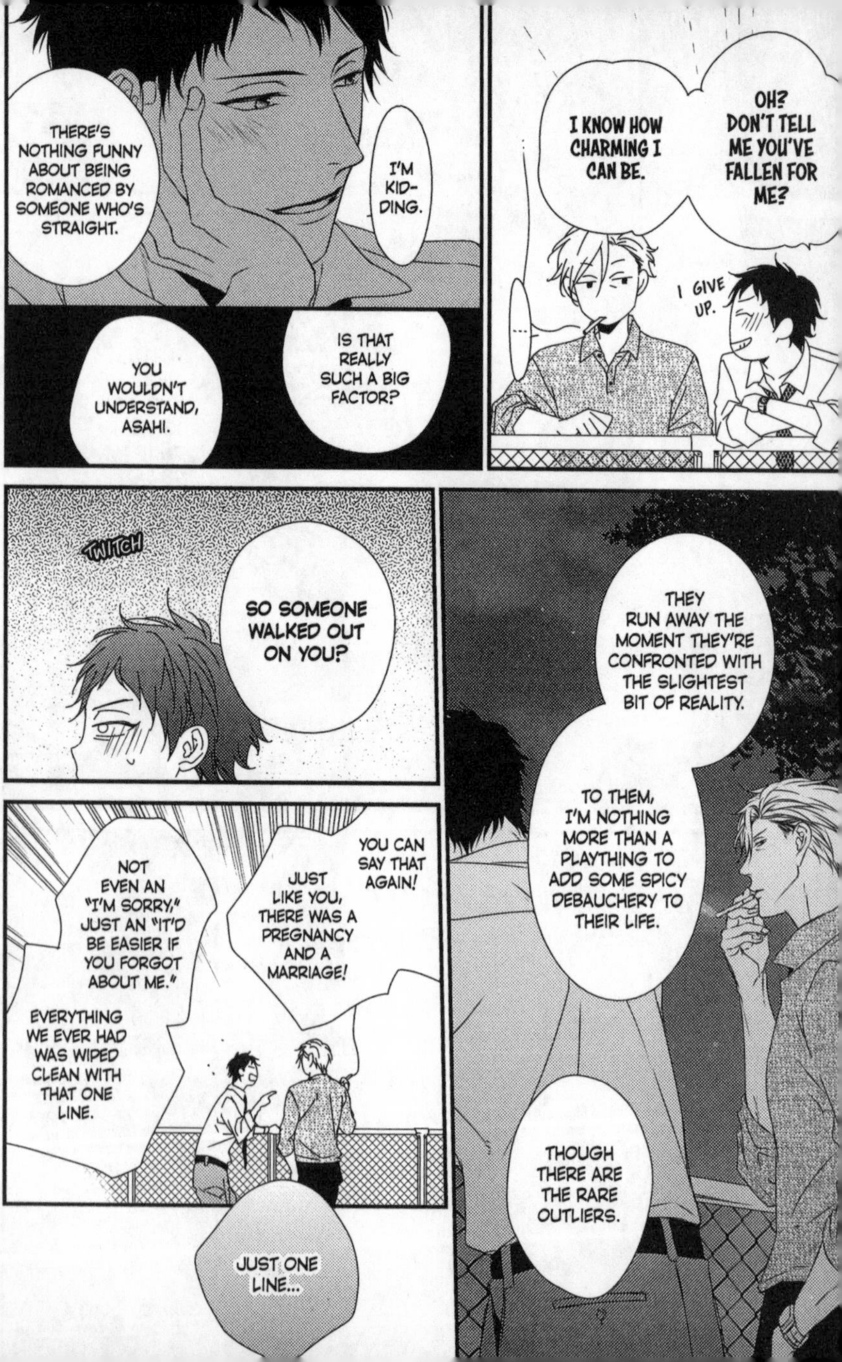
OH? DON'T TELL ME YOU'VE FALLEN FOR ME?
I KNOW HOW CHARMING I CAN BE.
...
I GIVE UP.
I'M KID-DING.
THERE'S NOTHING FUNNY ABOUT BEING ROMANCED BY SOMEONE WHO'S STRAIGHT.
IS THAT REALLY SUCH A BIG FACTOR?
YOU WOULDN'T UNDERSTAND, ASAHI.
THEY RUN AWAY THE MOMENT THEY'RE CONFRONTED WITH THE SLIGHTEST BIT OF REALITY.
TO THEM, I'M NOTHING MORE THAN A PLAYTHING TO ADD SOME SPICY DEBAUCHERY TO THEIR LIFE.
THOUGH THERE ARE THE RARE OUTLIERS.
TWITCH
SO SOMEONE WALKED OUT ON YOU?
YOU CAN SAY THAT AGAIN!
JUST LIKE YOU, THERE WAS A PREGNANCY AND A MARRIAGE!
NOT EVEN AN "I'M SORRY," JUST AN "IT'D BE EASIER IF YOU FORGOT ABOUT ME."
EVERYTHING WE EVER HAD WAS WIPED CLEAN WITH THAT ONE LINE.
JUST ONE LINE...

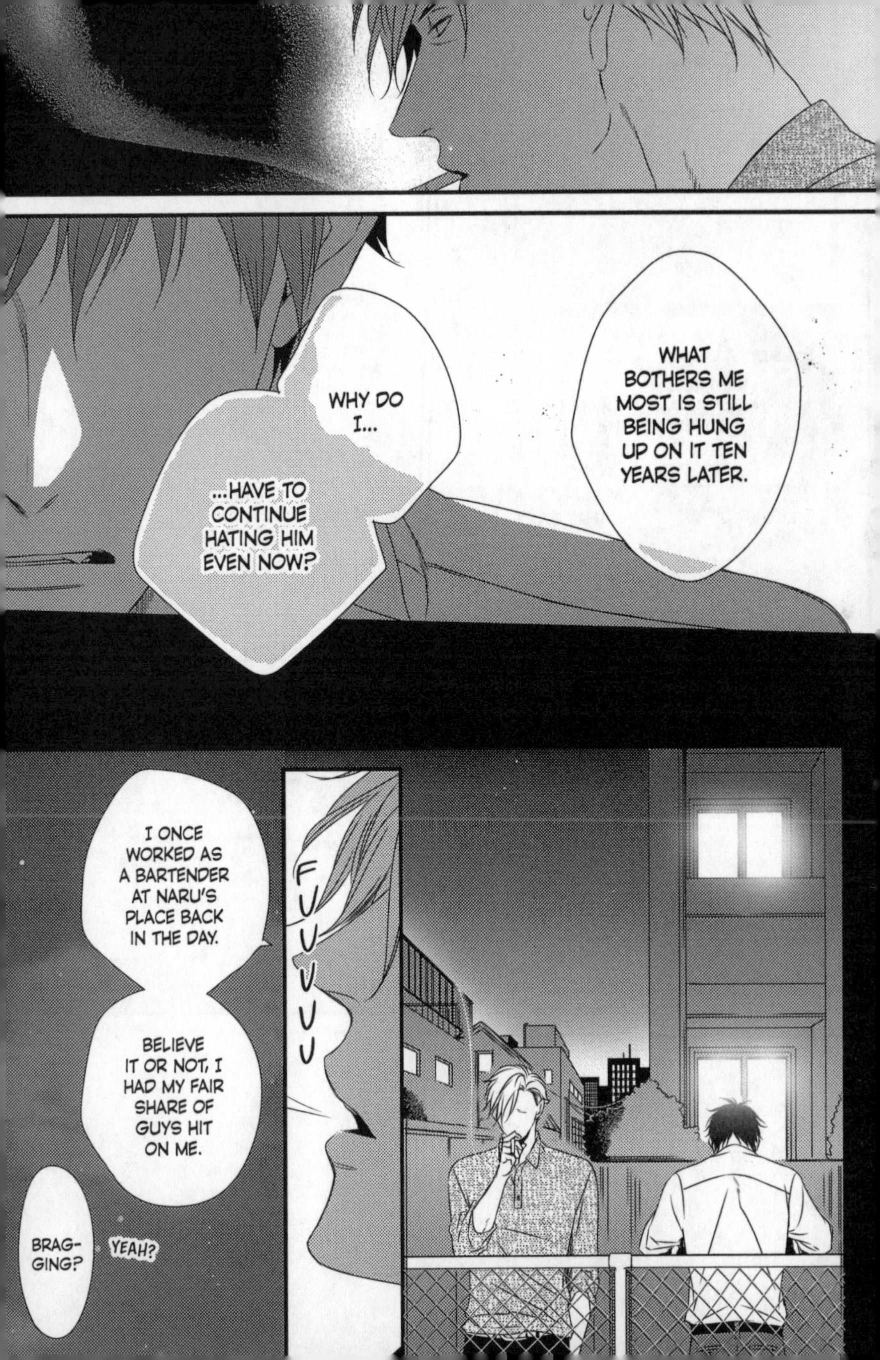
WHAT BOTHERS ME MOST IS STILL BEING HUNG UP ON IT TEN YEARS LATER.
WHY DO I...
...HAVE TO CONTINUE HATING HIM EVEN NOW?
FUUUUUUU
I ONCE WORKED AS A BARTENDER AT NARU'S PLACE BACK IN THE DAY.
BELIEVE IT OR NOT, I HAD MY FAIR SHARE OF GUYS HIT ON ME.
BRAG-GING?
YEAH?

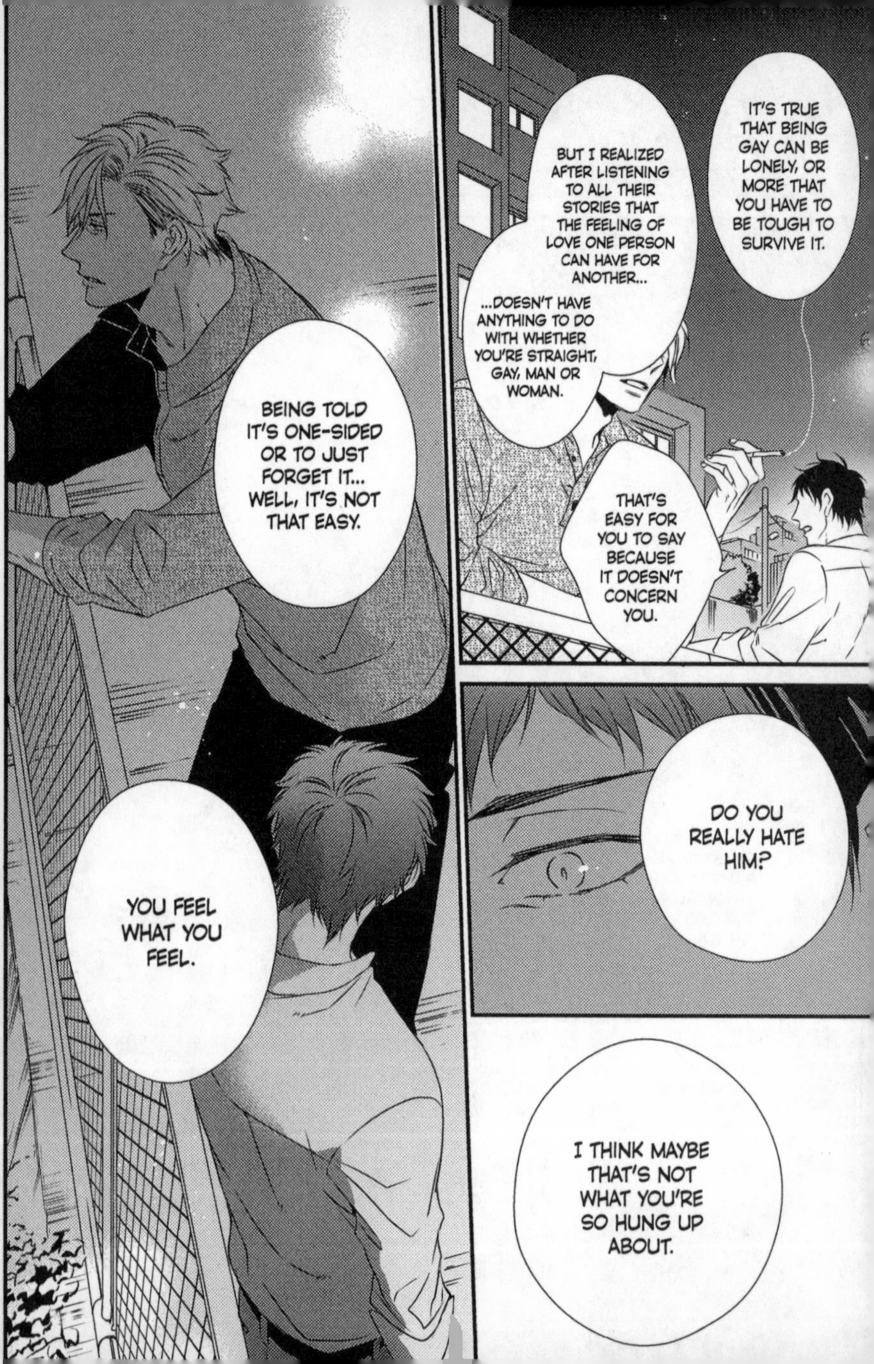
IT'S TRUE THAT BEING GAY CAN BE LONELY, OR MORE THAT YOU HAVE TO BE TOUGH TO SURVIVE IT.
BUT I REALIZED AFTER LISTENING TO ALL THEIR STORIES THAT THE FEELING OF LOVE ONE PERSON CAN HAVE FOR ANOTHER...
...DOESN'T HAVE ANYTHING TO DO WITH WHETHER YOU'RE STRAIGHT, GAY, MAN OR WOMAN.
THAT'S EASY FOR YOU TO SAY BECAUSE IT DOESN'T CONCERN YOU.
DO YOU REALLY HATE HIM?
I THINK MAYBE THAT'S NOT WHAT YOU'RE SO HUNG UP ABOUT.
BEING TOLD IT'S ONE-SIDED OR TO JUST FORGET IT... WELL, IT'S NOT THAT EASY.
YOU FEEL WHAT YOU FEEL.

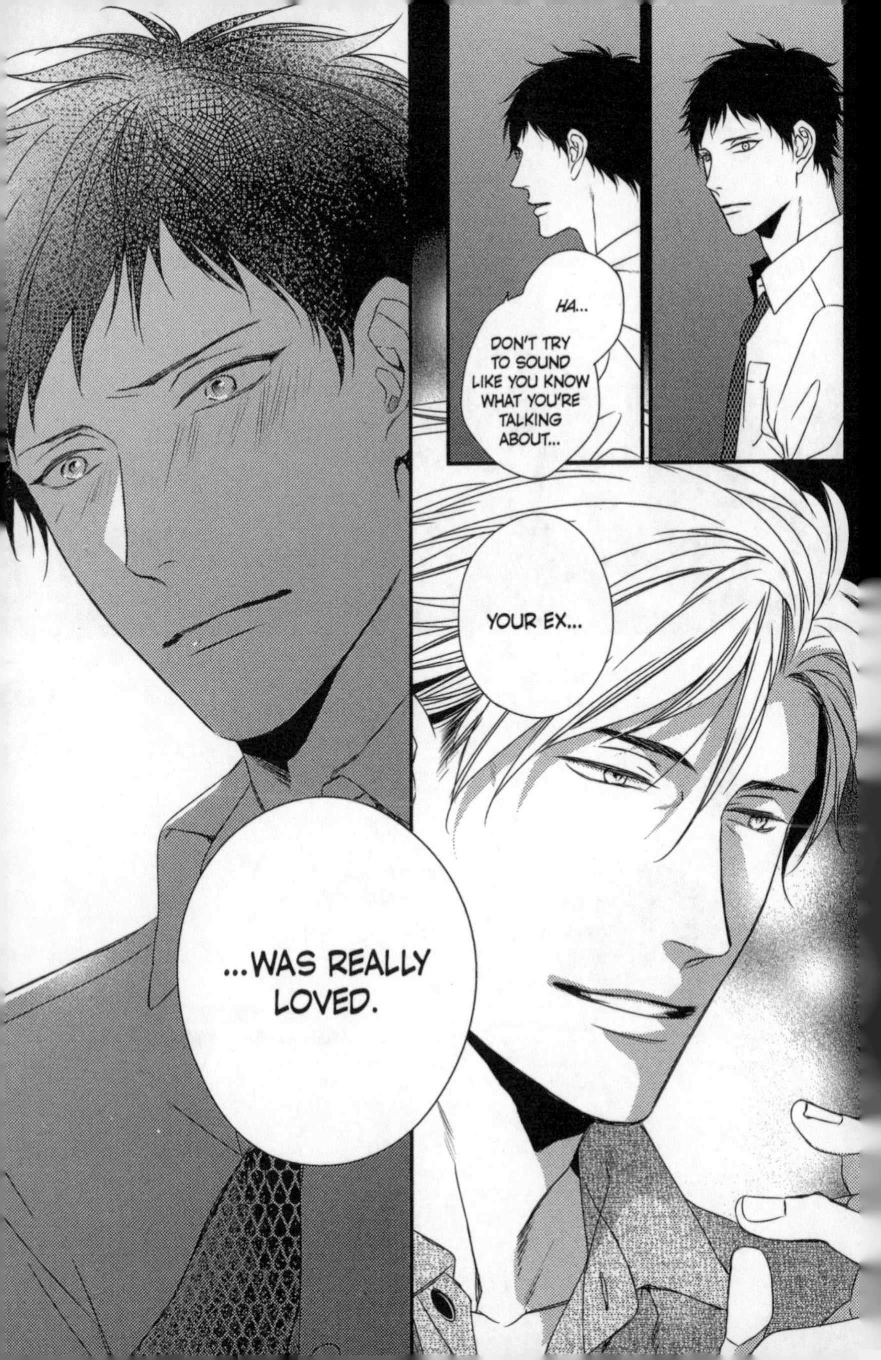
HA...
DON'T TRY TO SOUND LIKE YOU KNOW WHAT YOU'RE TALKING ABOUT...
YOUR EX...
...WAS REALLY LOVED.

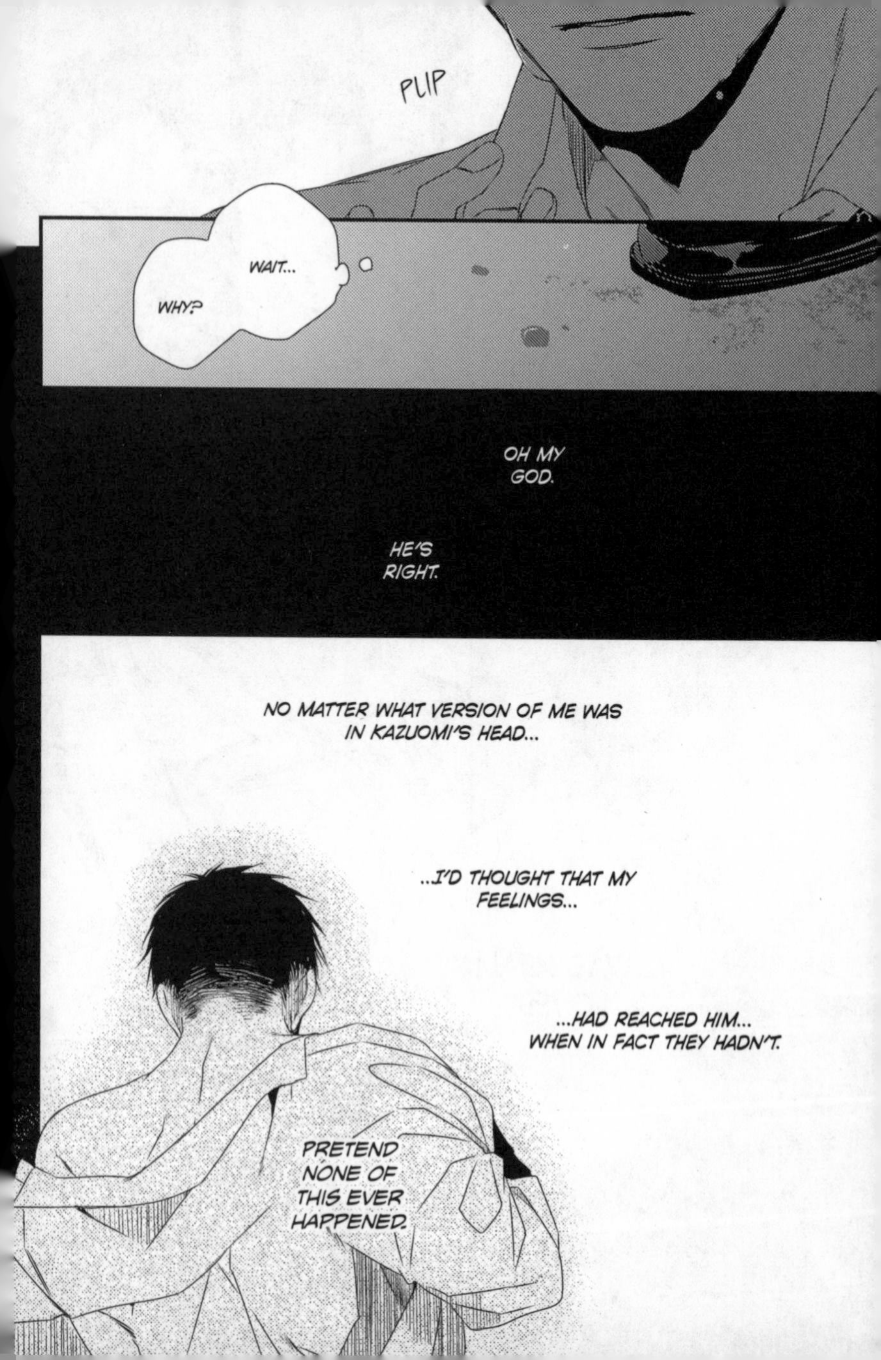
PLIP
WAIT...
WHY?
OH MY GOD.
HE'S RIGHT.
NO MATTER WHAT VERSION OF ME WAS IN KAZUOMI'S HEAD...
...I'D THOUGHT THAT MY FEELINGS...
...HAD REACHED HIM... WHEN IN FACT THEY HADN'T.
PRETEND NONE OF THIS EVER HAPPENED.

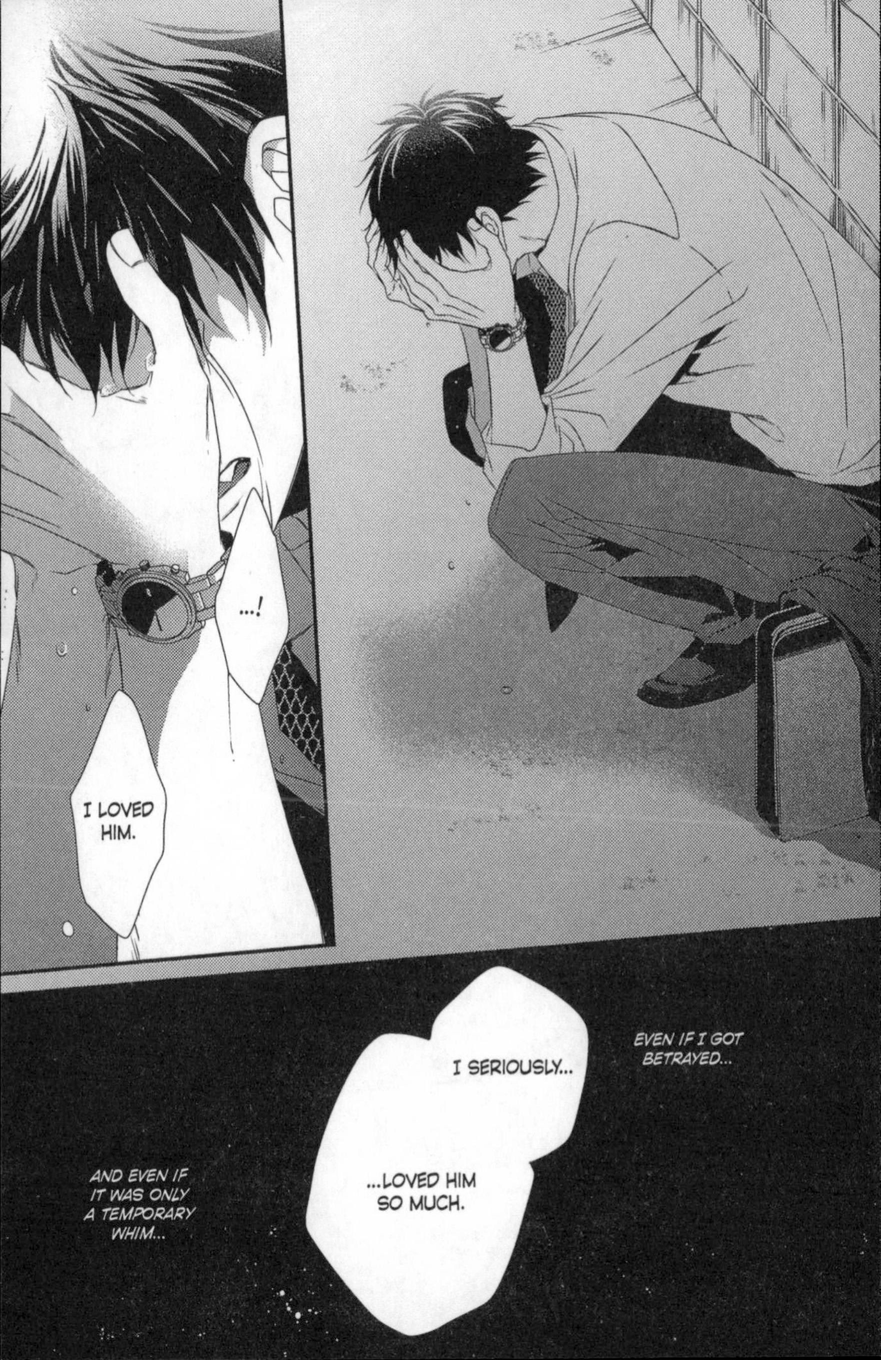
...!
I LOVED HIM.
EVEN IF I GOT BETRAYED...
I SERIOUSLY...
...LOVED HIM SO MUCH.
AND EVEN IF IT WAS ONLY A TEMPORARY WHIM...

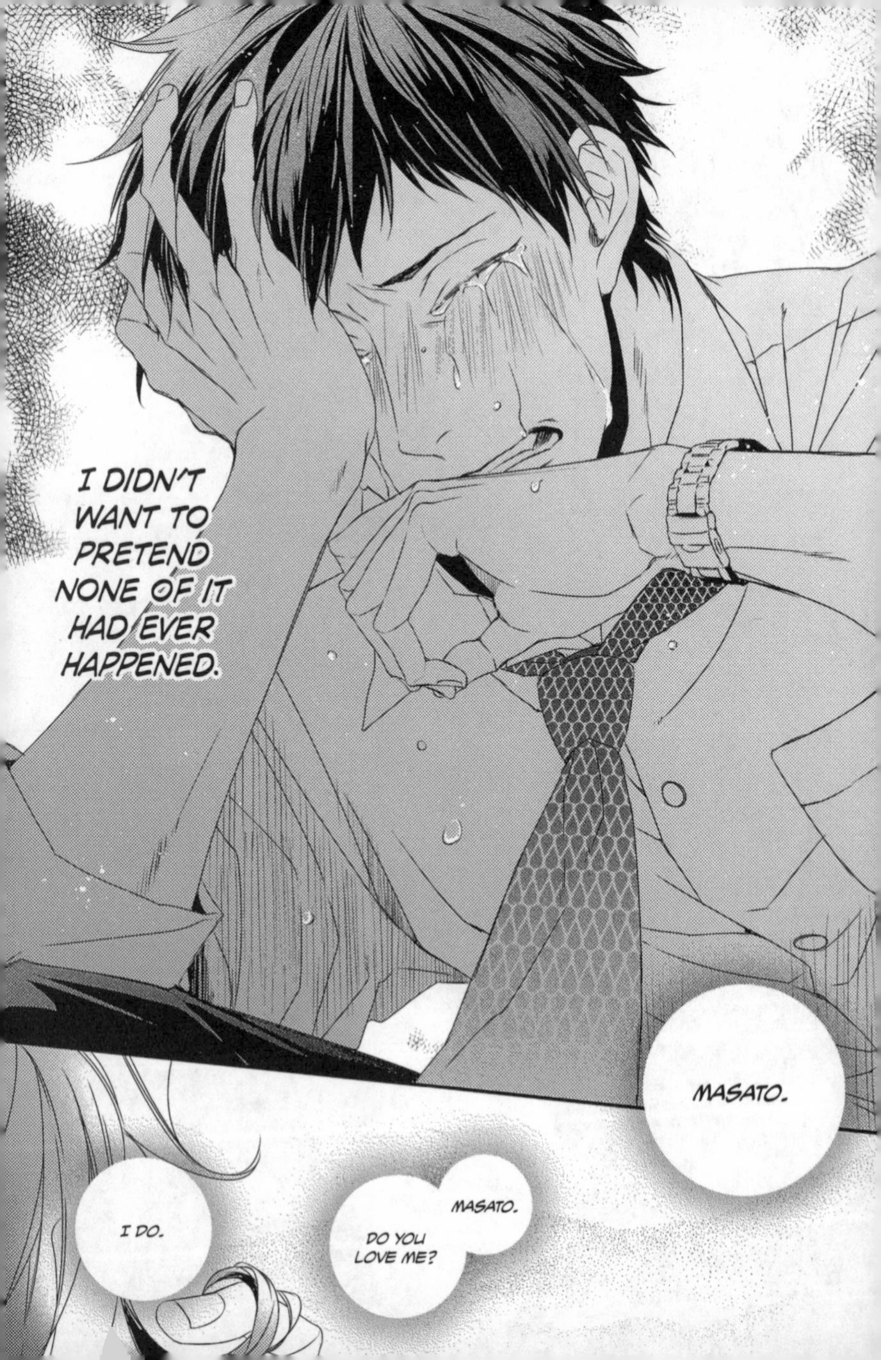
I DIDN'T WANT TO PRETEND NONE OF IT HAD EVER HAPPENED.
MASATO.
MASATO.
DO YOU LOVE ME?
I DO.

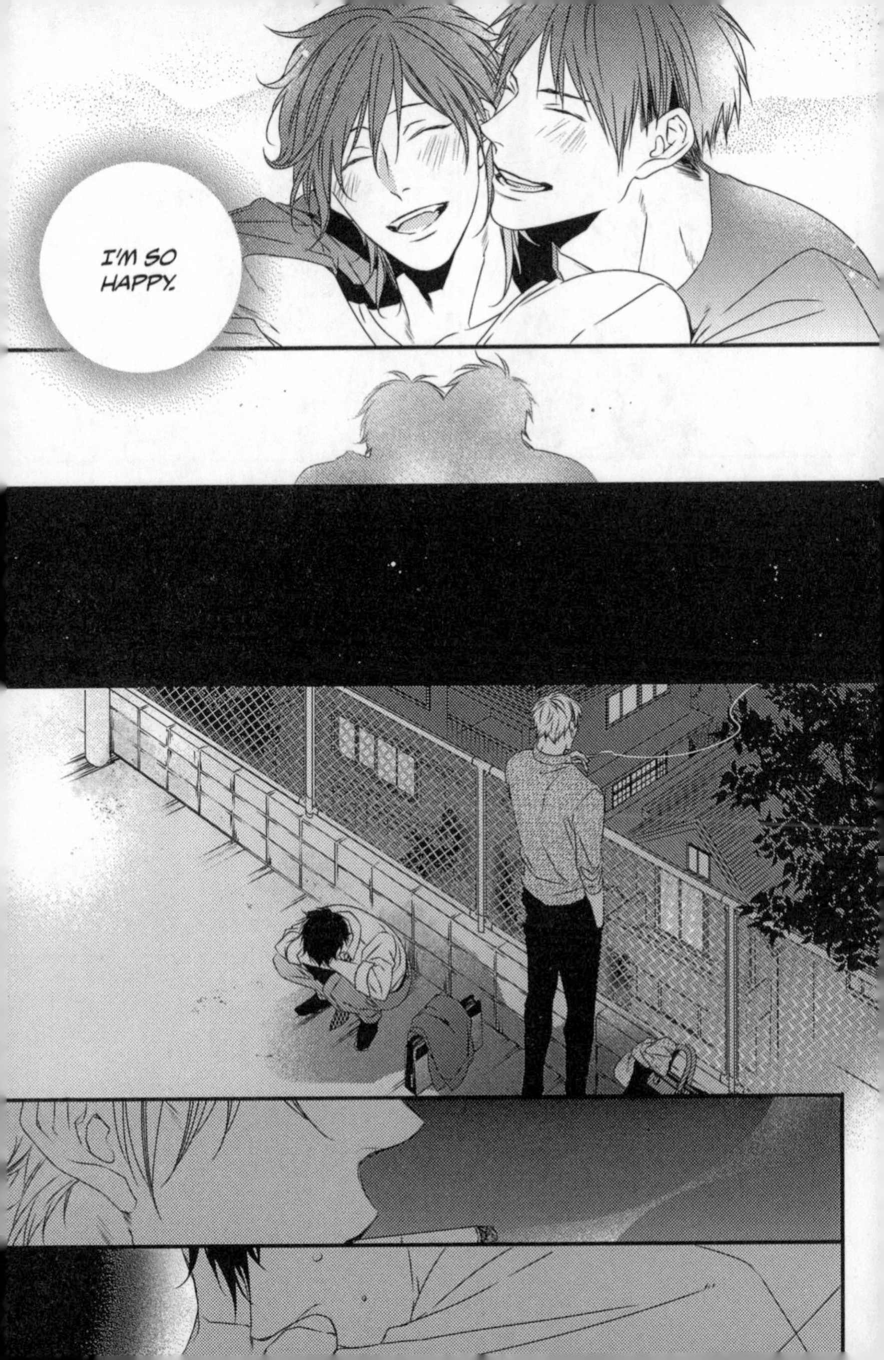
I'M SO
HAPPY.

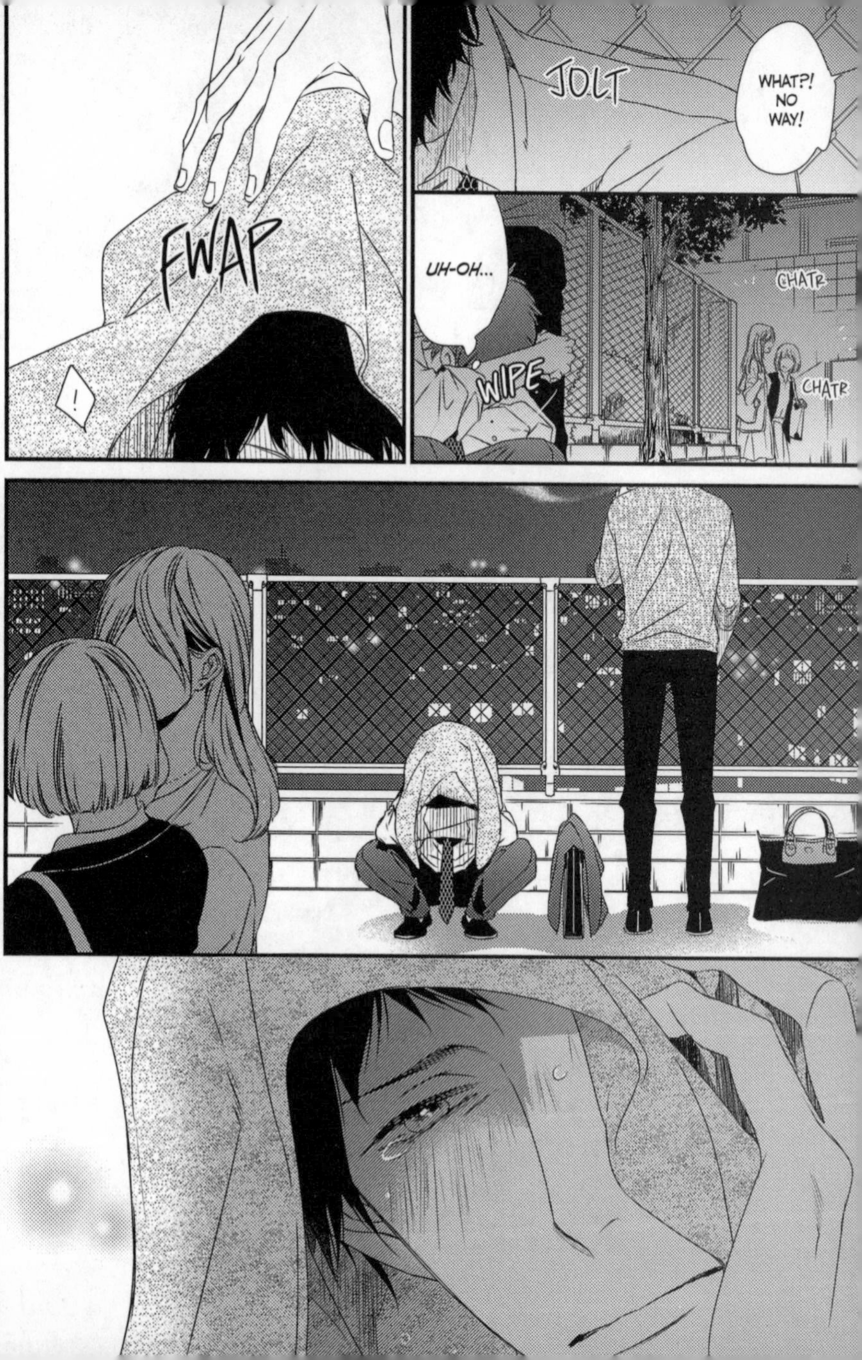
JOLT
WHAT?! NO WAY!
UH-OH...
WIPE
CHATR
CHATR
FWAP
!

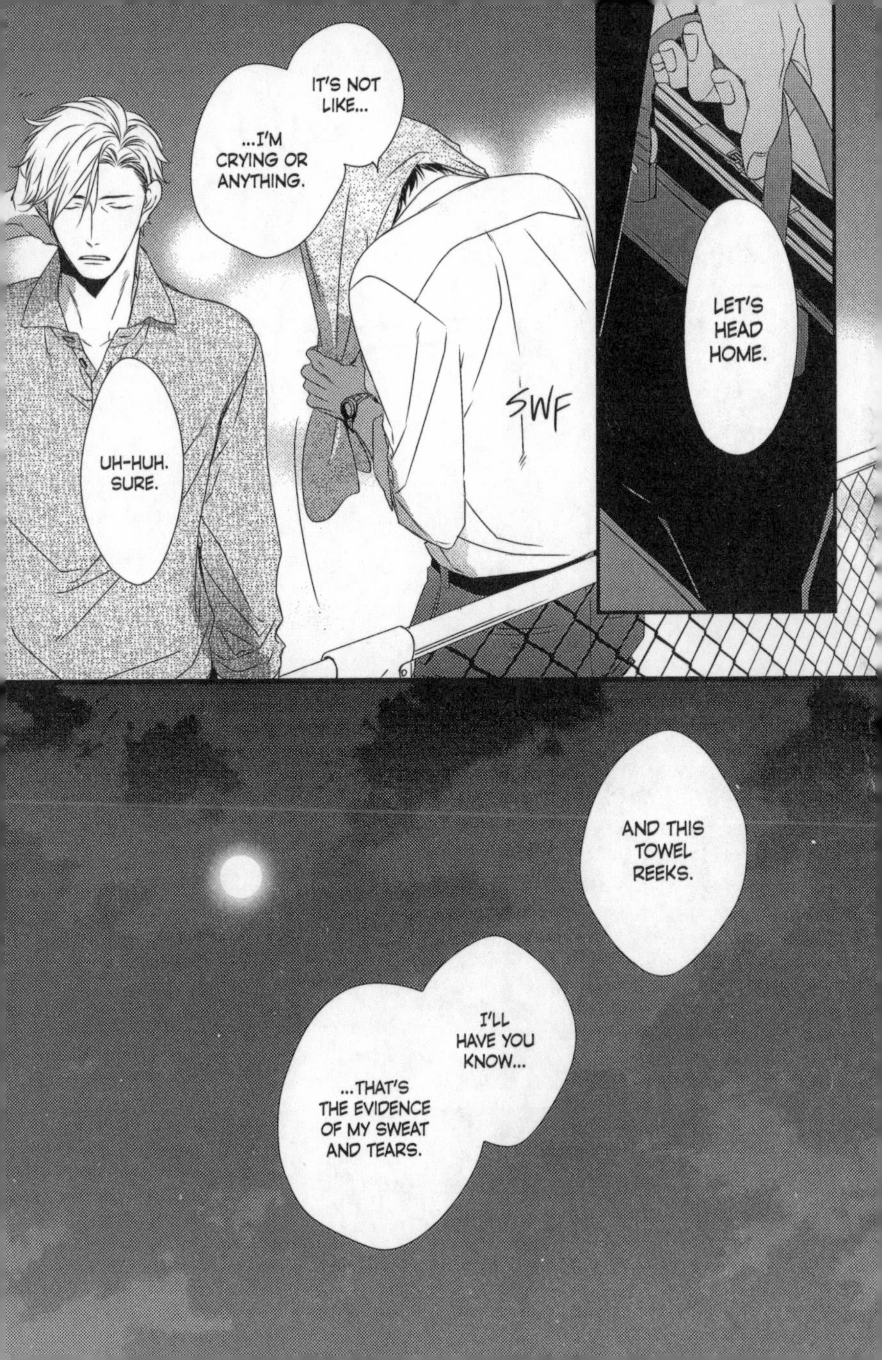
LET'S HEAD HOME.
IT'S NOT LIKE...
...I'M CRYING OR ANYTHING.
SWF
UH-HUH. SURE.
AND THIS TOWEL REEKS.
I'LL HAVE YOU KNOW...
...THAT'S THE EVIDENCE OF MY SWEAT AND TEARS.

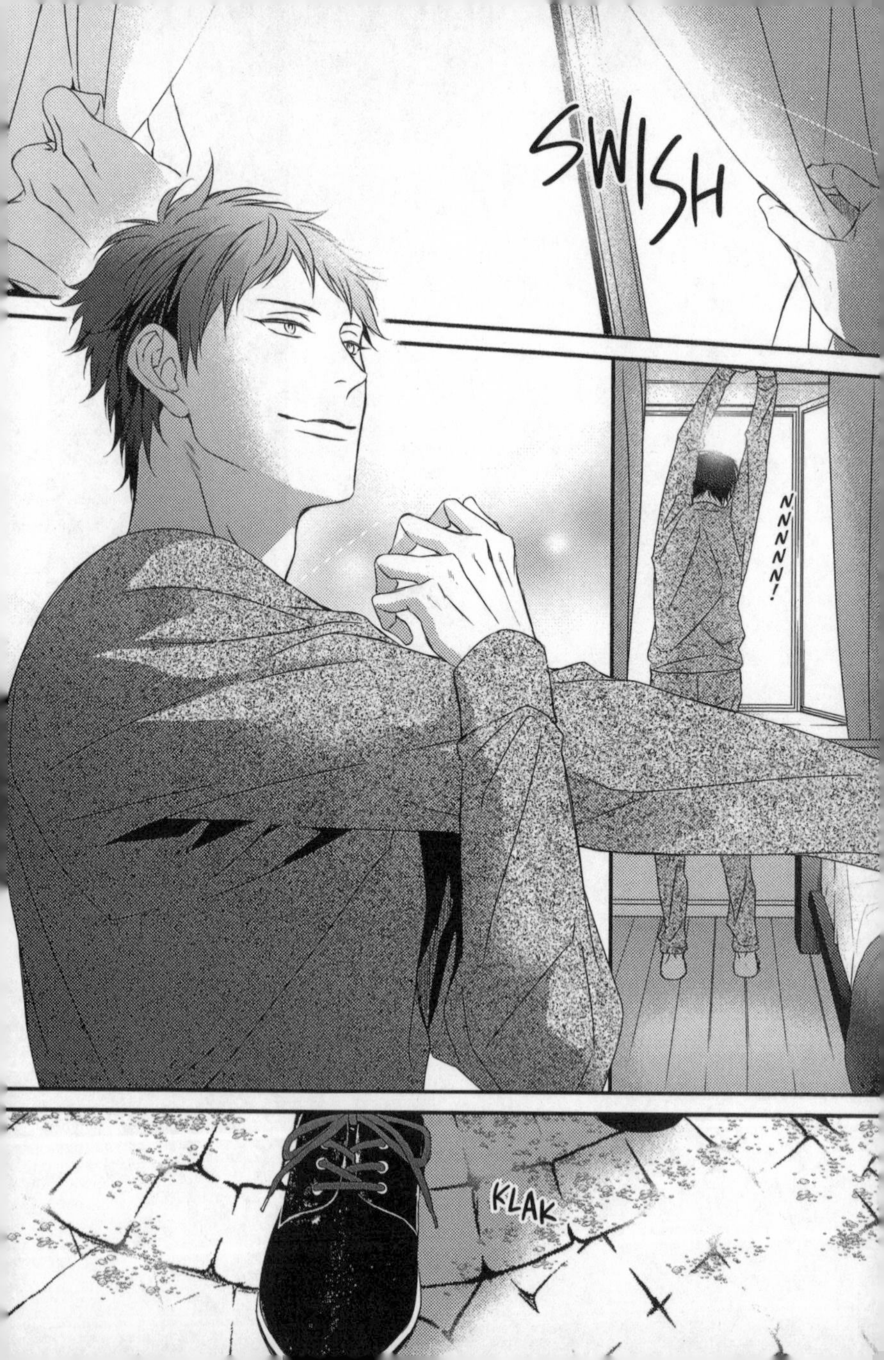
SWISH
NNNNN!
KLAK

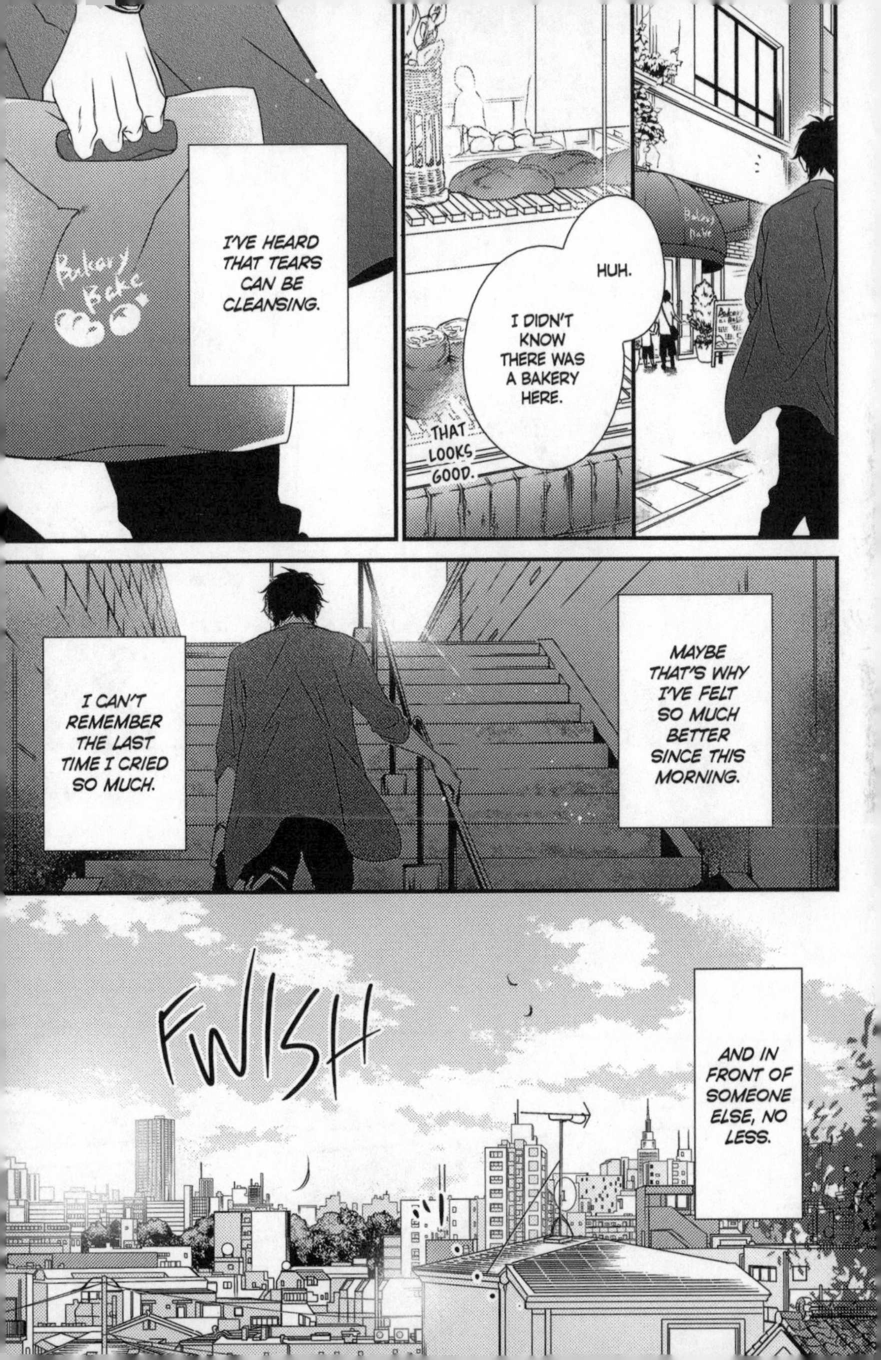
HUH.
I DIDN'T KNOW THERE WAS A BAKERY HERE.
THAT LOOKS GOOD.
I'VE HEARD THAT TEARS CAN BE CLEANSING.
Bakery Bake
MAYBE THAT'S WHY I'VE FELT SO MUCH BETTER SINCE THIS MORNING.
I CAN'T REMEMBER THE LAST TIME I CRIED SO MUCH.
AND IN FRONT OF SOMEONE ELSE, NO LESS.
FWISH

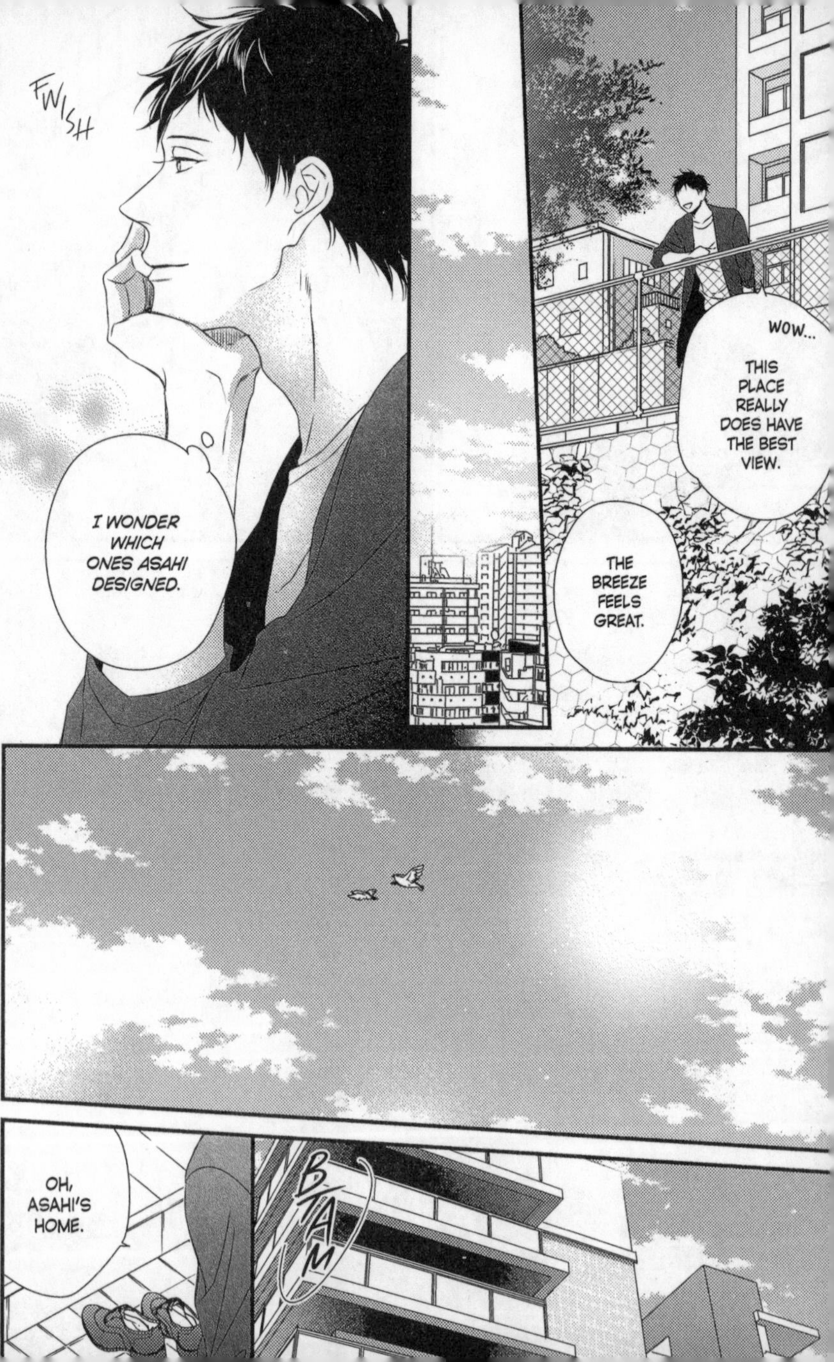
WOW...
THIS PLACE REALLY DOES HAVE THE BEST VIEW.
THE BREEZE FEELS GREAT.
FWISH
I WONDER WHICH ONES ASAHI DESIGNED.
BLAM
OH, ASAHI'S HOME.

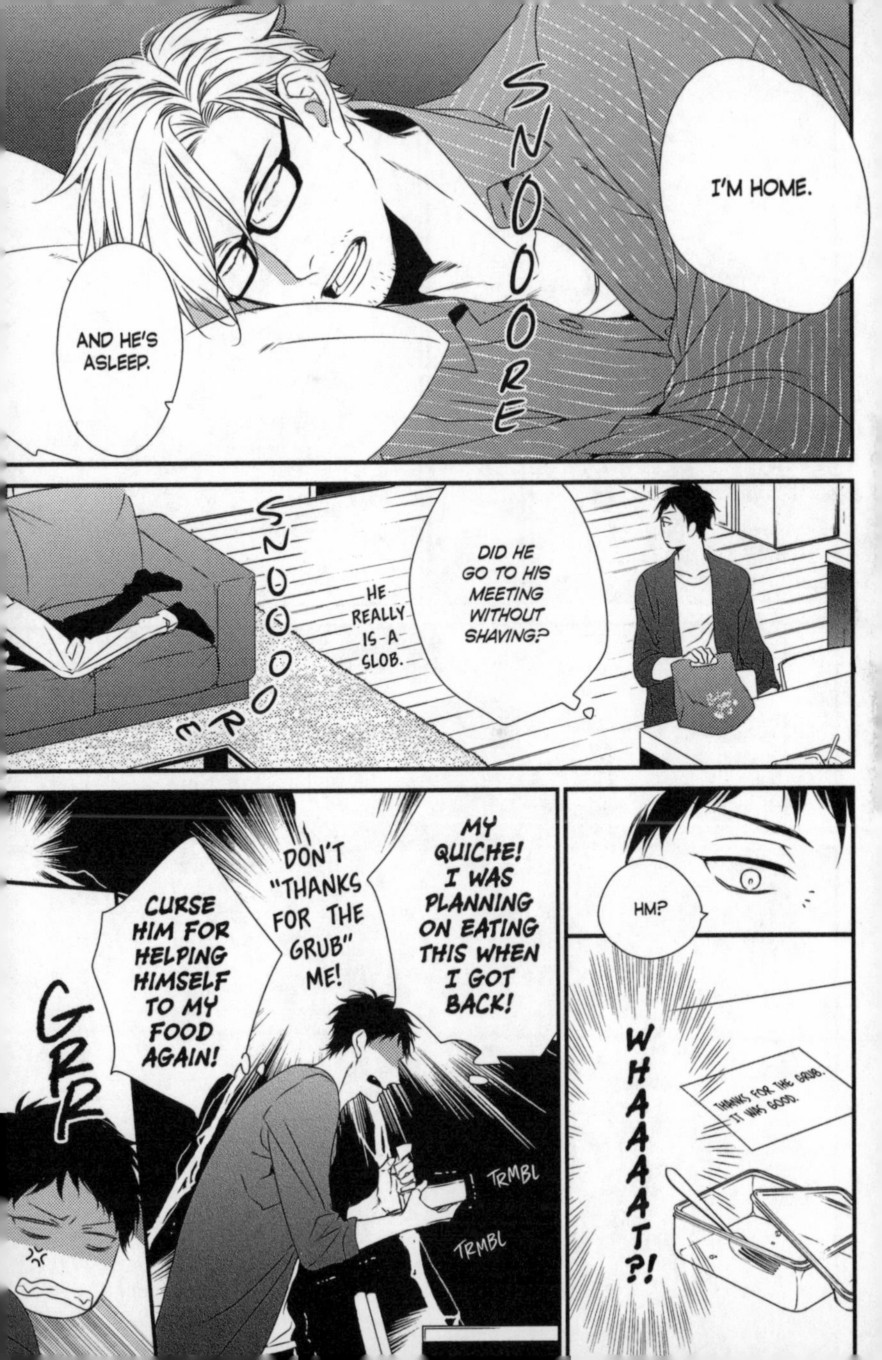
I'M HOME.
SNOOORE
AND HE'S ASLEEP.
DID HE GO TO HIS MEETING WITHOUT SHAVING?
HE REALLY IS-A SLOB.
SNOOOOORE
HM?
WHAAAAAT?!
THANKS FOR THE GRUB. IT WAS GOOD.
MY QUICHE! I WAS PLANNING ON EATING THIS WHEN I GOT BACK!
DON'T "THANKS FOR THE GRUB" ME!
CURSE HIM FOR HELPING HIMSELF TO MY FOOD AGAIN!
TRMBL
TRMBL
GRR

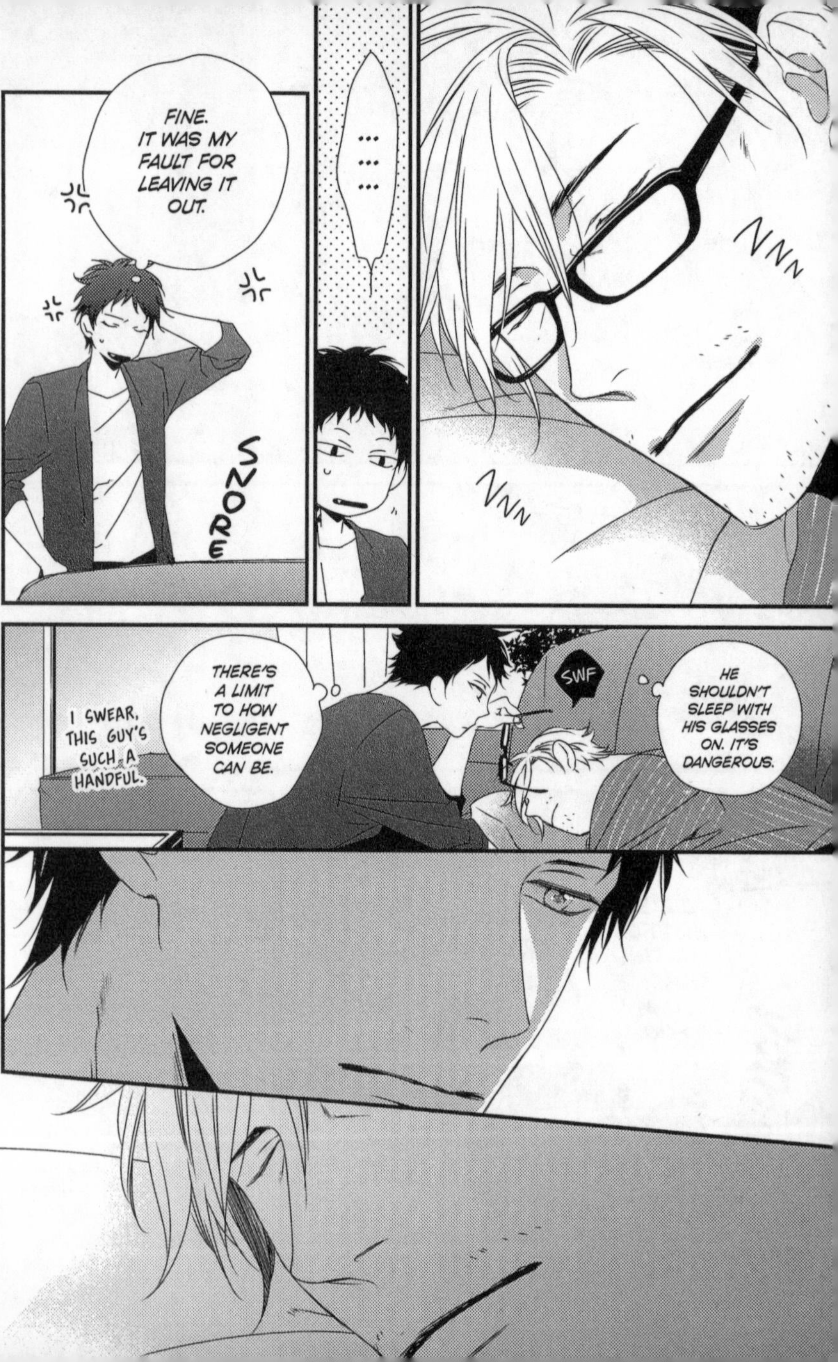
NNN
NNN
... ...
FINE. IT WAS MY FAULT FOR LEAVING IT OUT.
SNORE
SWF
HE SHOULDN'T SLEEP WITH HIS GLASSES ON. IT'S DANGEROUS.
THERE'S A LIMIT TO HOW NEGLIGENT SOMEONE CAN BE.
I SWEAR, THIS GUY'S SUCH A HANDFUL.

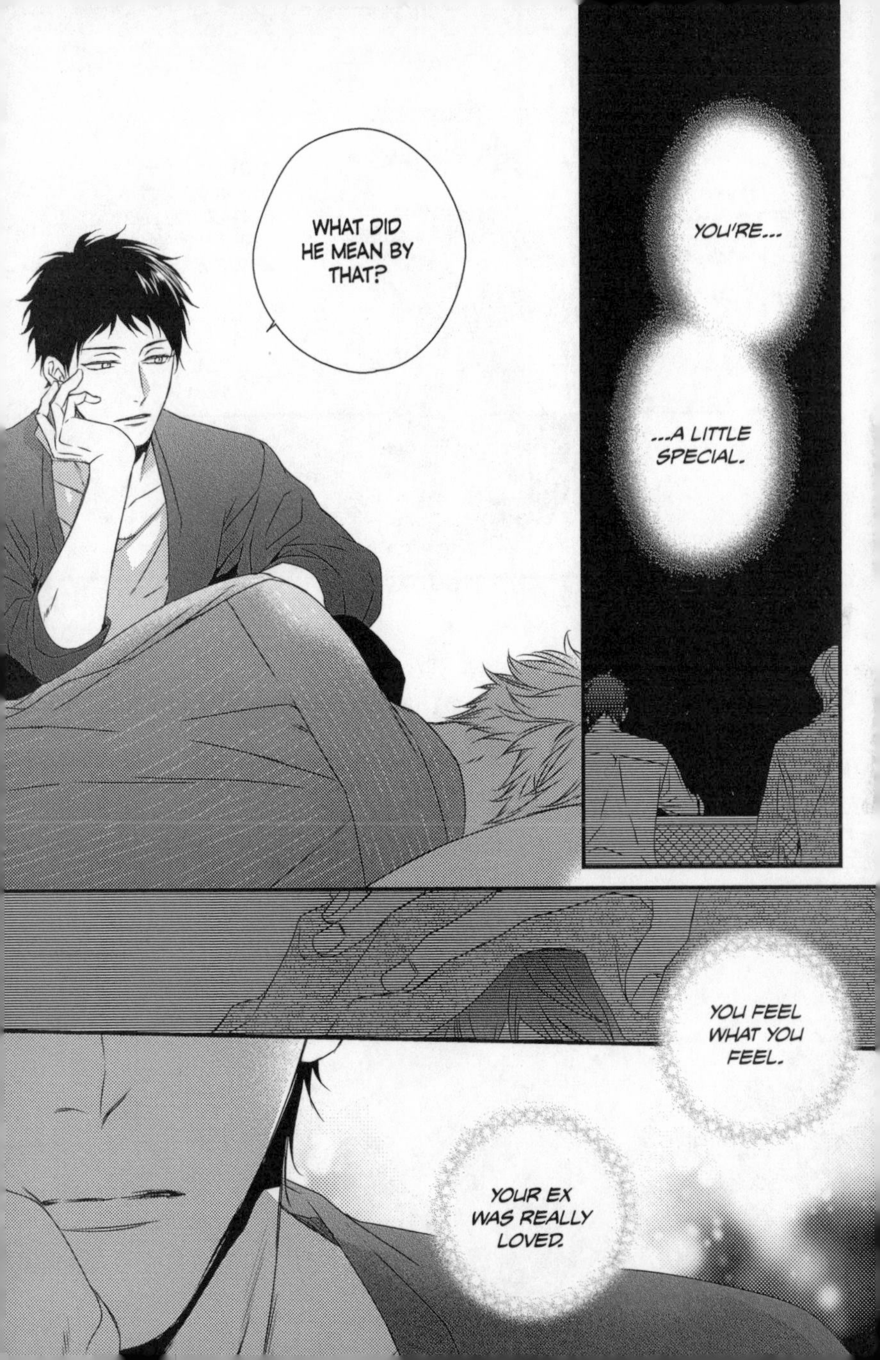
YOU'RE...
...A LITTLE SPECIAL.
WHAT DID HE MEAN BY THAT?
YOU FEEL WHAT YOU FEEL.
YOUR EX WAS REALLY LOVED.

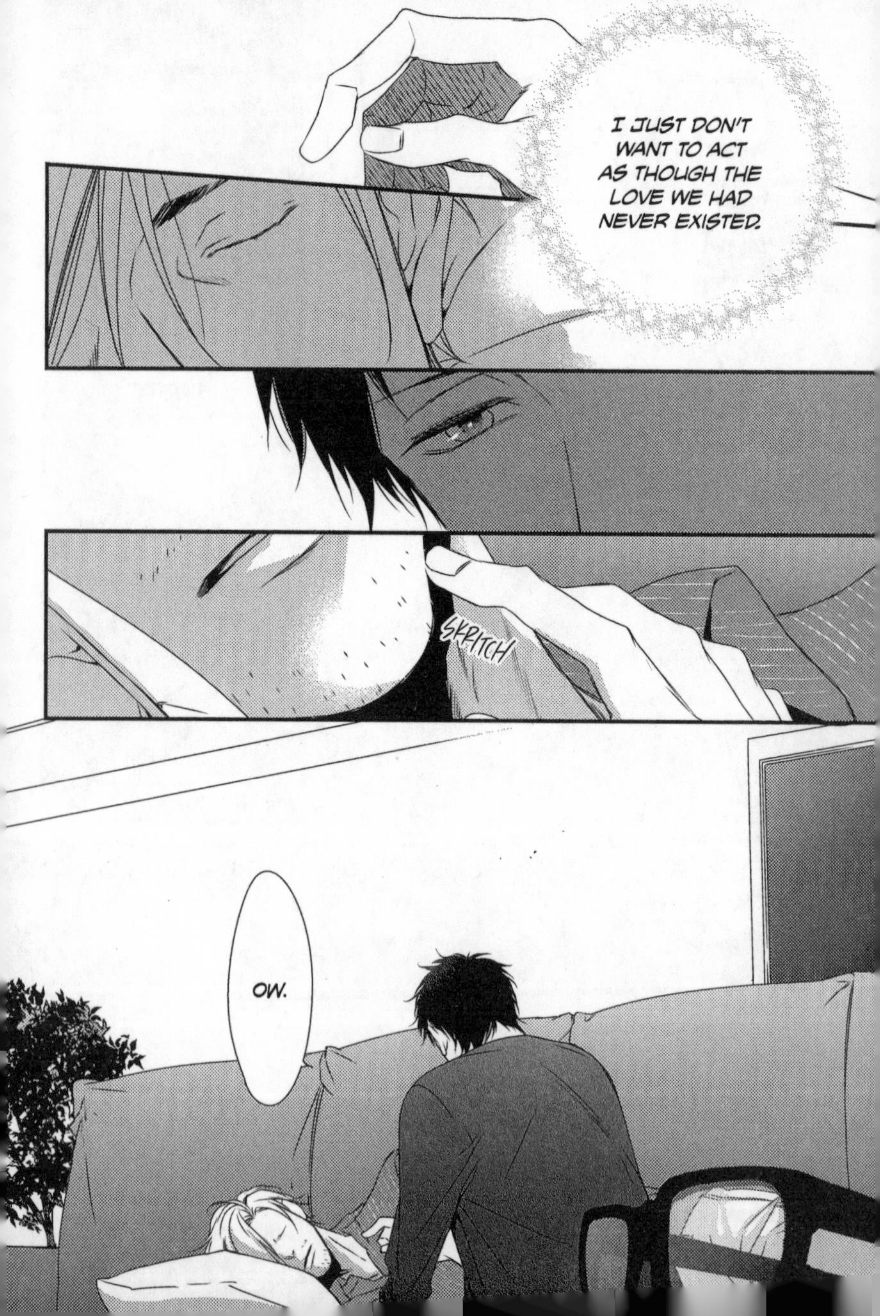
I JUST DON'T WANT TO ACT AS THOUGH THE LOVE WE HAD NEVER EXISTED.
SKRITCH
OW.

LOVE NEST

THE CORRELATION BETWEEN ONE'S USUAL SPOT ON THE SOFA AND EMOTIONAL DISTANCE ③

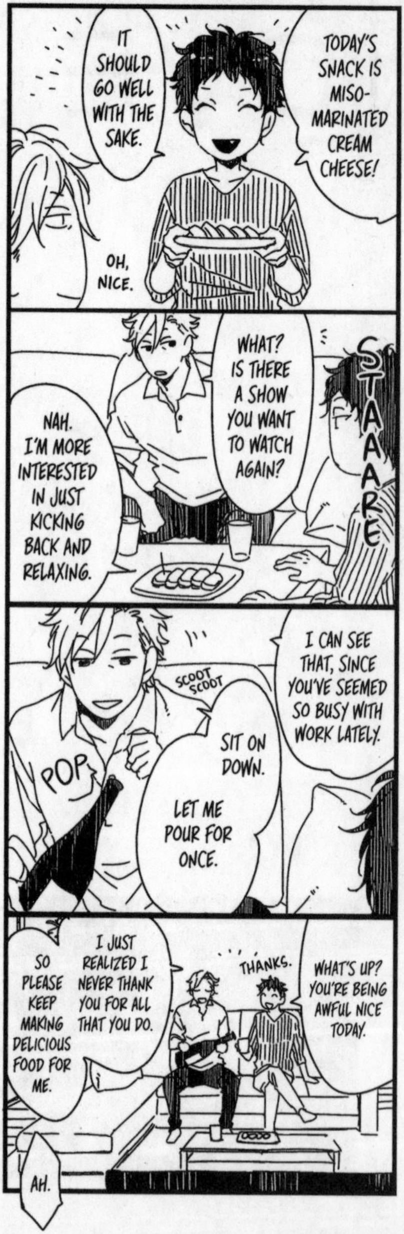
TODAY'S SNACK IS MISO-MARINATED CREAM CHEESE!
IT SHOULD GO WELL WITH THE SAKE.
OH, NICE.
STAAARE
WHAT? IS THERE A SHOW YOU WANT TO WATCH AGAIN?
NAH. I'M MORE INTERESTED IN JUST KICKING BACK AND RELAXING.
I CAN SEE THAT, SINCE YOU'VE SEEMED SO BUSY WITH WORK LATELY.
SCOOT SCOOT
SIT ON DOWN.
LET ME POUR FOR ONCE.
POP
WHAT'S UP? YOU'RE BEING AWFUL NICE TODAY.
THANKS.
I JUST REALIZED I NEVER THANK YOU FOR ALL THAT YOU DO.
SO PLEASE KEEP MAKING DELICIOUS FOOD FOR ME.
AH.

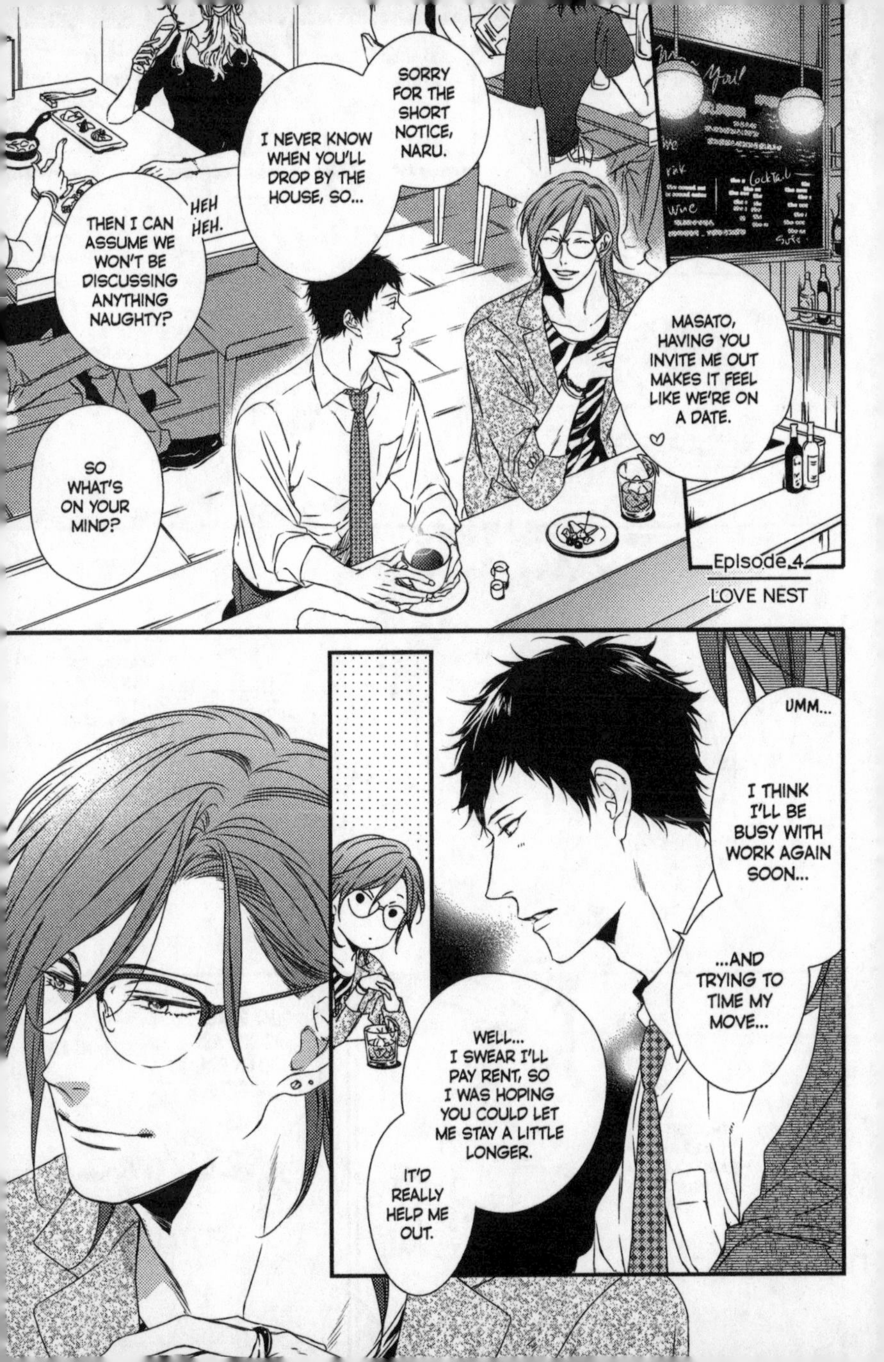
MASATO, HAVING YOU INVITE ME OUT MAKES IT FEEL LIKE WE'RE ON A DATE. ♡
SORRY FOR THE SHORT NOTICE, NARU.
I NEVER KNOW WHEN YOU'LL DROP BY THE HOUSE, SO...
HEH HEH.
THEN I CAN ASSUME WE WON'T BE DISCUSSING ANYTHING NAUGHTY?
SO WHAT'S ON YOUR MIND?
Episode 4
LOVE NEST
UMM...
I THINK I'LL BE BUSY WITH WORK AGAIN SOON...
...AND TRYING TO TIME MY MOVE...
WELL... I SWEAR I'LL PAY RENT, SO I WAS HOPING YOU COULD LET ME STAY A LITTLE LONGER.
IT'D REALLY HELP ME OUT.

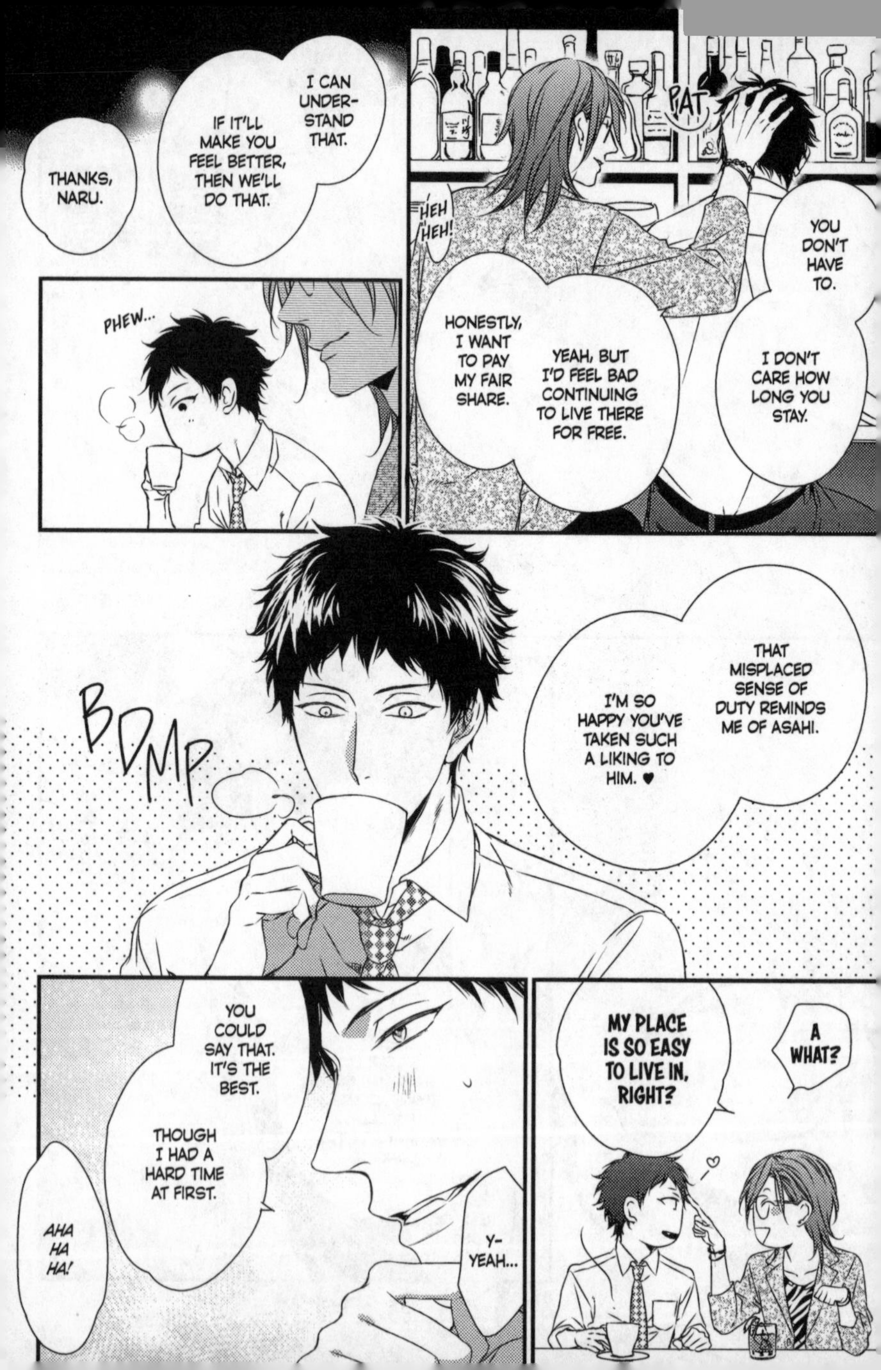
PAT
YOU DON'T HAVE TO.
I DON'T CARE HOW LONG YOU STAY.
HEH HEH!
YEAH, BUT I'D FEEL BAD CONTINUING TO LIVE THERE FOR FREE.
HONESTLY, I WANT TO PAY MY FAIR SHARE.
I CAN UNDER-STAND THAT.
IF IT'LL MAKE YOU FEEL BETTER, THEN WE'LL DO THAT.
THANKS, NARU.
PHEW...
THAT MISPLACED SENSE OF DUTY REMINDS ME OF ASAHI.
I'M SO HAPPY YOU'VE TAKEN SUCH A LIKING TO HIM. ♥
BDMP
A WHAT?
MY PLACE IS SO EASY TO LIVE IN, RIGHT?
YOU COULD SAY THAT. IT'S THE BEST.
THOUGH I HAD A HARD TIME AT FIRST.
Y-YEAH...
AHA HA HA!

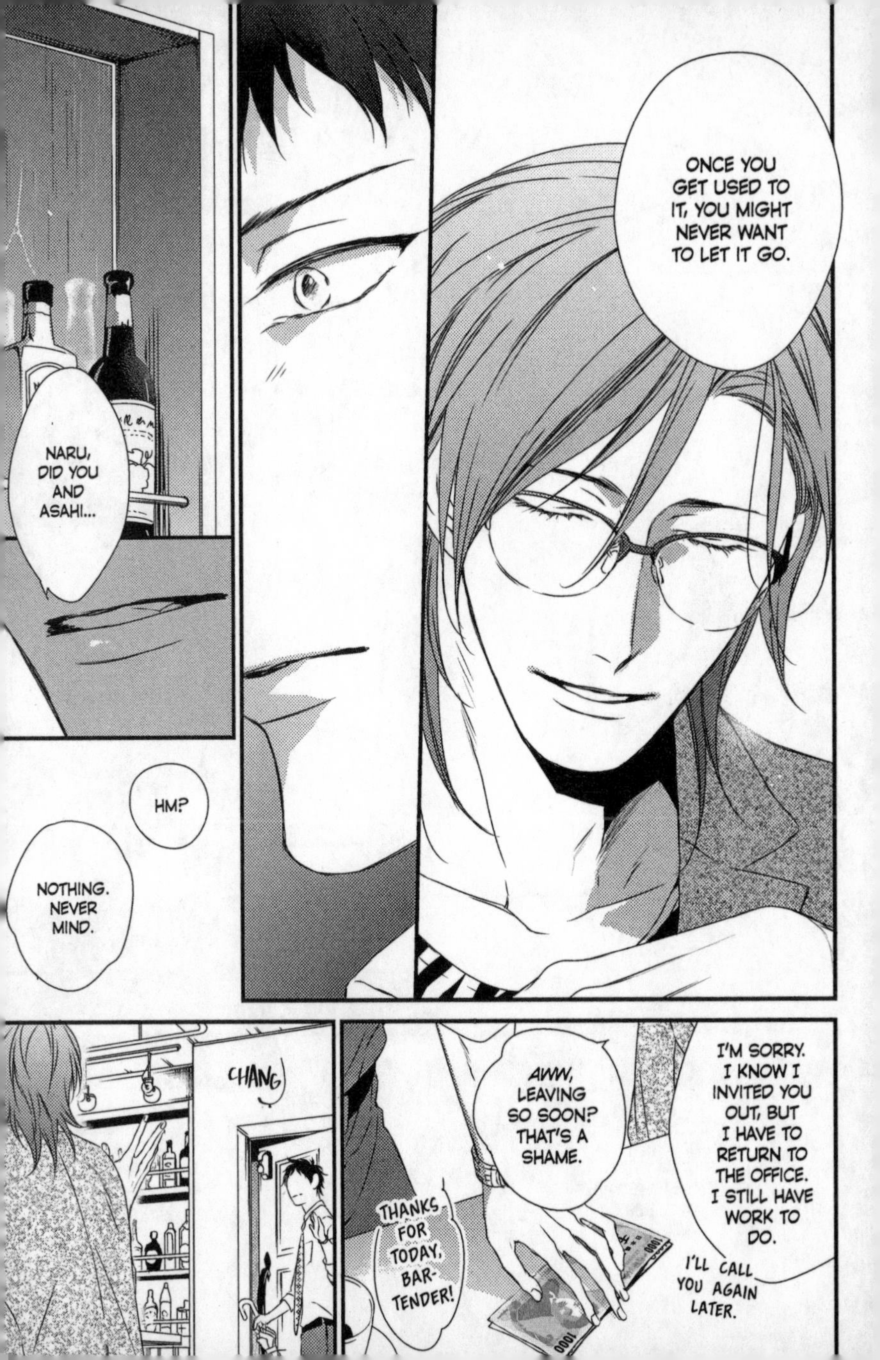
ONCE YOU GET USED TO IT, YOU MIGHT NEVER WANT TO LET IT GO.
NARU, DID YOU AND ASAHI...
HM?
NOTHING. NEVER MIND.
I'M SORRY. I KNOW I INVITED YOU OUT, BUT I HAVE TO RETURN TO THE OFFICE. I STILL HAVE WORK TO DO.
AWW, LEAVING SO SOON? THAT'S A SHAME.
I'LL CALL YOU AGAIN LATER.
THANKS FOR TODAY, BAR-TENDER!
CHANG

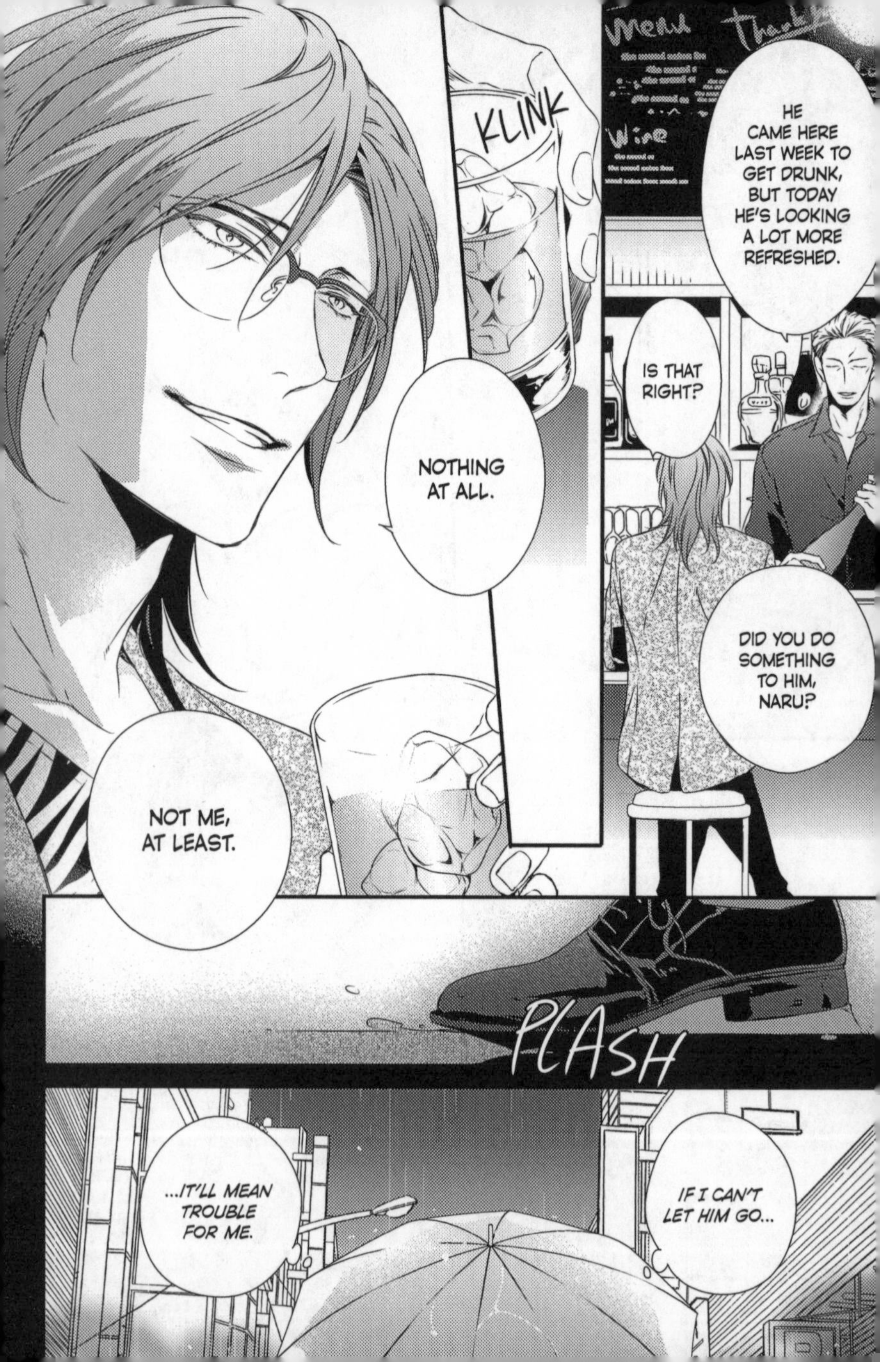
HE CAME HERE LAST WEEK TO GET DRUNK, BUT TODAY HE'S LOOKING A LOT MORE REFRESHED.
IS THAT RIGHT?
DID YOU DO SOMETHING TO HIM, NARU?
KLINK
NOTHING AT ALL.
NOT ME, AT LEAST.
PLASH
IF I CAN'T LET HIM GO...
...IT'LL MEAN TROUBLE FOR ME.

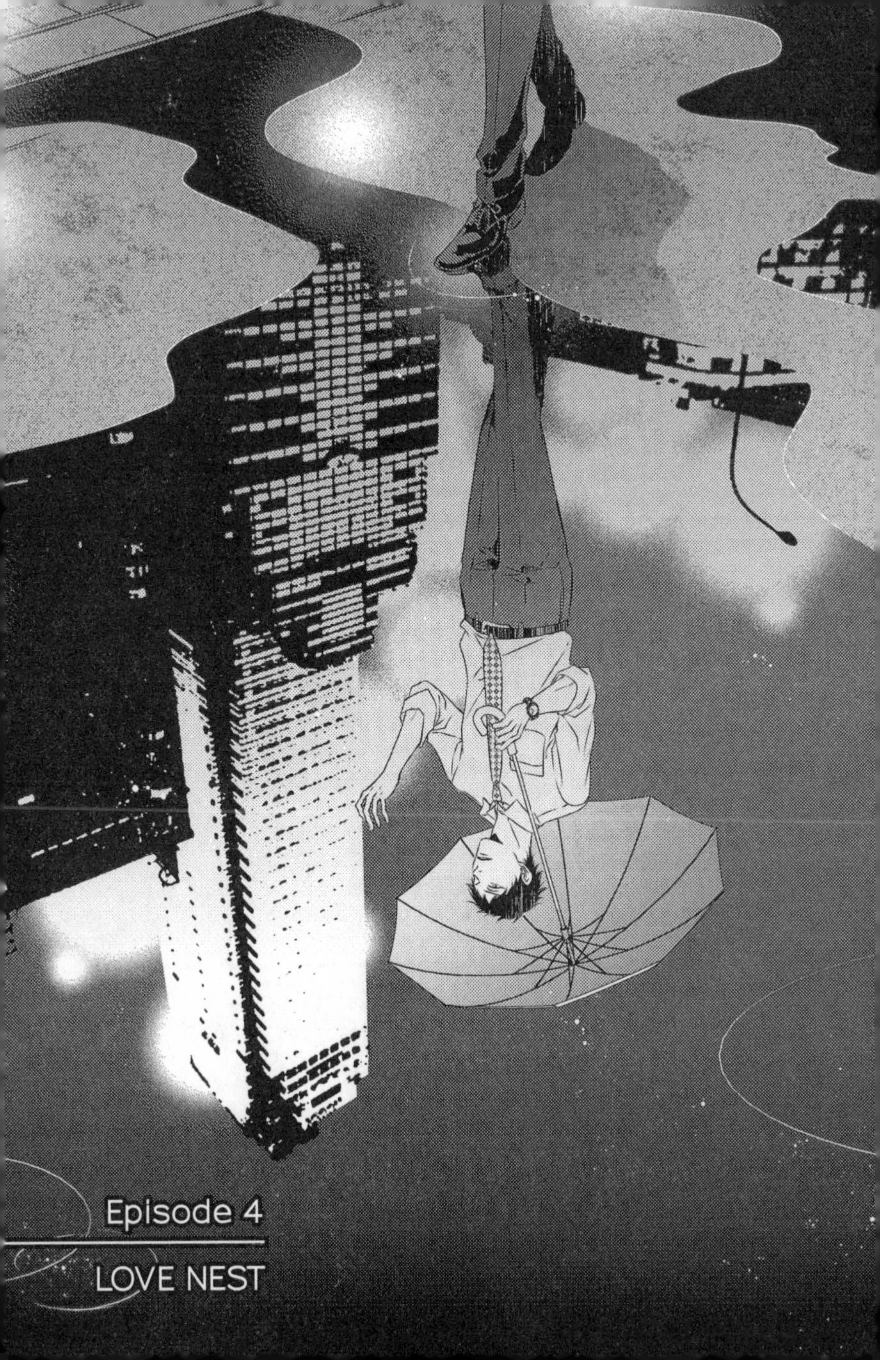
Episode 4
LOVE NEST

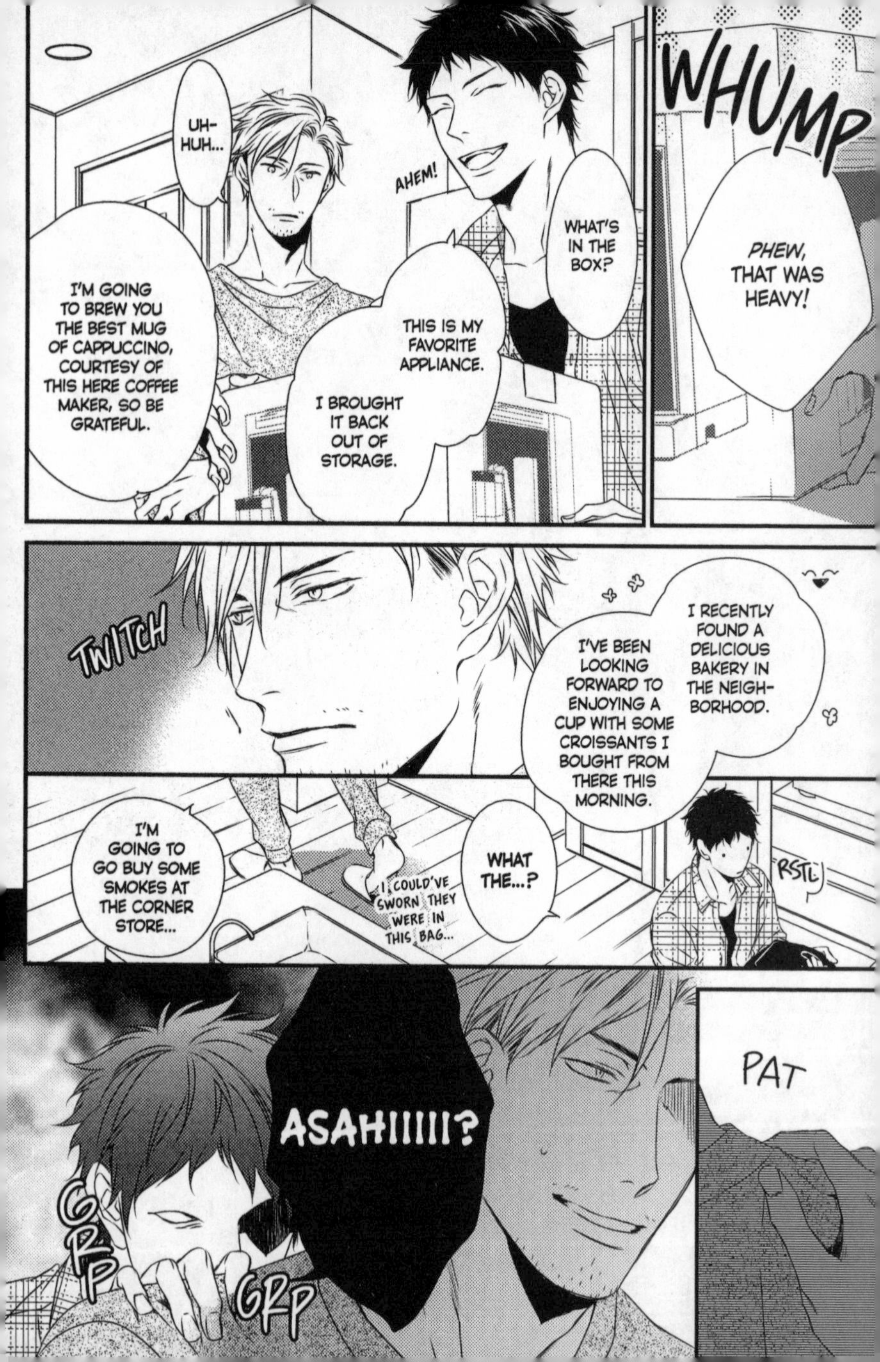
WHUMP
PHEW, THAT WAS HEAVY!
WHAT'S IN THE BOX?
AHEM!
THIS IS MY FAVORITE APPLIANCE.
I BROUGHT IT BACK OUT OF STORAGE.
UH-HUH...
I'M GOING TO BREW YOU THE BEST MUG OF CAPPUCCINO, COURTESY OF THIS HERE COFFEE MAKER, SO BE GRATEFUL.
I RECENTLY FOUND A DELICIOUS BAKERY IN THE NEIGH-BORHOOD.
I'VE BEEN LOOKING FORWARD TO ENJOYING A CUP WITH SOME CROISSANTS I BOUGHT FROM THERE THIS MORNING.
TWITCH
RSTL
WHAT THE...?
I COULD'VE SWORN THEY WERE IN THIS BAG...
I'M GOING TO GO BUY SOME SMOKES AT THE CORNER STORE...
PAT
ASAHIIIII?
GRP
GRP

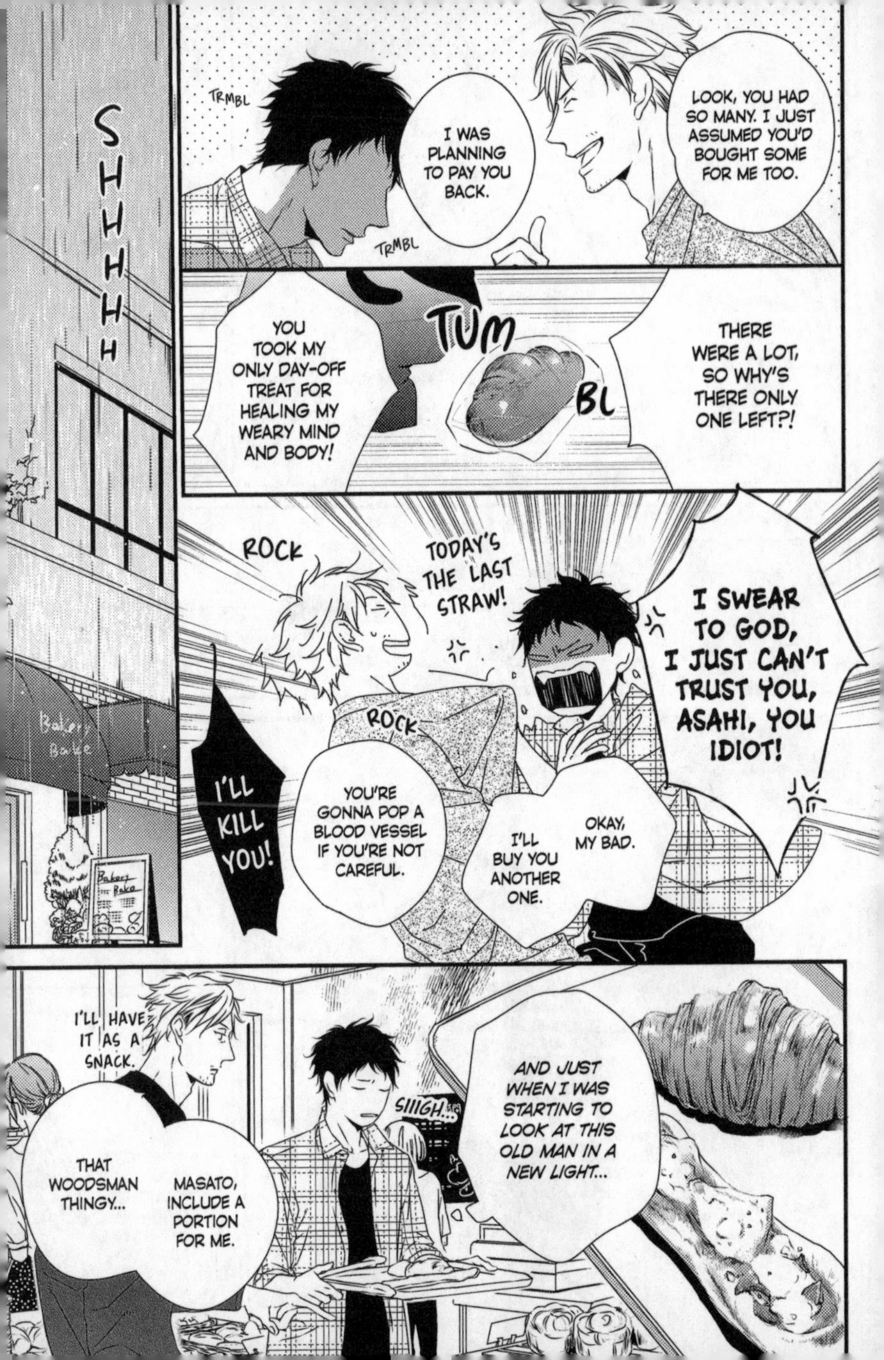
LOOK, YOU HAD SO MANY. I JUST ASSUMED YOU'D BOUGHT SOME FOR ME TOO.
I WAS PLANNING TO PAY YOU BACK.
TRMBL
TRMBL
THERE WERE A LOT, SO WHY'S THERE ONLY ONE LEFT?!
TUM
BL
YOU TOOK MY ONLY DAY-OFF TREAT FOR HEALING MY WEARY MIND AND BODY!
I SWEAR TO GOD, I JUST CAN'T TRUST YOU, ASAHI, YOU IDIOT!
TODAY'S THE LAST STRAW!
ROCK
ROCK
OKAY, MY BAD.
I'LL BUY YOU ANOTHER ONE.
YOU'RE GONNA POP A BLOOD VESSEL IF YOU'RE NOT CAREFUL.
I'LL KILL YOU!
SHHHHHH
AND JUST WHEN I WAS STARTING TO LOOK AT THIS OLD MAN IN A NEW LIGHT...
SIIIGH...
I'LL HAVE IT AS A SNACK.
MASATO, INCLUDE A PORTION FOR ME.
THAT WOODSMAN THINGY...

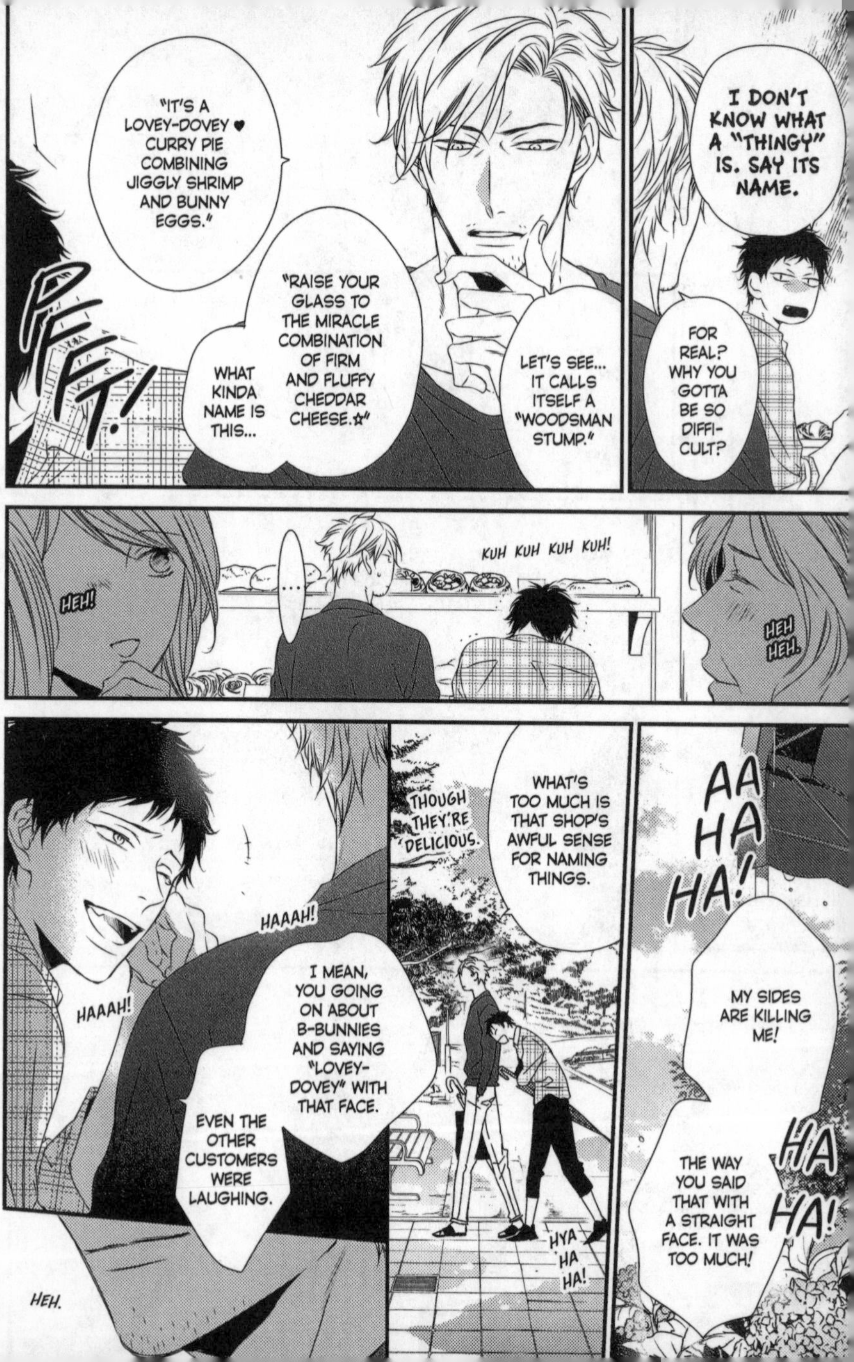
I DON'T KNOW WHAT A "THINGY" IS. SAY ITS NAME.
FOR REAL? WHY YOU GOTTA BE SO DIFFI-CULT?
LET'S SEE... IT CALLS ITSELF A "WOODSMAN STUMP."
"RAISE YOUR GLASS TO THE MIRACLE COMBINATION OF FIRM AND FLUFFY CHEDDAR CHEESE.☆"
WHAT KINDA NAME IS THIS...
"IT'S A LOVEY-DOVEY ♥ CURRY PIE COMBINING JIGGLY SHRIMP AND BUNNY EGGS."
PFFT!
HEH HEH.
KUH KUH KUH KUH!
...
HEH!
AA HA HA!
MY SIDES ARE KILLING ME!
HA HA!
THE WAY YOU SAID THAT WITH A STRAIGHT FACE. IT WAS TOO MUCH!
WHAT'S TOO MUCH IS THAT SHOP'S AWFUL SENSE FOR NAMING THINGS.
THOUGH THEY'RE DELICIOUS.
HYA HA HA!
HAAAH!
I MEAN, YOU GOING ON ABOUT B-BUNNIES AND SAYING "LOVEY-DOVEY" WITH THAT FACE.
HAAAH!
EVEN THE OTHER CUSTOMERS WERE LAUGHING.
HEH.

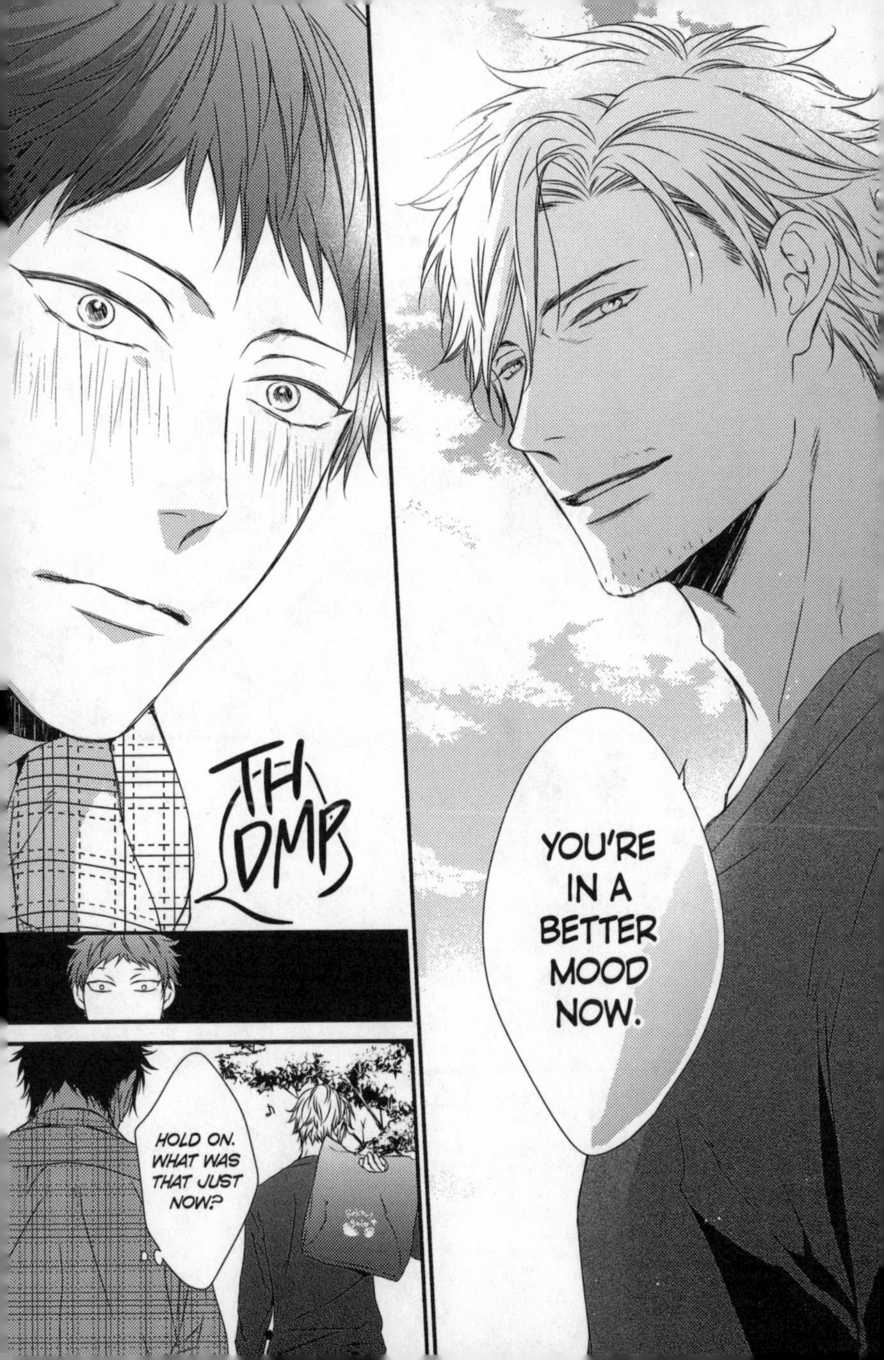
YOU'RE IN A BETTER MOOD NOW.
T-H DMP
HOLD ON. WHAT WAS THAT JUST NOW?

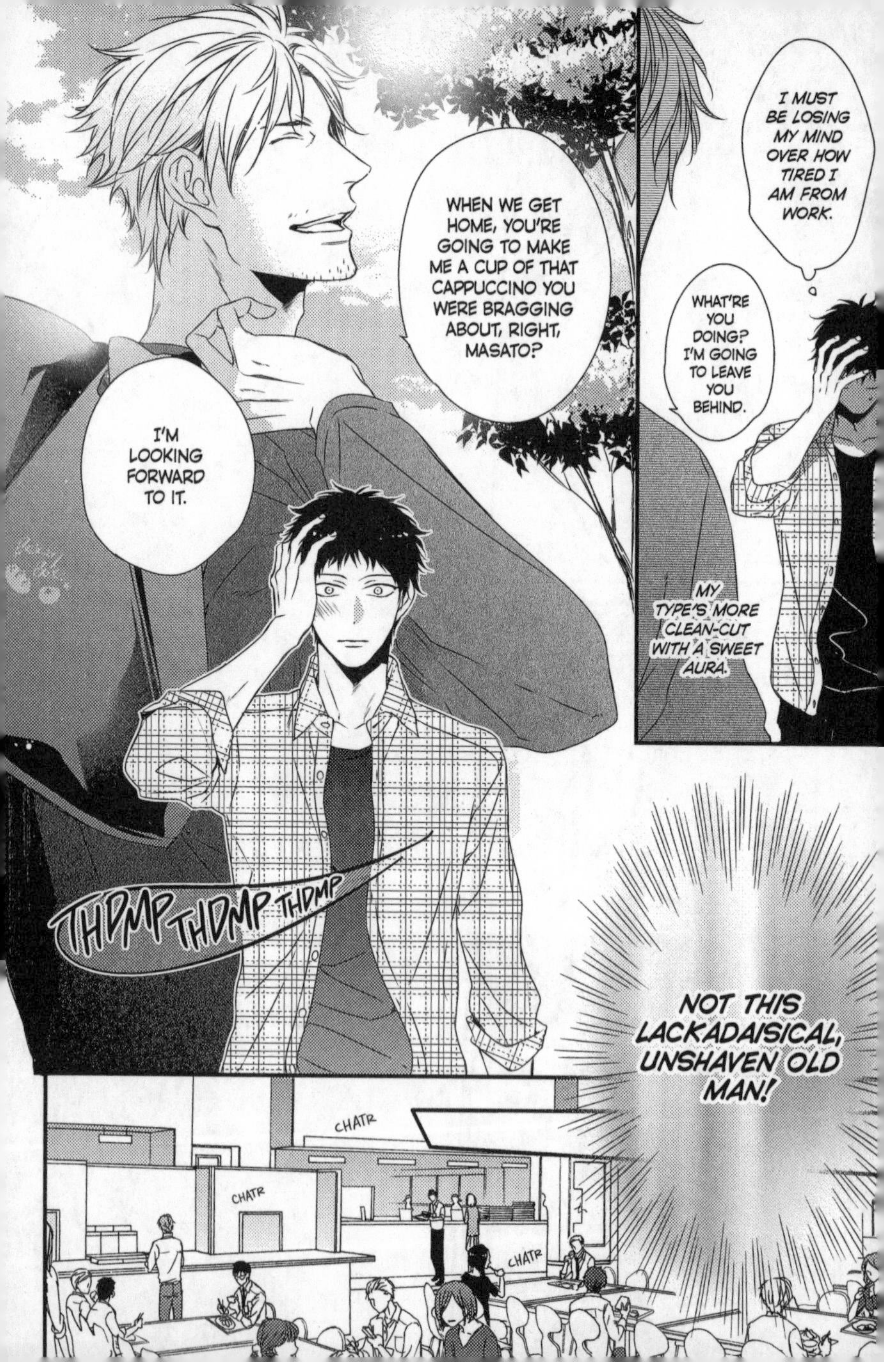
I MUST BE LOSING MY MIND OVER HOW TIRED I AM FROM WORK.
WHAT'RE YOU DOING? I'M GOING TO LEAVE YOU BEHIND.
MY TYPE'S MORE CLEAN-CUT WITH A SWEET AURA.
NOT THIS LACKADAISICAL, UNSHAVEN OLD MAN!
WHEN WE GET HOME, YOU'RE GOING TO MAKE ME A CUP OF THAT CAPPUCCINO YOU WERE BRAGGING ABOUT, RIGHT, MASATO?
I'M LOOKING FORWARD TO IT.
THDMP THDMP THDMP
CHATR
CHATR
CHATR

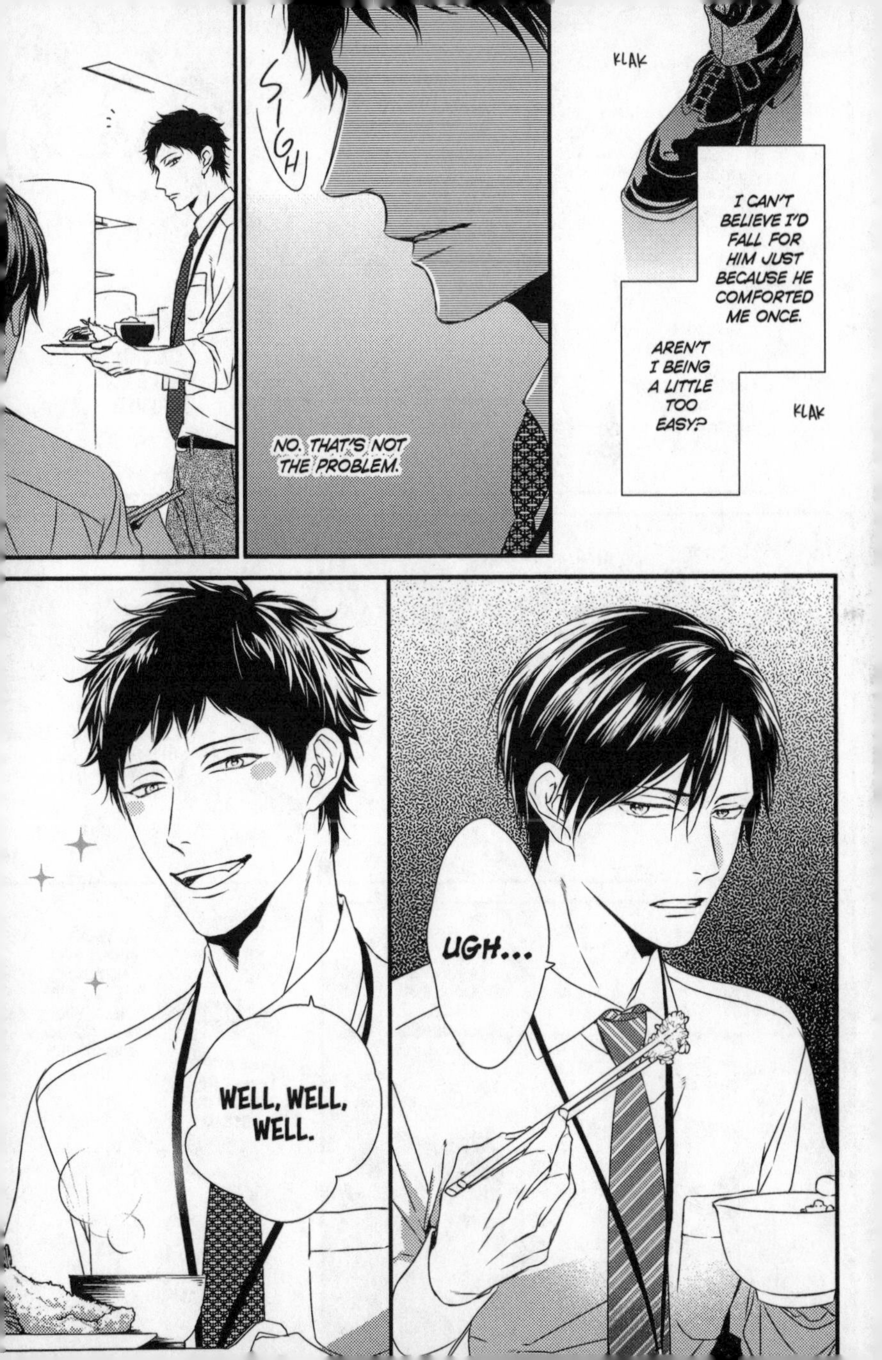
KLAK
I CAN'T BELIEVE I'D FALL FOR HIM JUST BECAUSE HE COMFORTED ME ONCE.
AREN'T I BEING A LITTLE TOO EASY?
KLAK
SIGH
NO. THAT'S NOT THE PROBLEM.
UGH...
WELL, WELL, WELL.

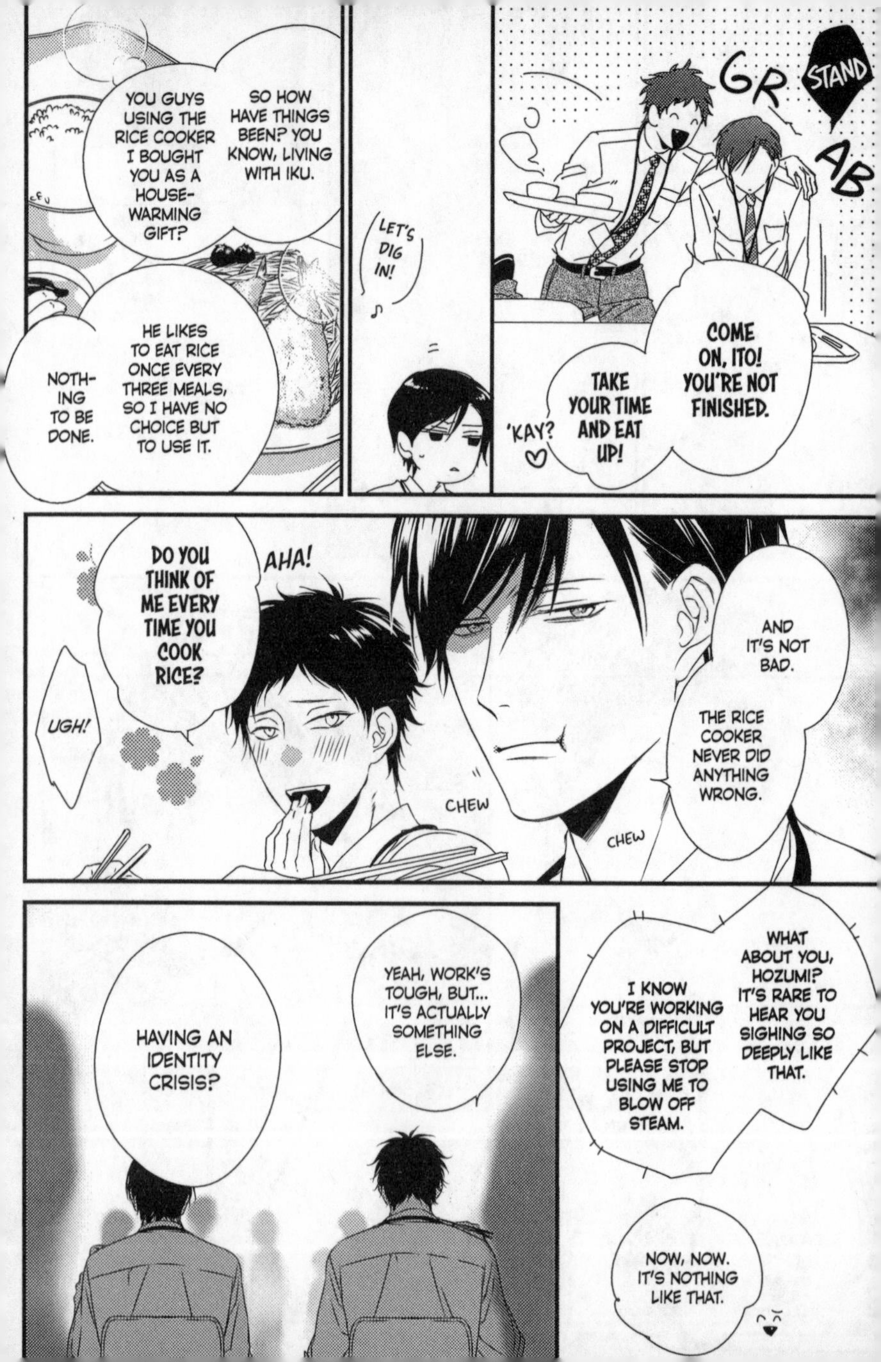
STAND
GR
AB
COME ON, ITO! YOU'RE NOT FINISHED.
TAKE YOUR TIME AND EAT UP!
'KAY?
LET'S DIG IN!
SO HOW HAVE THINGS BEEN? YOU KNOW, LIVING WITH IKU.
YOU GUYS USING THE RICE COOKER I BOUGHT YOU AS A HOUSE-WARMING GIFT?
HE LIKES TO EAT RICE ONCE EVERY THREE MEALS, SO I HAVE NO CHOICE BUT TO USE IT.
NOTH-ING TO BE DONE.
THE RICE COOKER NEVER DID ANYTHING WRONG.
AND IT'S NOT BAD.
CHEW
CHEW
AHA!
DO YOU THINK OF ME EVERY TIME YOU COOK RICE?
UGH!
WHAT ABOUT YOU, HOZUMI? IT'S RARE TO HEAR YOU SIGHING SO DEEPLY LIKE THAT.
I KNOW YOU'RE WORKING ON A DIFFICULT PROJECT, BUT PLEASE STOP USING ME TO BLOW OFF STEAM.
NOW, NOW. IT'S NOTHING LIKE THAT.
YEAH, WORK'S TOUGH, BUT... IT'S ACTUALLY SOMETHING ELSE.
HAVING AN IDENTITY CRISIS?

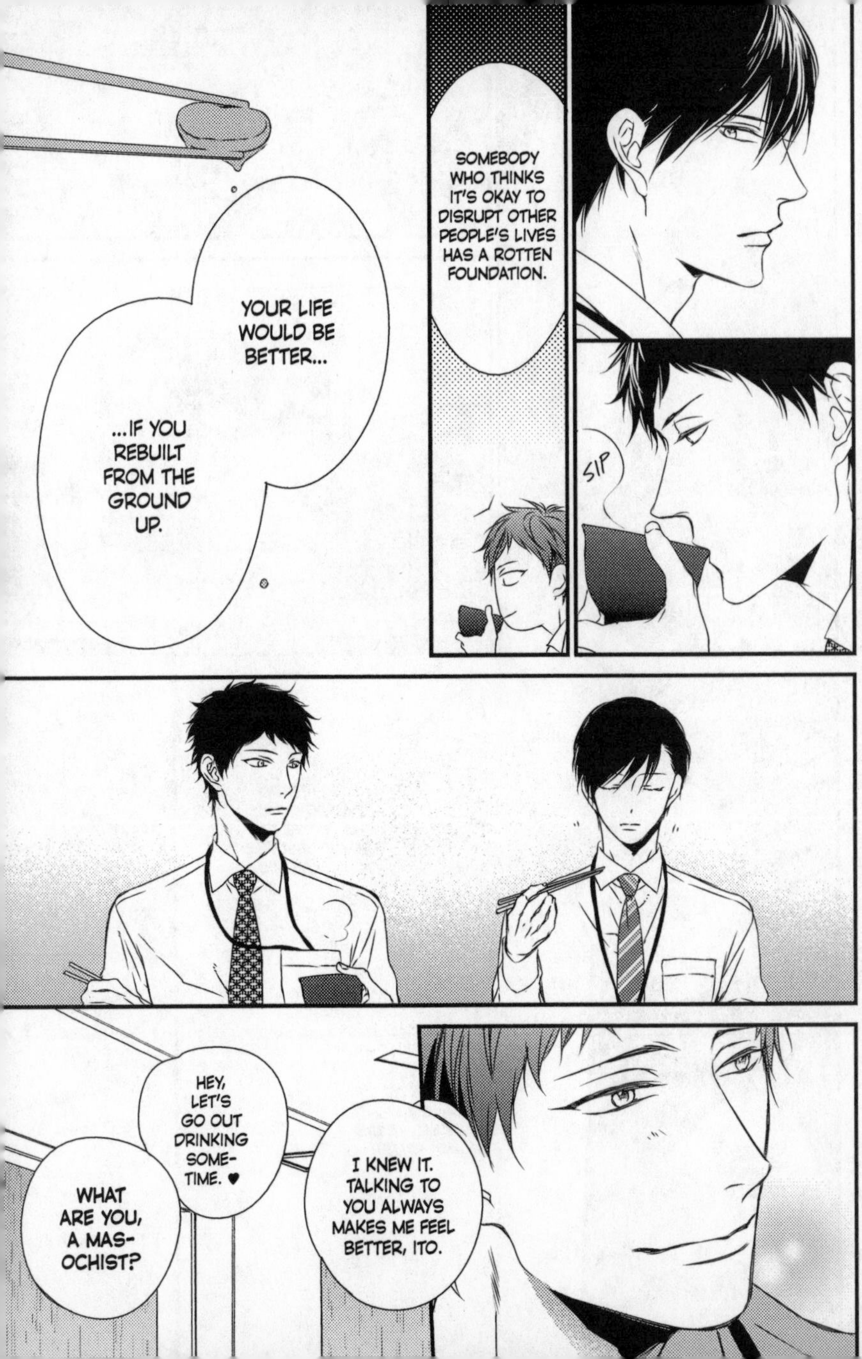
SOMEBODY WHO THINKS IT'S OKAY TO DISRUPT OTHER PEOPLE'S LIVES HAS A ROTTEN FOUNDATION.
SIP
YOUR LIFE WOULD BE BETTER...
...IF YOU REBUILT FROM THE GROUND UP.
I KNEW IT. TALKING TO YOU ALWAYS MAKES ME FEEL BETTER, ITO.
HEY, LET'S GO OUT DRINKING SOME-TIME. ♥
WHAT ARE YOU, A MAS-OCHIST?

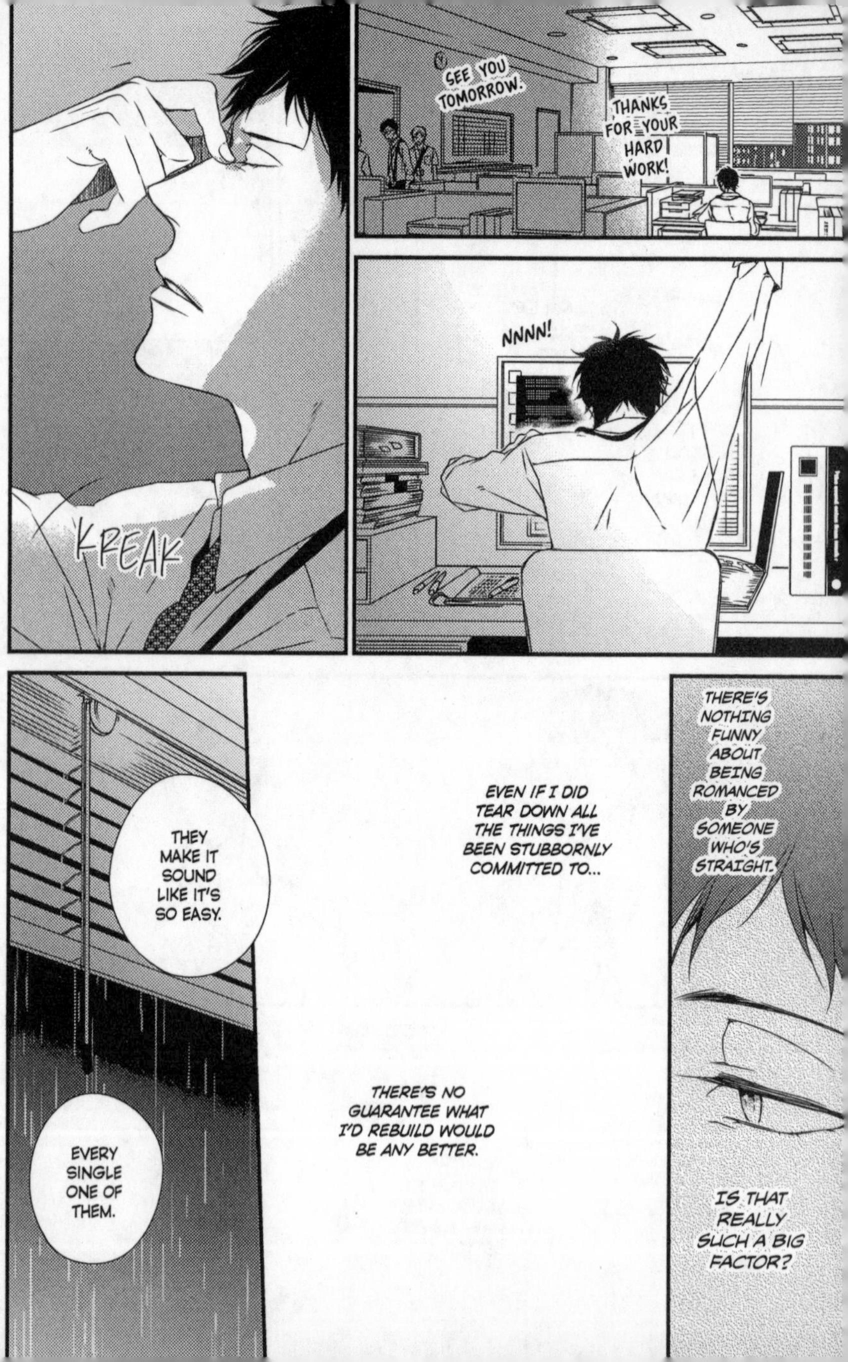
SEE YOU TOMORROW.
THANKS FOR YOUR HARD WORK!
NNNN!
KREAK
THERE'S NOTHING FUNNY ABOUT BEING ROMANCED BY SOMEONE WHO'S STRAIGHT.
IS THAT REALLY SUCH A BIG FACTOR?
EVEN IF I DID TEAR DOWN ALL THE THINGS I'VE BEEN STUBBORNLY COMMITTED TO...
THERE'S NO GUARANTEE WHAT I'D REBUILD WOULD BE ANY BETTER.
THEY MAKE IT SOUND LIKE IT'S SO EASY.
EVERY SINGLE ONE OF THEM.

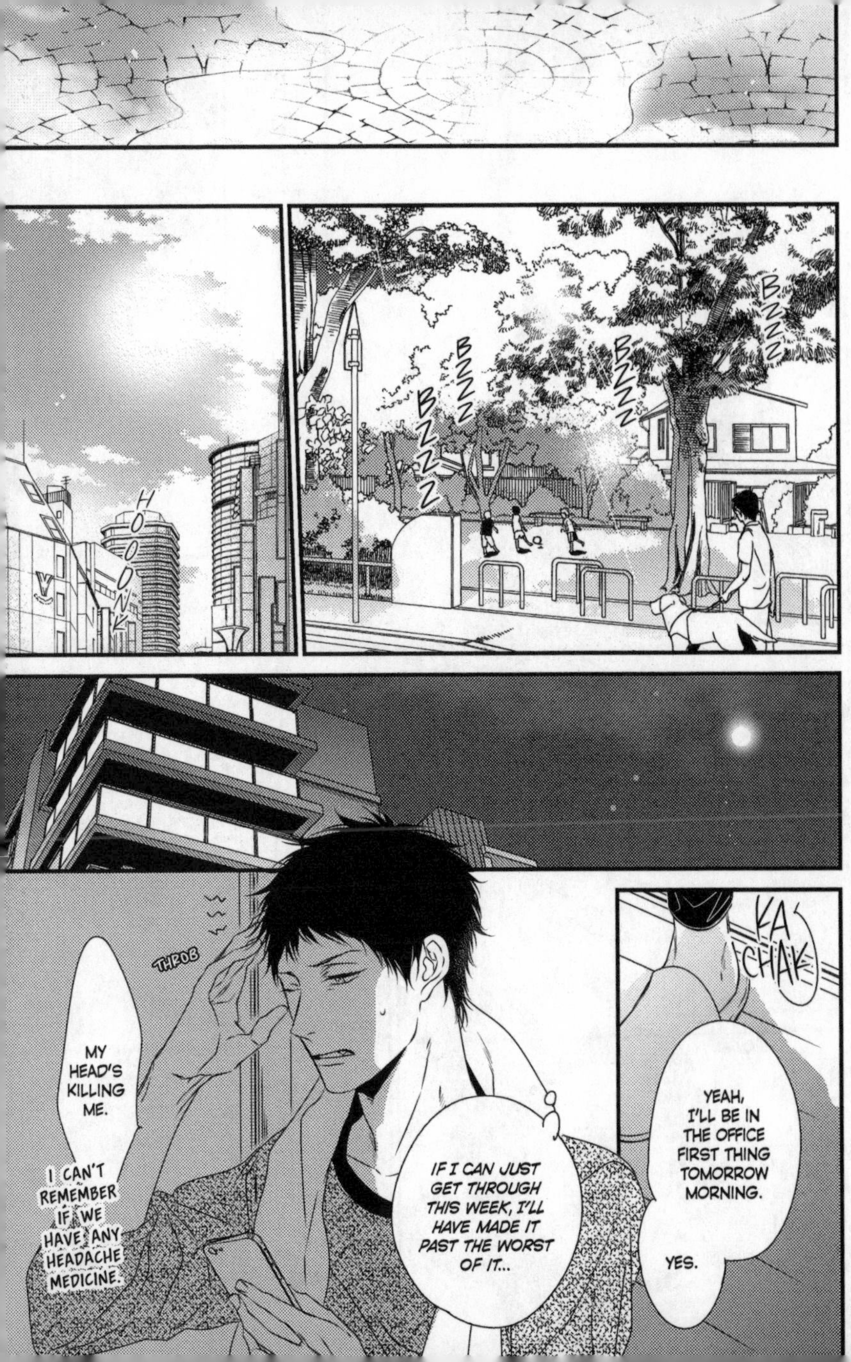
BZZZ
BZZZ
BZZZ
BZZZ
HOOOON
KA-CHAK
YEAH, I'LL BE IN THE OFFICE FIRST THING TOMORROW MORNING.
YES.
IF I CAN JUST GET THROUGH THIS WEEK, I'LL HAVE MADE IT PAST THE WORST OF IT...
THROB
MY HEAD'S KILLING ME.
I CAN'T REMEMBER IF WE HAVE ANY HEADACHE MEDICINE.

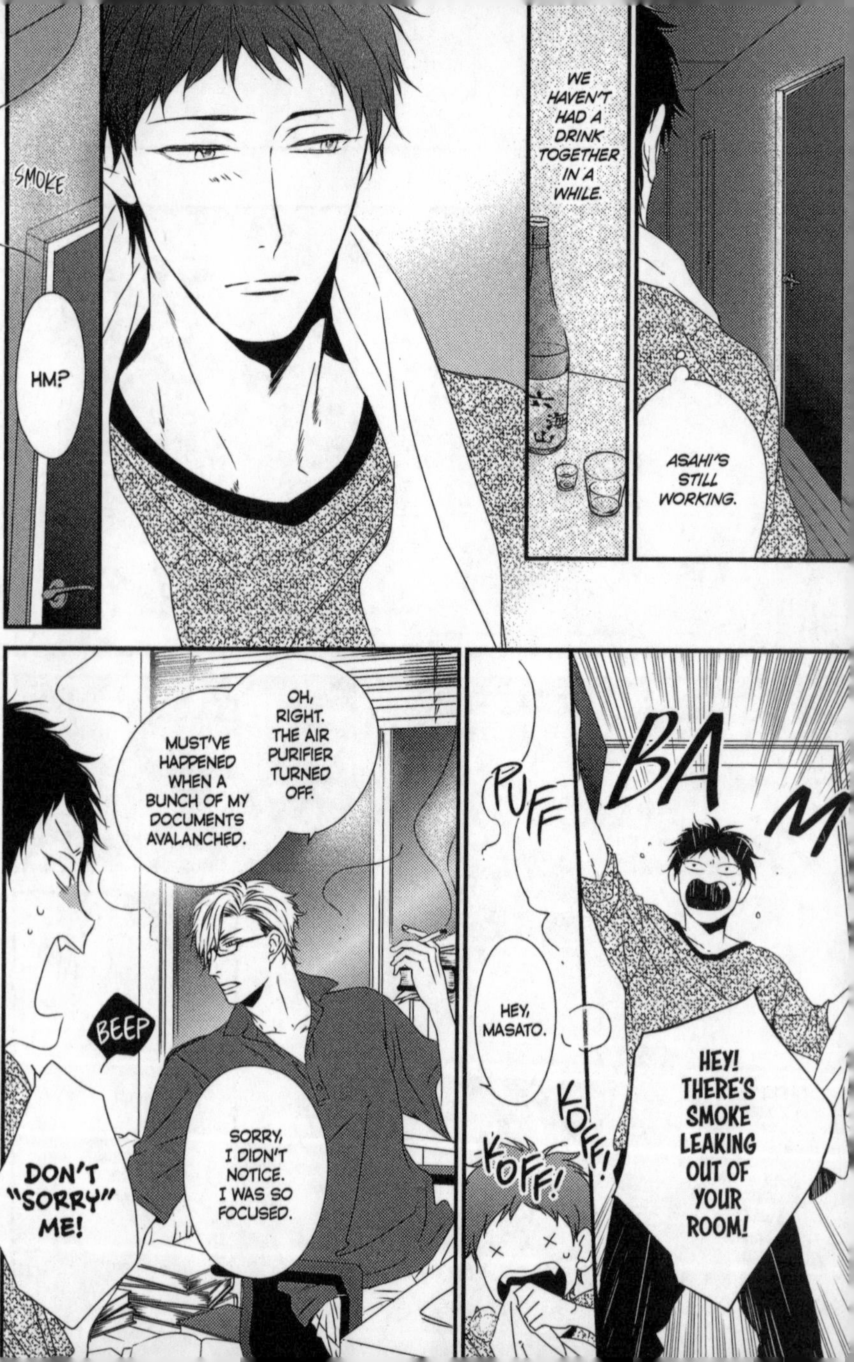
ASAHI'S STILL WORKING.
WE HAVEN'T HAD A DRINK TOGETHER IN A WHILE.
SMOKE
HM?
BAM
HEY! THERE'S SMOKE LEAKING OUT OF YOUR ROOM!
PUFF
HEY, MASATO.
KOFF!
KOFF!
OH, RIGHT. THE AIR PURIFIER TURNED OFF.
MUST'VE HAPPENED WHEN A BUNCH OF MY DOCUMENTS AVALANCHED.
SORRY, I DIDN'T NOTICE. I WAS SO FOCUSED.
BEEP
DON'T "SORRY" ME!

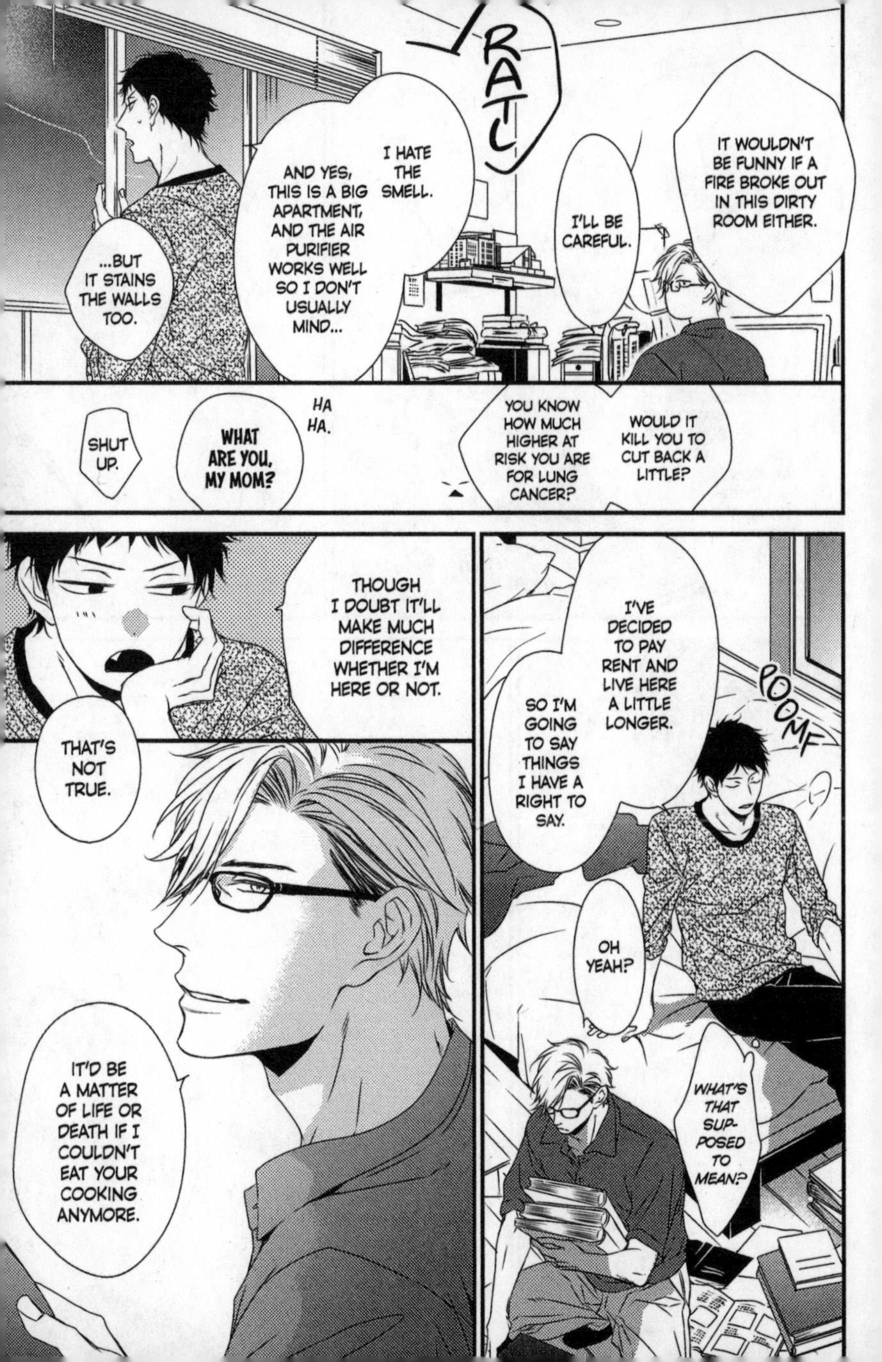
RATL
IT WOULDN'T BE FUNNY IF A FIRE BROKE OUT IN THIS DIRTY ROOM EITHER.
I'LL BE CAREFUL.
I HATE THE SMELL.
AND YES, THIS IS A BIG APARTMENT, AND THE AIR PURIFIER WORKS WELL SO I DON'T USUALLY MIND...
...BUT IT STAINS THE WALLS TOO.
WOULD IT KILL YOU TO CUT BACK A LITTLE?
YOU KNOW HOW MUCH HIGHER AT RISK YOU ARE FOR LUNG CANCER?
HA HA.
WHAT ARE YOU, MY MOM?
SHUT UP.
I'VE DECIDED TO PAY RENT AND LIVE HERE A LITTLE LONGER.
SO I'M GOING TO SAY THINGS I HAVE A RIGHT TO SAY.
POOMF
OH YEAH?
WHAT'S THAT SUP-POSED TO MEAN?
THOUGH I DOUBT IT'LL MAKE MUCH DIFFERENCE WHETHER I'M HERE OR NOT.
THAT'S NOT TRUE.
IT'D BE A MATTER OF LIFE OR DEATH IF I COULDN'T EAT YOUR COOKING ANYMORE.

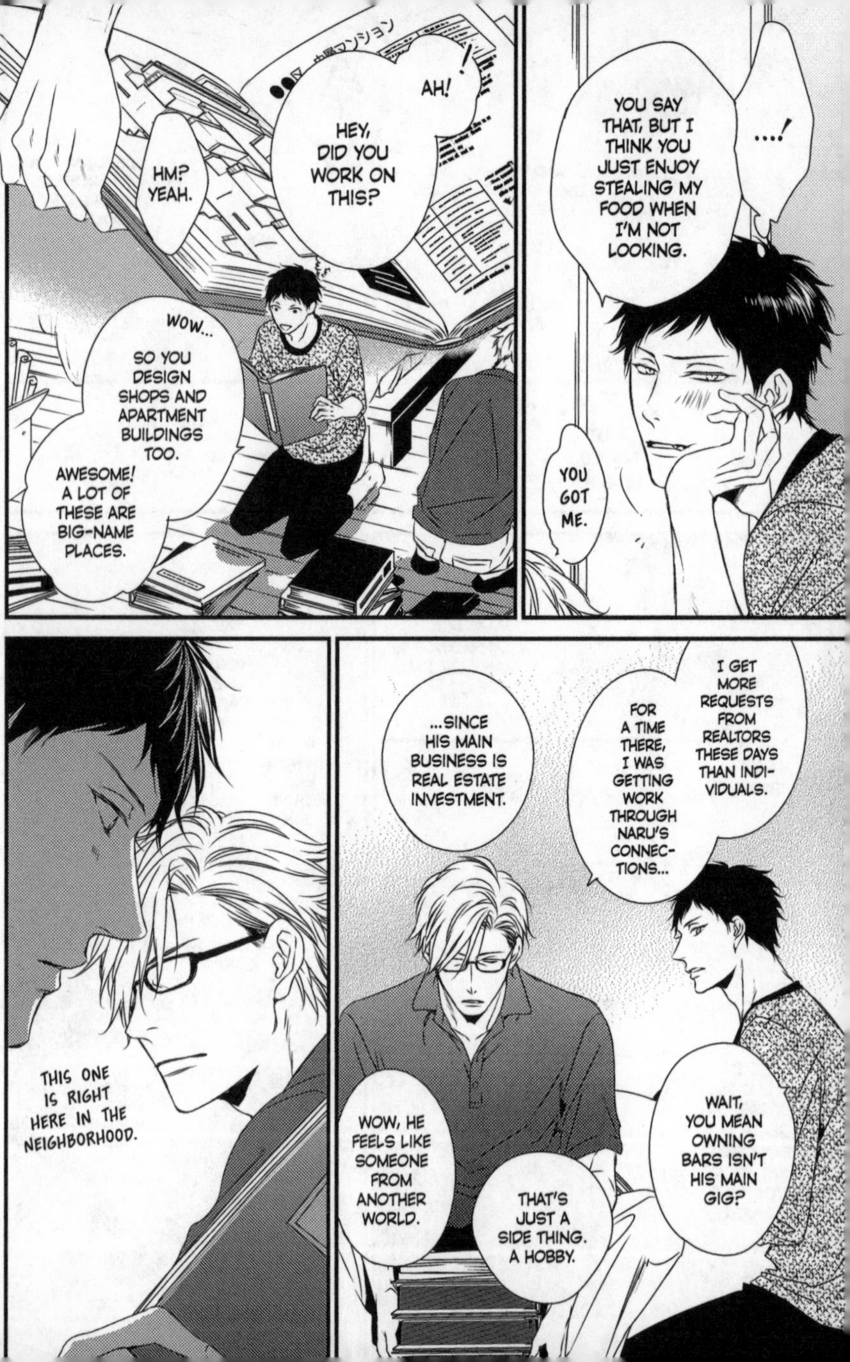
YOU SAY THAT, BUT I THINK YOU JUST ENJOY STEALING MY FOOD WHEN I'M NOT LOOKING.
...!
YOU GOT ME.
AH!
HEY, DID YOU WORK ON THIS?
HM? YEAH.
WOW...
SO YOU DESIGN SHOPS AND APARTMENT BUILDINGS TOO.
AWESOME! A LOT OF THESE ARE BIG-NAME PLACES.
I GET MORE REQUESTS FROM REALTORS THESE DAYS THAN INDIVIDUALS.
FOR A TIME THERE, I WAS GETTING WORK THROUGH NARU'S CONNECTIONS...
...SINCE HIS MAIN BUSINESS IS REAL ESTATE INVESTMENT.
WAIT, YOU MEAN OWNING BARS ISN'T HIS MAIN GIG?
THAT'S JUST A SIDE THING. A HOBBY.
WOW, HE FEELS LIKE SOMEONE FROM ANOTHER WORLD.
THIS ONE IS RIGHT HERE IN THE NEIGHBORHOOD.

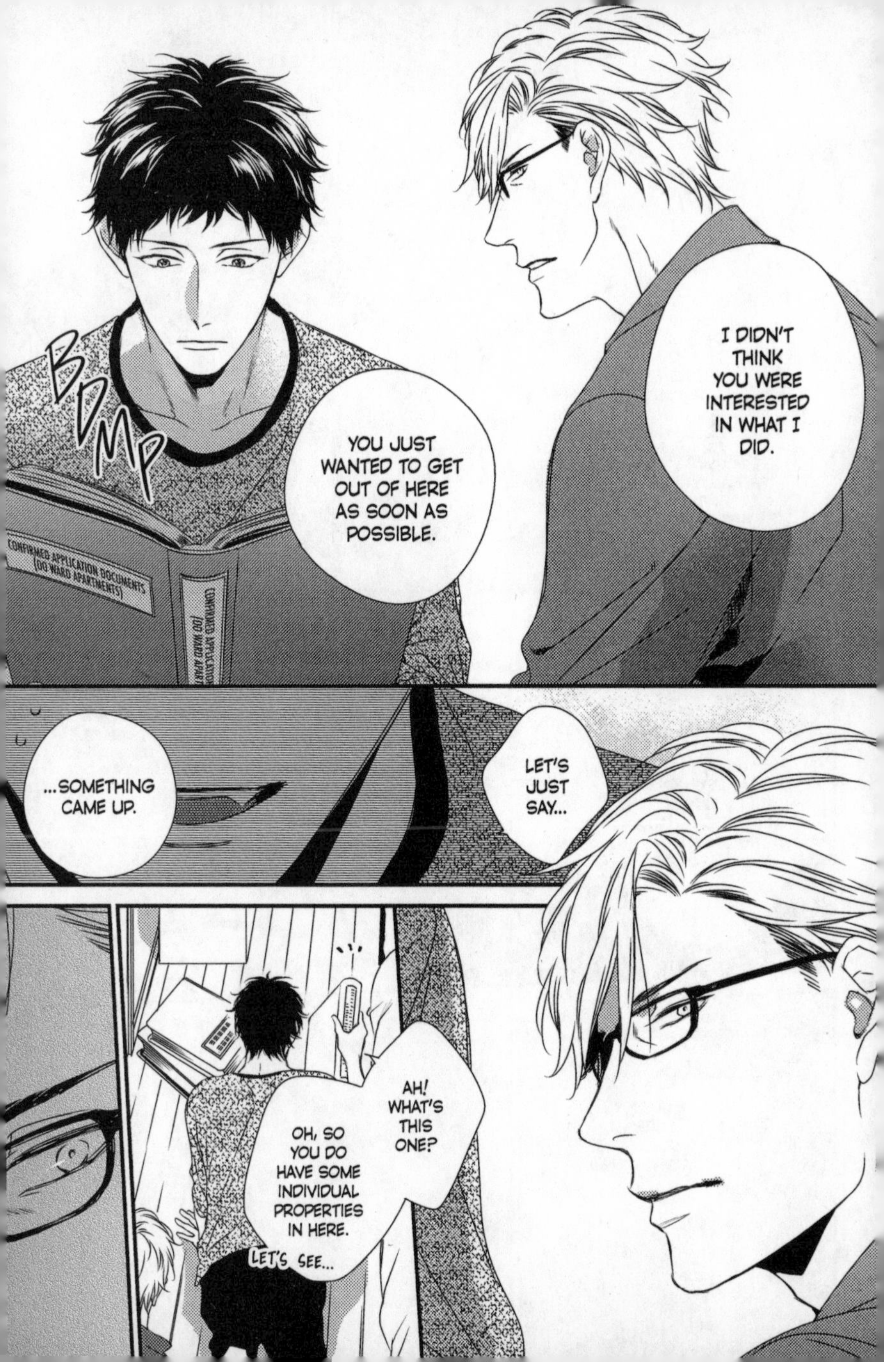
I DIDN'T THINK YOU WERE INTERESTED IN WHAT I DID.
YOU JUST WANTED TO GET OUT OF HERE AS SOON AS POSSIBLE.
BDMP
CONFIRMED APPLICATION DOCUMENTS (OO WARD APARTMENTS)
LET'S JUST SAY...
...SOMETHING CAME UP.
AH! WHAT'S THIS ONE?
OH, SO YOU DO HAVE SOME INDIVIDUAL PROPERTIES IN HERE.
LET'S SEE...

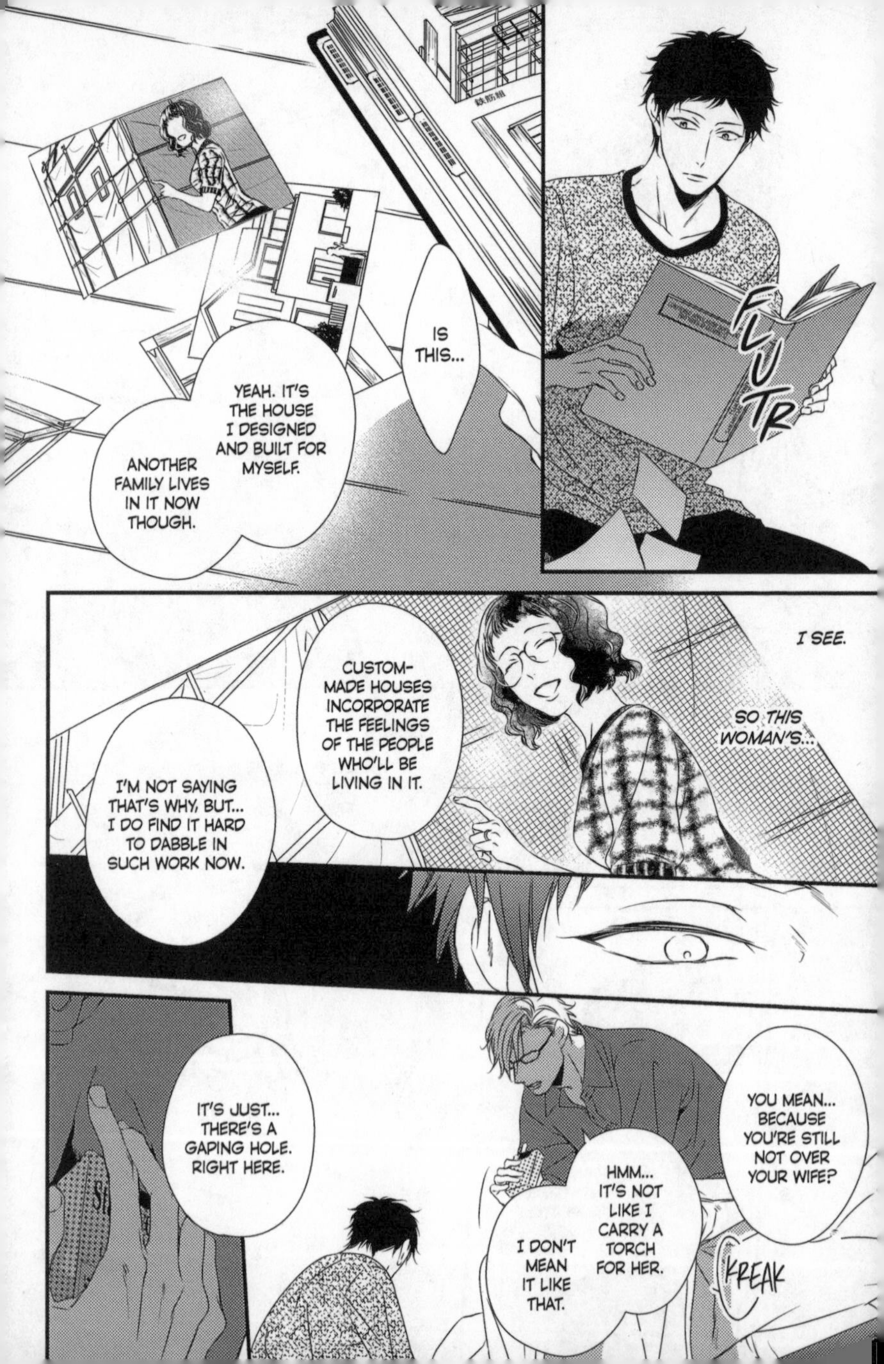
FLUTR
IS THIS...
YEAH. IT'S THE HOUSE I DESIGNED AND BUILT FOR MYSELF.
ANOTHER FAMILY LIVES IN IT NOW THOUGH.
I SEE.
SO THIS WOMAN'S...
CUSTOM-MADE HOUSES INCORPORATE THE FEELINGS OF THE PEOPLE WHO'LL BE LIVING IN IT.
I'M NOT SAYING THAT'S WHY, BUT... I DO FIND IT HARD TO DABBLE IN SUCH WORK NOW.
YOU MEAN... BECAUSE YOU'RE STILL NOT OVER YOUR WIFE?
KREAK
HMM... IT'S NOT LIKE I CARRY A TORCH FOR HER.
I DON'T MEAN IT LIKE THAT.
IT'S JUST... THERE'S A GAPING HOLE. RIGHT HERE.

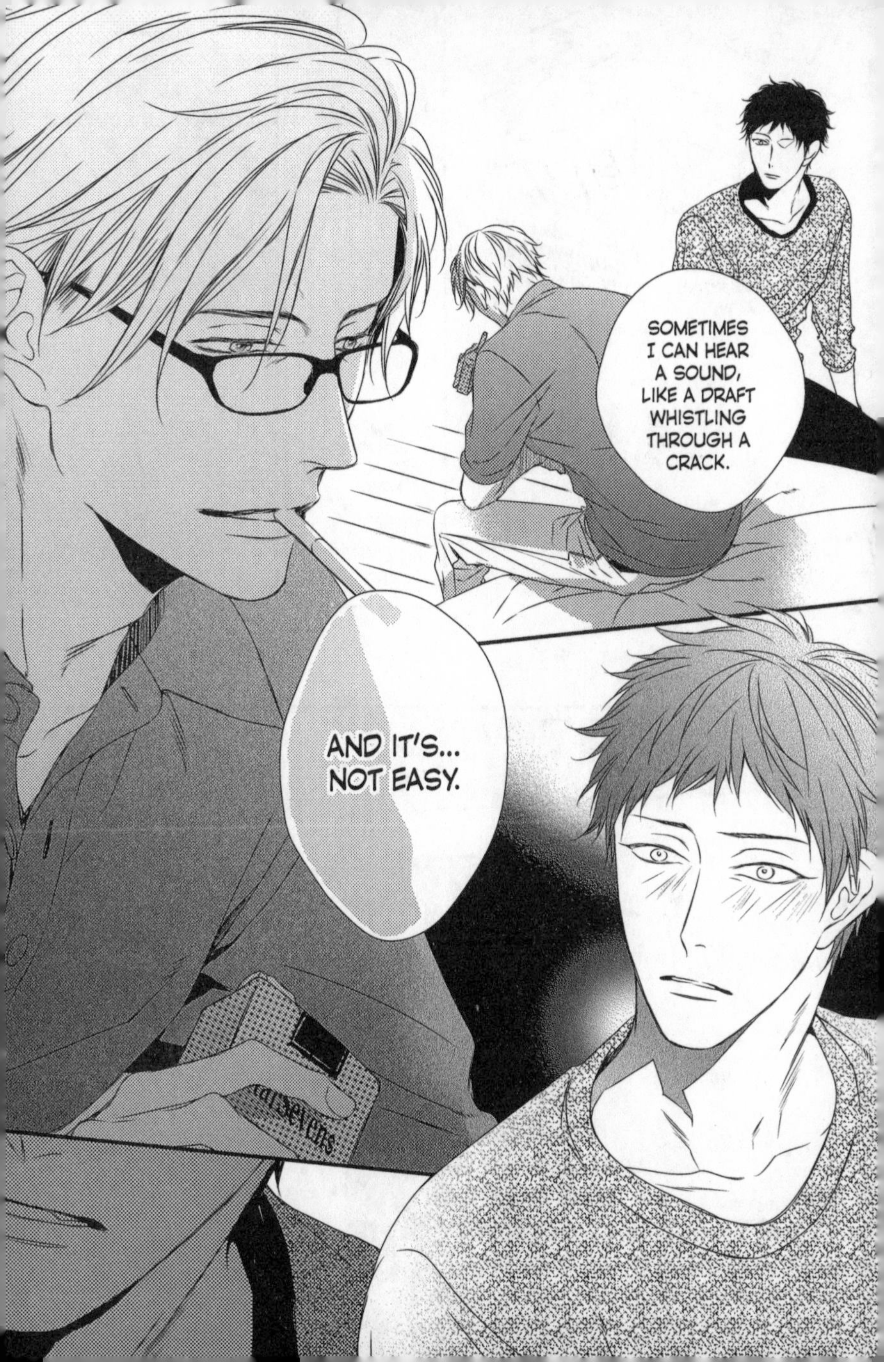
SOMETIMES I CAN HEAR A SOUND, LIKE A DRAFT WHISTLING THROUGH A CRACK.
AND IT'S... NOT EASY.

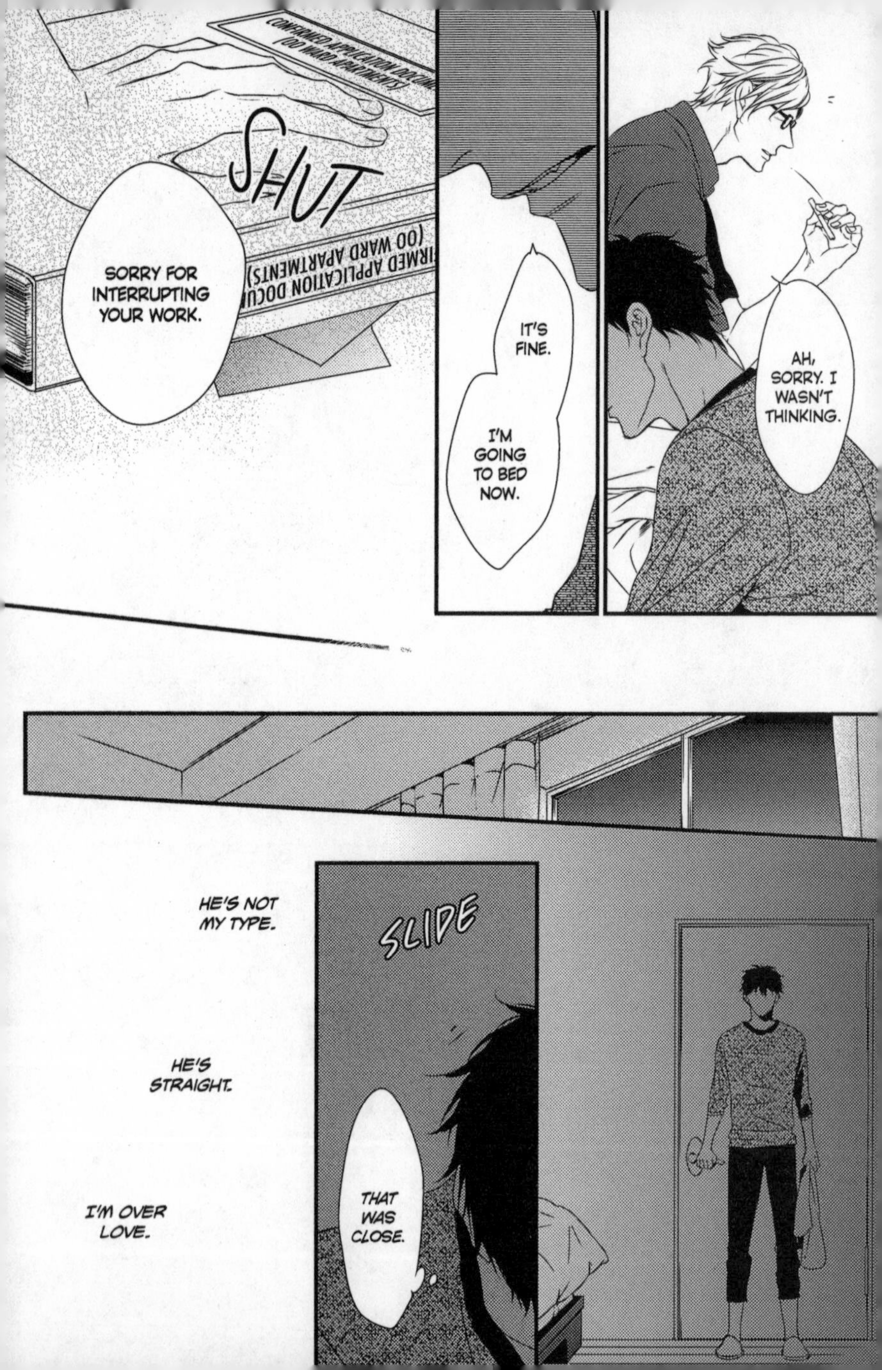
AH, SORRY. I WASN'T THINKING.
IT'S FINE.
I'M GOING TO BED NOW.
CONFIRMED APPLICATION DOCUM
(OO WARD APARTMENTS)
SHUT
FIRMED APPLICATION DOCU
(OO WARD APARTMENTS)
SORRY FOR INTERRUPTING YOUR WORK.
SLIDE
THAT WAS CLOSE.
HE'S NOT MY TYPE.
HE'S STRAIGHT.
I'M OVER LOVE.

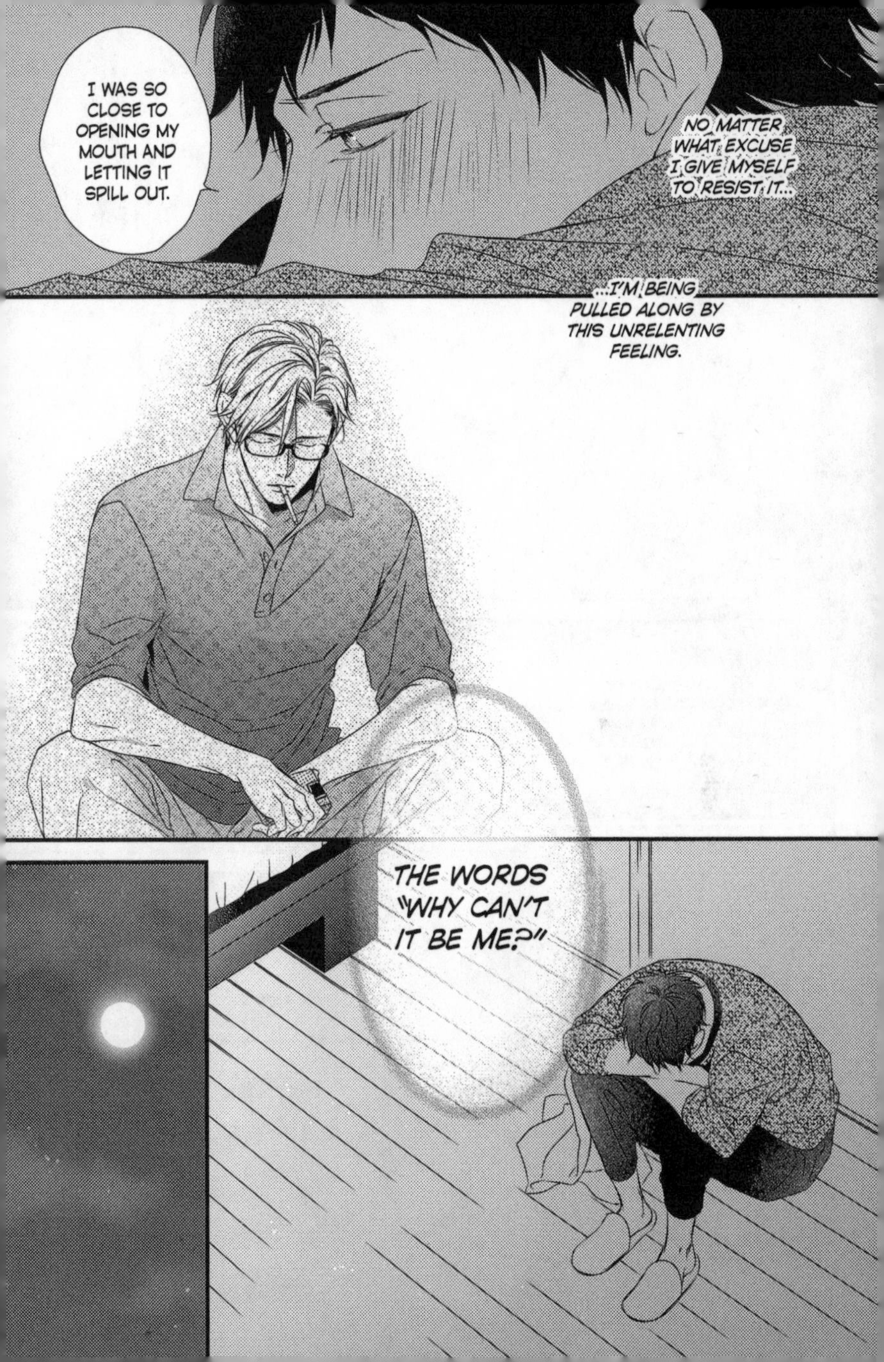
I WAS SO CLOSE TO OPENING MY MOUTH AND LETTING IT SPILL OUT.
NO MATTER WHAT EXCUSE I GIVE MYSELF TO RESIST IT...
...I'M BEING PULLED ALONG BY THIS UNRELENTING FEELING.
THE WORDS "WHY CAN'T IT BE ME?"

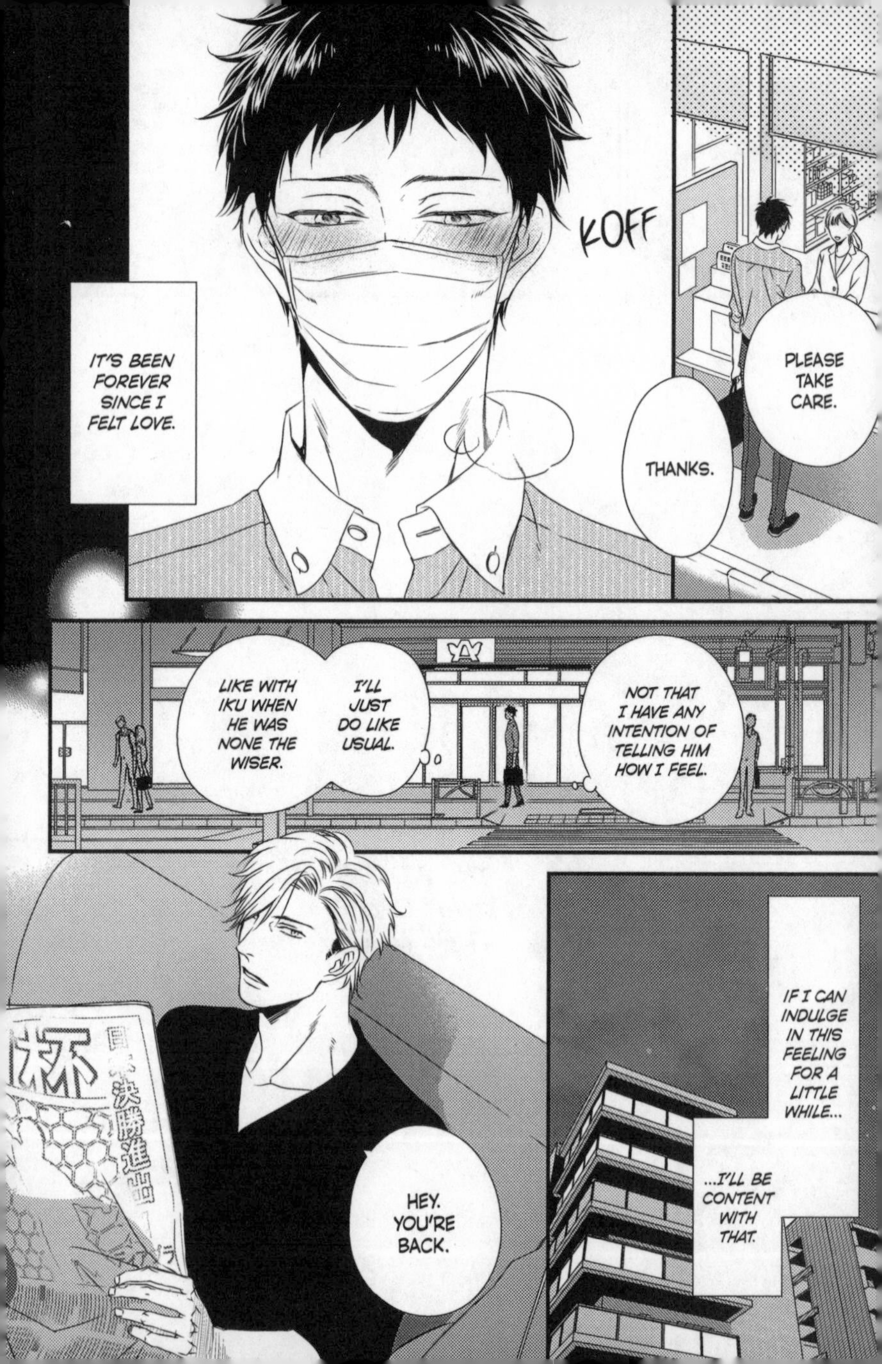
PLEASE TAKE CARE.
THANKS.
KOFF
IT'S BEEN FOREVER SINCE I FELT LOVE.
NOT THAT I HAVE ANY INTENTION OF TELLING HIM HOW I FEEL.
I'LL JUST DO LIKE USUAL.
LIKE WITH IKU WHEN HE WAS NONE THE WISER.
IF I CAN INDULGE IN THIS FEELING FOR A LITTLE WHILE...
...I'LL BE CONTENT WITH THAT.
HEY. YOU'RE BACK.

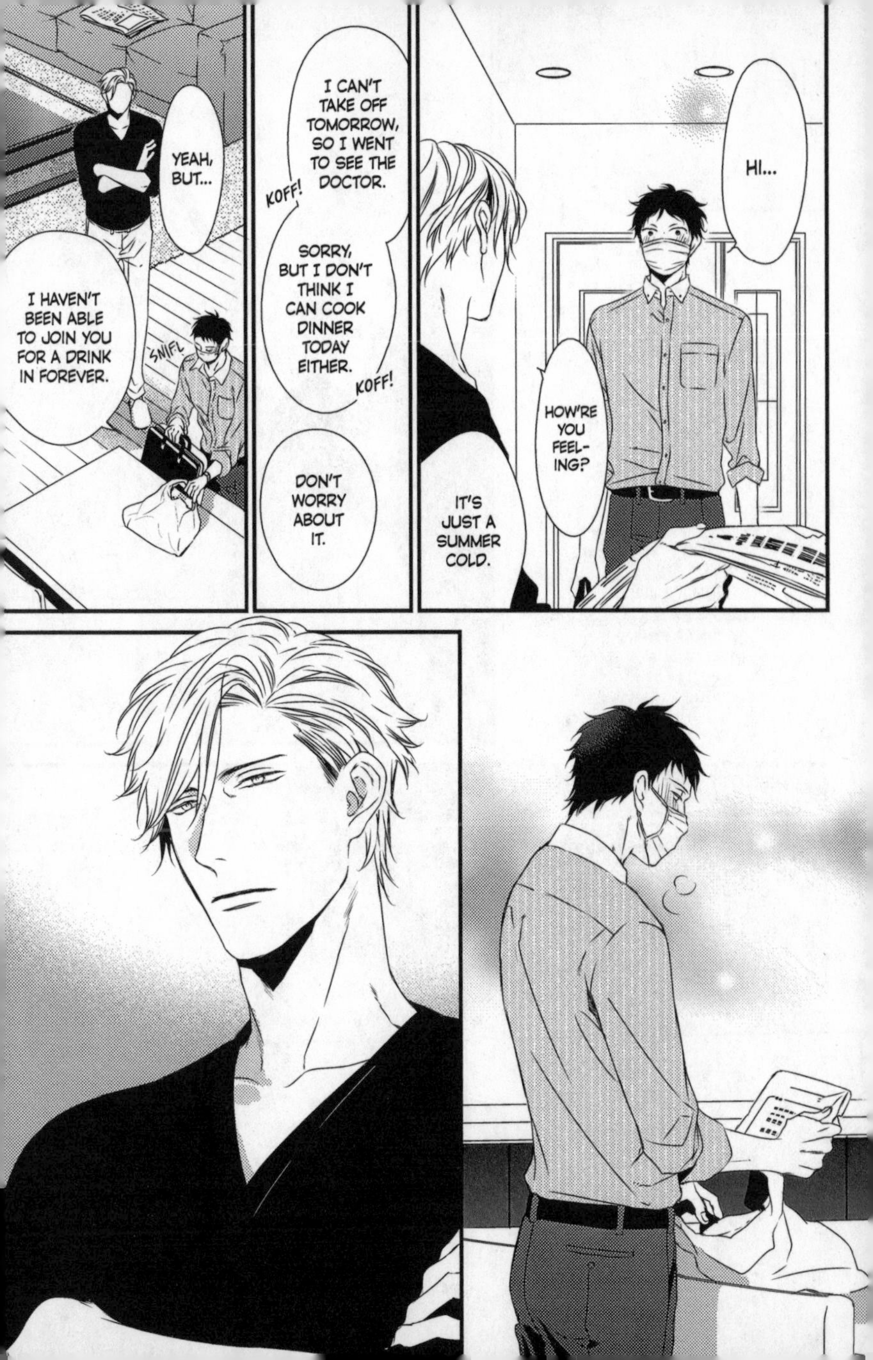
HI...
HOW'RE YOU FEEL-ING?
IT'S JUST A SUMMER COLD.
I CAN'T TAKE OFF TOMORROW, SO I WENT TO SEE THE DOCTOR.
KOFF!
SORRY, BUT I DON'T THINK I CAN COOK DINNER TODAY EITHER.
KOFF!
DON'T WORRY ABOUT IT.
YEAH, BUT...
SNIFL
I HAVEN'T BEEN ABLE TO JOIN YOU FOR A DRINK IN FOREVER.

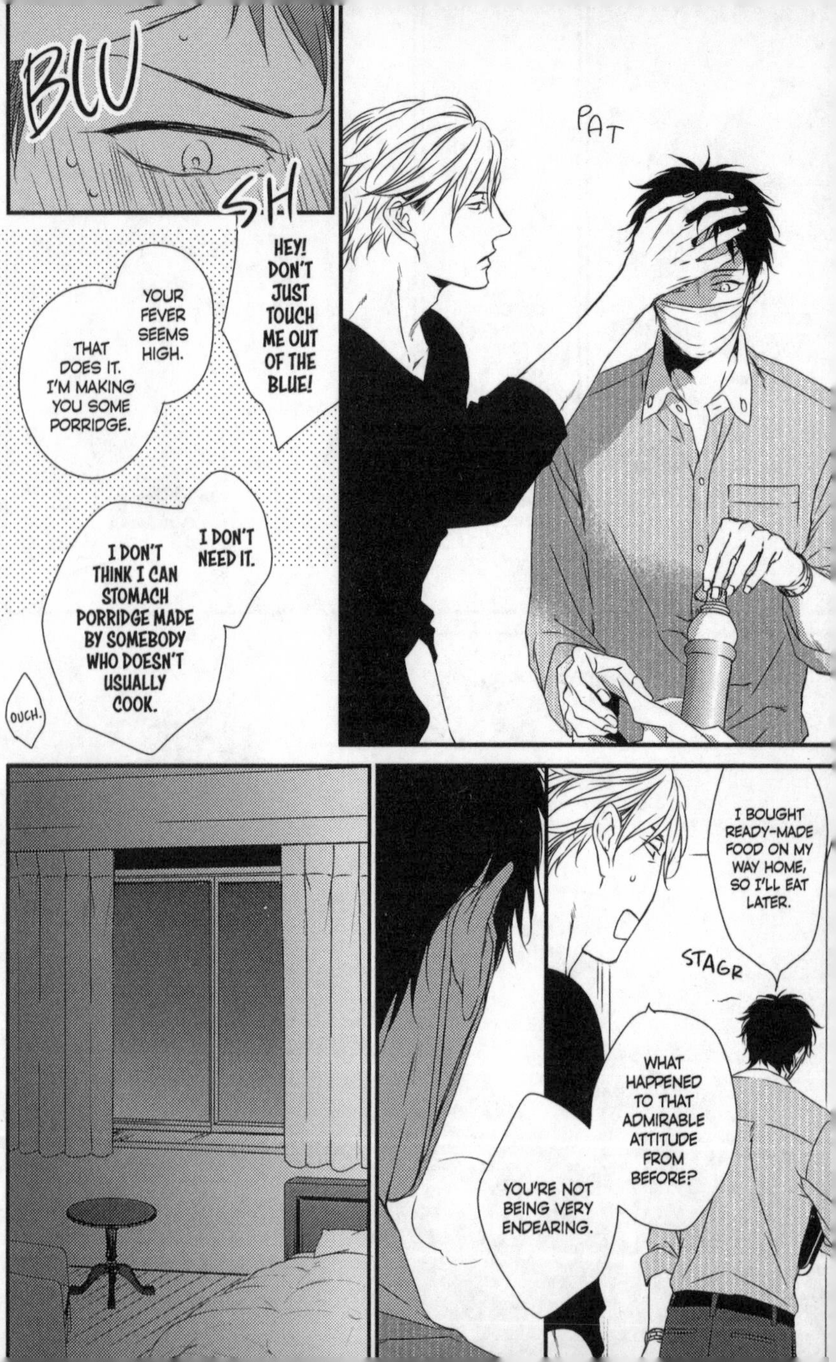
PAT
HEY! DON'T JUST TOUCH ME OUT OF THE BLUE!
BLU
SH
YOUR FEVER SEEMS HIGH.
THAT DOES IT. I'M MAKING YOU SOME PORRIDGE.
I DON'T NEED IT.
I DON'T THINK I CAN STOMACH PORRIDGE MADE BY SOMEBODY WHO DOESN'T USUALLY COOK.
OUCH.
I BOUGHT READY-MADE FOOD ON MY WAY HOME, SO I'LL EAT LATER.
STAGR
WHAT HAPPENED TO THAT ADMIRABLE ATTITUDE FROM BEFORE?
YOU'RE NOT BEING VERY ENDEARING.

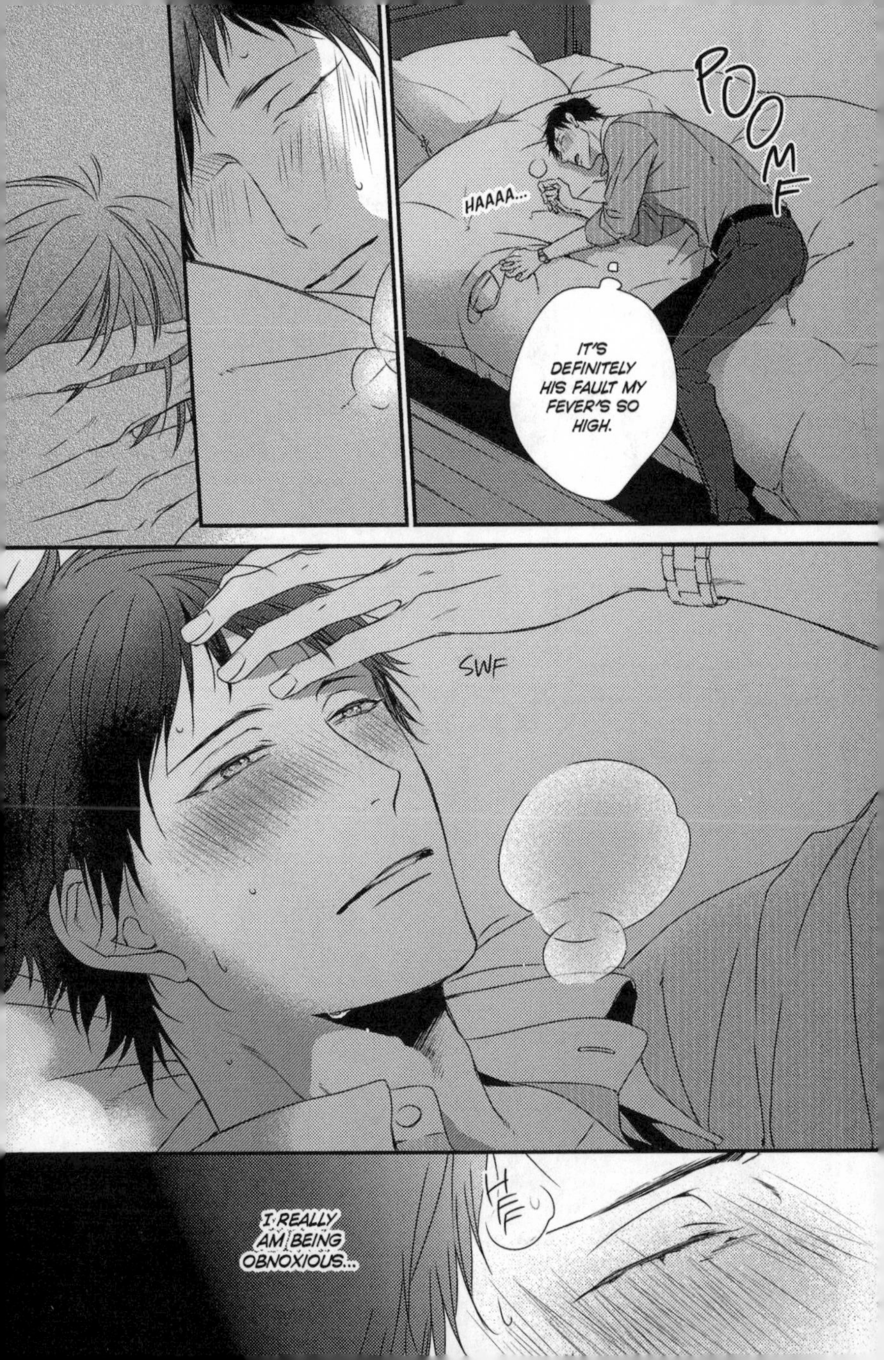
POOMF
HAAAA...
IT'S DEFINITELY HIS FAULT MY FEVER'S SO HIGH.
SWF
HFF
I REALLY AM BEING OBNOXIOUS...

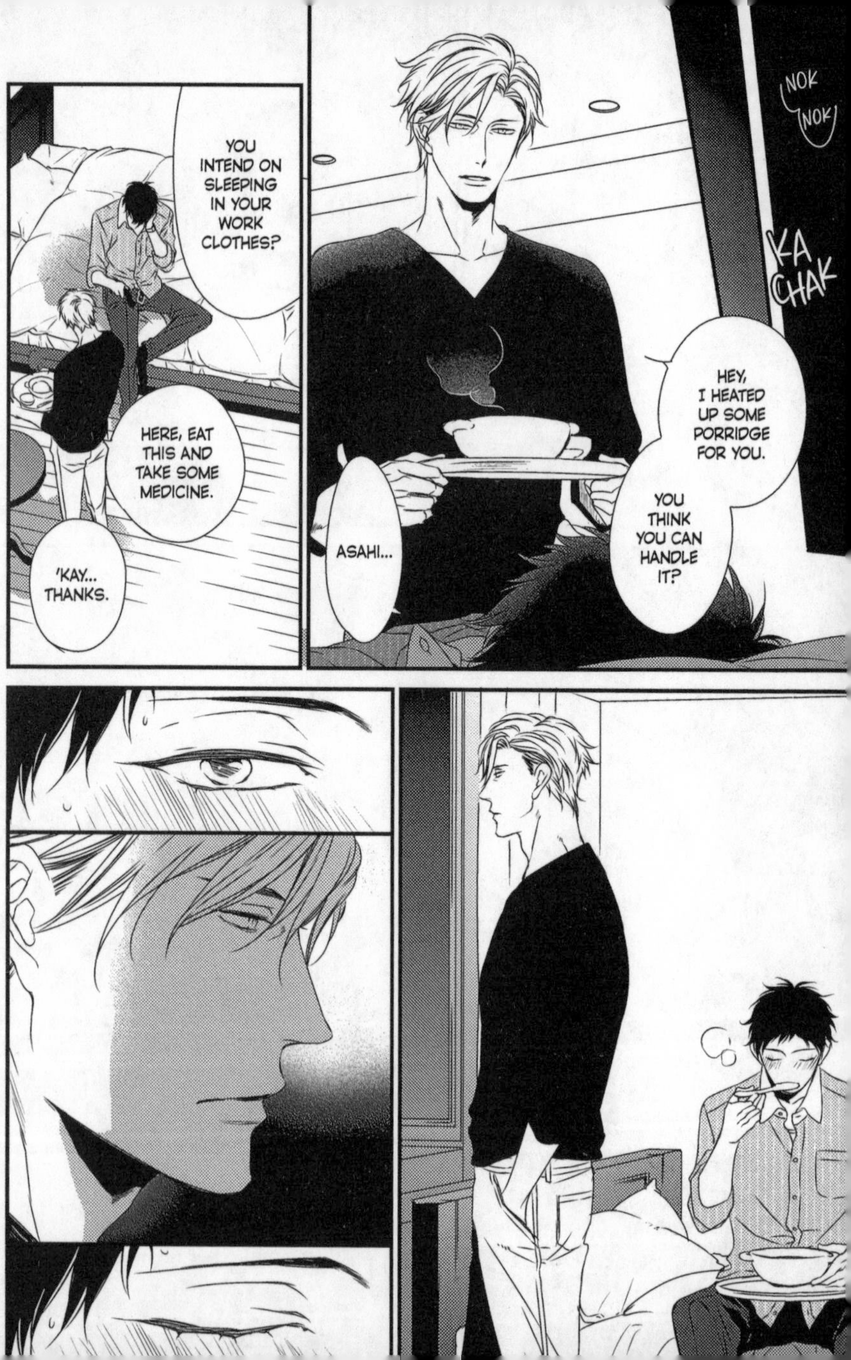
NOK NOK
KA CHAK
HEY, I HEATED UP SOME PORRIDGE FOR YOU.
YOU THINK YOU CAN HANDLE IT?
ASAHI...
YOU INTEND ON SLEEPING IN YOUR WORK CLOTHES?
HERE, EAT THIS AND TAKE SOME MEDICINE.
'KAY... THANKS.

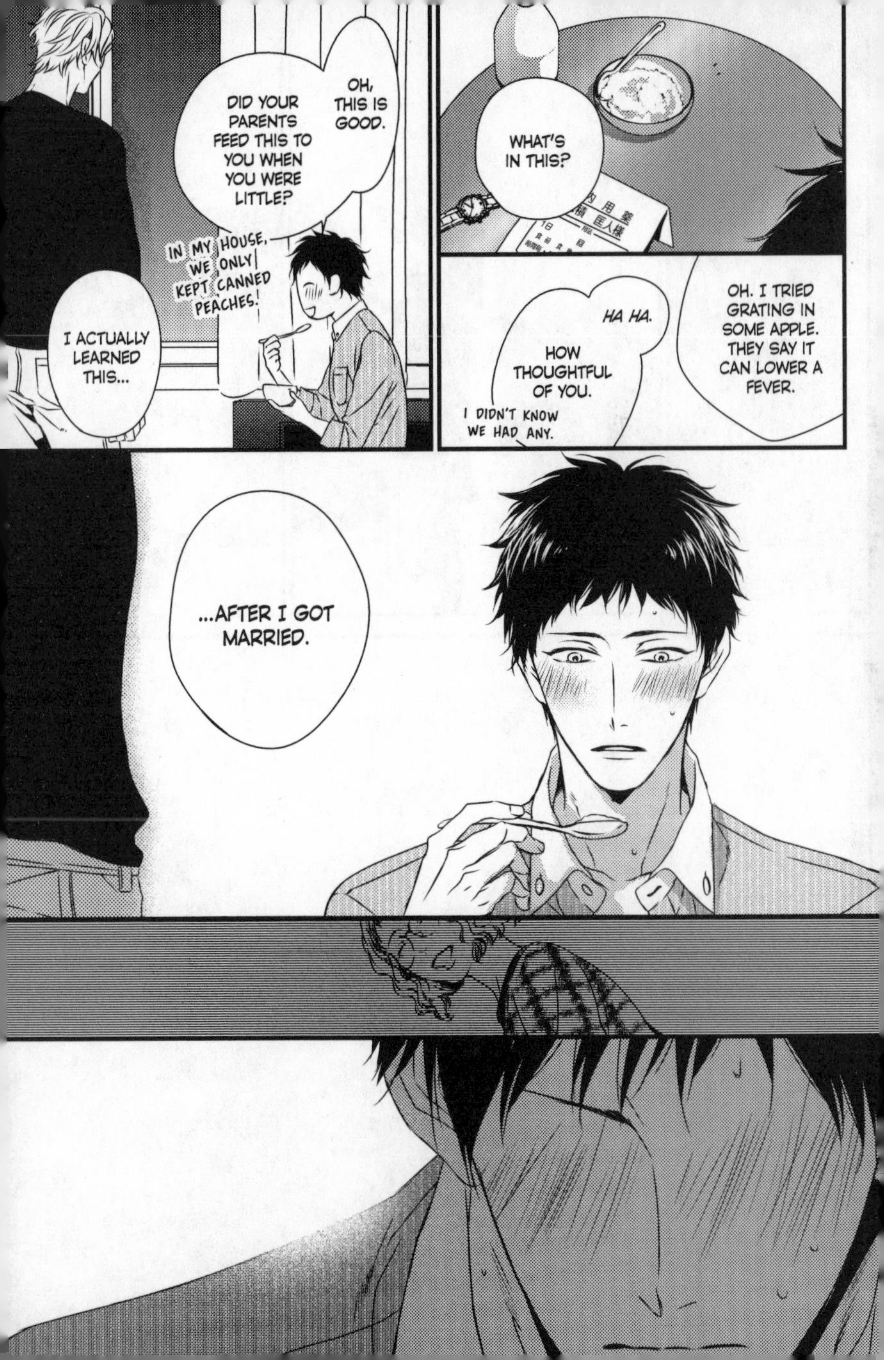
WHAT'S IN THIS?
OH. I TRIED GRATING IN SOME APPLE. THEY SAY IT CAN LOWER A FEVER.
HA HA.
HOW THOUGHTFUL OF YOU.
I DIDN'T KNOW WE HAD ANY.
OH, THIS IS GOOD.
DID YOUR PARENTS FEED THIS TO YOU WHEN YOU WERE LITTLE?
IN MY HOUSE, WE ONLY KEPT CANNED PEACHES!
I ACTUALLY LEARNED THIS...
...AFTER I GOT MARRIED.

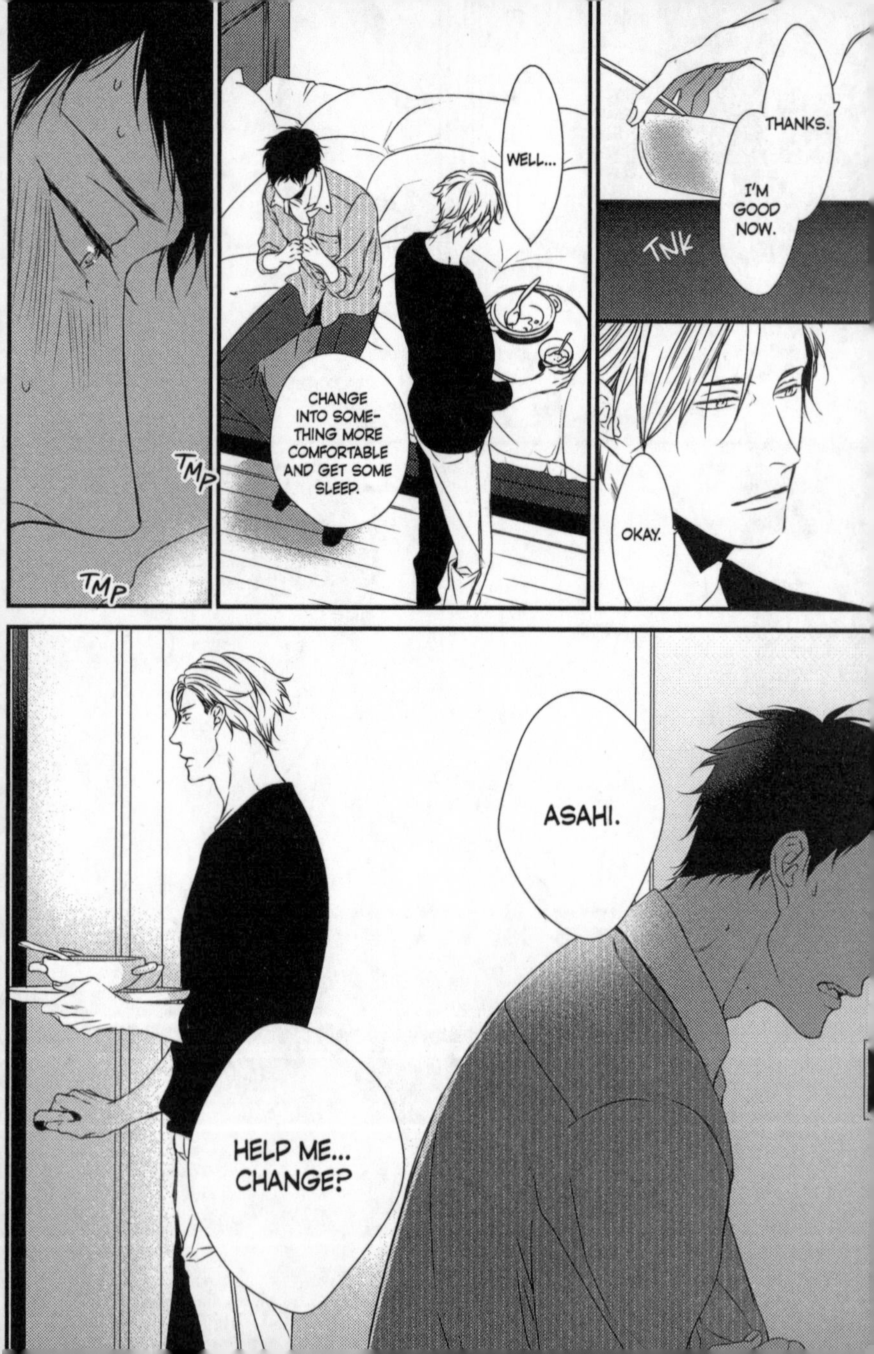
THANKS.
I'M GOOD NOW.
TNK
OKAY.
WELL...
CHANGE INTO SOME-THING MORE COMFORTABLE AND GET SOME SLEEP.
TMP
TMP
ASAHI.
HELP ME... CHANGE?

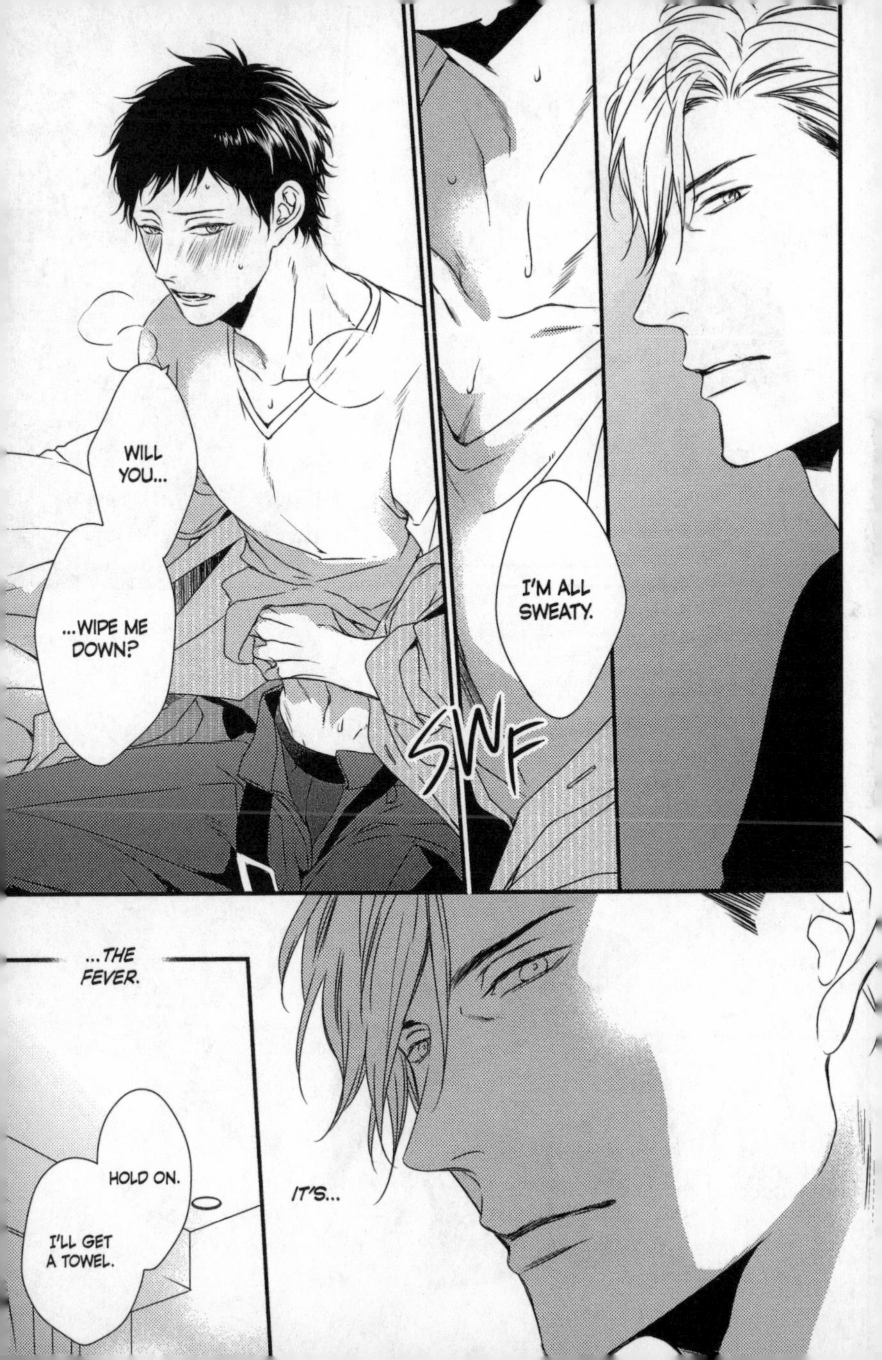
I'M ALL SWEATY.
SWF
WILL YOU...
...WIPE ME DOWN?
IT'S...
...THE FEVER.
HOLD ON.
I'LL GET A TOWEL.

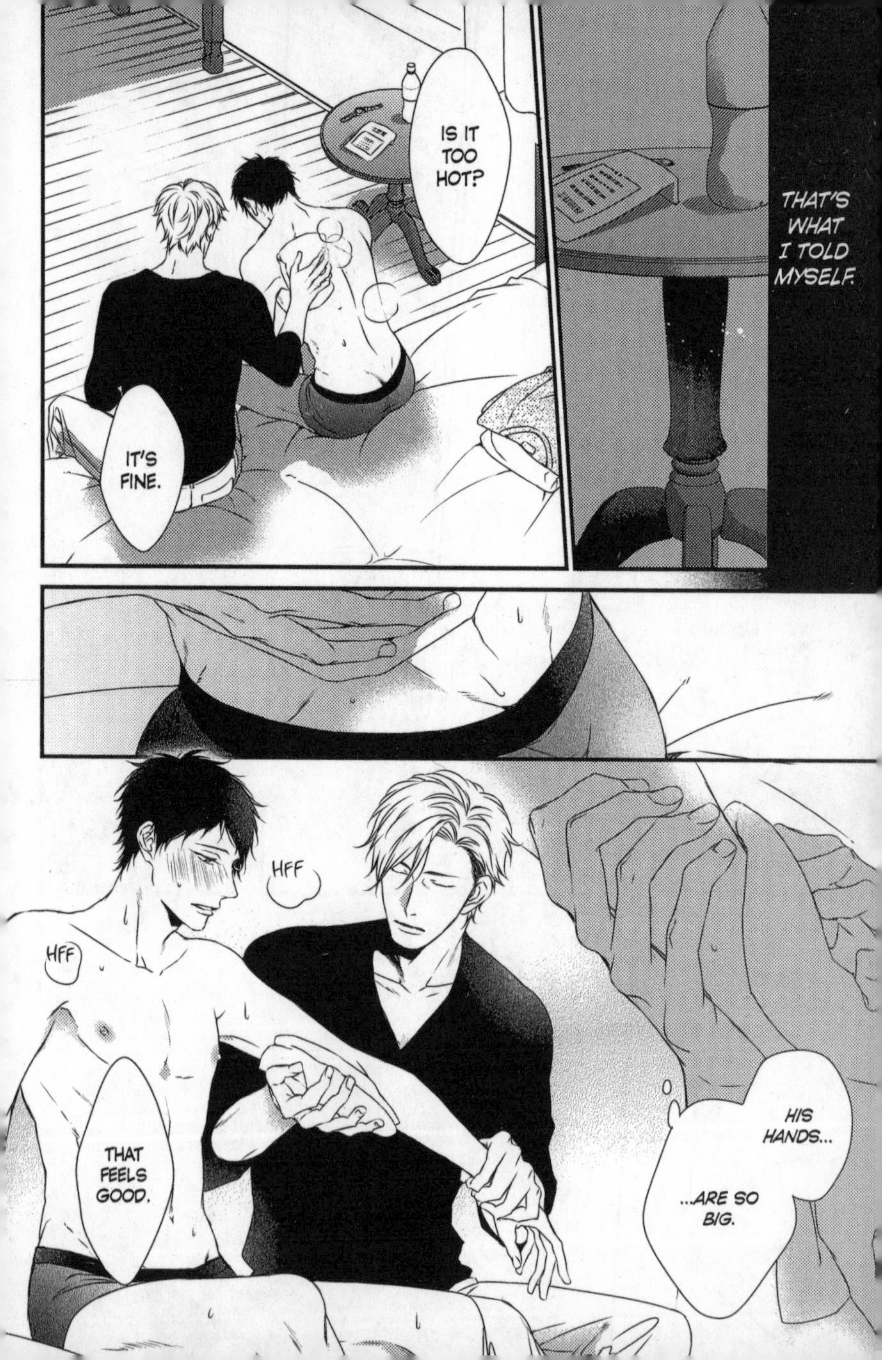
THAT'S WHAT I TOLD MYSELF.
IS IT TOO HOT?
IT'S FINE.
HIS HANDS...
...ARE SO BIG.
HFF
HFF
THAT FEELS GOOD.

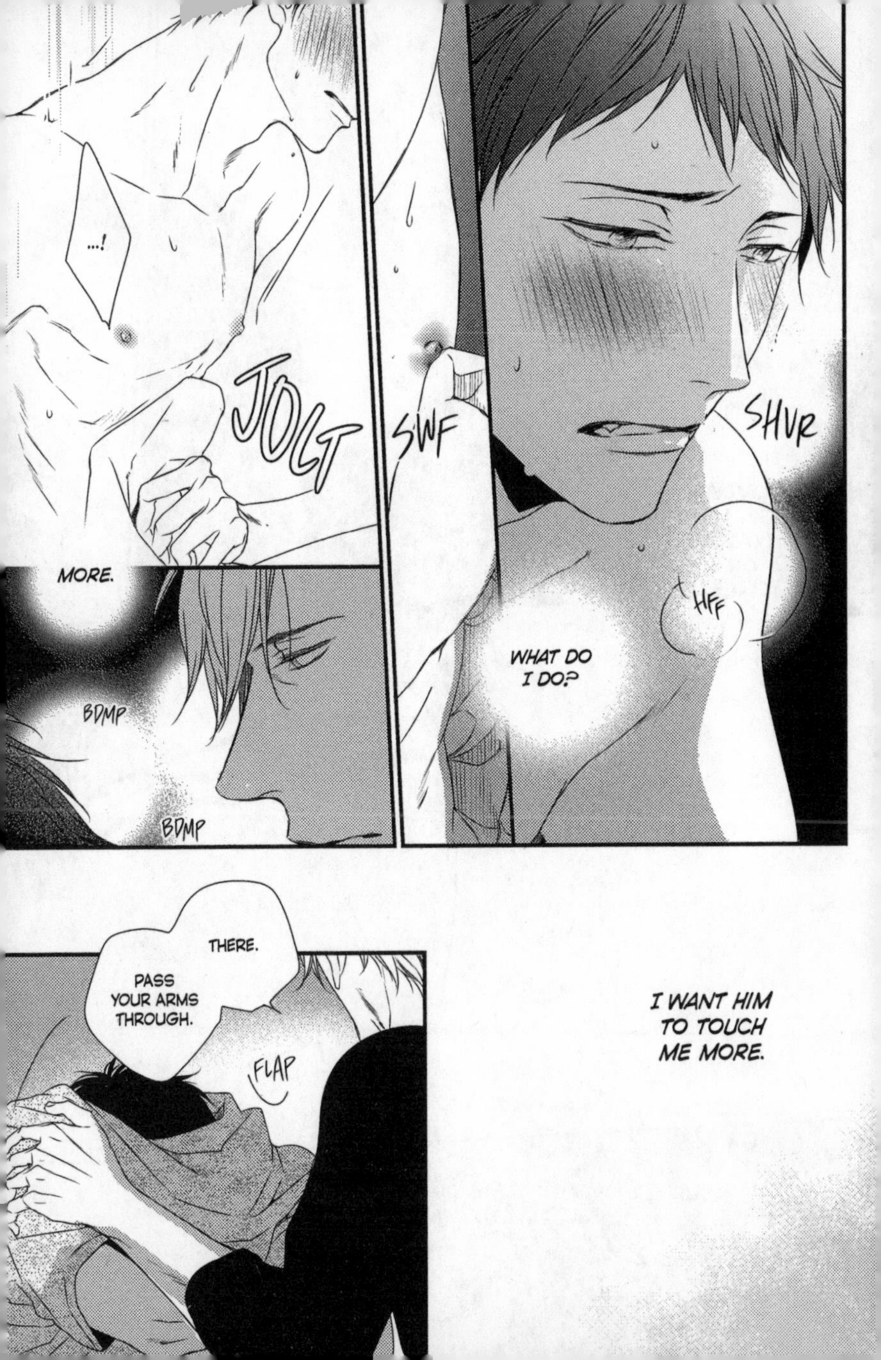
SHVR
SWF
HFF
WHAT DO I DO?
...!
JOLT
MORE.
BDMP
BDMP
I WANT HIM TO TOUCH ME MORE.
THERE.
PASS YOUR ARMS THROUGH.
FLAP

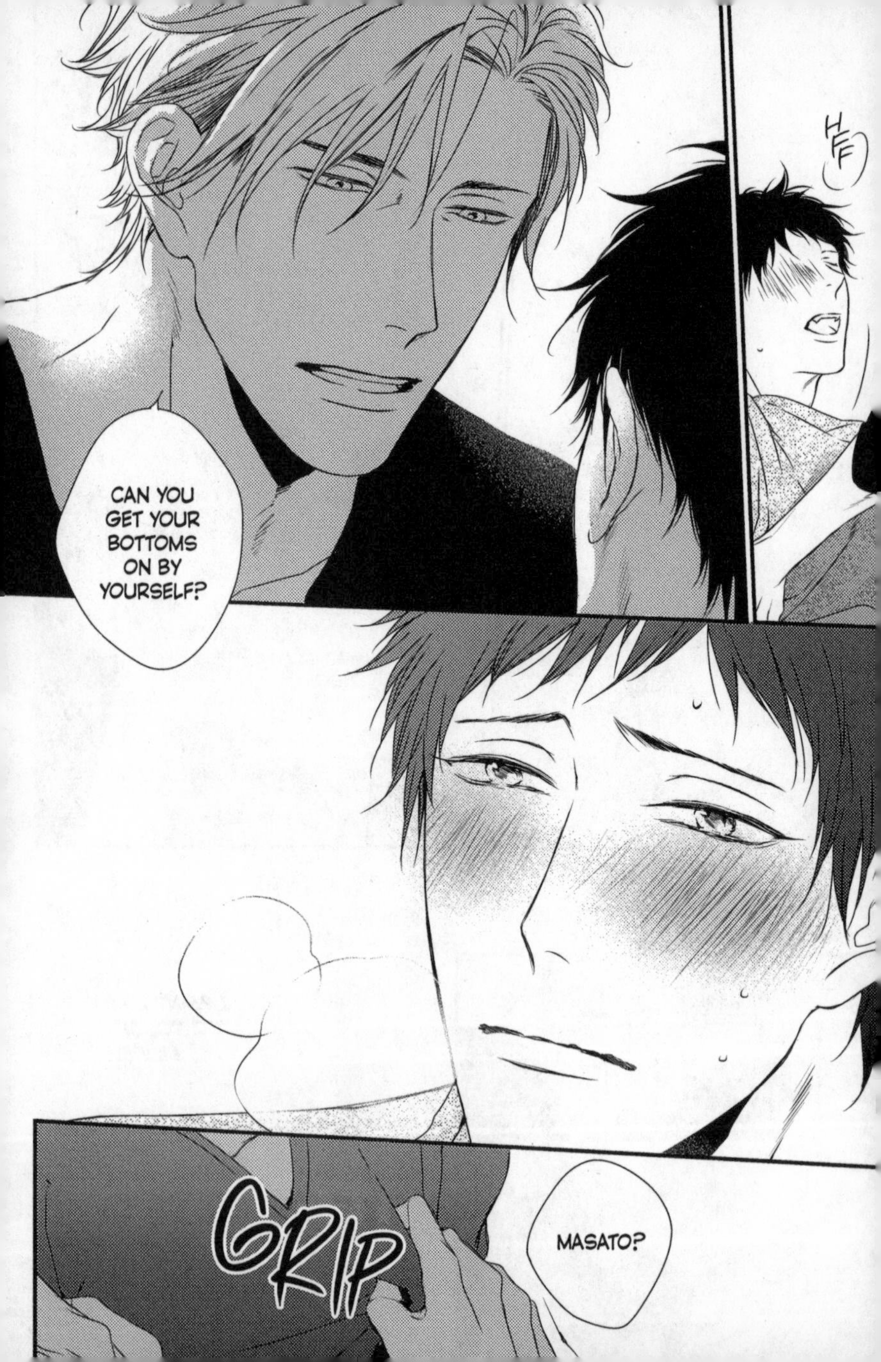
HFF
CAN YOU GET YOUR BOTTOMS ON BY YOURSELF?
MASATO?
GRIP

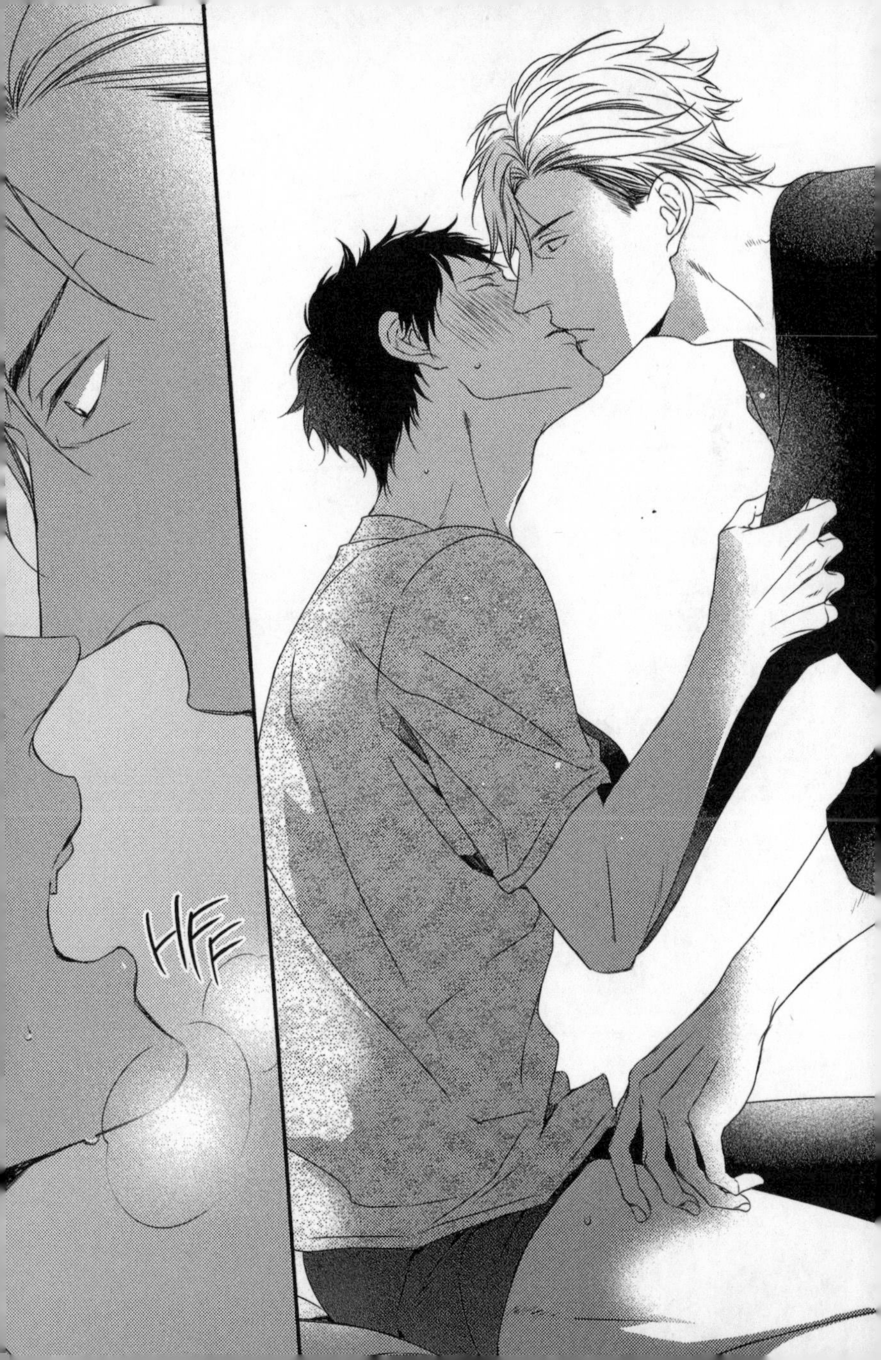
HFF

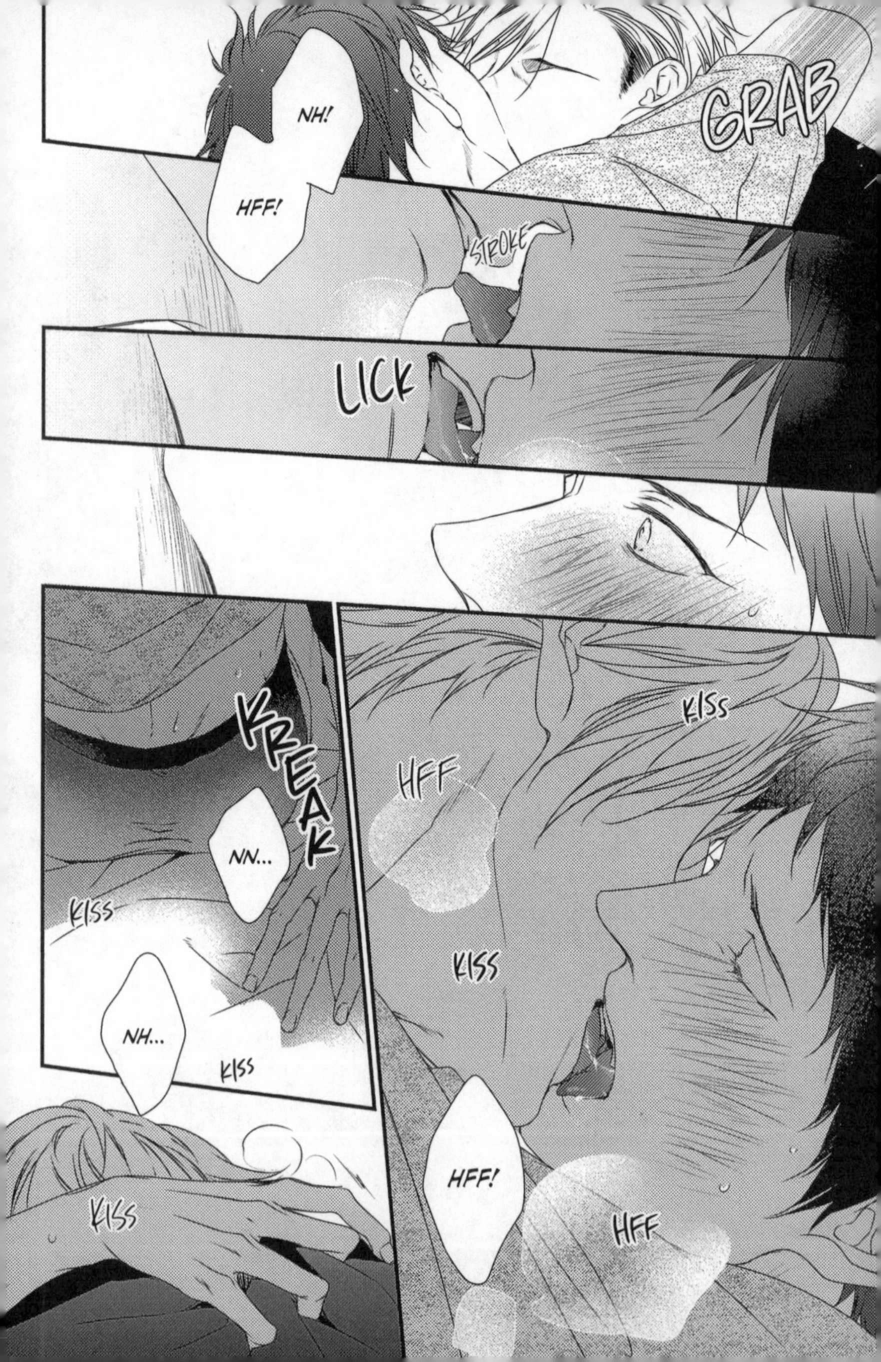
GRAB
NH!
HFF!
STROKE
LICK
KISS
HFF
KISS
HFF!
HFF
KREAK
NN...
KISS
NH...
KISS
KISS

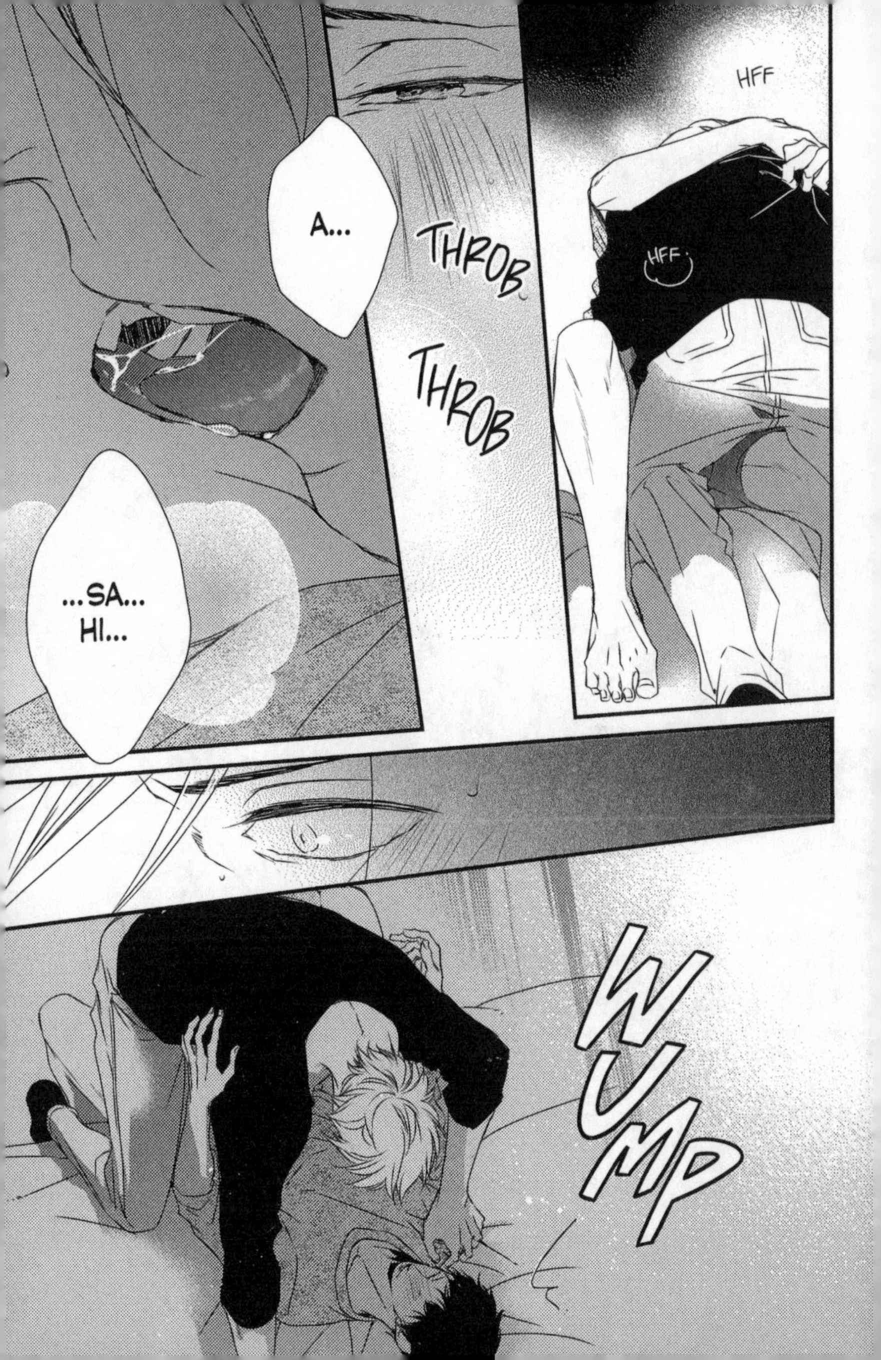
HFF
HFF
THROB
THROB
A...
...SA... HI...
WUMP

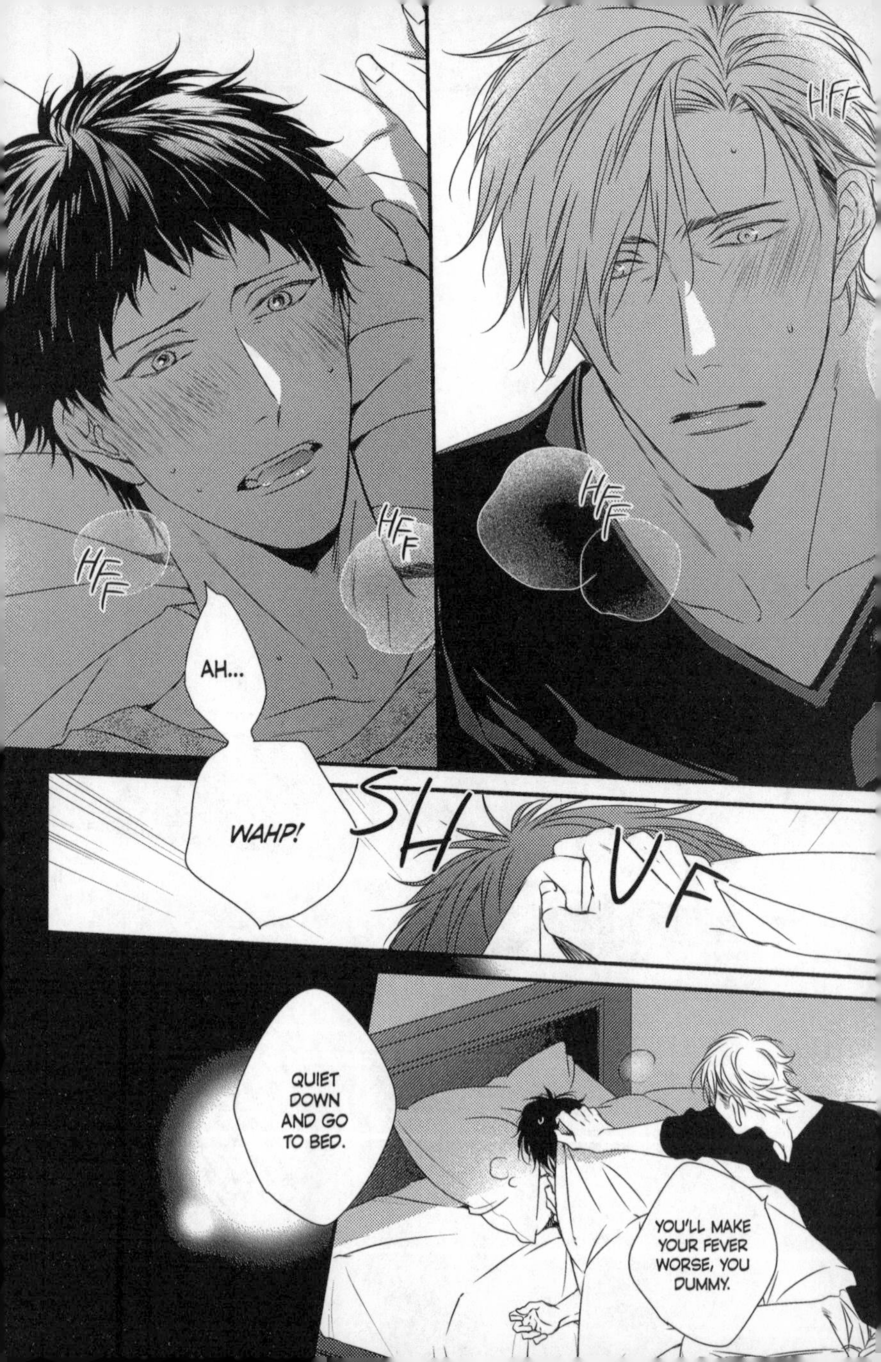
HFF
HFF
HFF
HFF
AH...
SHUF
WAHP!
QUIET DOWN AND GO TO BED.
YOU'LL MAKE YOUR FEVER WORSE, YOU DUMMY.

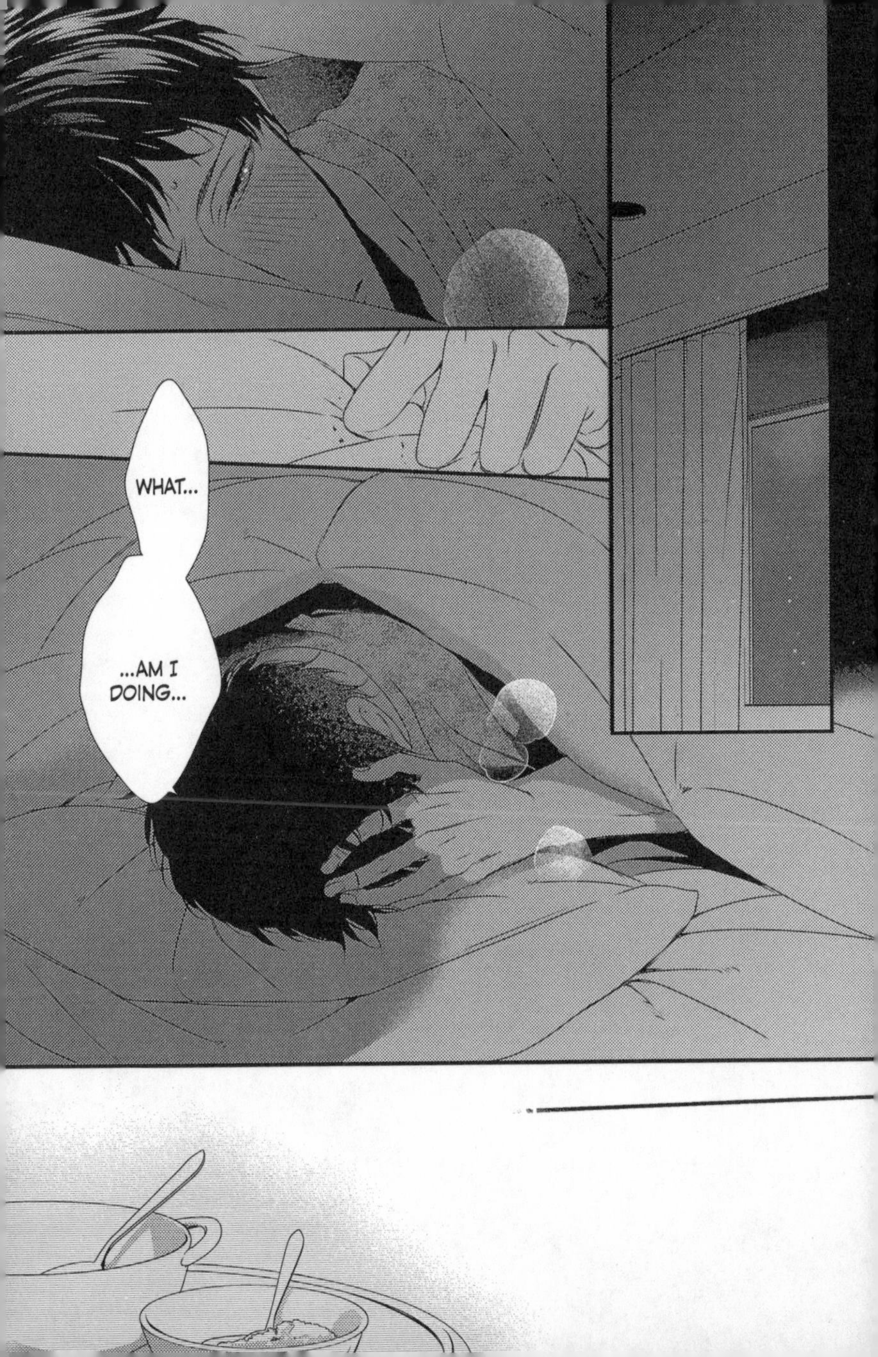
WHAT...
...AM I DOING...

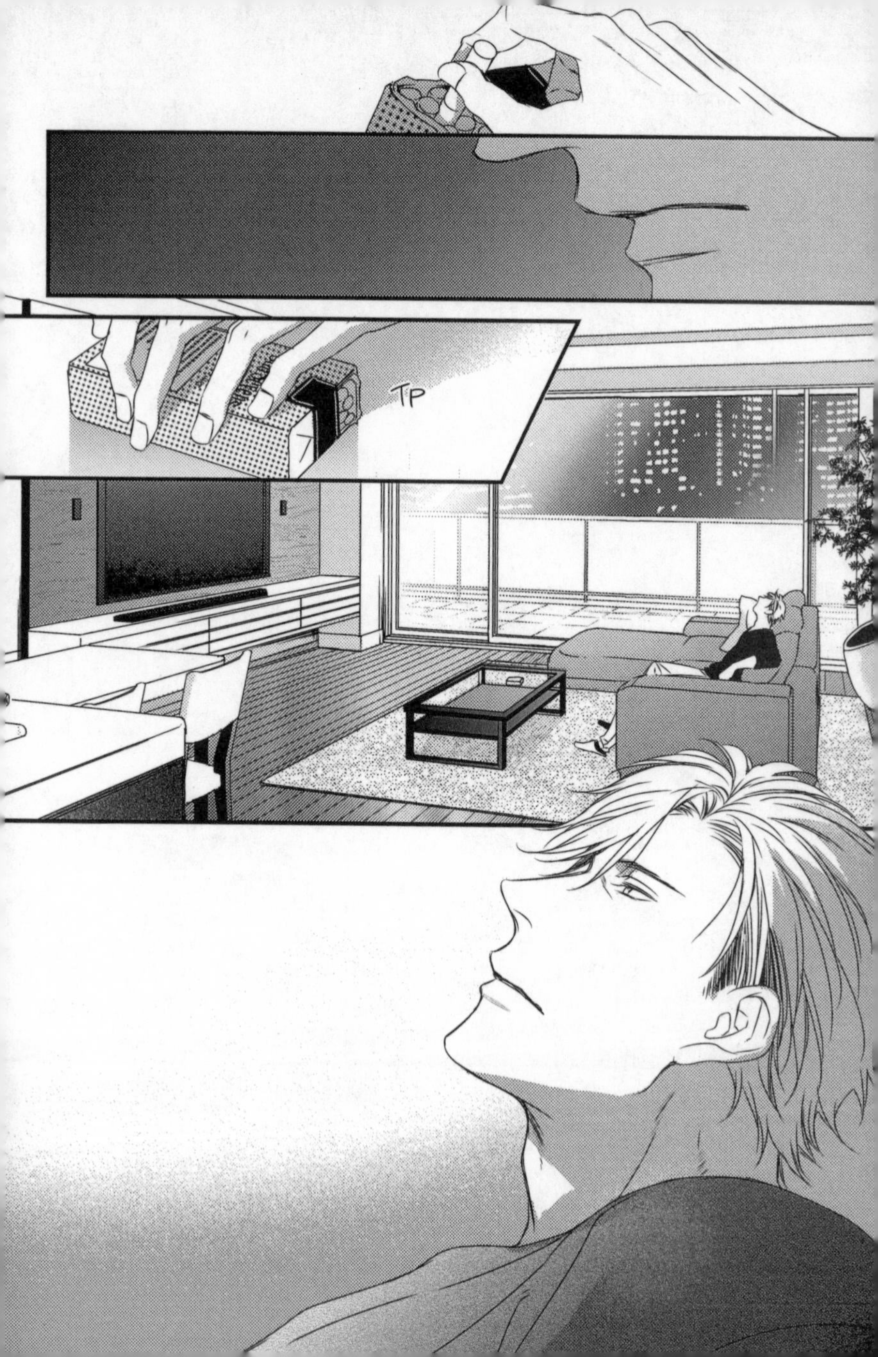
TP

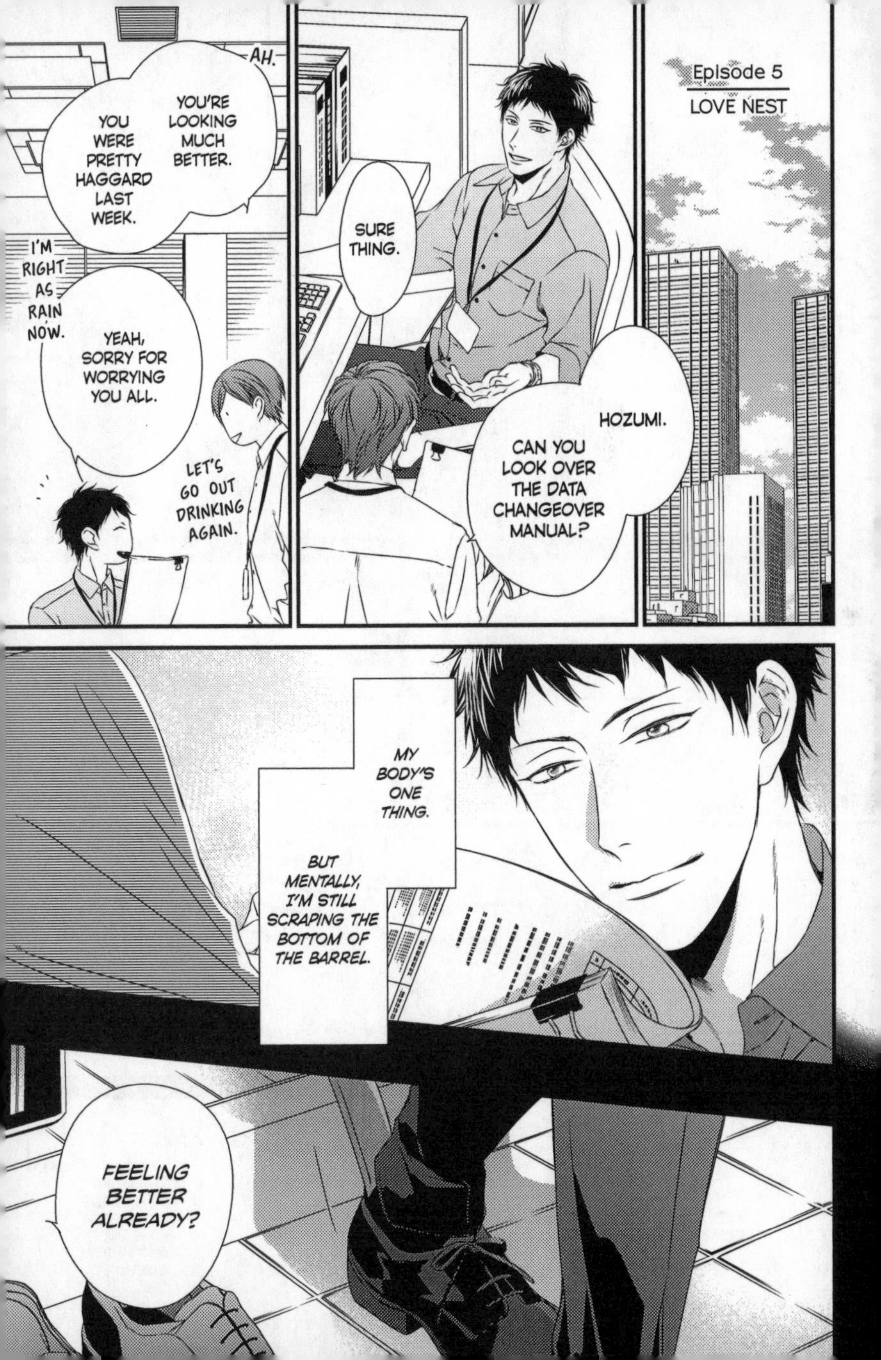
Episode 5
LOVE NEST
HOZUMI. CAN YOU LOOK OVER THE DATA CHANGEOVER MANUAL?
SURE THING.
AH.
YOU'RE LOOKING MUCH BETTER.
YOU WERE PRETTY HAGGARD LAST WEEK.
YEAH, SORRY FOR WORRYING YOU ALL.
I'M RIGHT AS RAIN NOW.
LET'S GO OUT DRINKING AGAIN.
MY BODY'S ONE THING.
BUT MENTALLY, I'M STILL SCRAPING THE BOTTOM OF THE BARREL.
FEELING BETTER ALREADY?

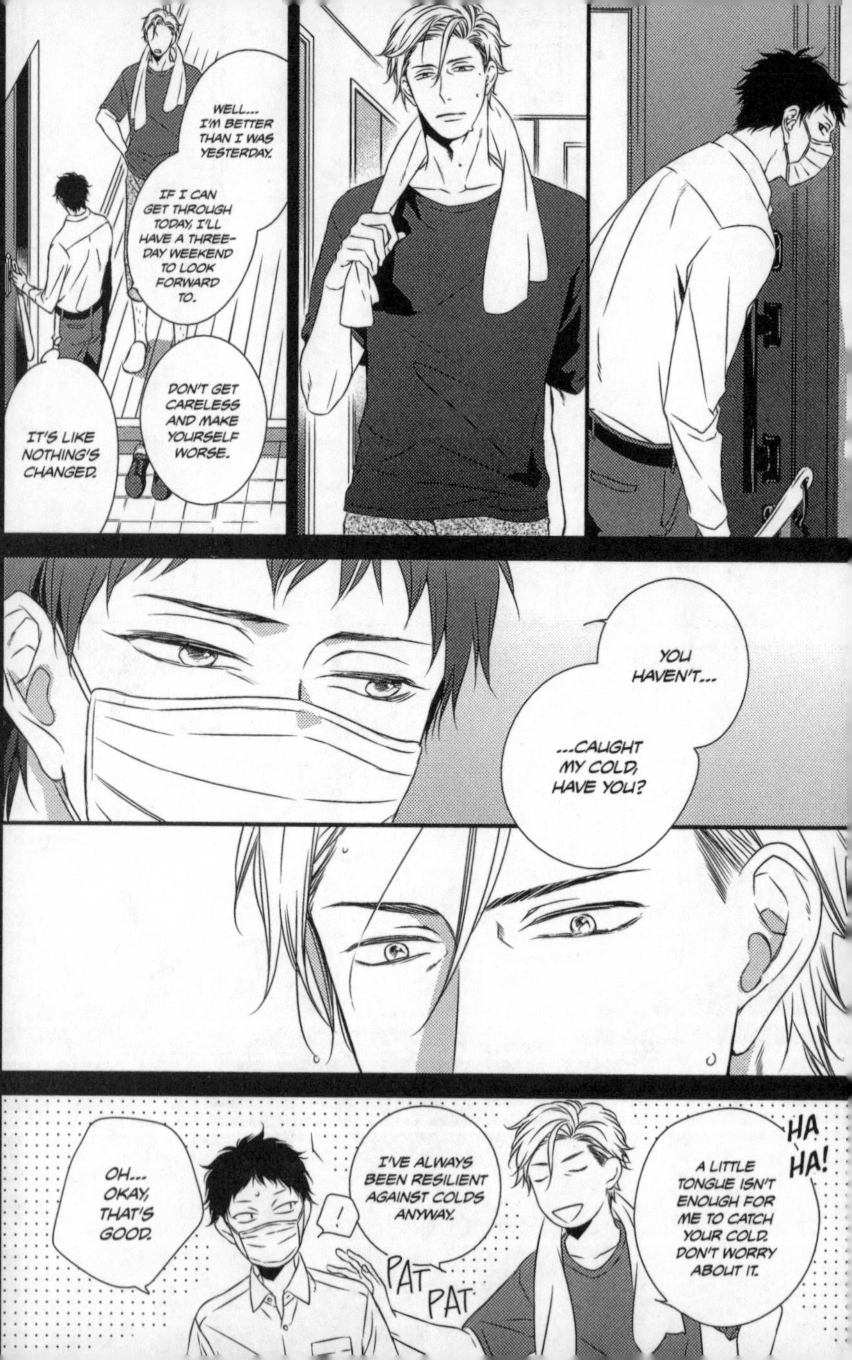
WELL... I'M BETTER THAN I WAS YESTERDAY.
IF I CAN GET THROUGH TODAY, I'LL HAVE A THREE-DAY WEEKEND TO LOOK FORWARD TO.
DON'T GET CARELESS AND MAKE YOURSELF WORSE.
IT'S LIKE NOTHING'S CHANGED.
YOU HAVEN'T...
...CAUGHT MY COLD, HAVE YOU?
HA HA!
A LITTLE TONGUE ISN'T ENOUGH FOR ME TO CATCH YOUR COLD. DON'T WORRY ABOUT IT.
I'VE ALWAYS BEEN RESILIENT AGAINST COLDS ANYWAY.
!
PAT PAT
OH... OKAY, THAT'S GOOD.

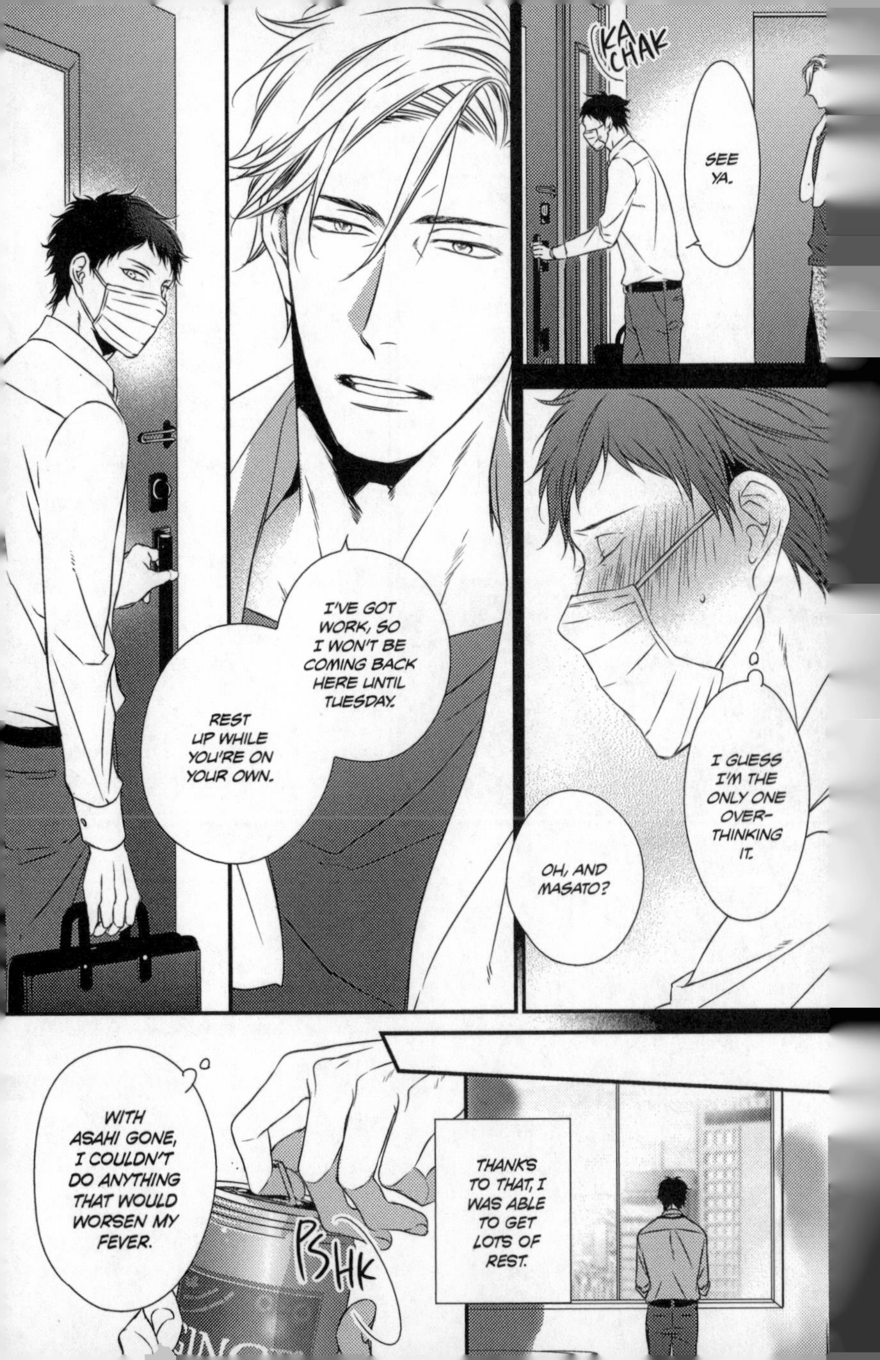
KA CHAK
SEE YA.
I GUESS I'M THE ONLY ONE OVER-THINKING IT.
OH, AND MASATO?
I'VE GOT WORK, SO I WON'T BE COMING BACK HERE UNTIL TUESDAY.
REST UP WHILE YOU'RE ON YOUR OWN.
WITH ASAHI GONE, I COULDN'T DO ANYTHING THAT WOULD WORSEN MY FEVER.
PSHK
THANKS TO THAT, I WAS ABLE TO GET LOTS OF REST.

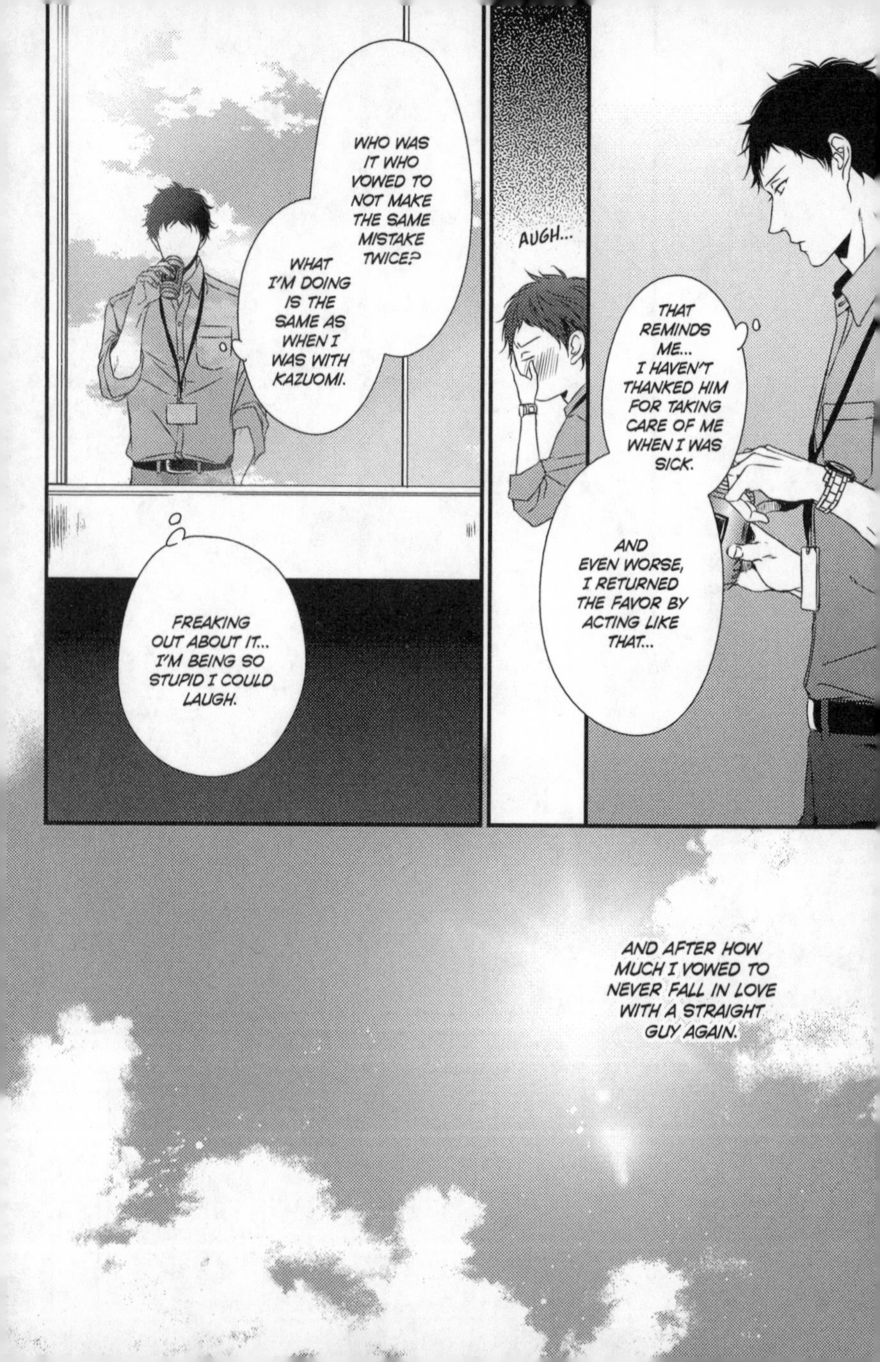
AUGH...
THAT REMINDS ME... I HAVEN'T THANKED HIM FOR TAKING CARE OF ME WHEN I WAS SICK.
AND EVEN WORSE, I RETURNED THE FAVOR BY ACTING LIKE THAT...
WHO WAS IT WHO VOWED TO NOT MAKE THE SAME MISTAKE TWICE?
WHAT I'M DOING IS THE SAME AS WHEN I WAS WITH KAZUOMI.
FREAKING OUT ABOUT IT... I'M BEING SO STUPID I COULD LAUGH.
AND AFTER HOW MUCH I VOWED TO NEVER FALL IN LOVE WITH A STRAIGHT GUY AGAIN.

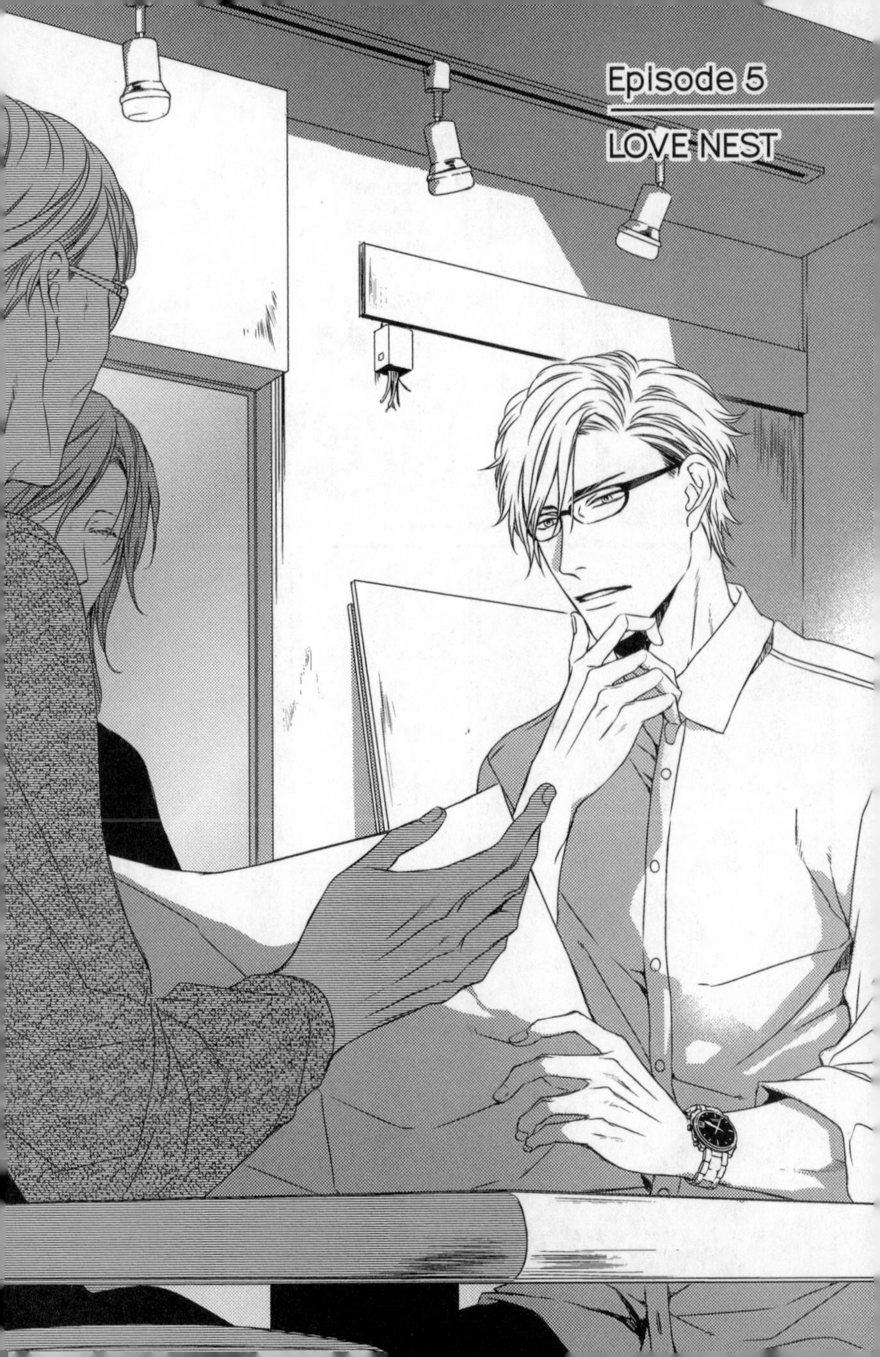
Episode 5
LOVE NEST

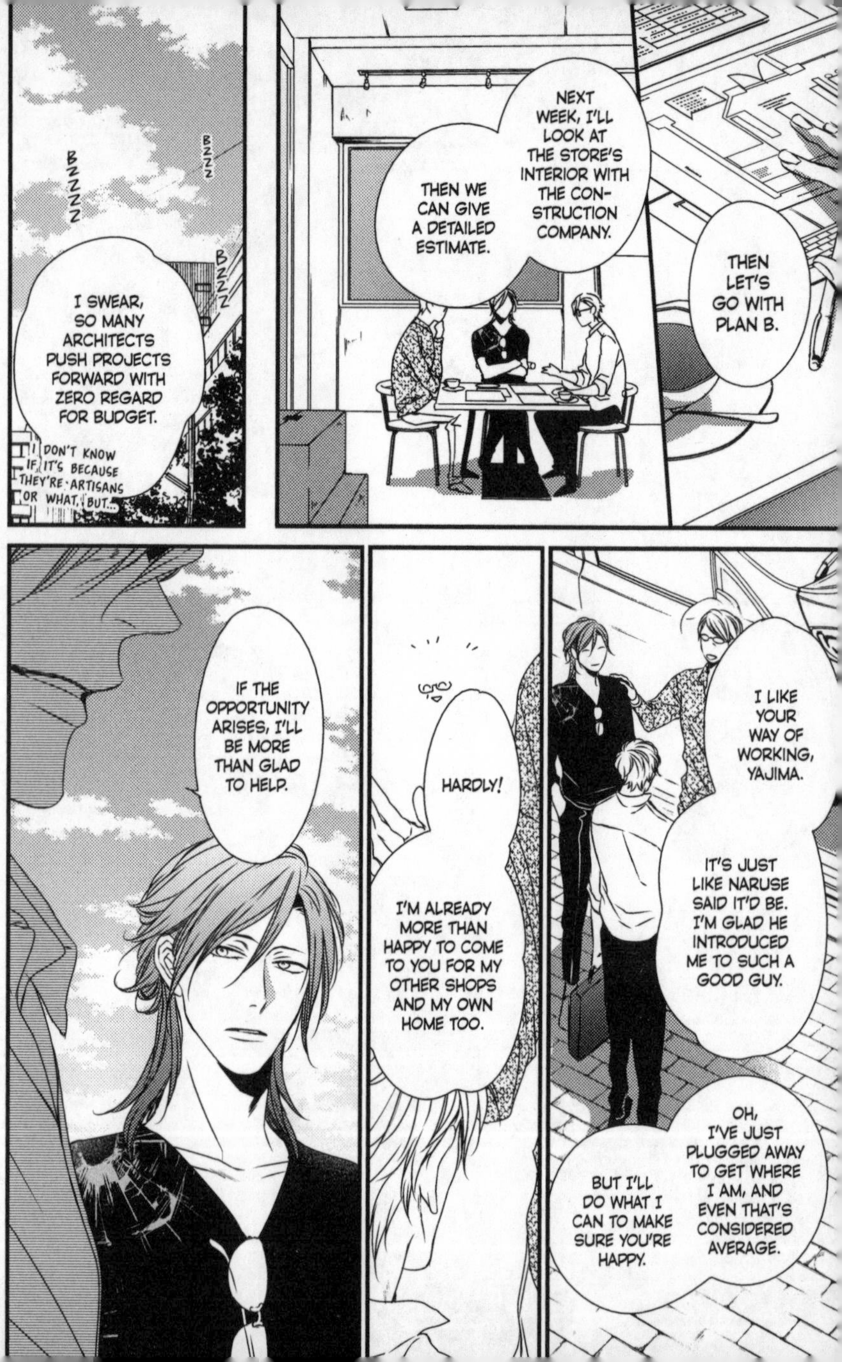
THEN LET'S GO WITH PLAN B.
NEXT WEEK, I'LL LOOK AT THE STORE'S INTERIOR WITH THE CON-STRUCTION COMPANY.
THEN WE CAN GIVE A DETAILED ESTIMATE.
BZZZ
BZZZZ
BZZZ
I SWEAR, SO MANY ARCHITECTS PUSH PROJECTS FORWARD WITH ZERO REGARD FOR BUDGET.
I DON'T KNOW IF IT'S BECAUSE THEY'RE ARTISANS OR WHAT, BUT...
I LIKE YOUR WAY OF WORKING, YAJIMA.
IT'S JUST LIKE NARUSE SAID IT'D BE. I'M GLAD HE INTRODUCED ME TO SUCH A GOOD GUY.
OH, I'VE JUST PLUGGED AWAY TO GET WHERE I AM, AND EVEN THAT'S CONSIDERED AVERAGE.
BUT I'LL DO WHAT I CAN TO MAKE SURE YOU'RE HAPPY.
HARDLY!
I'M ALREADY MORE THAN HAPPY TO COME TO YOU FOR MY OTHER SHOPS AND MY OWN HOME TOO.
IF THE OPPORTUNITY ARISES, I'LL BE MORE THAN GLAD TO HELP.

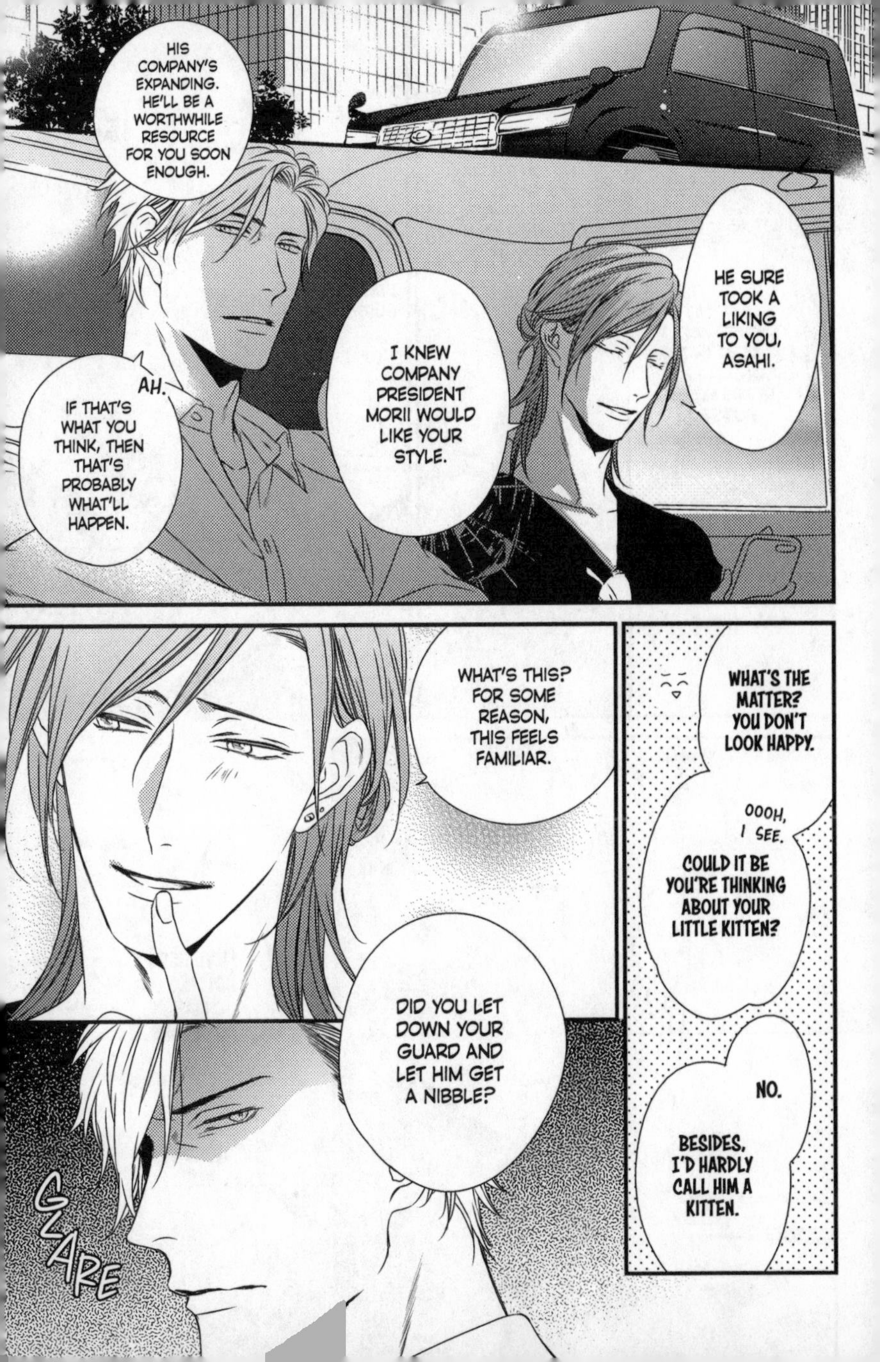

HIS COMPANY'S EXPANDING. HE'LL BE A WORTHWHILE RESOURCE FOR YOU SOON ENOUGH.
HE SURE TOOK A LIKING TO YOU, ASAHI.
I KNEW COMPANY PRESIDENT MORII WOULD LIKE YOUR STYLE.
AH.
IF THAT'S WHAT YOU THINK, THEN THAT'S PROBABLY WHAT'LL HAPPEN.
WHAT'S THE MATTER? YOU DON'T LOOK HAPPY.
OOOH, I SEE.
COULD IT BE YOU'RE THINKING ABOUT YOUR LITTLE KITTEN?
NO.
BESIDES, I'D HARDLY CALL HIM A KITTEN.
WHAT'S THIS? FOR SOME REASON, THIS FEELS FAMILIAR.
DID YOU LET DOWN YOUR GUARD AND LET HIM GET A NIBBLE?
GLARE

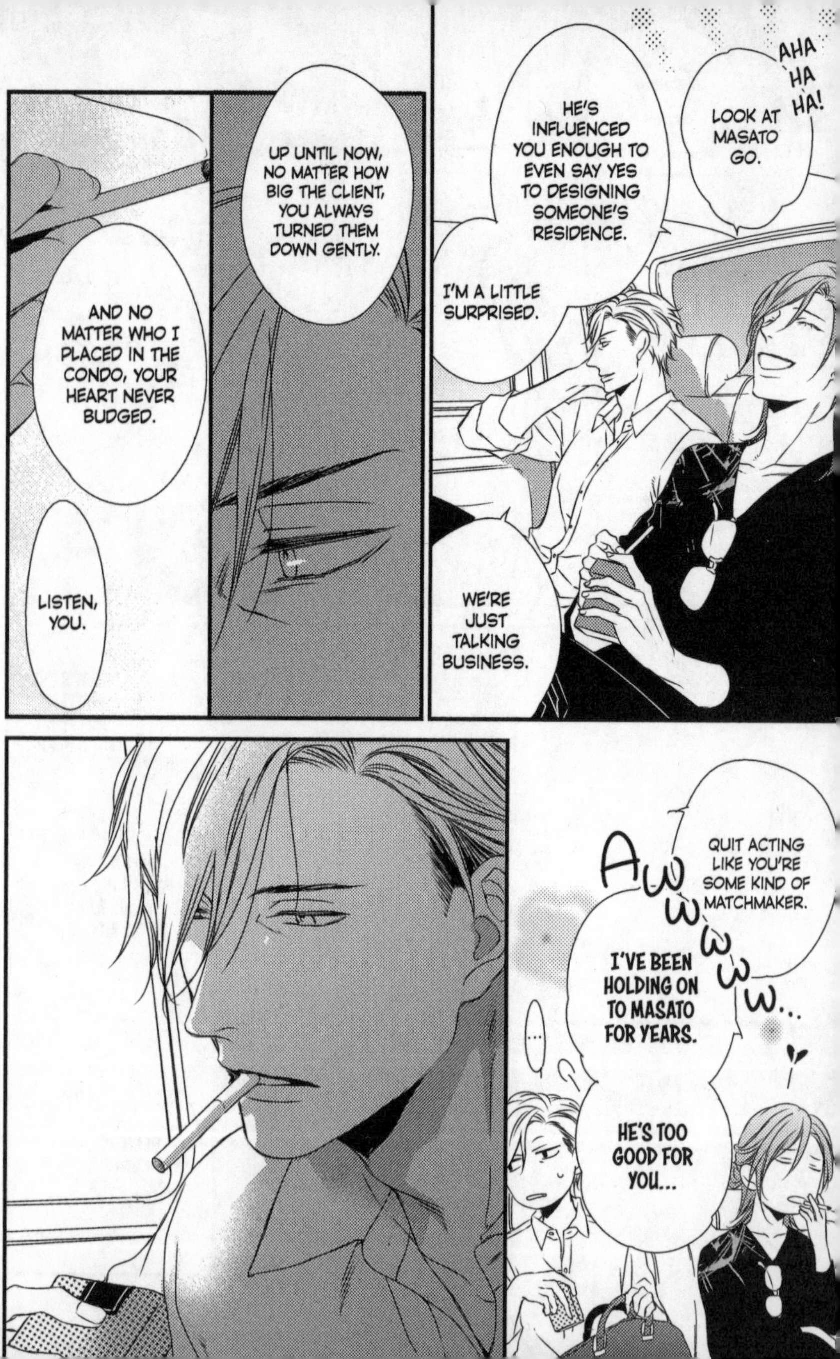
AHA HA HA!
LOOK AT MASATO GO.
HE'S INFLUENCED YOU ENOUGH TO EVEN SAY YES TO DESIGNING SOMEONE'S RESIDENCE.
I'M A LITTLE SURPRISED.
WE'RE JUST TALKING BUSINESS.
UP UNTIL NOW, NO MATTER HOW BIG THE CLIENT, YOU ALWAYS TURNED THEM DOWN GENTLY.
AND NO MATTER WHO I PLACED IN THE CONDO, YOUR HEART NEVER BUDGED.
LISTEN, YOU.
QUIT ACTING LIKE YOU'RE SOME KIND OF MATCHMAKER.
AWWWWWW...
I'VE BEEN HOLDING ON TO MASATO FOR YEARS.
HE'S TOO GOOD FOR YOU...
...

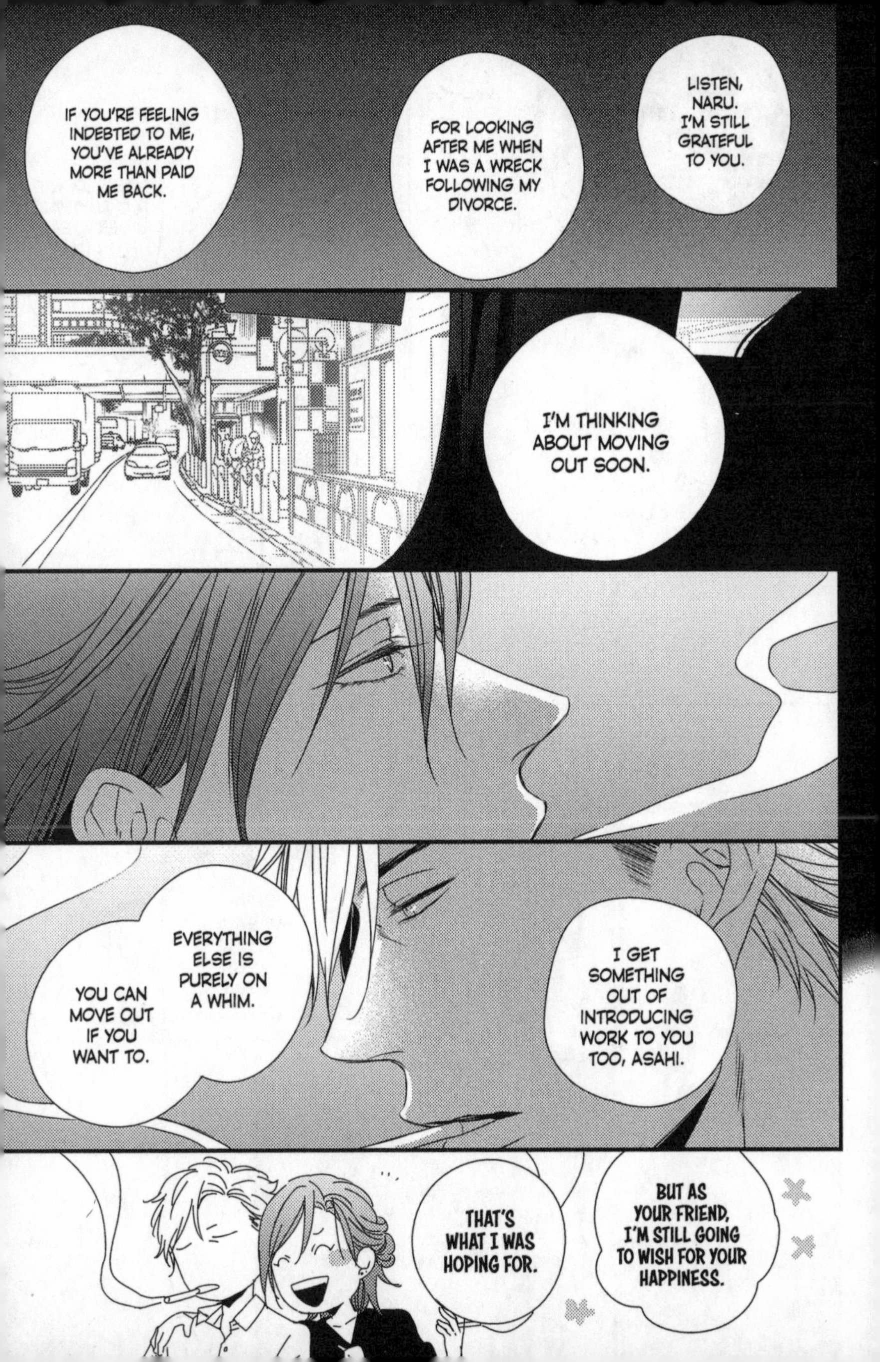
LISTEN, NARU. I'M STILL GRATEFUL TO YOU.
FOR LOOKING AFTER ME WHEN I WAS A WRECK FOLLOWING MY DIVORCE.
IF YOU'RE FEELING INDEBTED TO ME, YOU'VE ALREADY MORE THAN PAID ME BACK.
I'M THINKING ABOUT MOVING OUT SOON.
I GET SOMETHING OUT OF INTRODUCING WORK TO YOU TOO, ASAHI.
EVERYTHING ELSE IS PURELY ON A WHIM.
YOU CAN MOVE OUT IF YOU WANT TO.
BUT AS YOUR FRIEND, I'M STILL GOING TO WISH FOR YOUR HAPPINESS.
THAT'S WHAT I WAS HOPING FOR.

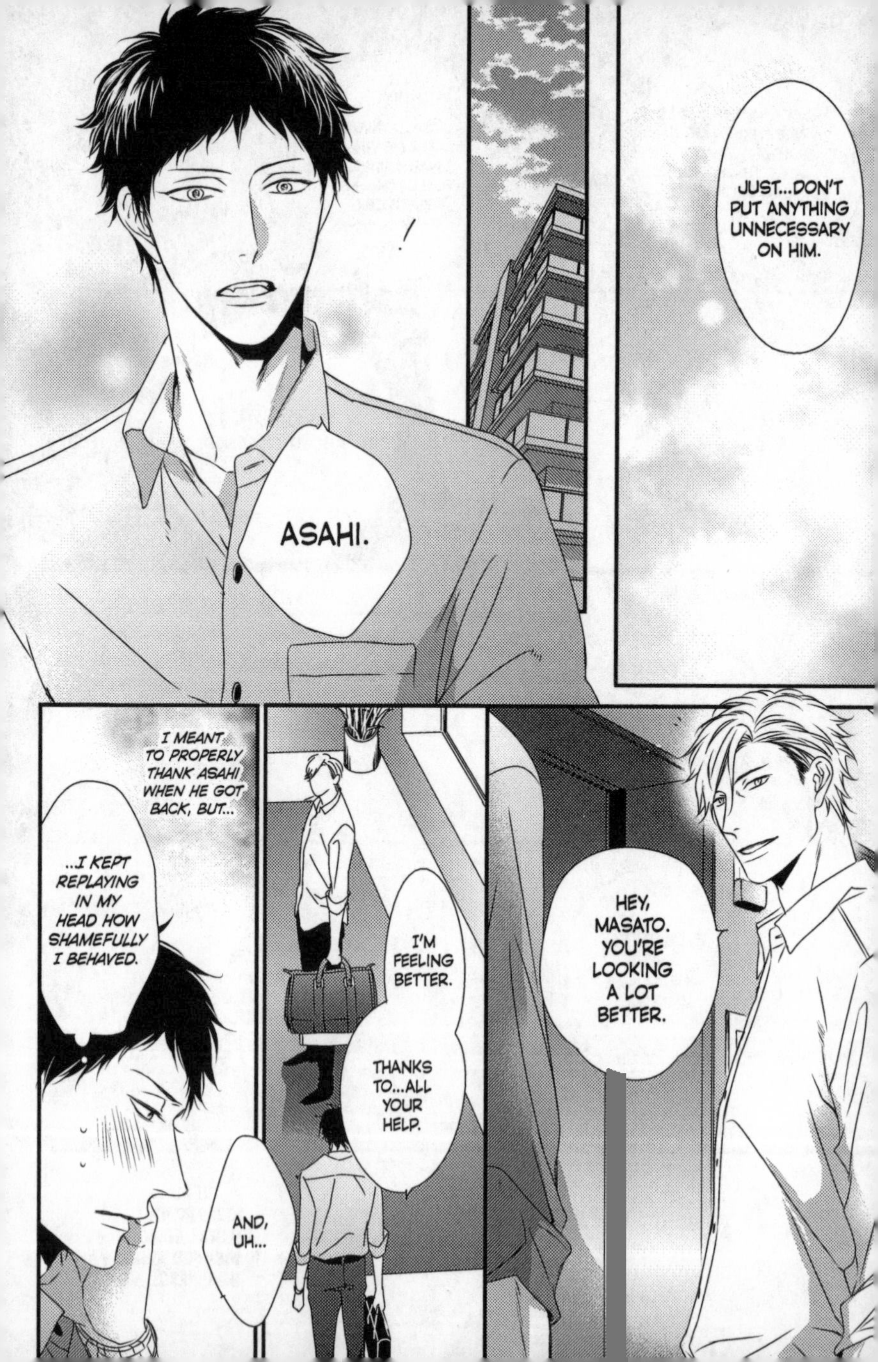
JUST...DON'T PUT ANYTHING UNNECESSARY ON HIM.
ASAHI.
HEY, MASATO. YOU'RE LOOKING A LOT BETTER.
I'M FEELING BETTER.
THANKS TO...ALL YOUR HELP.
AND, UH...
I MEANT TO PROPERLY THANK ASAHI WHEN HE GOT BACK, BUT...
...I KEPT REPLAYING IN MY HEAD HOW SHAMEFULLY I BEHAVED.

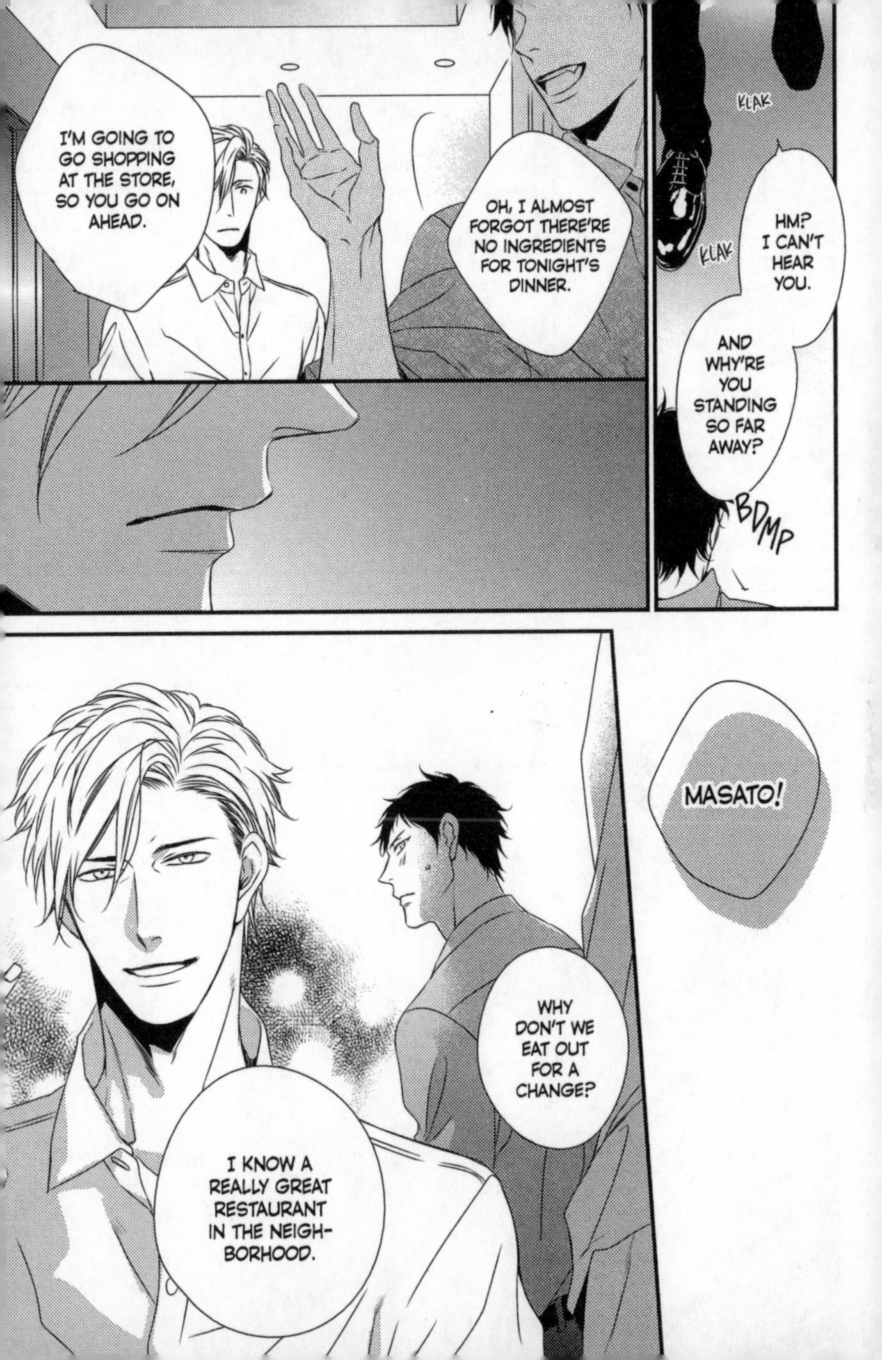
KLAK
KLAK
HM? I CAN'T HEAR YOU.
AND WHY'RE YOU STANDING SO FAR AWAY?
BDMP
OH, I ALMOST FORGOT THERE'RE NO INGREDIENTS FOR TONIGHT'S DINNER.
I'M GOING TO GO SHOPPING AT THE STORE, SO YOU GO ON AHEAD.
MASATO!
WHY DON'T WE EAT OUT FOR A CHANGE?
I KNOW A REALLY GREAT RESTAURANT IN THE NEIGH-BORHOOD.

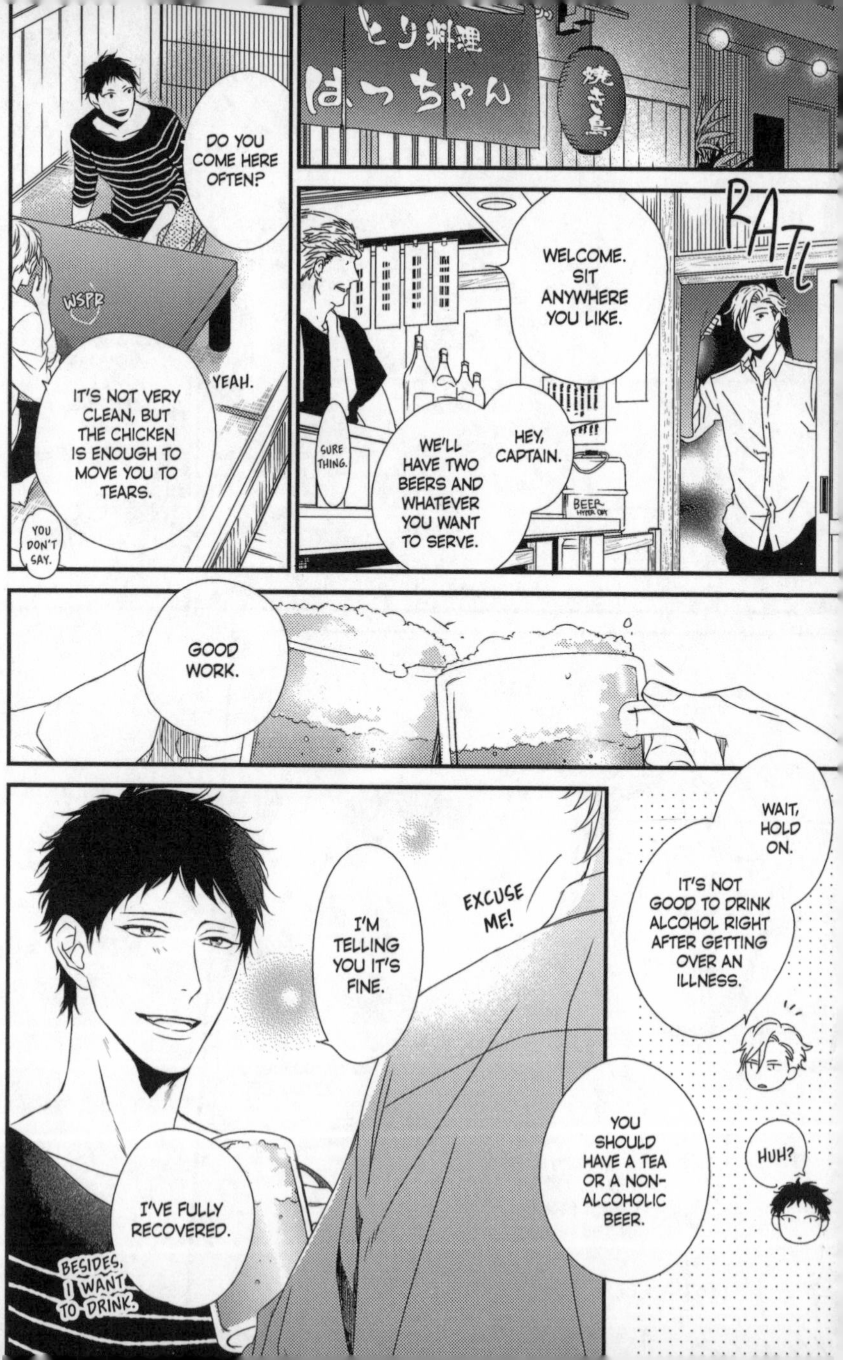

とり料理
はっちゃん
焼き鳥
RATTL
WELCOME. SIT ANYWHERE YOU LIKE.
HEY, CAPTAIN.
WE'LL HAVE TWO BEERS AND WHATEVER YOU WANT TO SERVE.
SURE THING.
DO YOU COME HERE OFTEN?
YEAH.
WSPR
IT'S NOT VERY CLEAN, BUT THE CHICKEN IS ENOUGH TO MOVE YOU TO TEARS.
YOU DON'T SAY.
GOOD WORK.
WAIT, HOLD ON.
IT'S NOT GOOD TO DRINK ALCOHOL RIGHT AFTER GETTING OVER AN ILLNESS.
YOU SHOULD HAVE A TEA OR A NON-ALCOHOLIC BEER.
HUH?
EXCUSE ME!
I'M TELLING YOU IT'S FINE.
I'VE FULLY RECOVERED.
BESIDES, I WANT TO DRINK.

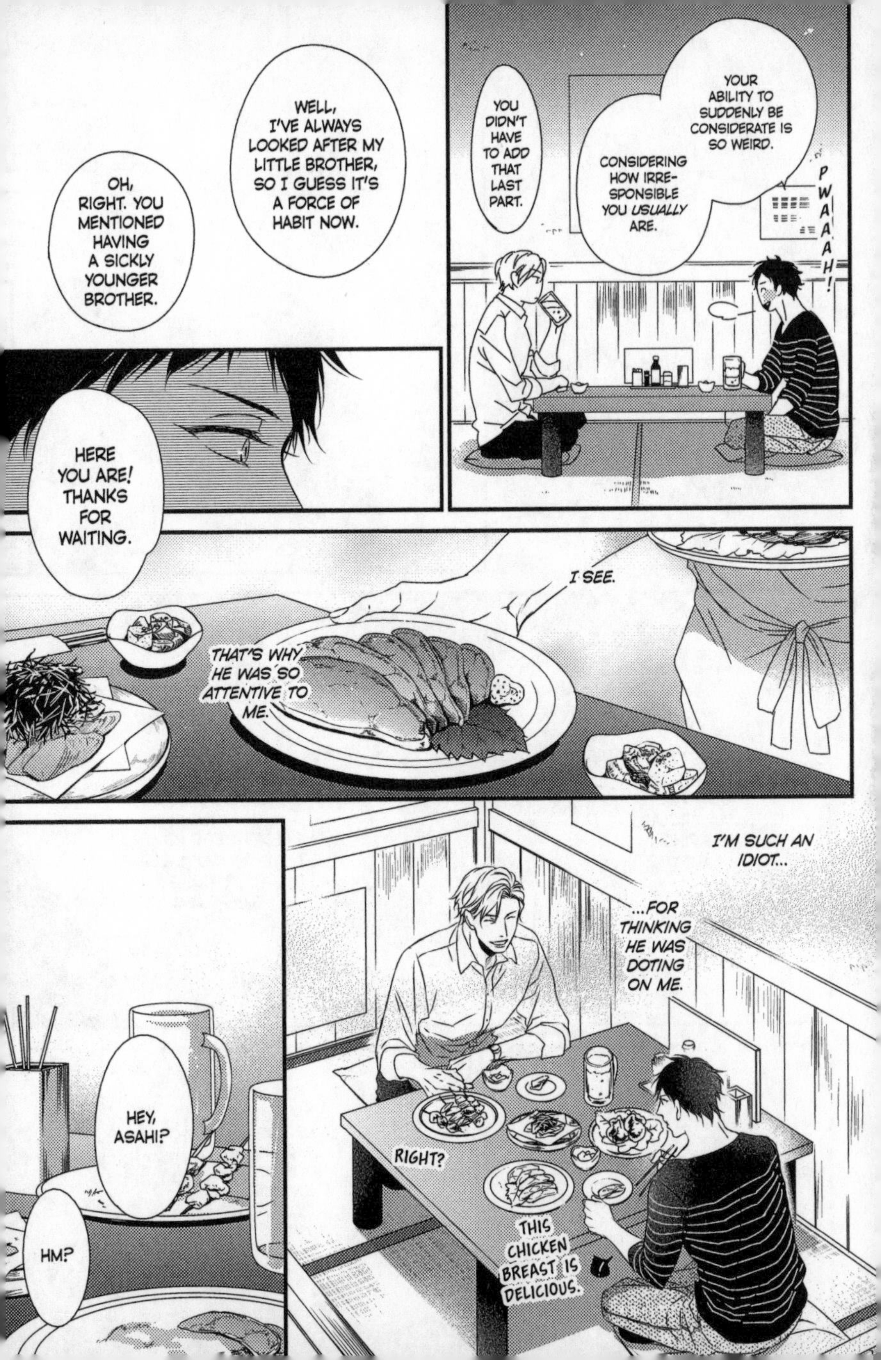
YOUR ABILITY TO SUDDENLY BE CONSIDERATE IS SO WEIRD.
CONSIDERING HOW IRRE-SPONSIBLE YOU *USUALLY* ARE.
PWAAAH!
YOU DIDN'T HAVE TO ADD THAT LAST PART.
WELL, I'VE ALWAYS LOOKED AFTER MY LITTLE BROTHER, SO I GUESS IT'S A FORCE OF HABIT NOW.
OH, RIGHT. YOU MENTIONED HAVING A SICKLY YOUNGER BROTHER.
HERE YOU ARE! THANKS FOR WAITING.
I SEE.
THAT'S WHY HE WAS SO ATTENTIVE TO ME.
I'M SUCH AN IDIOT...
...FOR THINKING HE WAS DOTING ON ME.
RIGHT?
THIS CHICKEN BREAST IS DELICIOUS.
HEY, ASAHI?
HM?

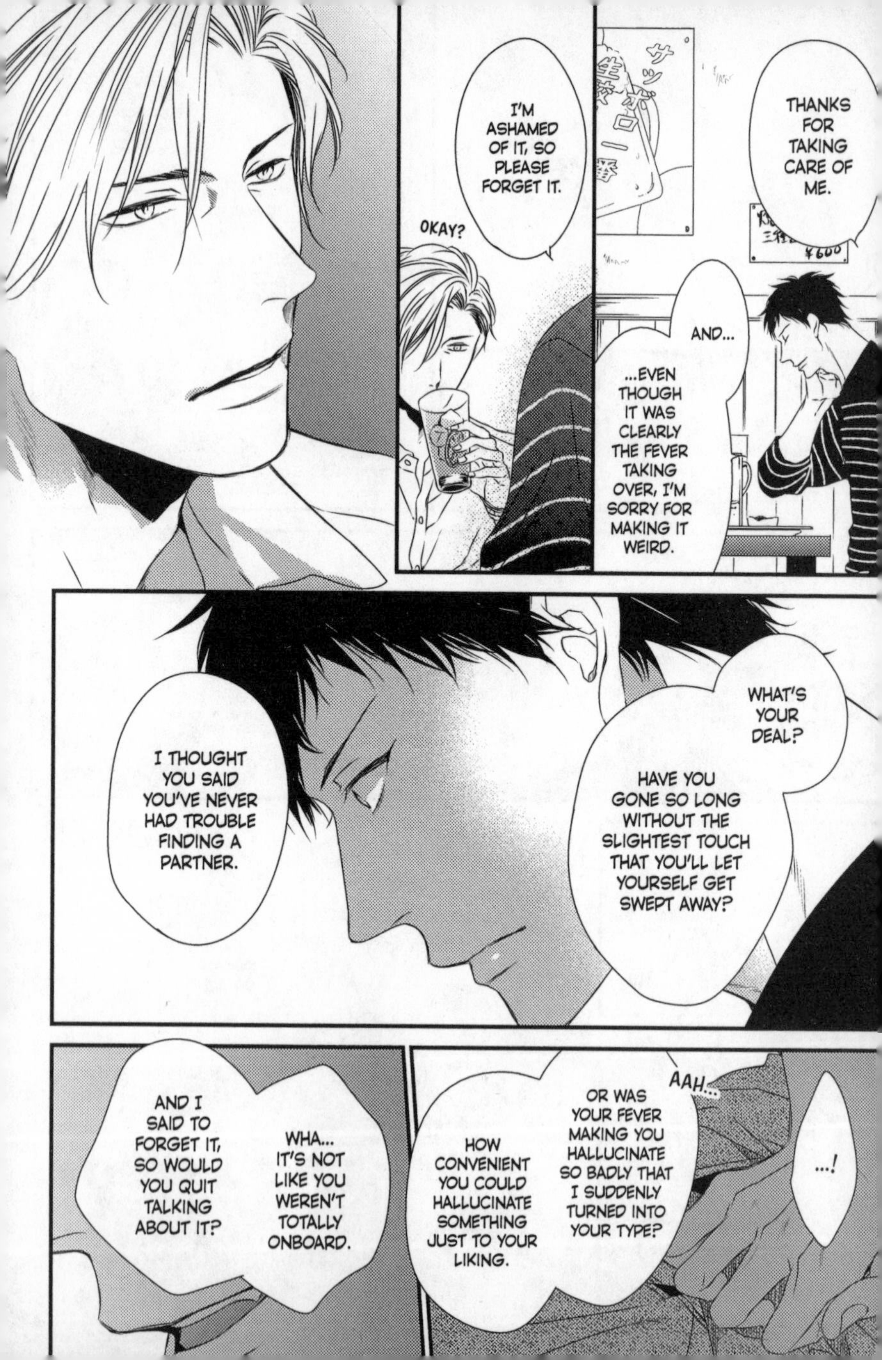
THANKS FOR TAKING CARE OF ME.
AND...
...EVEN THOUGH IT WAS CLEARLY THE FEVER TAKING OVER, I'M SORRY FOR MAKING IT WEIRD.
I'M ASHAMED OF IT, SO PLEASE FORGET IT.
OKAY?
WHAT'S YOUR DEAL?
HAVE YOU GONE SO LONG WITHOUT THE SLIGHTEST TOUCH THAT YOU'LL LET YOURSELF GET SWEPT AWAY?
I THOUGHT YOU SAID YOU'VE NEVER HAD TROUBLE FINDING A PARTNER.
...!
AAH...
OR WAS YOUR FEVER MAKING YOU HALLUCINATE SO BADLY THAT I SUDDENLY TURNED INTO YOUR TYPE?
HOW CONVENIENT YOU COULD HALLUCINATE SOMETHING JUST TO YOUR LIKING.
WHA... IT'S NOT LIKE YOU WEREN'T TOTALLY ONBOARD.
AND I SAID TO FORGET IT, SO WOULD YOU QUIT TALKING ABOUT IT?

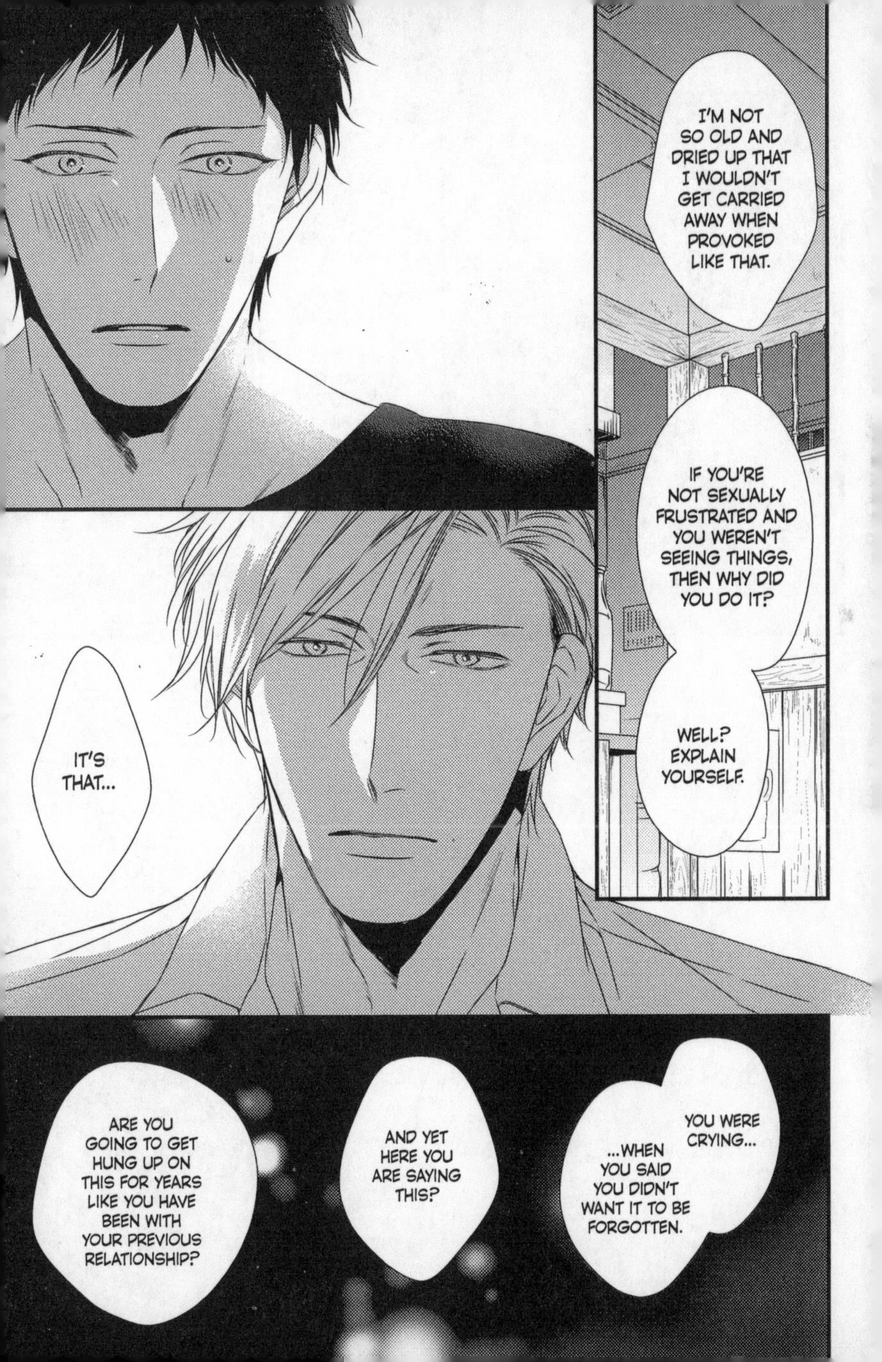
I'M NOT SO OLD AND DRIED UP THAT I WOULDN'T GET CARRIED AWAY WHEN PROVOKED LIKE THAT.
IF YOU'RE NOT SEXUALLY FRUSTRATED AND YOU WEREN'T SEEING THINGS, THEN WHY DID YOU DO IT?
WELL? EXPLAIN YOURSELF.
IT'S THAT...
YOU WERE CRYING...
...WHEN YOU SAID YOU DIDN'T WANT IT TO BE FORGOTTEN.
AND YET HERE YOU ARE SAYING THIS?
ARE YOU GOING TO GET HUNG UP ON THIS FOR YEARS LIKE YOU HAVE BEEN WITH YOUR PREVIOUS RELATIONSHIP?

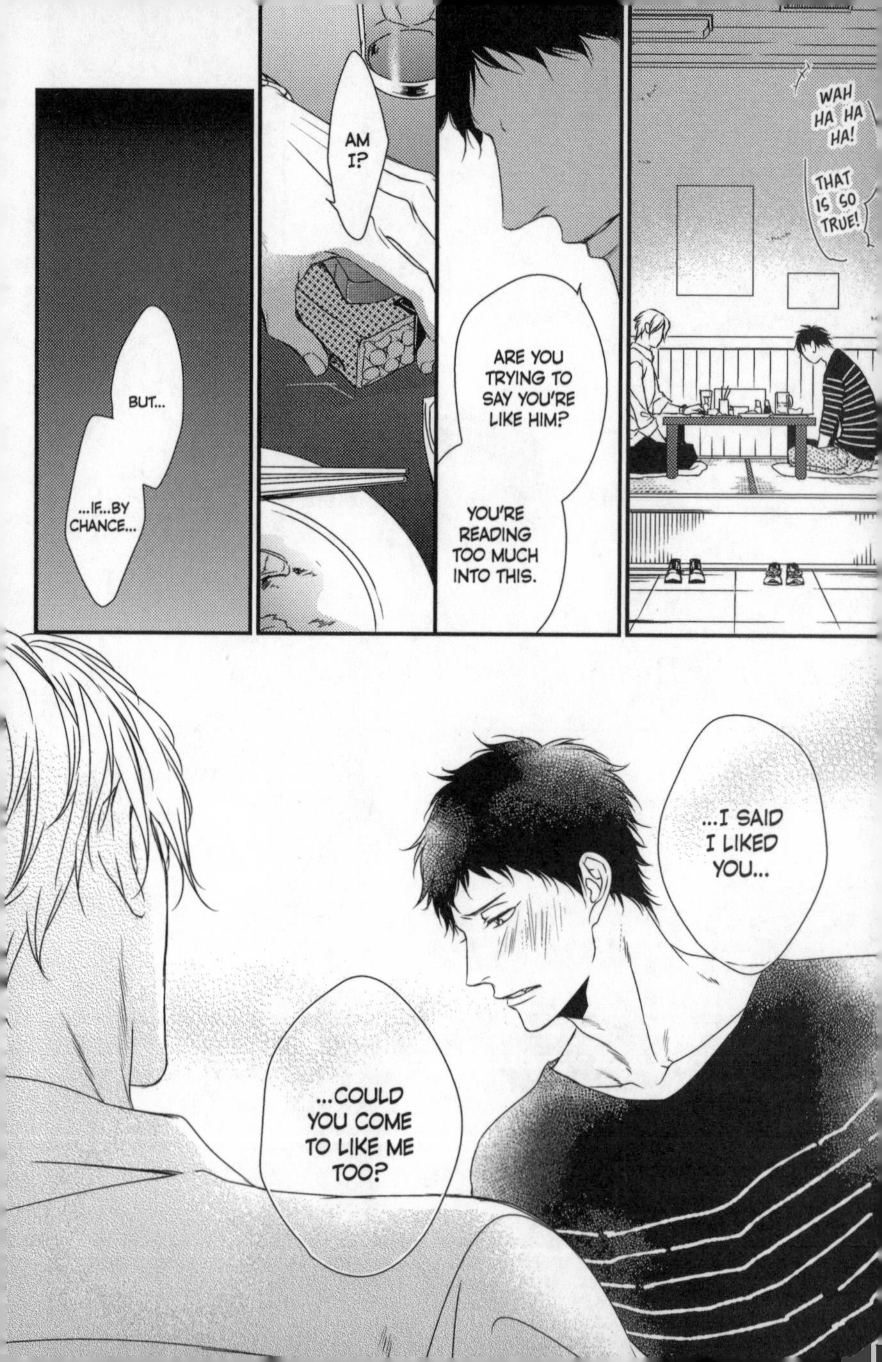
WAH HA HA HA!
THAT IS SO TRUE!
ARE YOU TRYING TO SAY YOU'RE LIKE HIM?
YOU'RE READING TOO MUCH INTO THIS.
AM I?
BUT...
...IF...BY CHANCE...
...I SAID I LIKED YOU...
...COULD YOU COME TO LIKE ME TOO?

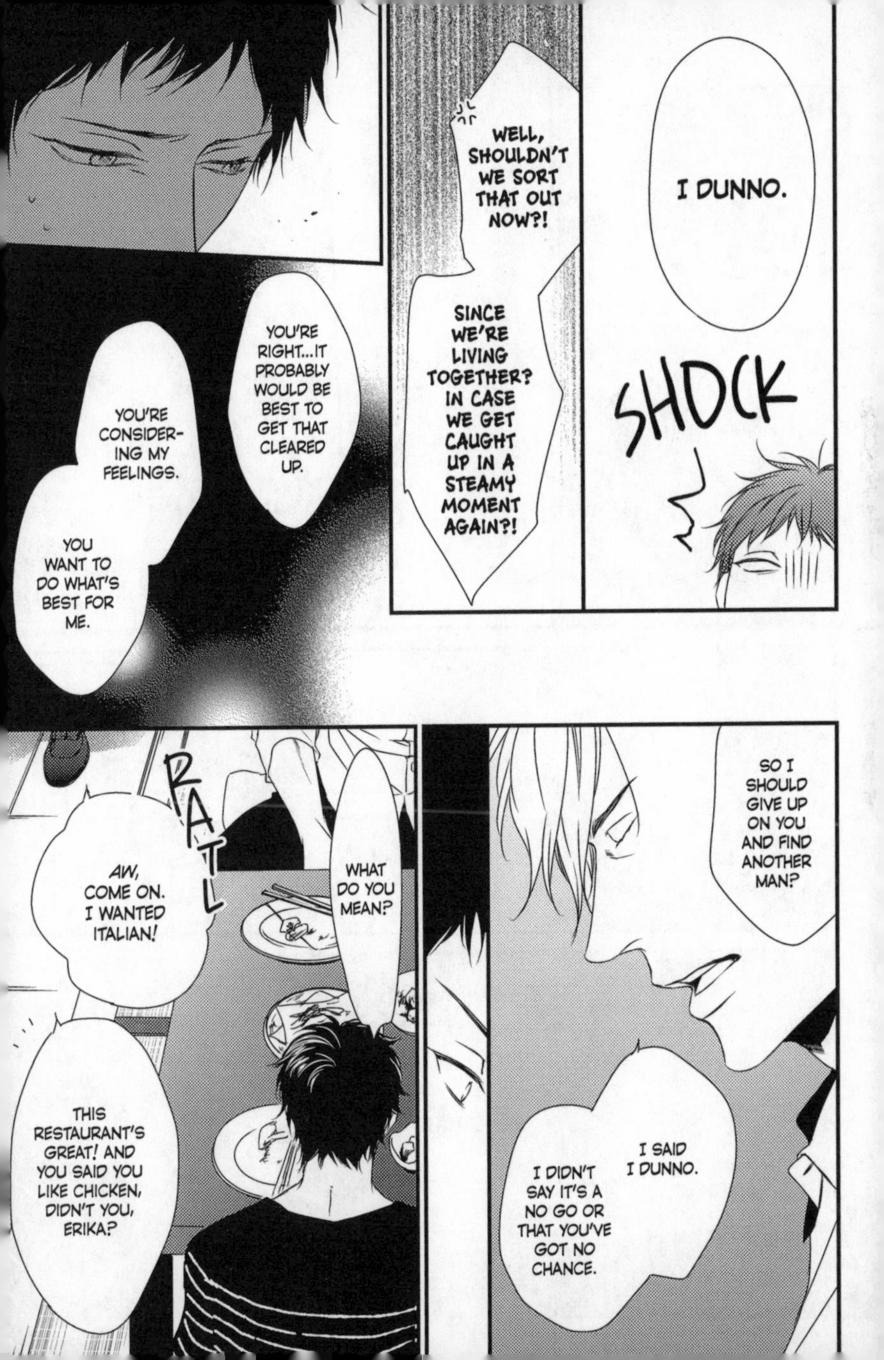
I DUNNO.
SHOCK
WELL, SHOULDN'T WE SORT THAT OUT NOW?!
SINCE WE'RE LIVING TOGETHER? IN CASE WE GET CAUGHT UP IN A STEAMY MOMENT AGAIN?!
YOU'RE RIGHT...IT PROBABLY WOULD BE BEST TO GET THAT CLEARED UP.
YOU'RE CONSIDER-ING MY FEELINGS.
YOU WANT TO DO WHAT'S BEST FOR ME.
SO I SHOULD GIVE UP ON YOU AND FIND ANOTHER MAN?
I SAID I DUNNO.
I DIDN'T SAY IT'S A NO GO OR THAT YOU'VE GOT NO CHANCE.
WHAT DO YOU MEAN?
RATTL
AW, COME ON. I WANTED ITALIAN!
THIS RESTAURANT'S GREAT! AND YOU SAID YOU LIKE CHICKEN, DIDN'T YOU, ERIKA?

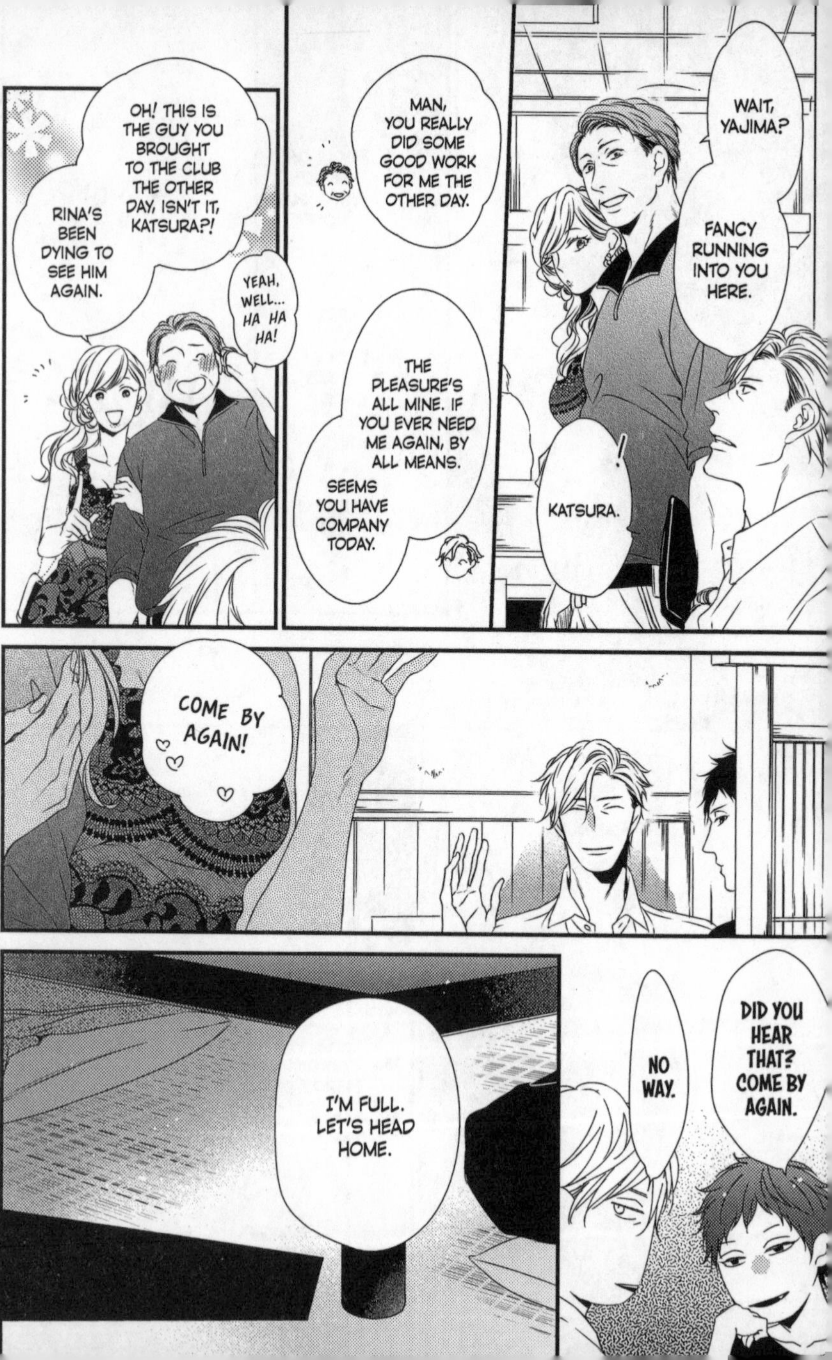
WAIT, YAJIMA?
FANCY RUNNING INTO YOU HERE.
!
KATSURA.
MAN, YOU REALLY DID SOME GOOD WORK FOR ME THE OTHER DAY.
THE PLEASURE'S ALL MINE. IF YOU EVER NEED ME AGAIN, BY ALL MEANS.
SEEMS YOU HAVE COMPANY TODAY.
OH! THIS IS THE GUY YOU BROUGHT TO THE CLUB THE OTHER DAY, ISN'T IT, KATSURA?!
RINA'S BEEN DYING TO SEE HIM AGAIN.
YEAH, WELL... HA HA HA!
COME BY AGAIN!
DID YOU HEAR THAT? COME BY AGAIN.
NO WAY.
I'M FULL. LET'S HEAD HOME.

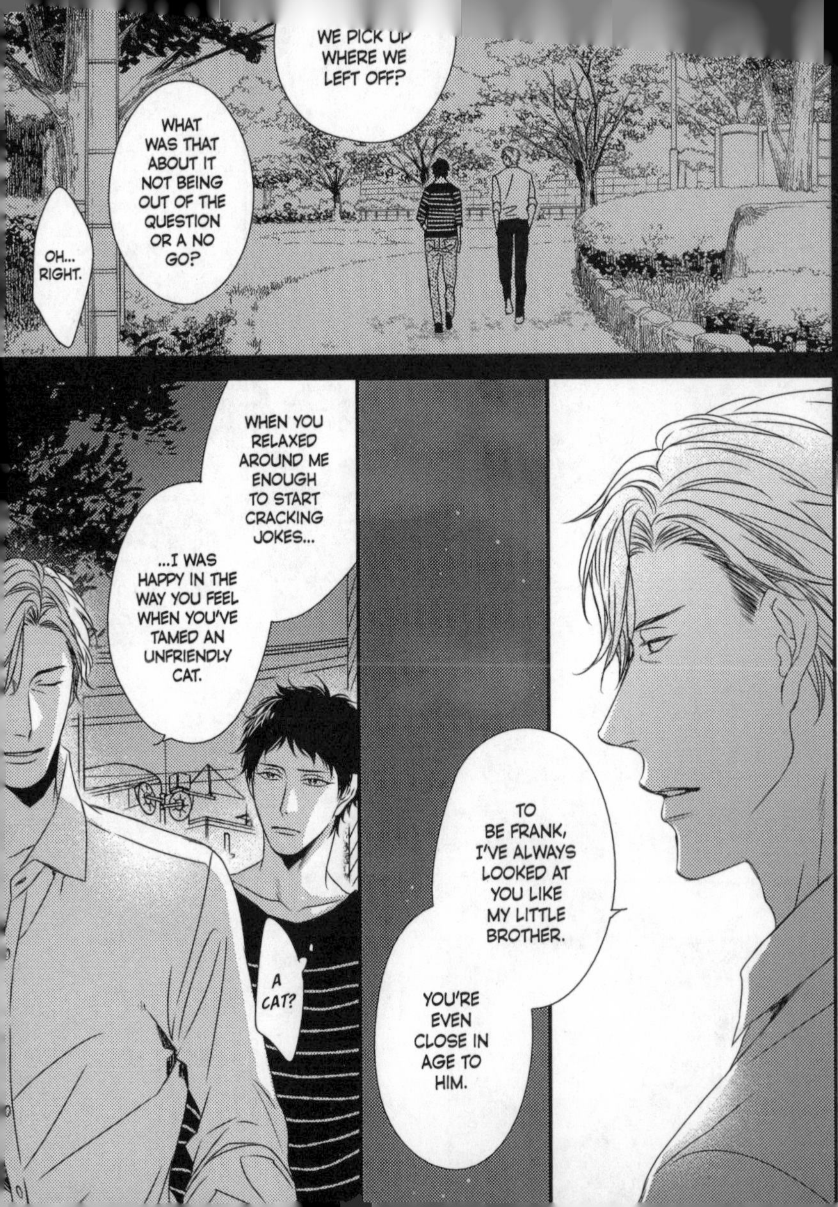
WE PICK UP WHERE WE LEFT OFF?
WHAT WAS THAT ABOUT IT NOT BEING OUT OF THE QUESTION OR A NO GO?
OH... RIGHT.
TO BE FRANK, I'VE ALWAYS LOOKED AT YOU LIKE MY LITTLE BROTHER.
YOU'RE EVEN CLOSE IN AGE TO HIM.
WHEN YOU RELAXED AROUND ME ENOUGH TO START CRACKING JOKES...
...I WAS HAPPY IN THE WAY YOU FEEL WHEN YOU'VE TAMED AN UNFRIENDLY CAT.
A CAT?

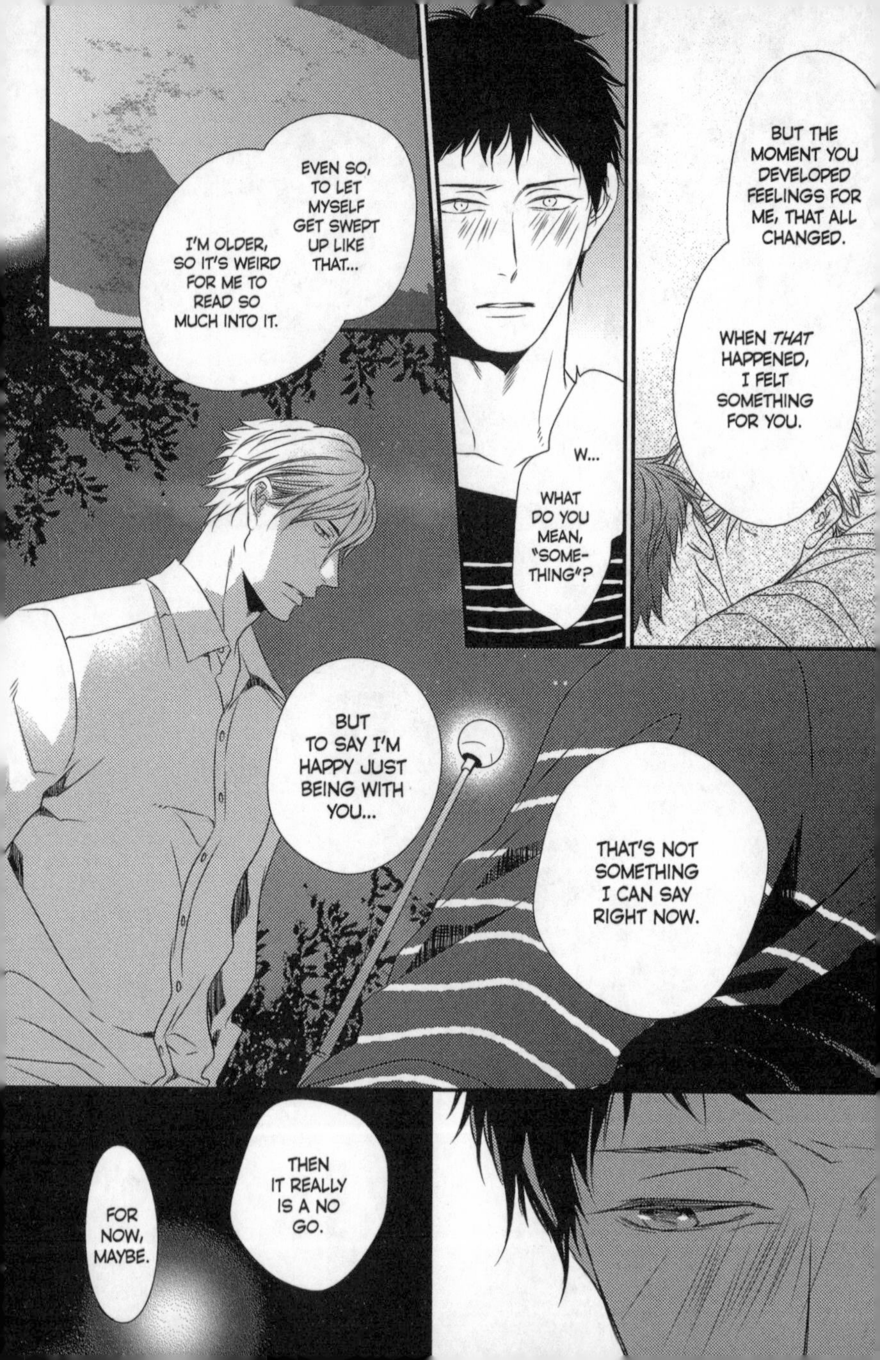
BUT THE MOMENT YOU DEVELOPED FEELINGS FOR ME, THAT ALL CHANGED.
WHEN *THAT* HAPPENED, I FELT SOMETHING FOR YOU.
W...
WHAT DO YOU MEAN, "SOMETHING"?
EVEN SO, TO LET MYSELF GET SWEPT UP LIKE THAT...
I'M OLDER, SO IT'S WEIRD FOR ME TO READ SO MUCH INTO IT.
BUT TO SAY I'M HAPPY JUST BEING WITH YOU...
THAT'S NOT SOMETHING I CAN SAY RIGHT NOW.
THEN IT REALLY IS A NO GO.
FOR NOW, MAYBE.

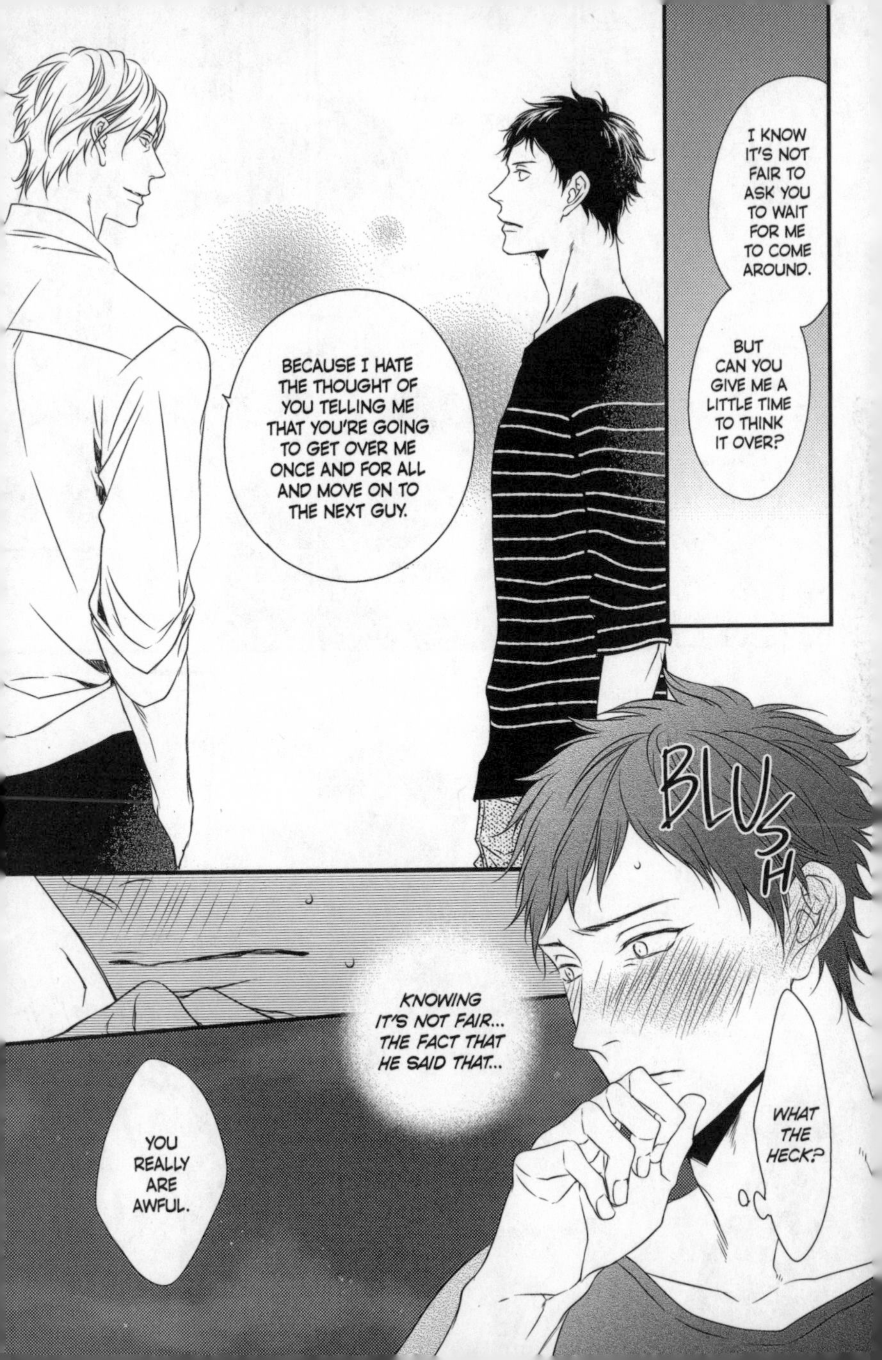
I KNOW IT'S NOT FAIR TO ASK YOU TO WAIT FOR ME TO COME AROUND.
BUT CAN YOU GIVE ME A LITTLE TIME TO THINK IT OVER?
BECAUSE I HATE THE THOUGHT OF YOU TELLING ME THAT YOU'RE GOING TO GET OVER ME ONCE AND FOR ALL AND MOVE ON TO THE NEXT GUY.
BLUSH
WHAT THE HECK?
KNOWING IT'S NOT FAIR... THE FACT THAT HE SAID THAT...
YOU REALLY ARE AWFUL.

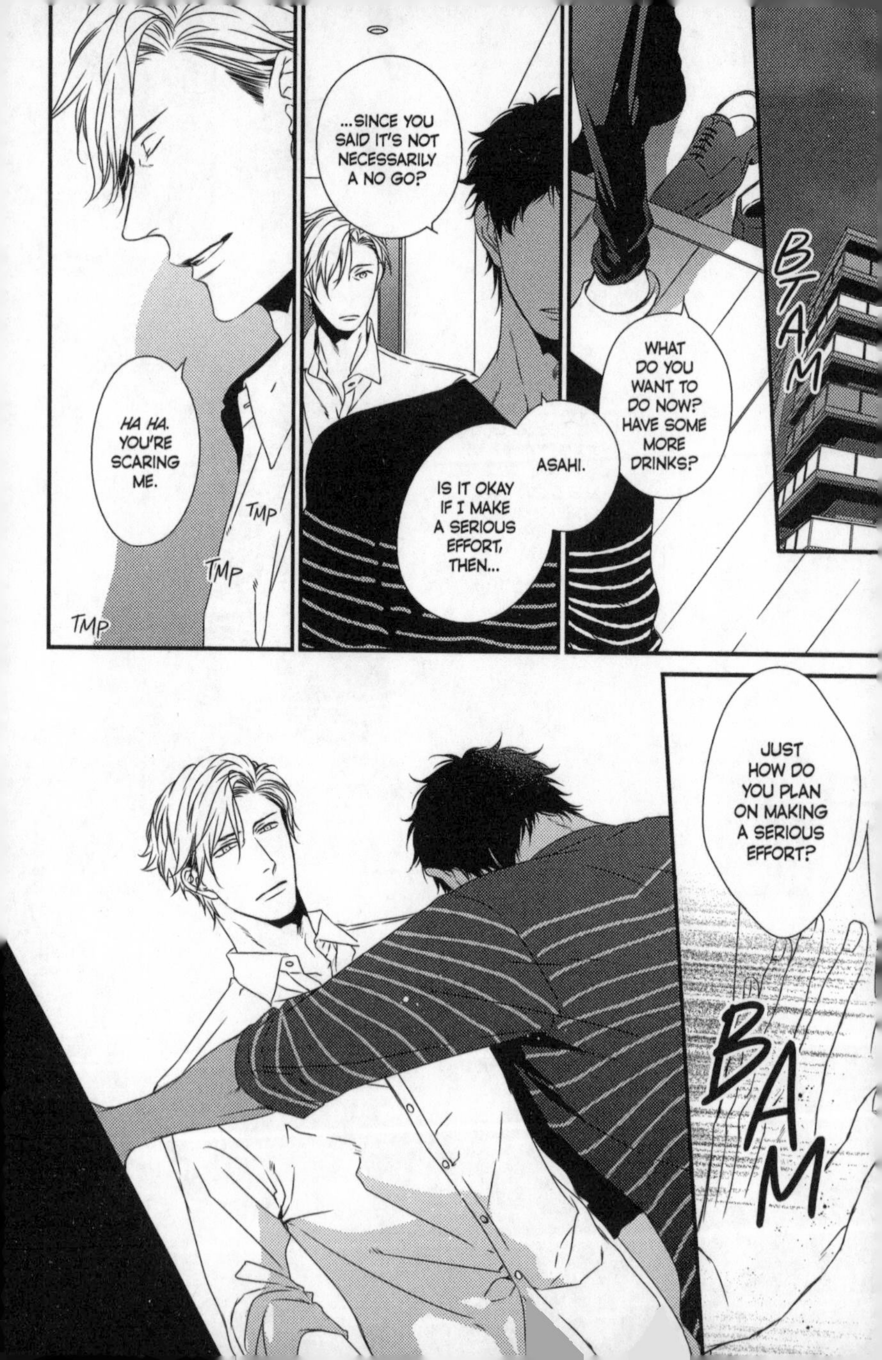
BTAM
WHAT DO YOU WANT TO DO NOW? HAVE SOME MORE DRINKS?
ASAHI.
IS IT OKAY IF I MAKE A SERIOUS EFFORT, THEN...
...SINCE YOU SAID IT'S NOT NECESSARILY A NO GO?
HA HA. YOU'RE SCARING ME.
TMP
TMP
TMP
JUST HOW DO YOU PLAN ON MAKING A SERIOUS EFFORT?
BAM

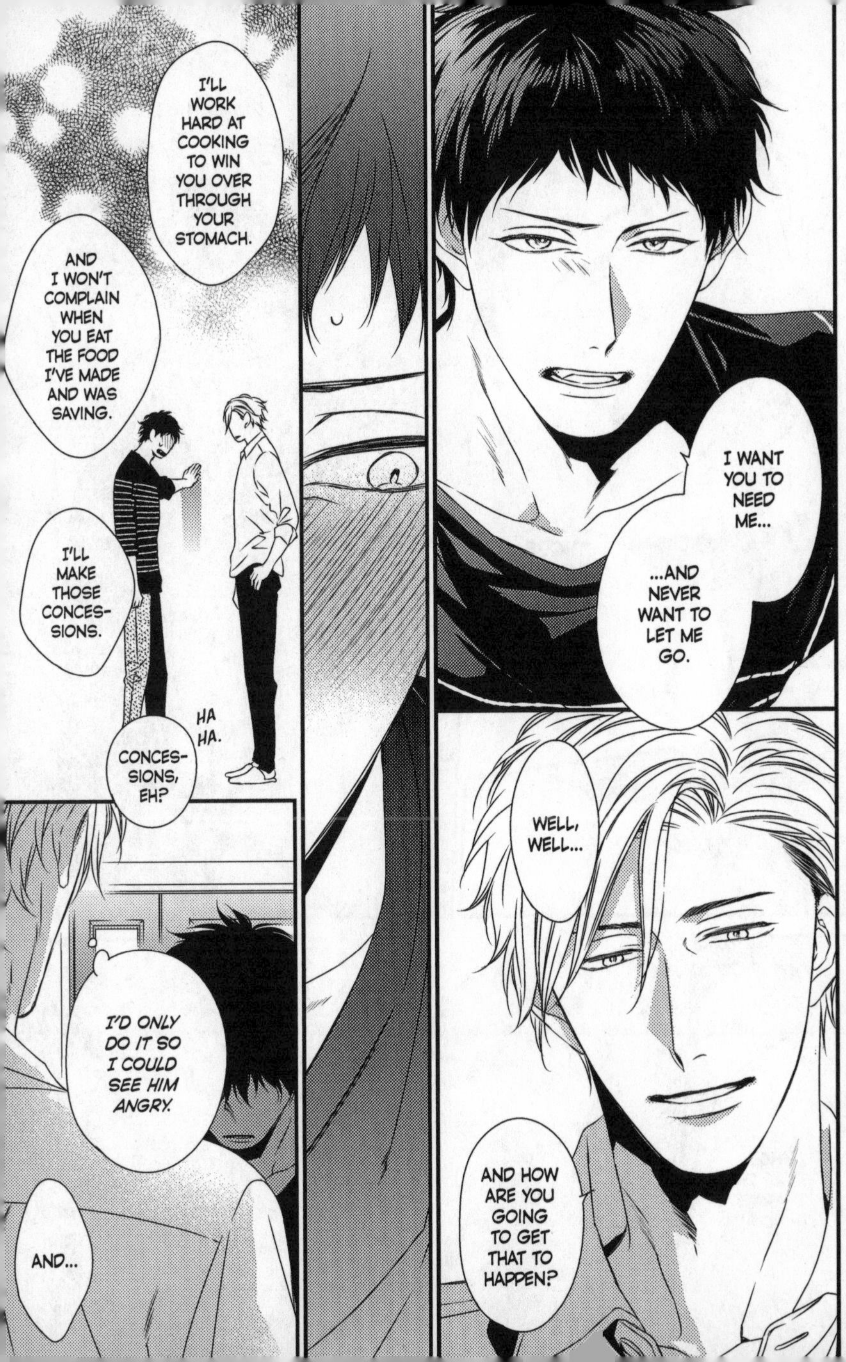
I WANT YOU TO NEED ME...
...AND NEVER WANT TO LET ME GO.
WELL, WELL...
AND HOW ARE YOU GOING TO GET THAT TO HAPPEN?
I'LL WORK HARD AT COOKING TO WIN YOU OVER THROUGH YOUR STOMACH.
AND I WON'T COMPLAIN WHEN YOU EAT THE FOOD I'VE MADE AND WAS SAVING.
I'LL MAKE THOSE CONCES-SIONS.
HA HA.
CONCES-SIONS, EH?
I'D ONLY DO IT SO I COULD SEE HIM ANGRY.
AND...

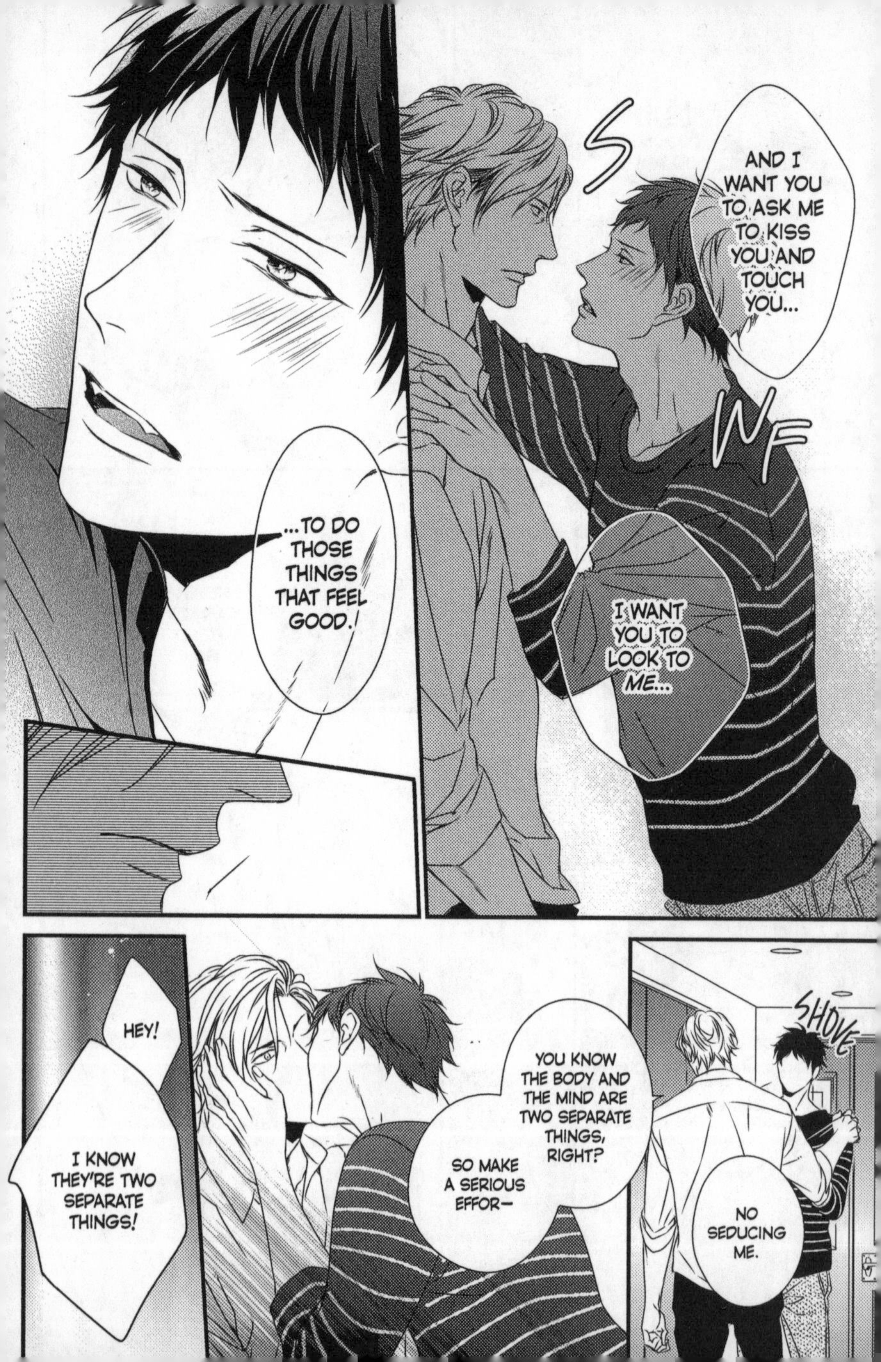
S
AND I WANT YOU TO ASK ME TO KISS YOU AND TOUCH YOU...
WF
I WANT YOU TO LOOK TO ME...
...TO DO THOSE THINGS THAT FEEL GOOD.
SHOVE
NO SEDUCING ME.
YOU KNOW THE BODY AND THE MIND ARE TWO SEPARATE THINGS, RIGHT?
SO MAKE A SERIOUS EFFOR—
HEY!
I KNOW THEY'RE TWO SEPARATE THINGS!

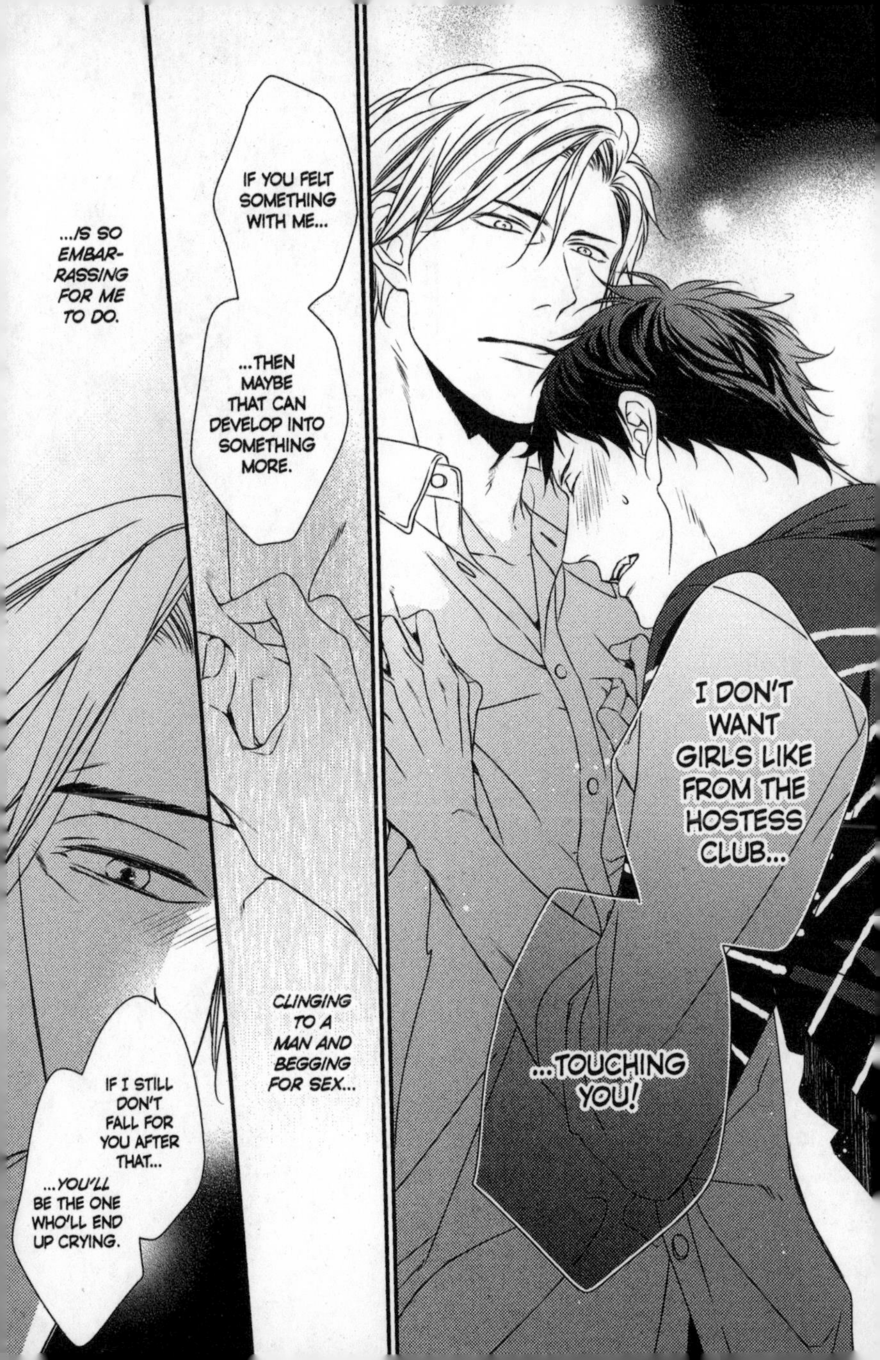
I DON'T WANT GIRLS LIKE FROM THE HOSTESS CLUB...
...TOUCHING YOU!
IF YOU FELT SOMETHING WITH ME...
...THEN MAYBE THAT CAN DEVELOP INTO SOMETHING MORE.
CLINGING TO A MAN AND BEGGING FOR SEX...
...IS SO EMBAR-RASSING FOR ME TO DO.
IF I STILL DON'T FALL FOR YOU AFTER THAT...
...YOU'LL BE THE ONE WHO'LL END UP CRYING.

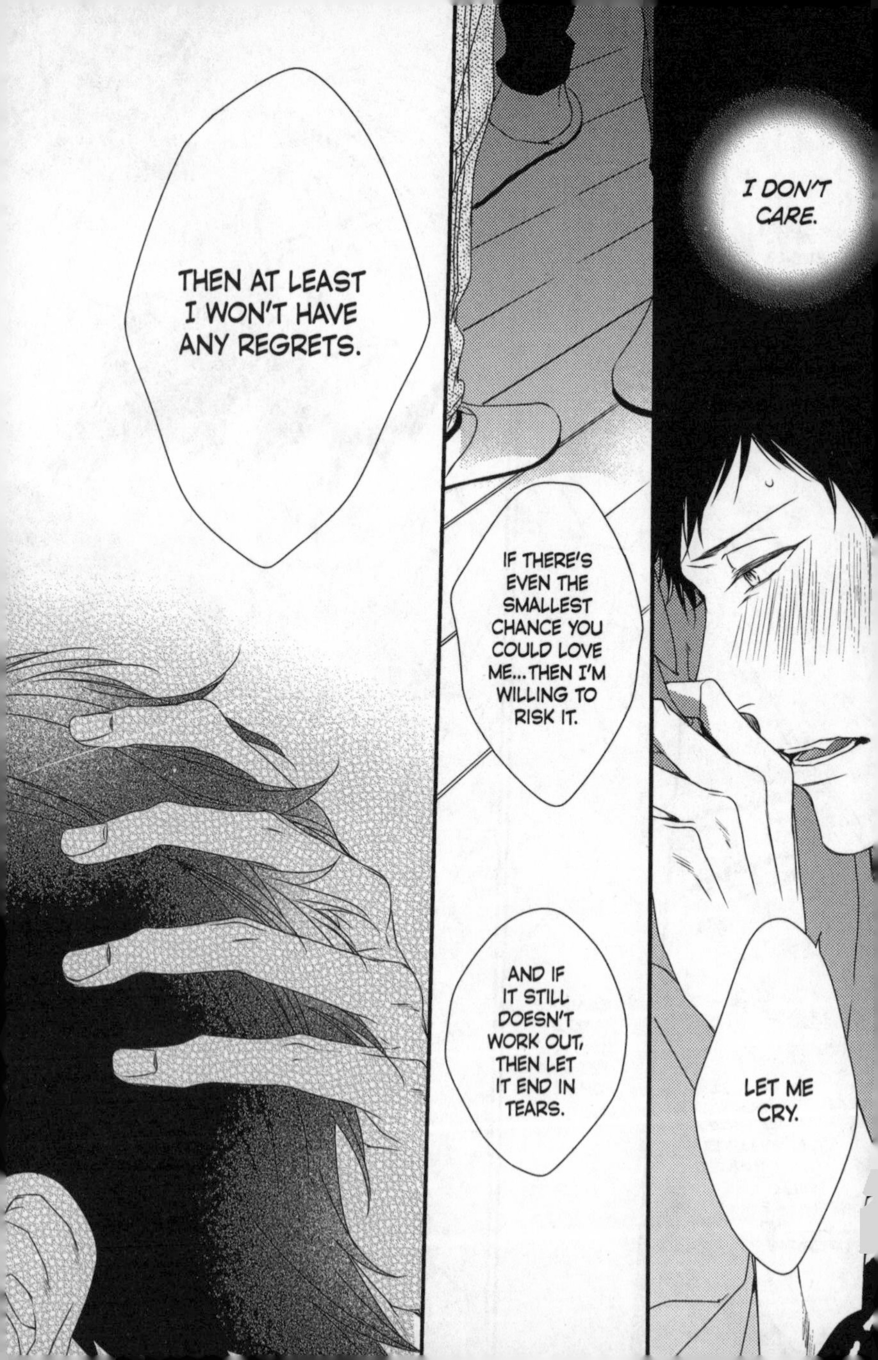
I DON'T CARE.
LET ME CRY.
IF THERE'S EVEN THE SMALLEST CHANCE YOU COULD LOVE ME...THEN I'M WILLING TO RISK IT.
AND IF IT STILL DOESN'T WORK OUT, THEN LET IT END IN TEARS.
THEN AT LEAST I WON'T HAVE ANY REGRETS.

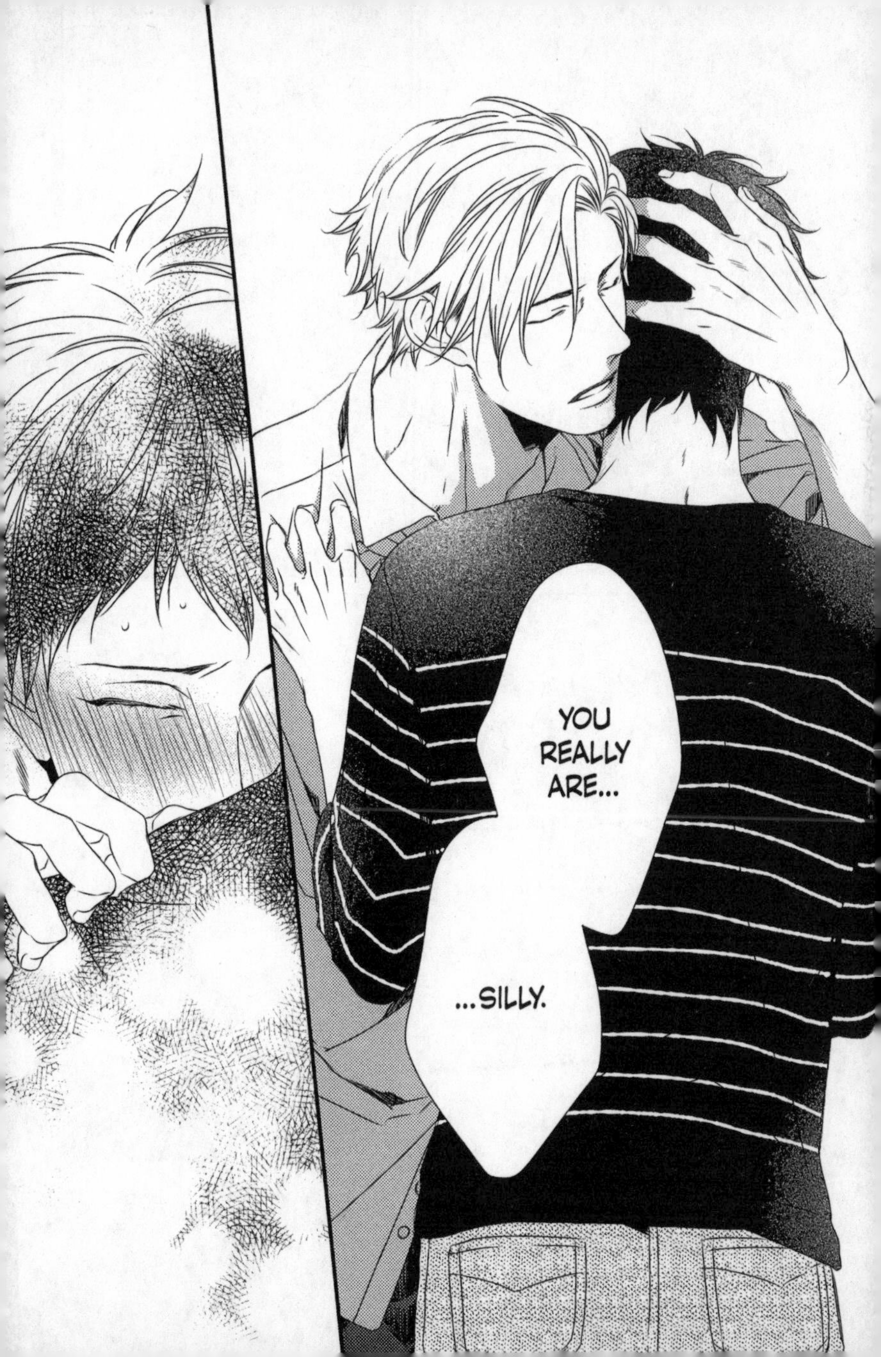
YOU REALLY ARE...
...SILLY.

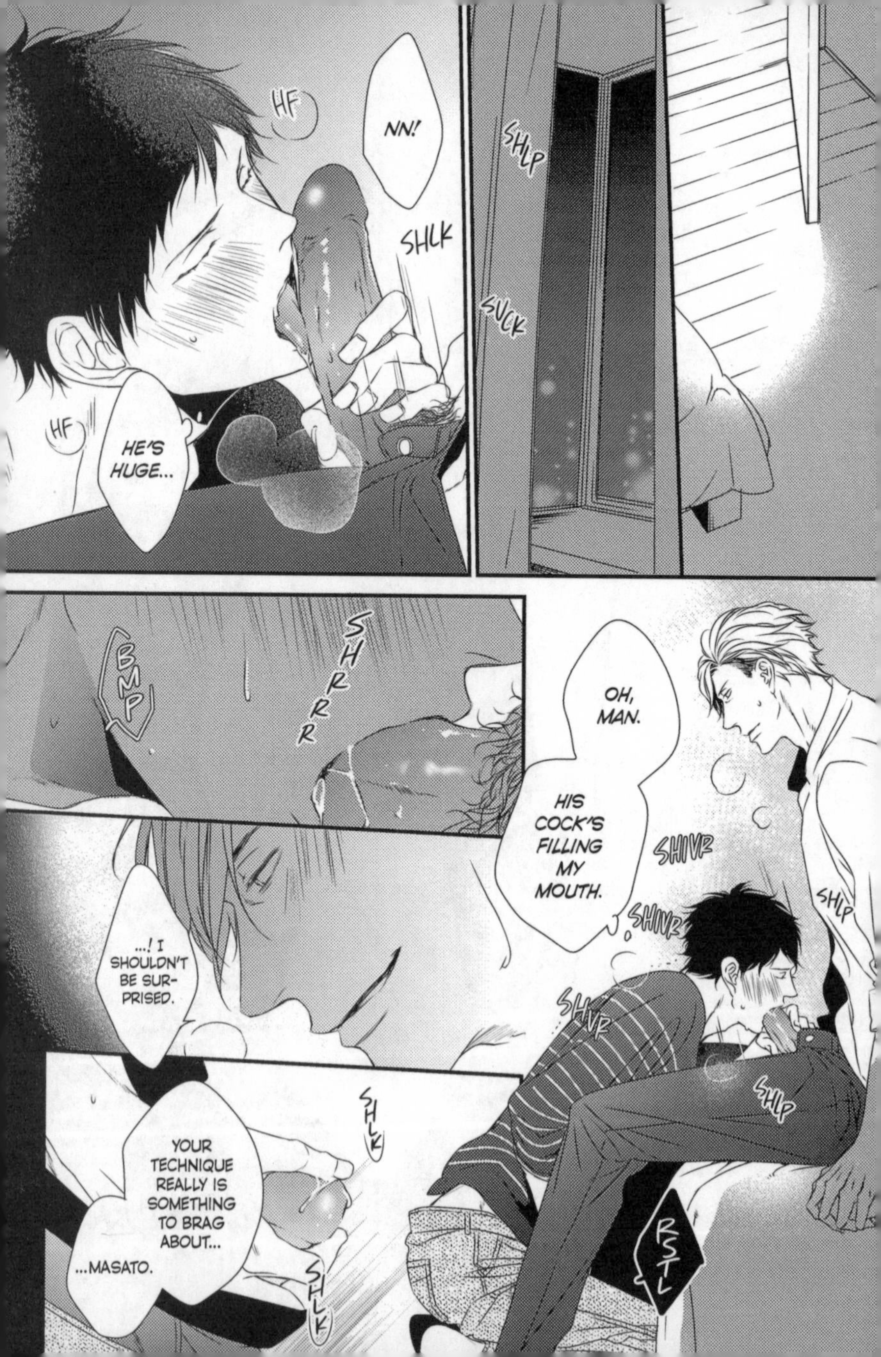
SHLP
SUCK
HF
NN!
SHLK
HF
HE'S HUGE...
OH, MAN.
HIS COCK'S FILLING MY MOUTH.
SHIVR
SHLP
SHIVR
SHIVR
SHLP
RSTL
SHRRRR
BMP
...! I SHOULDN'T BE SUR-PRISED.
SHLK
YOUR TECHNIQUE REALLY IS SOMETHING TO BRAG ABOUT...
...MASATO.
SHLK

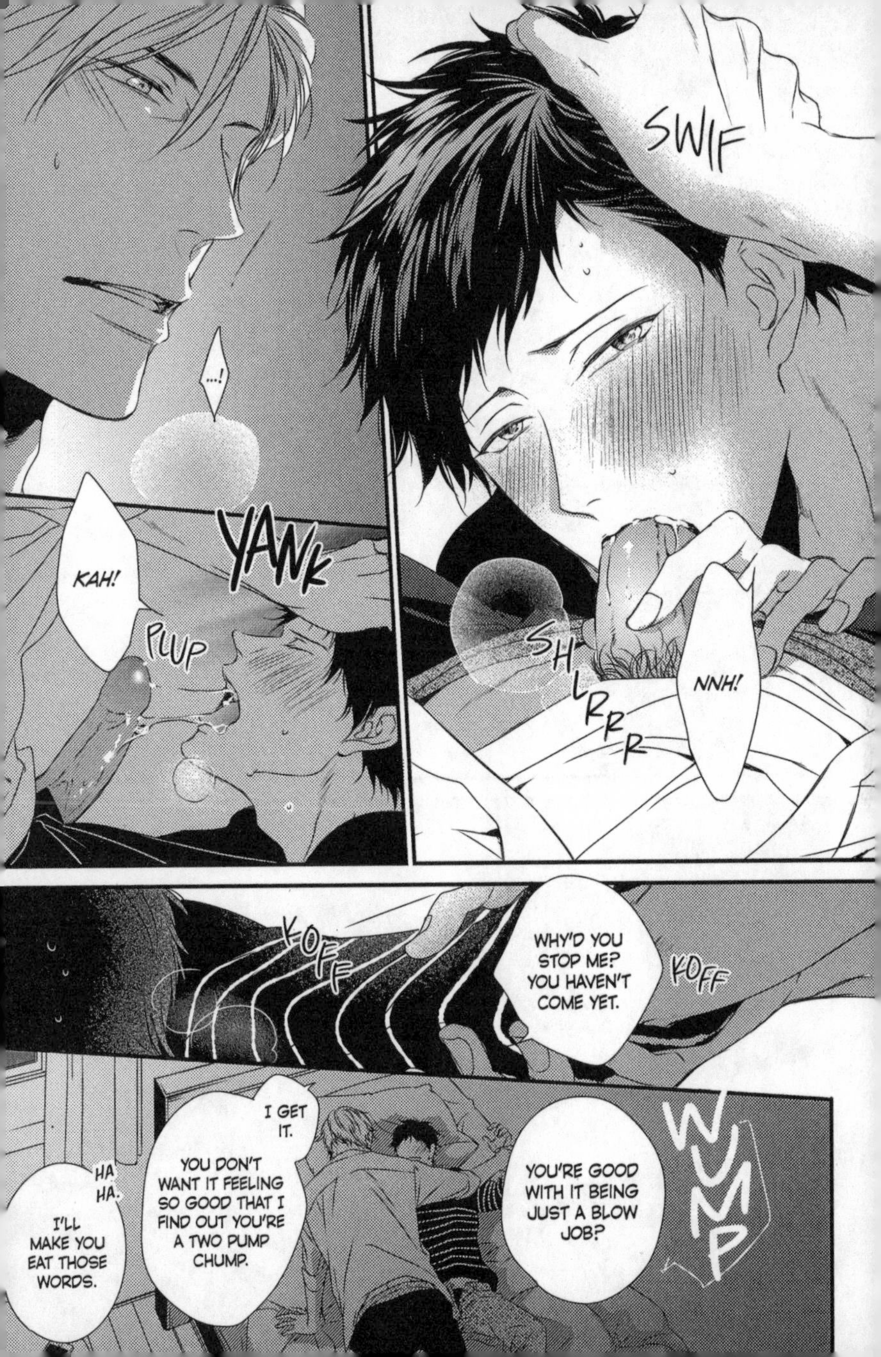
SWIF
NNH!
SHLRRRR
...!
YANK
KAH!
PLUP
K'OFF
WHY'D YOU STOP ME? YOU HAVEN'T COME YET.
K'OFF
WUMP
YOU'RE GOOD WITH IT BEING JUST A BLOW JOB?
I GET IT.
YOU DON'T WANT IT FEELING SO GOOD THAT I FIND OUT YOU'RE A TWO PUMP CHUMP.
HA HA.
I'LL MAKE YOU EAT THOSE WORDS.

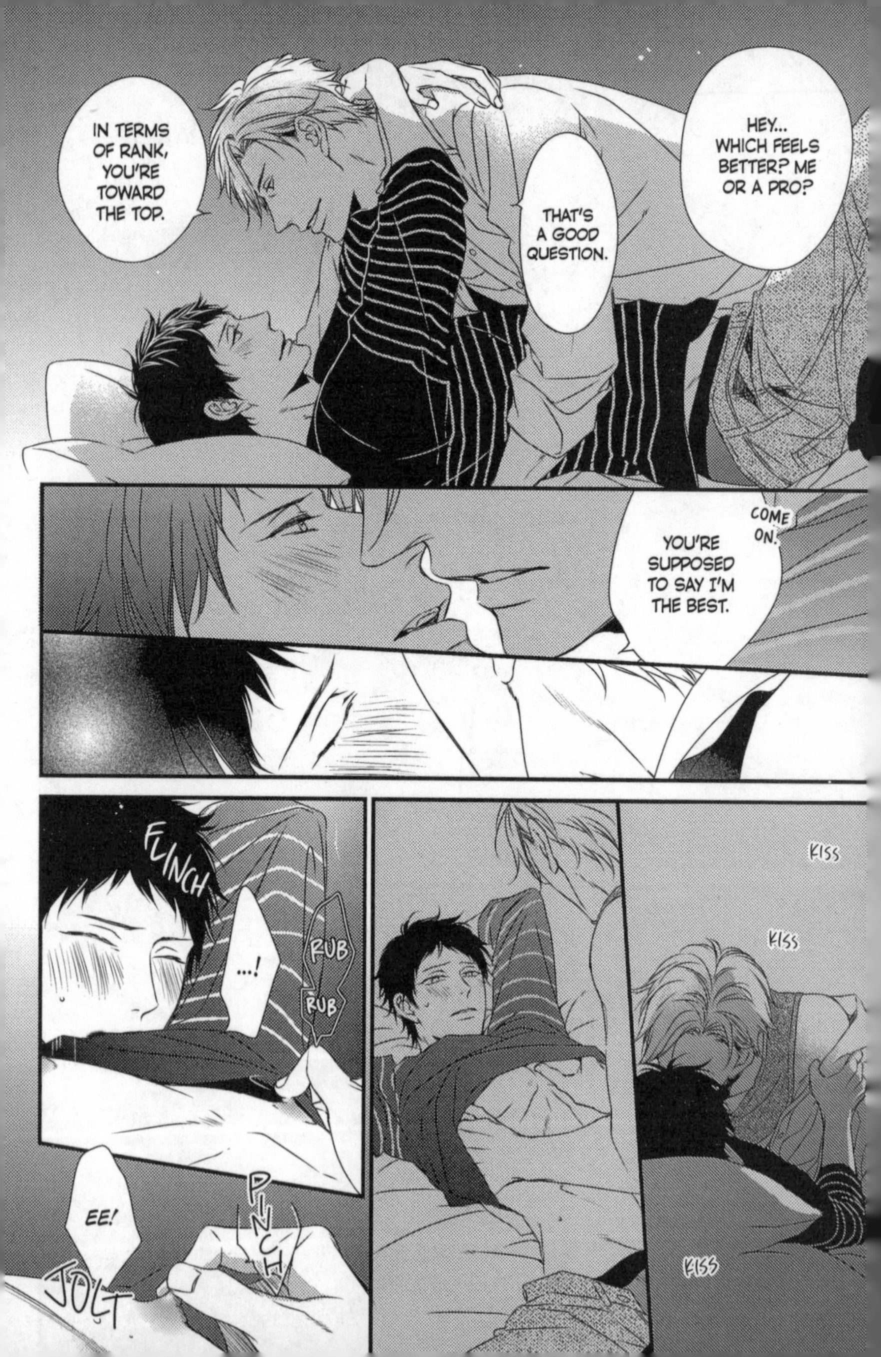
HEY... WHICH FEELS BETTER? ME OR A PRO?
THAT'S A GOOD QUESTION.
IN TERMS OF RANK, YOU'RE TOWARD THE TOP.
COME ON.
YOU'RE SUPPOSED TO SAY I'M THE BEST.
KISS
KISS
KISS
RUB
RUB
...!
FLINCH
PINCH
EE!
JOLT

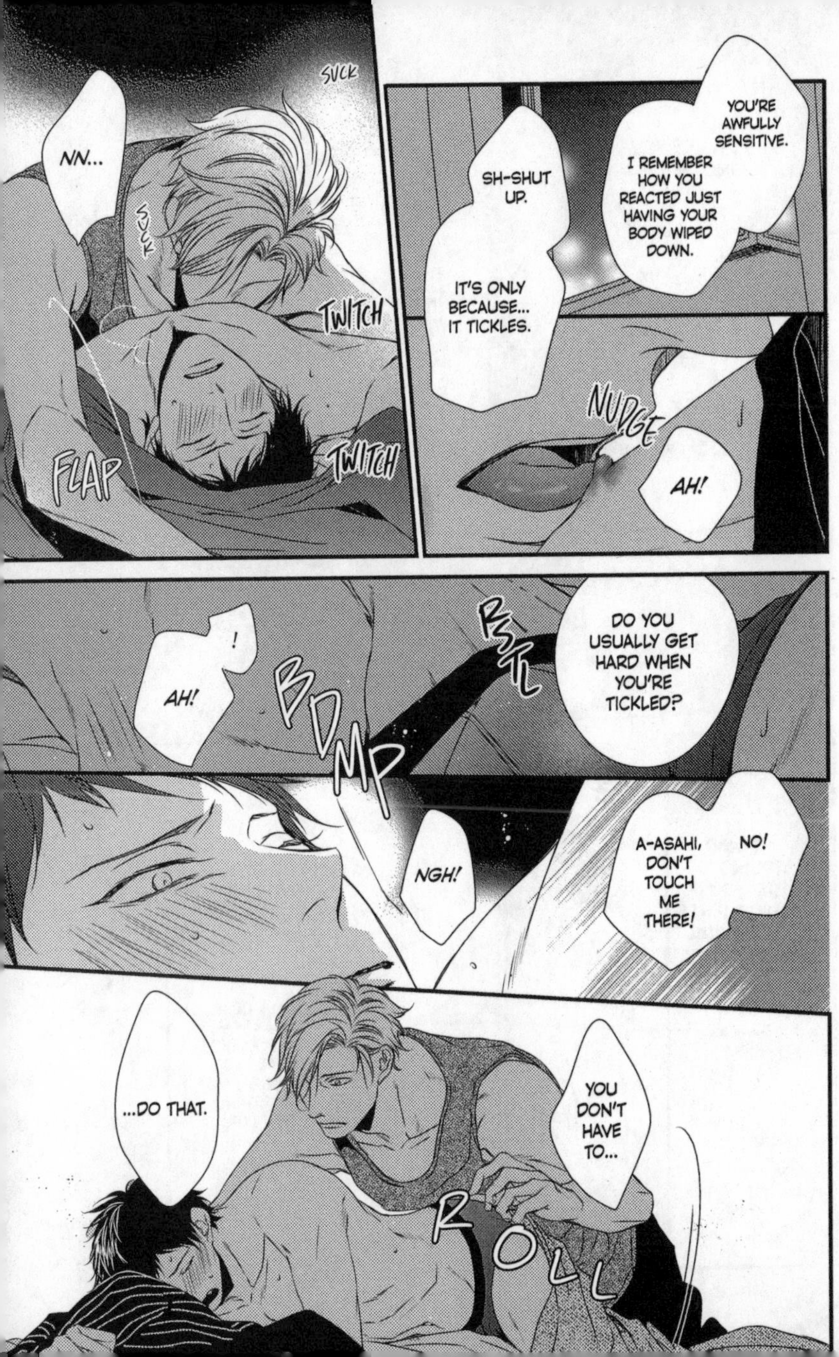
YOU'RE AWFULLY SENSITIVE.
I REMEMBER HOW YOU REACTED JUST HAVING YOUR BODY WIPED DOWN.
SH-SHUT UP.
IT'S ONLY BECAUSE... IT TICKLES.
NUDGE
AH!
SUCK
NN...
SUCK
TWITCH
TWITCH
FLAP
DO YOU USUALLY GET HARD WHEN YOU'RE TICKLED?
BSTL
BDMP
!
AH!
NO!
A-ASAHI, DON'T TOUCH ME THERE!
NGH!
YOU DON'T HAVE TO...
ROLL
...DO THAT.

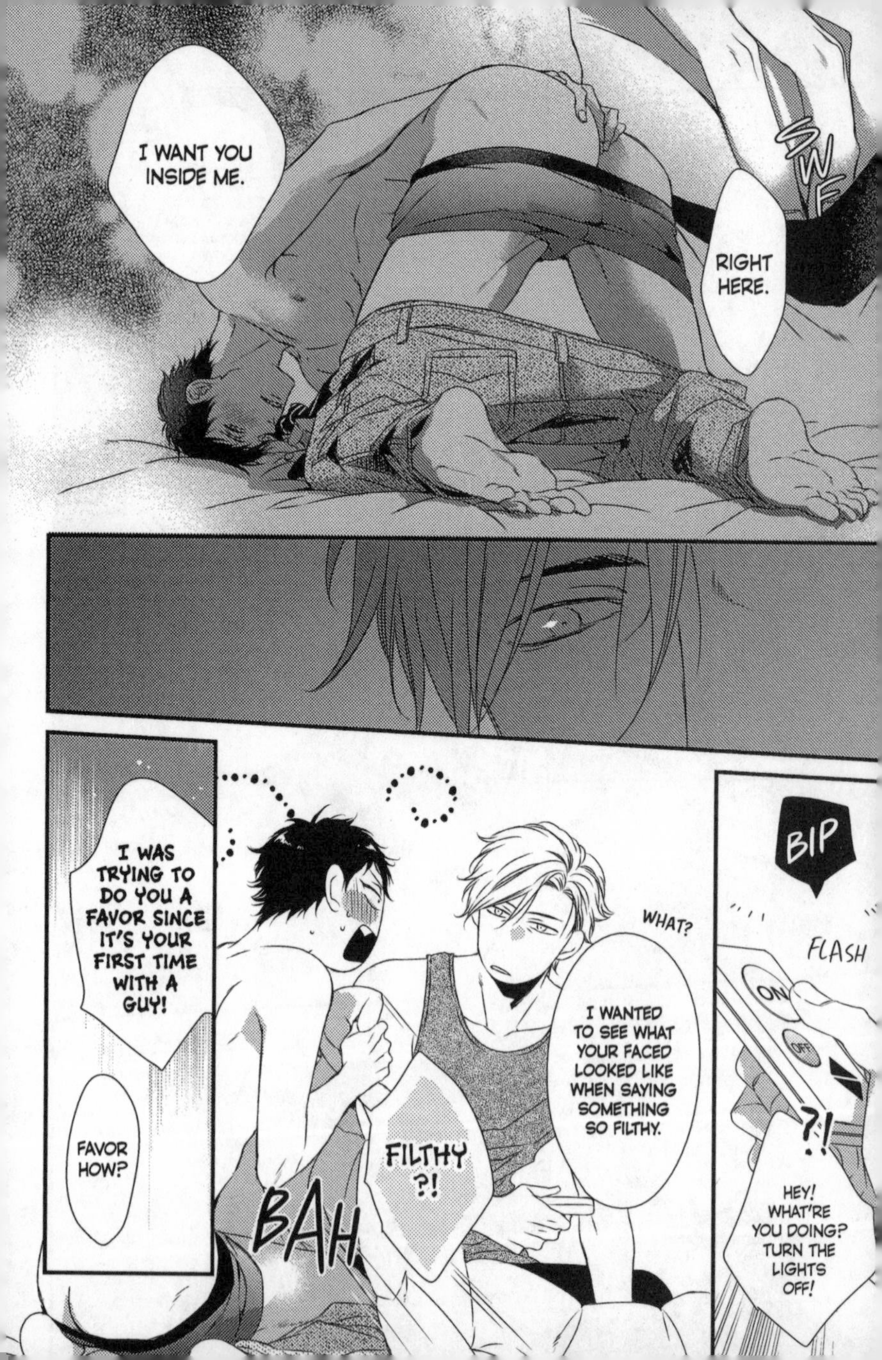
SWF
I WANT YOU INSIDE ME.
RIGHT HERE.
BIP
FLASH
?!
HEY! WHAT'RE YOU DOING? TURN THE LIGHTS OFF!
WHAT?
I WANTED TO SEE WHAT YOUR FACED LOOKED LIKE WHEN SAYING SOMETHING SO FILTHY.
FILTHY ?!
BAH
I WAS TRYING TO DO YOU A FAVOR SINCE IT'S YOUR FIRST TIME WITH A GUY!
FAVOR HOW?

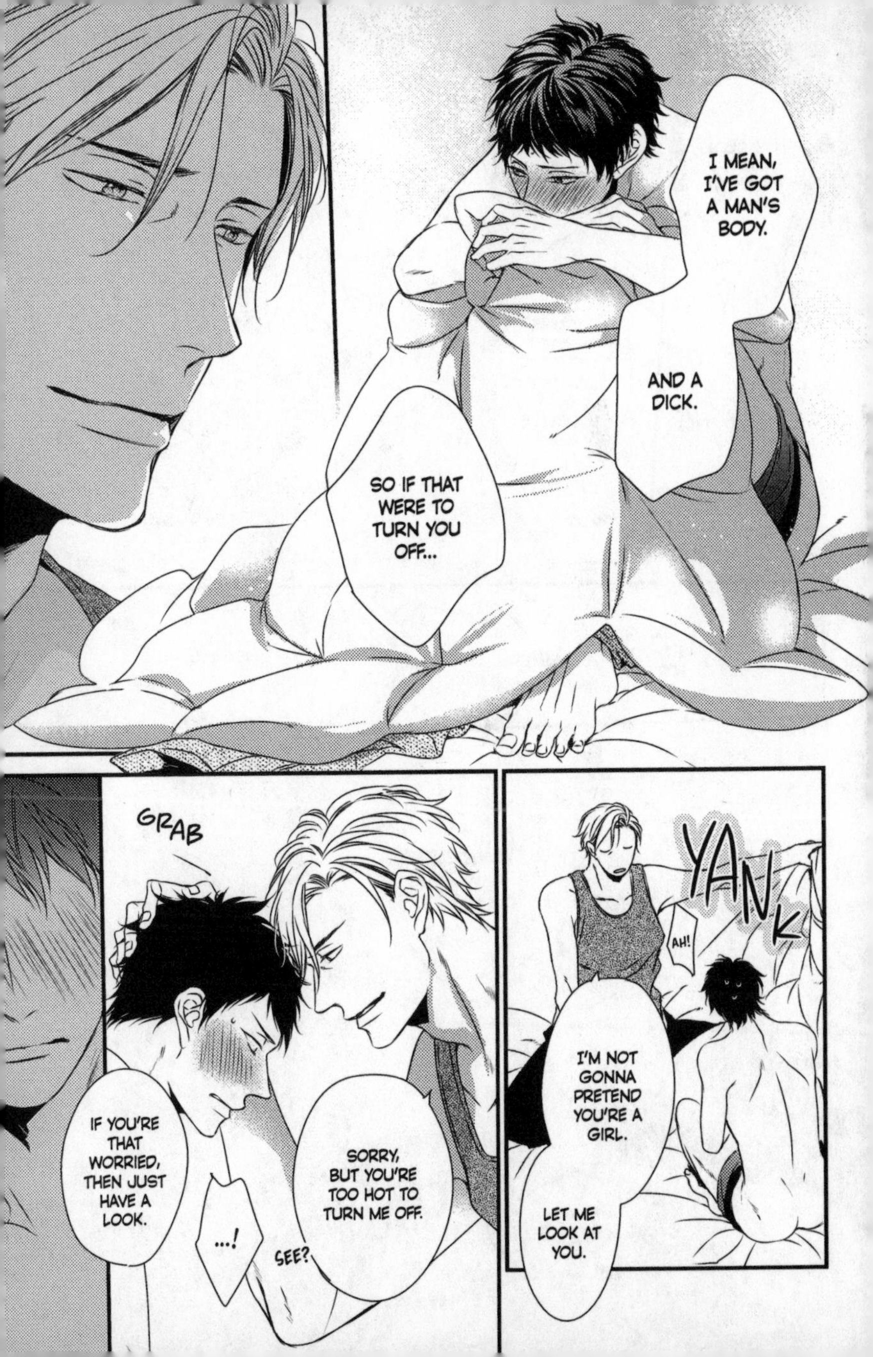
I MEAN, I'VE GOT A MAN'S BODY.
AND A DICK.
SO IF THAT WERE TO TURN YOU OFF...
YANK
AH!
I'M NOT GONNA PRETEND YOU'RE A GIRL.
LET ME LOOK AT YOU.
GRAB
SORRY, BUT YOU'RE TOO HOT TO TURN ME OFF.
SEE?
...!
IF YOU'RE THAT WORRIED, THEN JUST HAVE A LOOK.

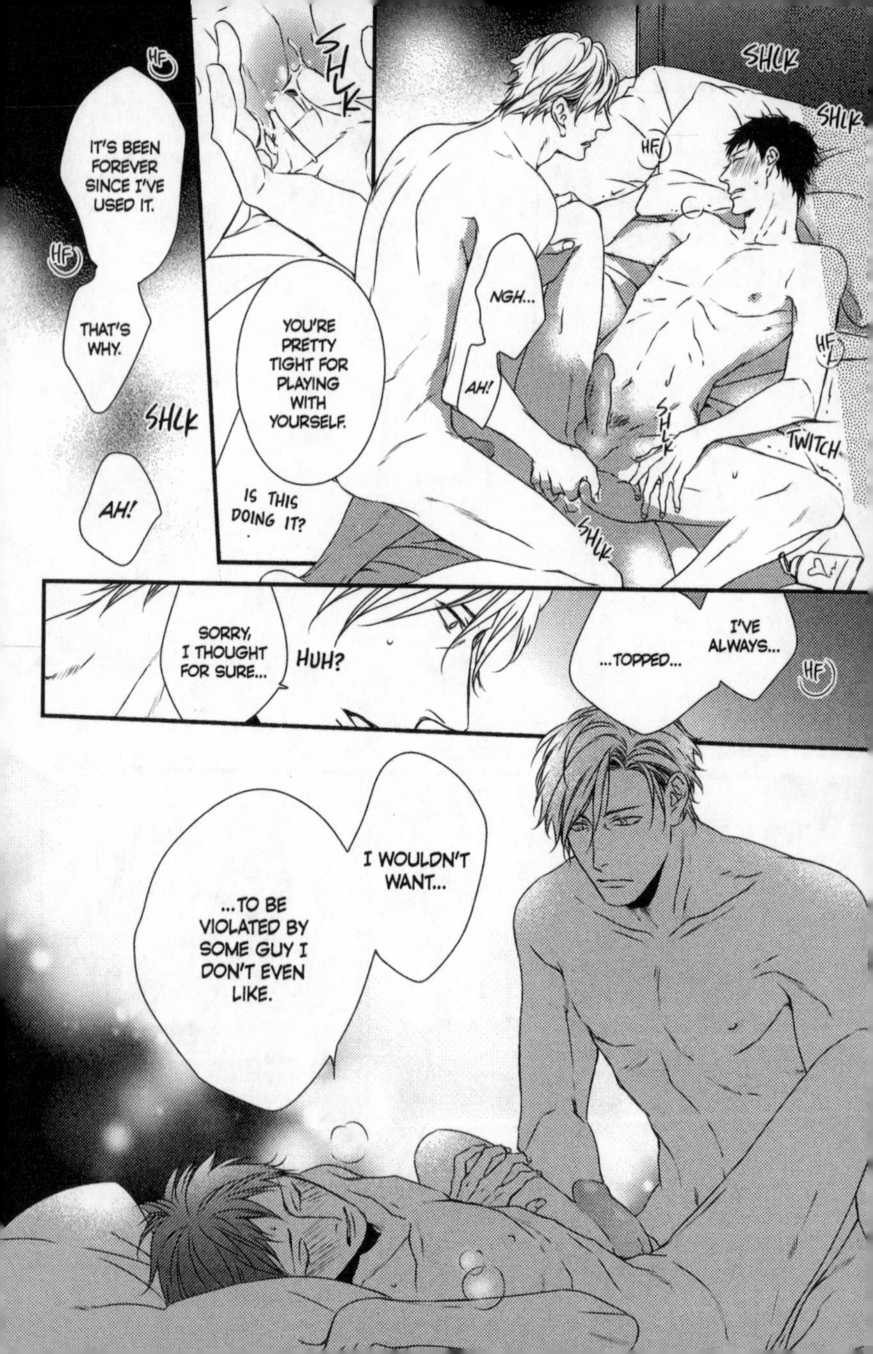
SHLK
SHLK
HF
SHLK
NGH...
AH!
YOU'RE PRETTY TIGHT FOR PLAYING WITH YOURSELF.
HF
TWITCH
SHLK
SHLK
IS THIS DOING IT?
HF
IT'S BEEN FOREVER SINCE I'VE USED IT.
HF
THAT'S WHY.
SHLK
AH!
HF
I'VE ALWAYS...
...TOPPED...
HUH?
SORRY, I THOUGHT FOR SURE...
I WOULDN'T WANT...
...TO BE VIOLATED BY SOME GUY I DON'T EVEN LIKE.

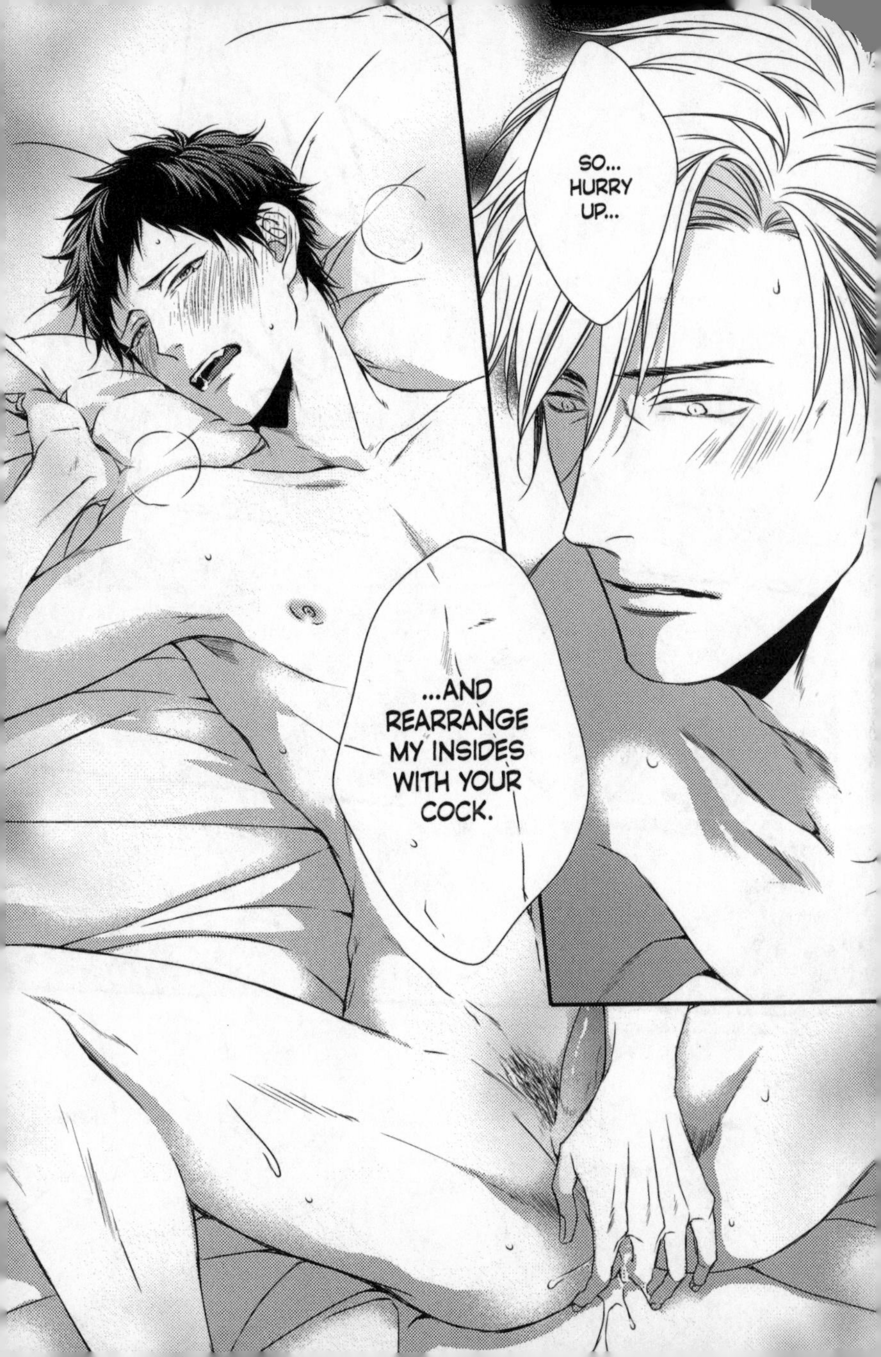
SO... HURRY UP...
...AND REARRANGE MY INSIDES WITH YOUR COCK.

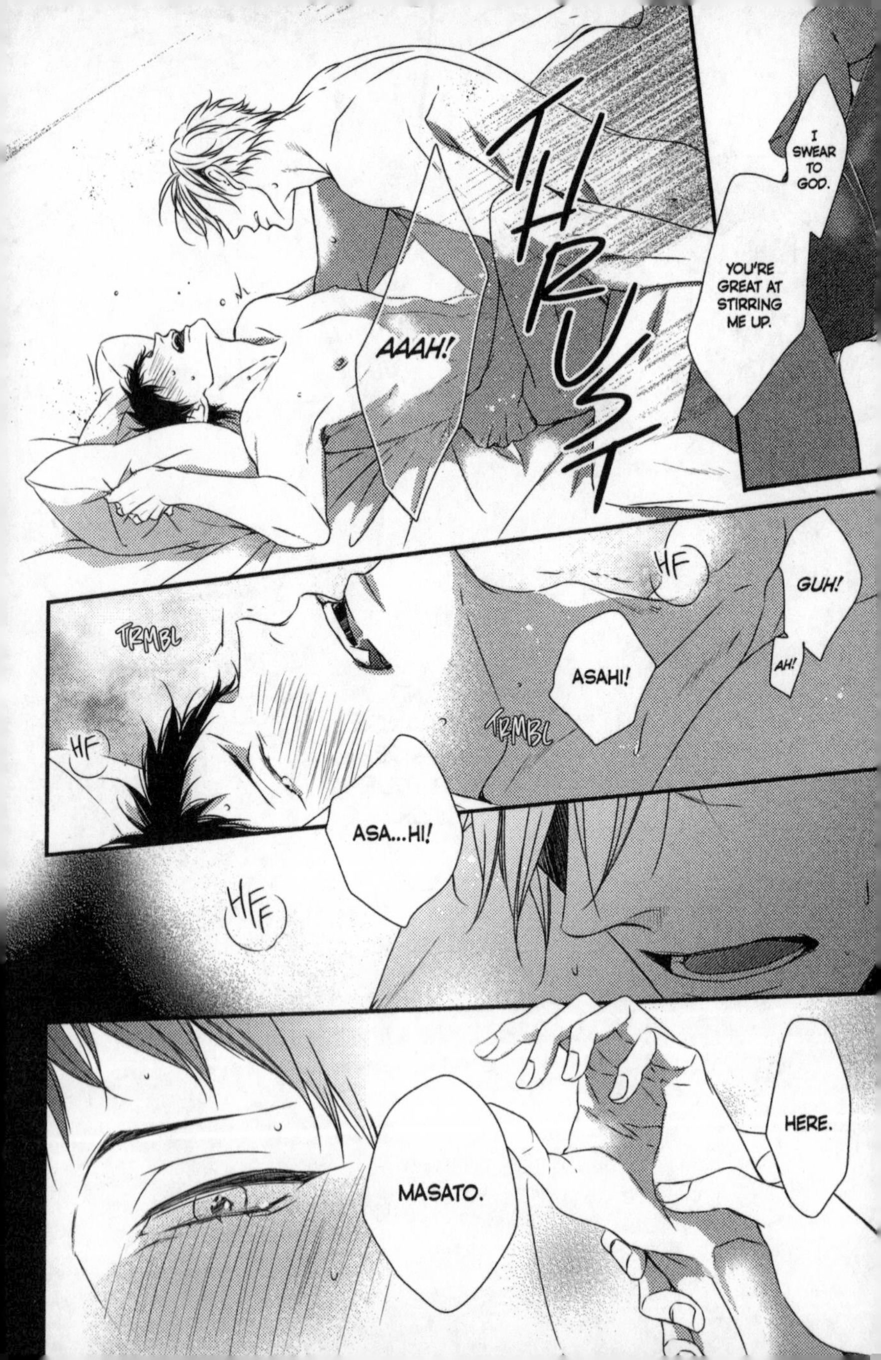
I SWEAR TO GOD.
YOU'RE GREAT AT STIRRING ME UP.
THRUST
AAAH!
GUH!
HF
AH!
ASAHI!
TRMBL
TRMBL
HF
ASA...HI!
HFF
HERE.
MASATO.

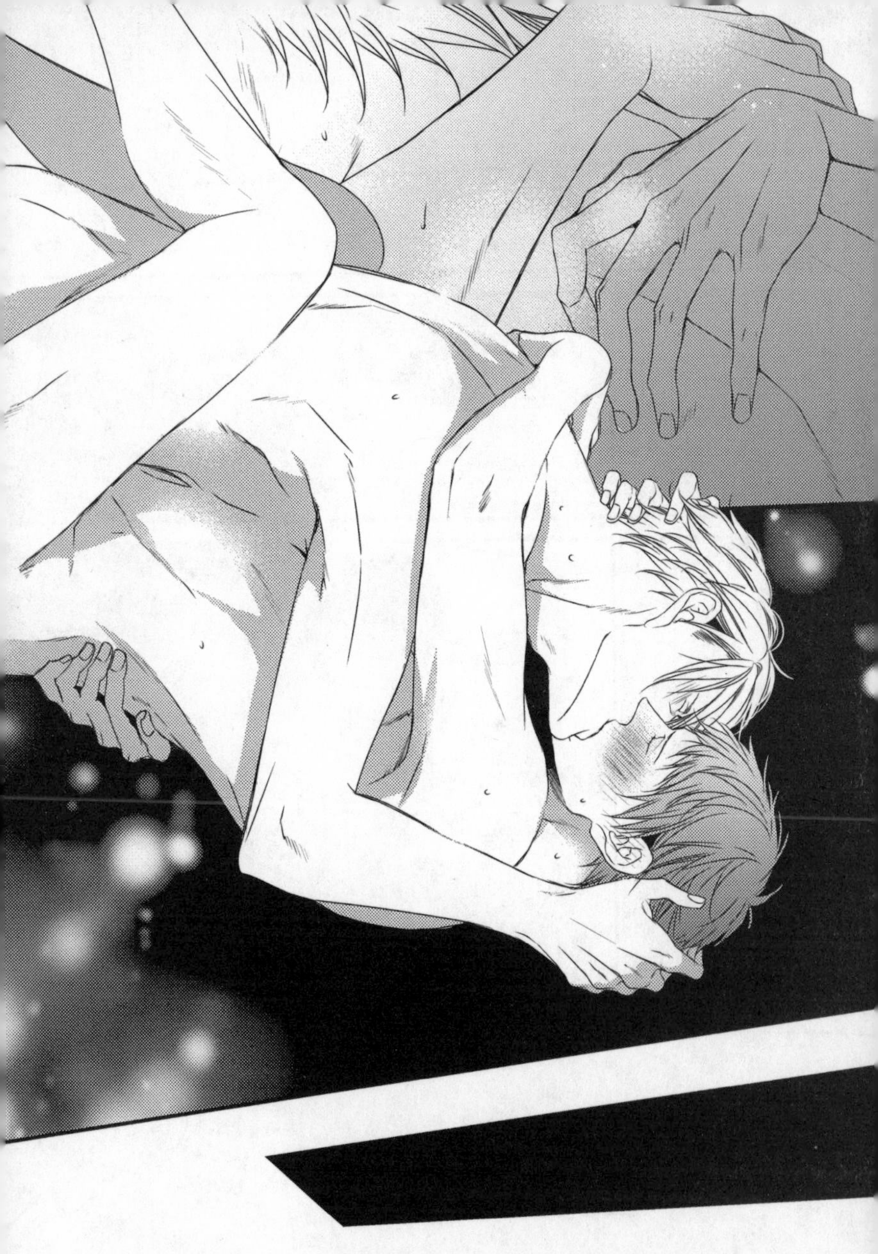

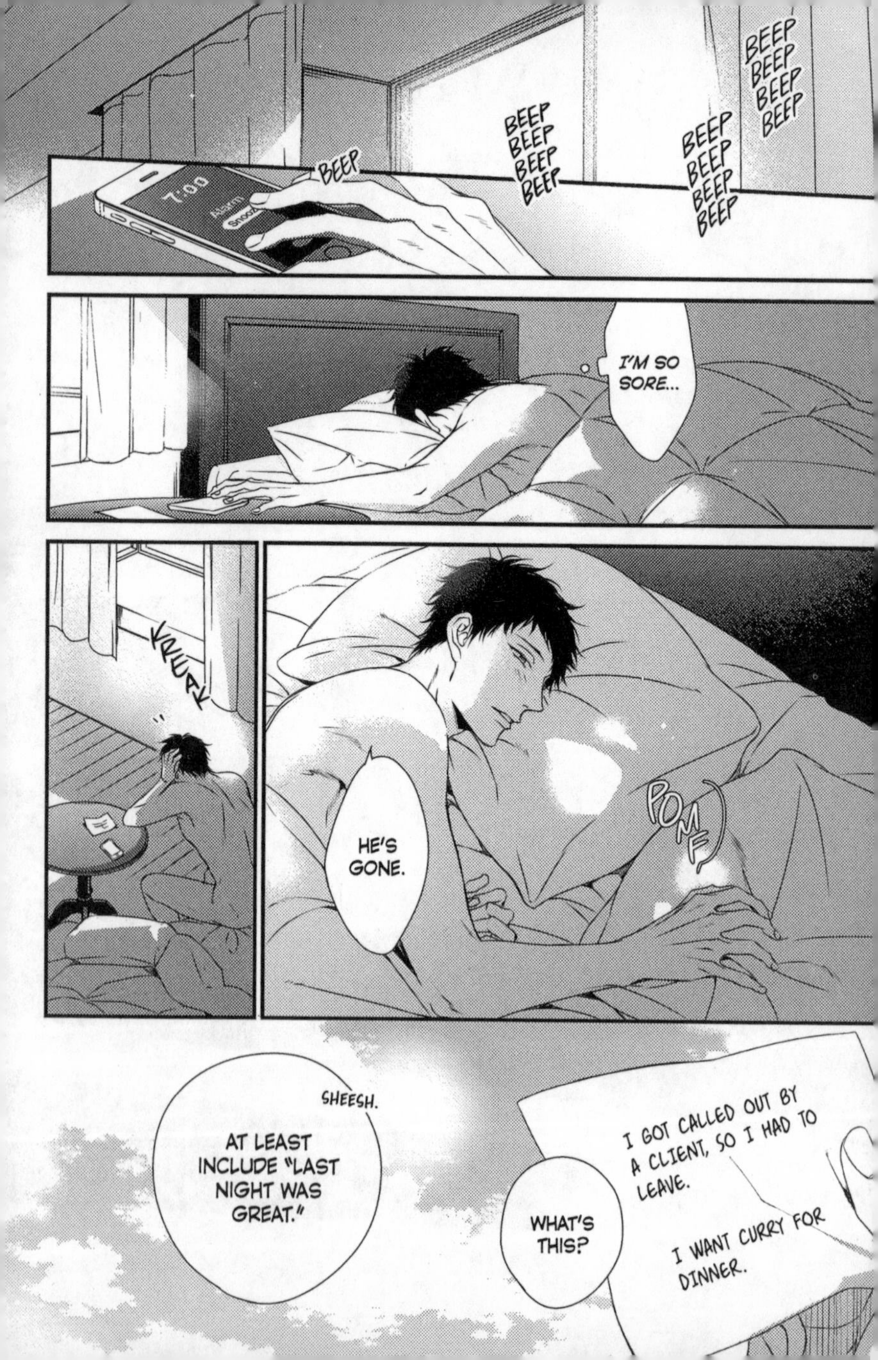
BEEP BEEP BEEP BEEP
BEEP BEEP BEEP BEEP
BEEP BEEP BEEP BEEP
BEEP
7:00
Alarm
I'M SO SORE...
POMF
HE'S GONE.
KREAK
I GOT CALLED OUT BY A CLIENT, SO I HAD TO LEAVE.
I WANT CURRY FOR DINNER.
WHAT'S THIS?
SHEESH.
AT LEAST INCLUDE "LAST NIGHT WAS GREAT."

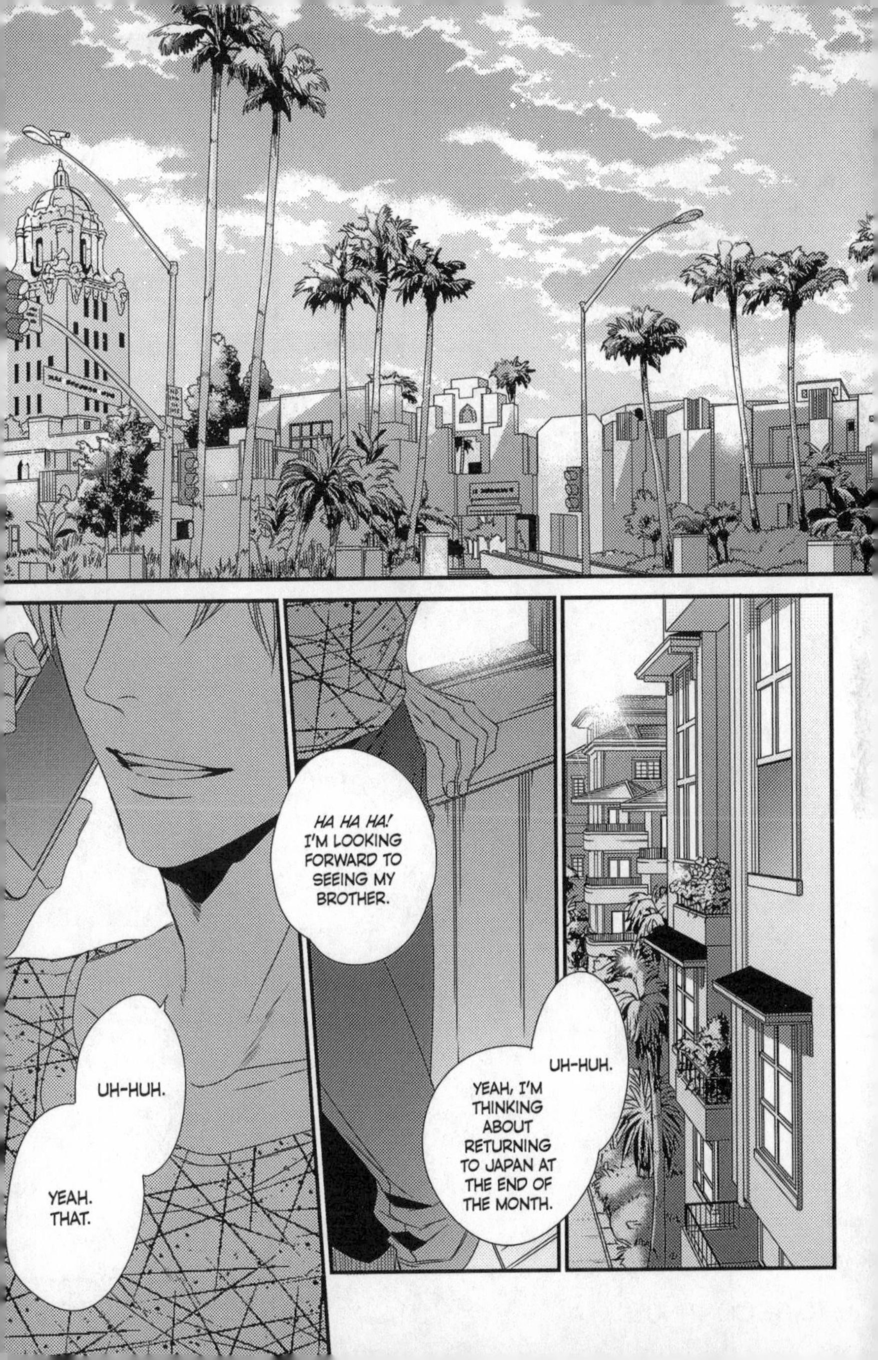
UH-HUH.
YEAH, I'M THINKING ABOUT RETURNING TO JAPAN AT THE END OF THE MONTH.
HA HA HA! I'M LOOKING FORWARD TO SEEING MY BROTHER.
UH-HUH.
YEAH. THAT.

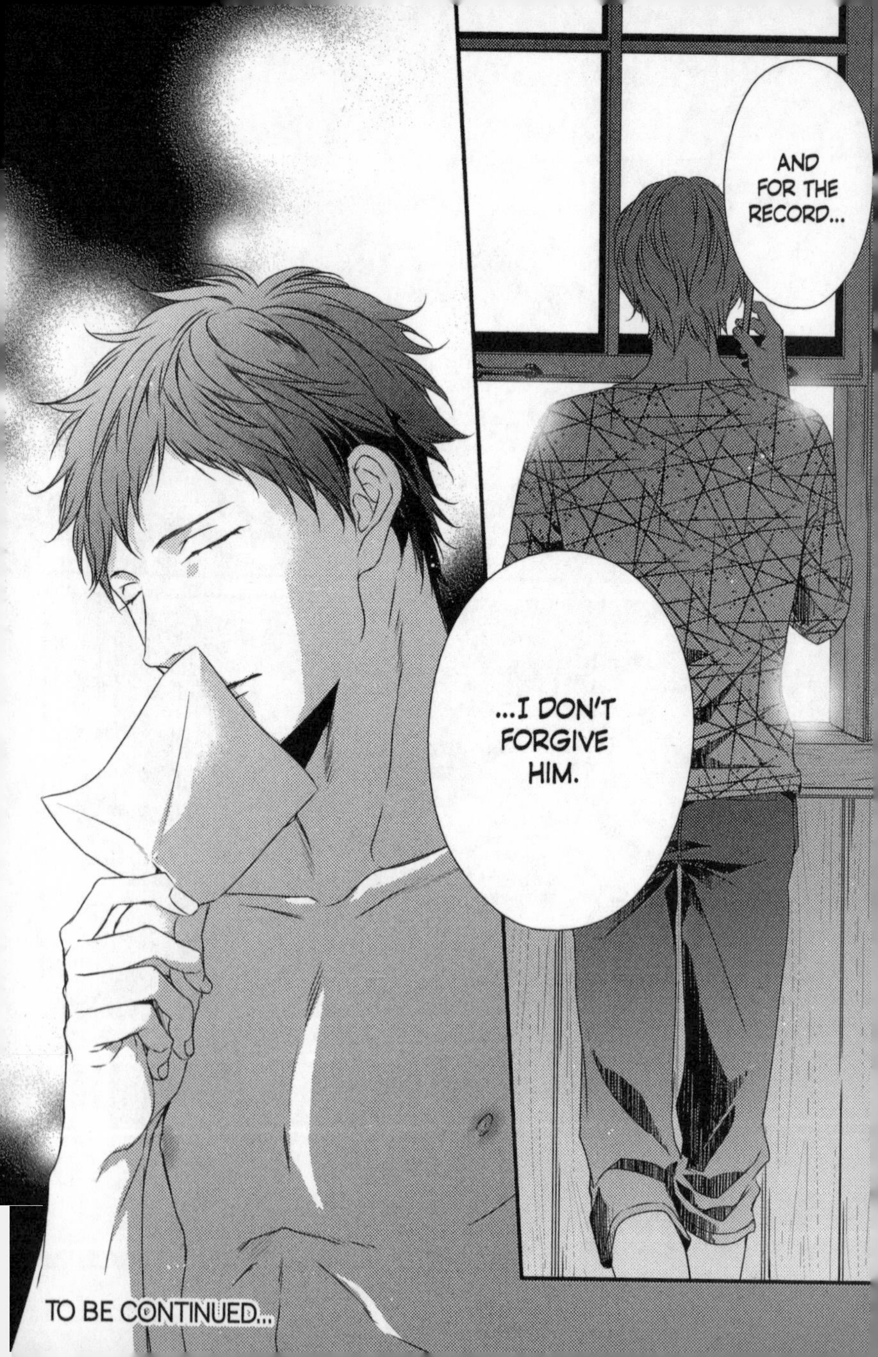
AND FOR THE RECORD...
...I DON'T FORGIVE HIM.
TO BE CONTINUED...

LOVE NEST

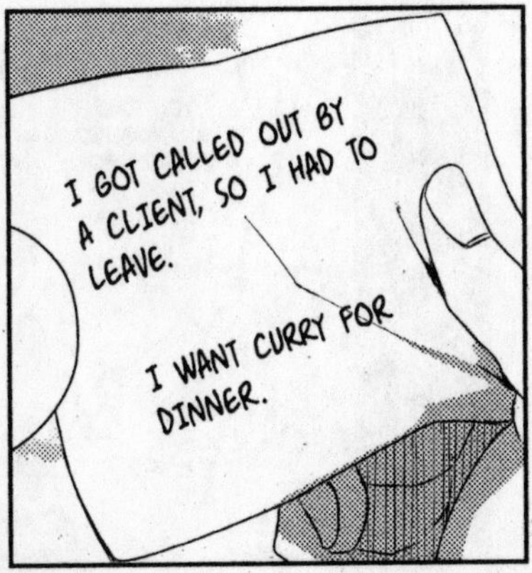
I GOT CALLED OUT BY A CLIENT, SO I HAD TO LEAVE.
I WANT CURRY FOR DINNER.

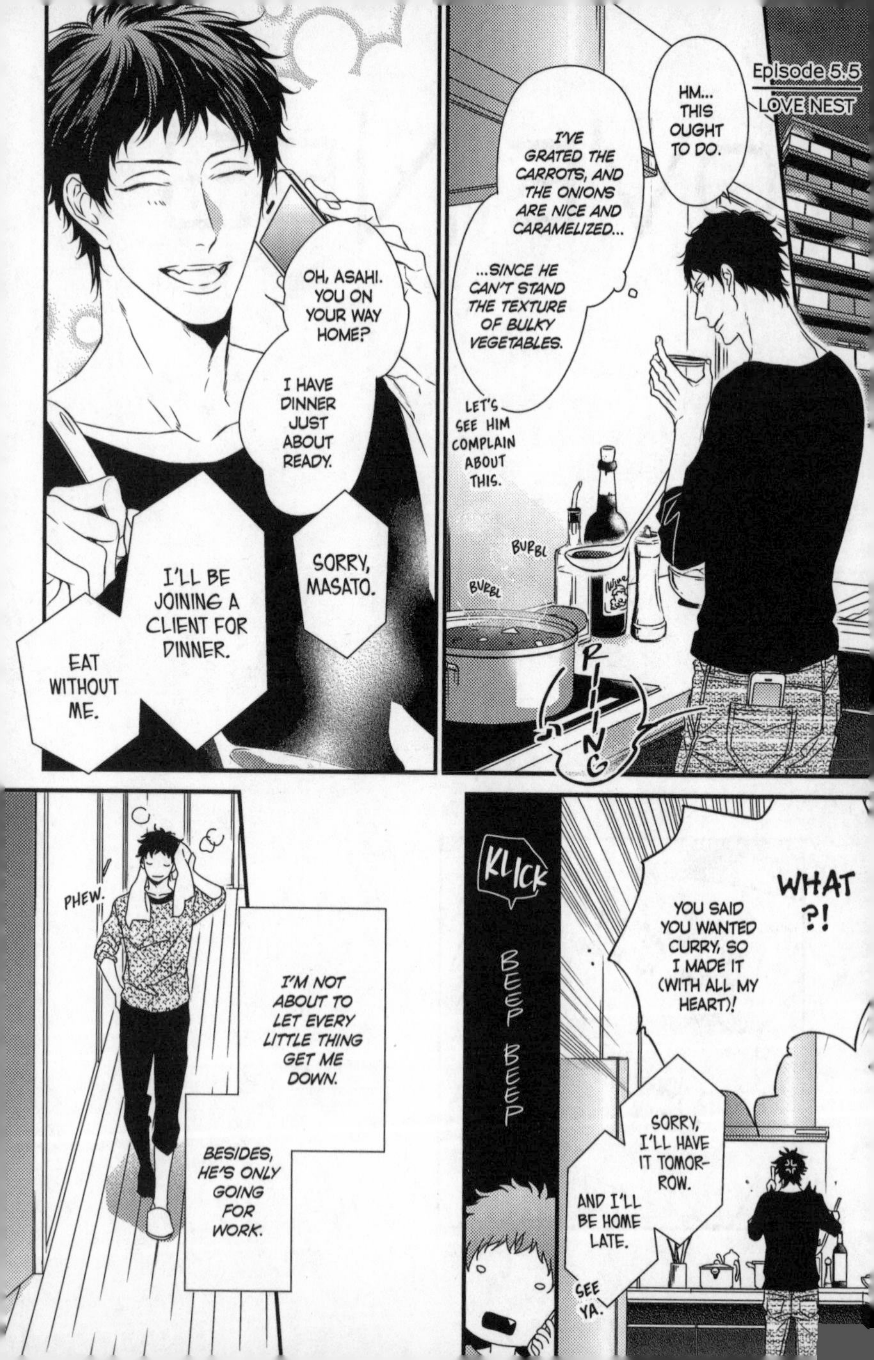
Episode 5.5
LOVE NEST
HM... THIS OUGHT TO DO.
I'VE GRATED THE CARROTS, AND THE ONIONS ARE NICE AND CARAMELIZED...
...SINCE HE CAN'T STAND THE TEXTURE OF BULKY VEGETABLES.
LET'S SEE HIM COMPLAIN ABOUT THIS.
BURBL
BURBL
RIIING
OH, ASAHI. YOU ON YOUR WAY HOME?
I HAVE DINNER JUST ABOUT READY.
SORRY, MASATO.
I'LL BE JOINING A CLIENT FOR DINNER.
EAT WITHOUT ME.
KLICK
BEEP BEEP
WHAT ?!
YOU SAID YOU WANTED CURRY, SO I MADE IT (WITH ALL MY HEART)!
SORRY, I'LL HAVE IT TOMOR-ROW.
AND I'LL BE HOME LATE.
SEE YA.
PHEW.
I'M NOT ABOUT TO LET EVERY LITTLE THING GET ME DOWN.
BESIDES, HE'S ONLY GOING FOR WORK.

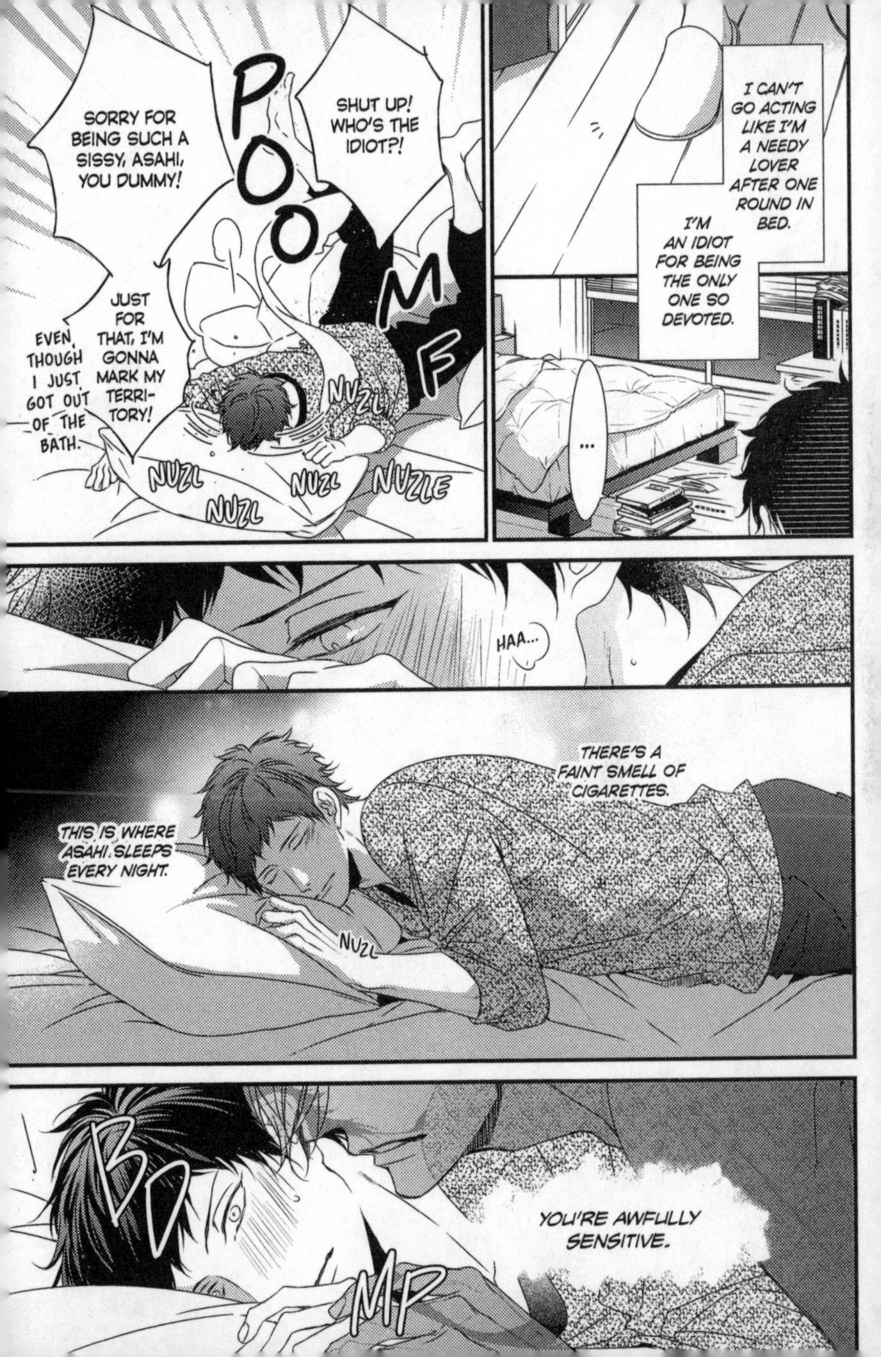
I CAN'T GO ACTING LIKE I'M A NEEDY LOVER AFTER ONE ROUND IN BED.
I'M AN IDIOT FOR BEING THE ONLY ONE SO DEVOTED.
...
SHUT UP! WHO'S THE IDIOT?!
POOMF
SORRY FOR BEING SUCH A SISSY, ASAHI, YOU DUMMY!
JUST FOR THAT, I'M GONNA MARK MY TERRITORY!
EVEN THOUGH I JUST GOT OUT OF THE BATH.
NUZL
NUZLE
NUZL
NUZL
NUZL
HAA...
THERE'S A FAINT SMELL OF CIGARETTES.
THIS IS WHERE ASAHI SLEEPS EVERY NIGHT.
NUZL
!
BOMP
YOU'RE AWFULLY SENSITIVE.

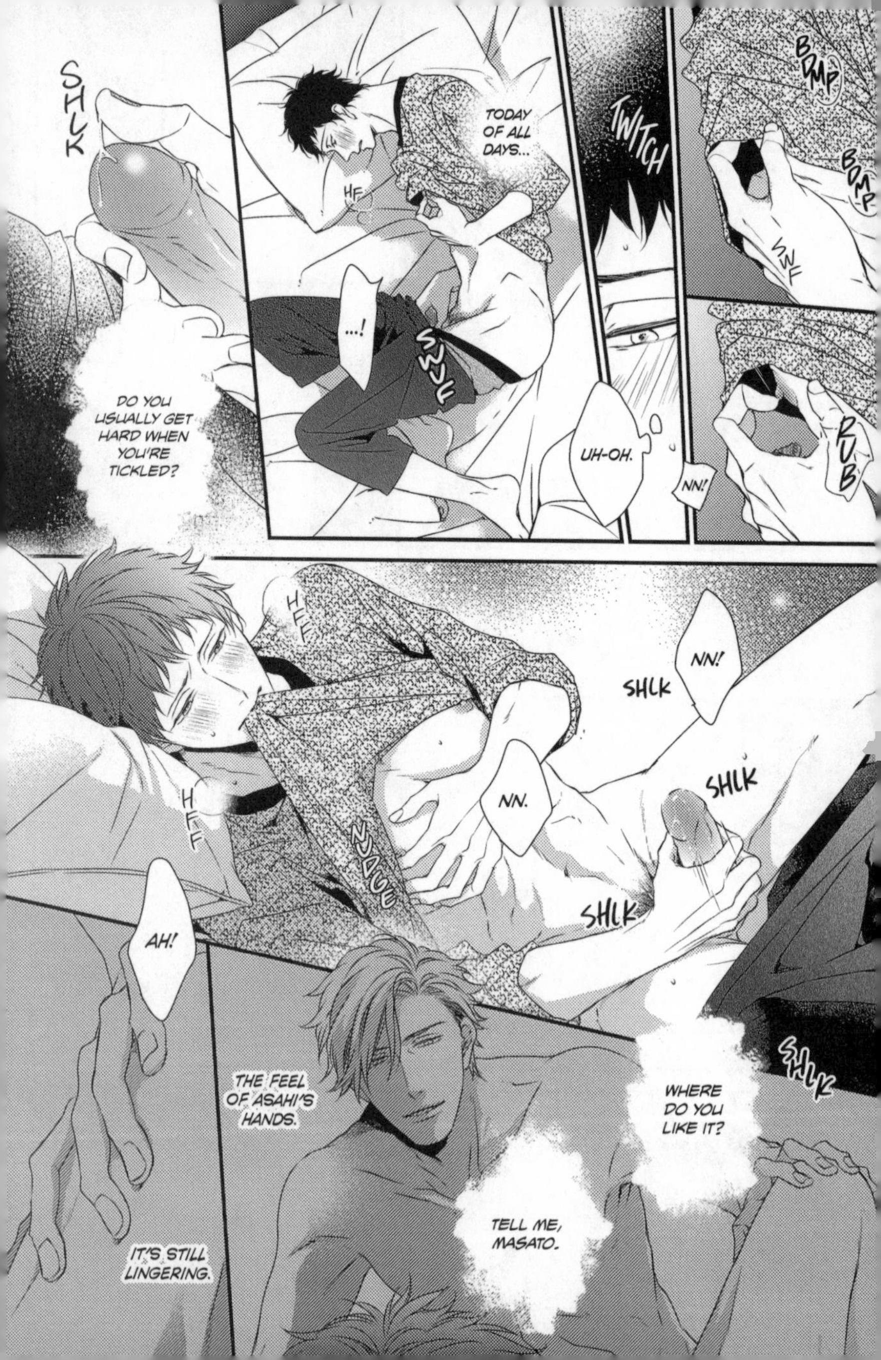
BOMP
BOMP
SNK
RUB
NN!
TWITCH
UH-OH.
TODAY OF ALL DAYS...
HF
...!
SWUF
SHLK
DO YOU USUALLY GET HARD WHEN YOU'RE TICKLED?
NN!
SHLK
HFF
SHLK
NN.
NUDGE
HFF
SHLK
AH!
SHLK
WHERE DO YOU LIKE IT?
TELL ME, MASATO.
THE FEEL OF ASAHI'S HANDS.
IT'S STILL LINGERING.

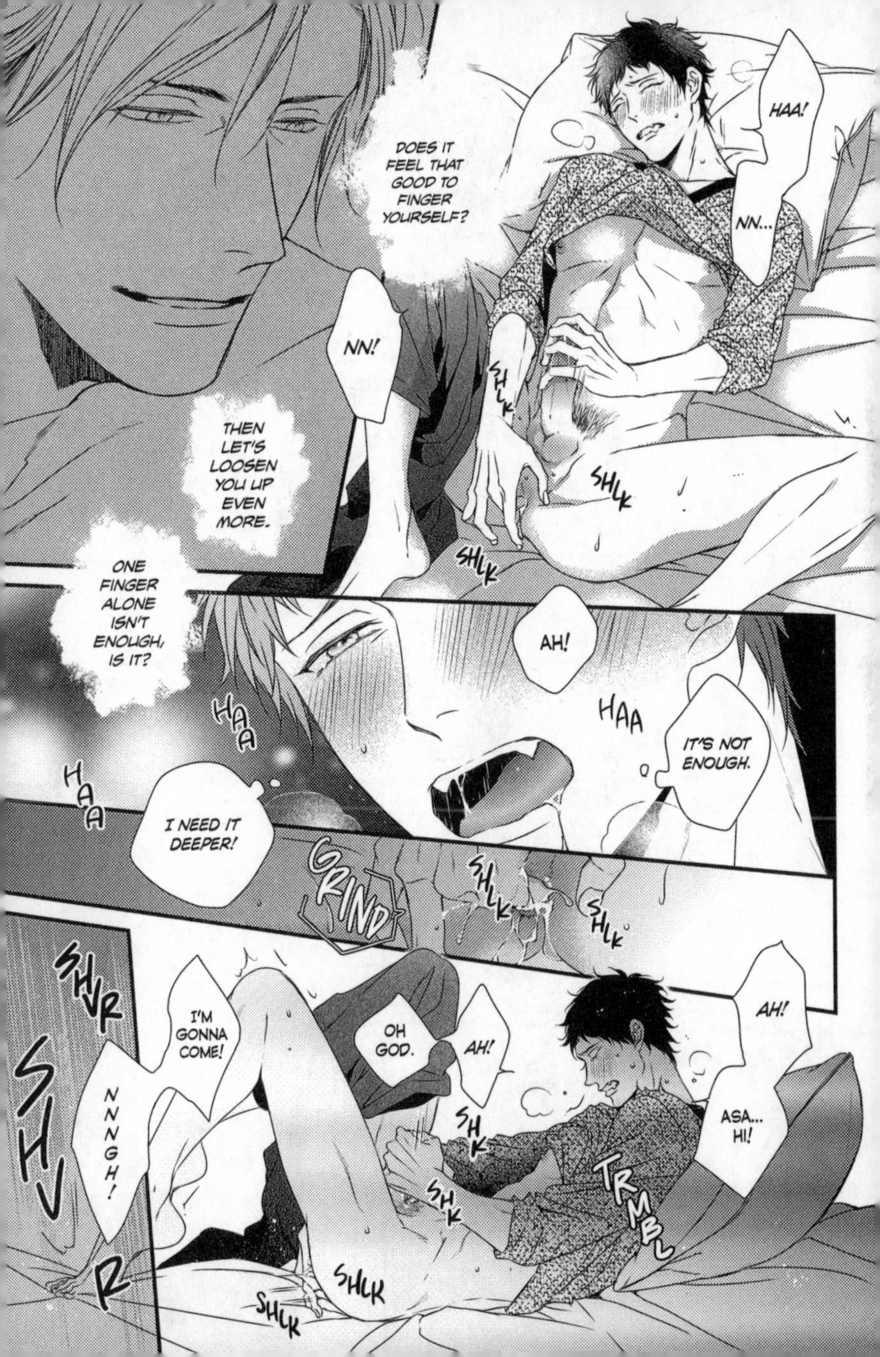
HAA!
NN...
DOES IT FEEL THAT GOOD TO FINGER YOURSELF?
NN!
SHLK
SHLK
SHLK
THEN LET'S LOOSEN YOU UP EVEN MORE.
AH!
IT'S NOT ENOUGH.
HAA
ONE FINGER ALONE ISN'T ENOUGH, IS IT?
HAA
HAA
I NEED IT DEEPER!
SHLK
SHLK
GRIND
AH!
ASA... HI!
TRMBL
AH!
OH GOD.
SHK
SHK
I'M GONNA COME!
NNNGH!
SHVR
SHVR
SHLK
SHLK

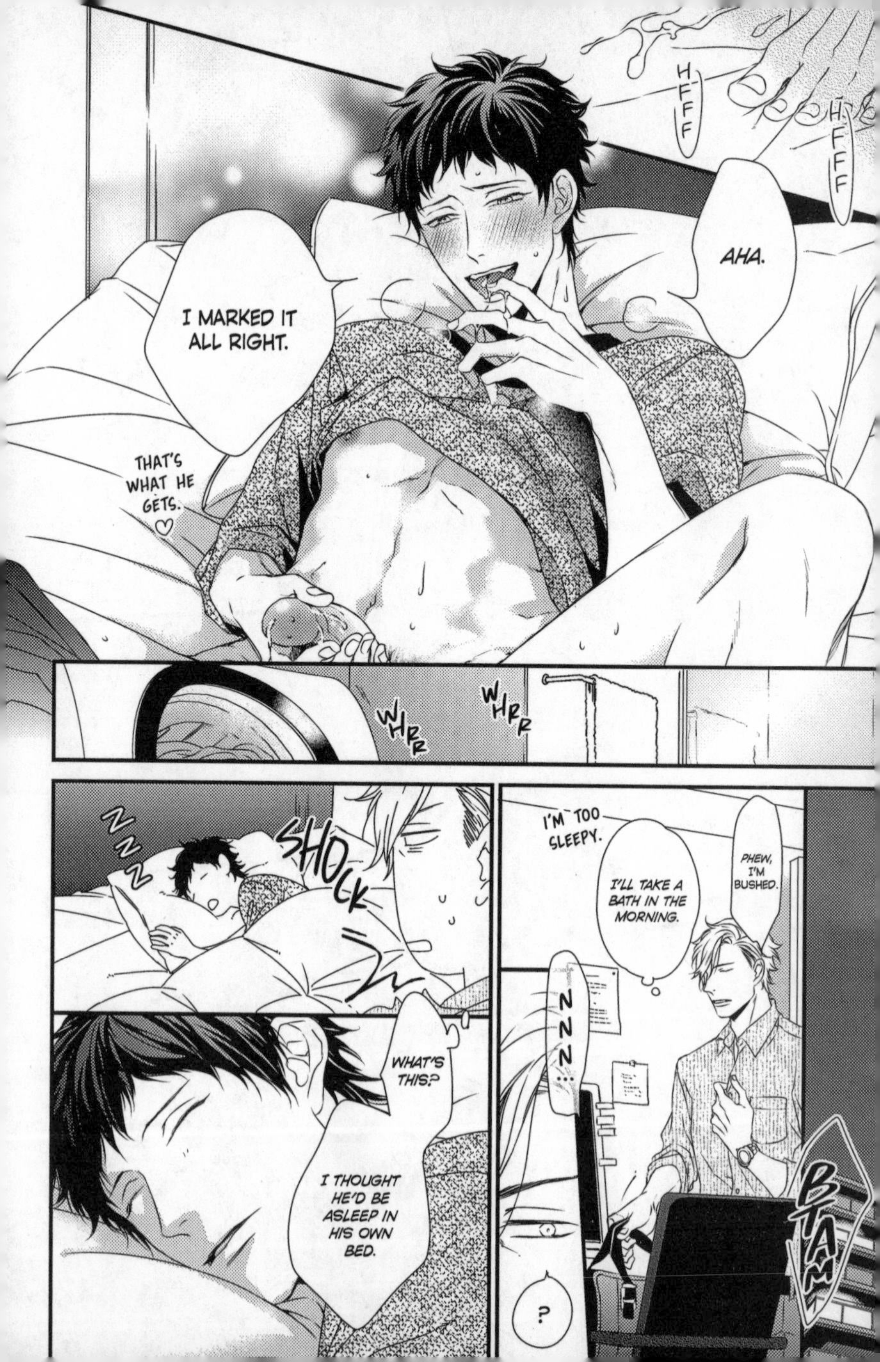

HFFF
HFFF
AHA.
I MARKED IT ALL RIGHT.
THAT'S WHAT HE GETS. ♡
WHRR
WHRR
PHEW, I'M BUSHED.
I'M TOO SLEEPY.
I'LL TAKE A BATH IN THE MORNING.
BLAM
NNN...
?
SHOCK
ZZZ
WHAT'S THIS?
I THOUGHT HE'D BE ASLEEP IN HIS OWN BED.

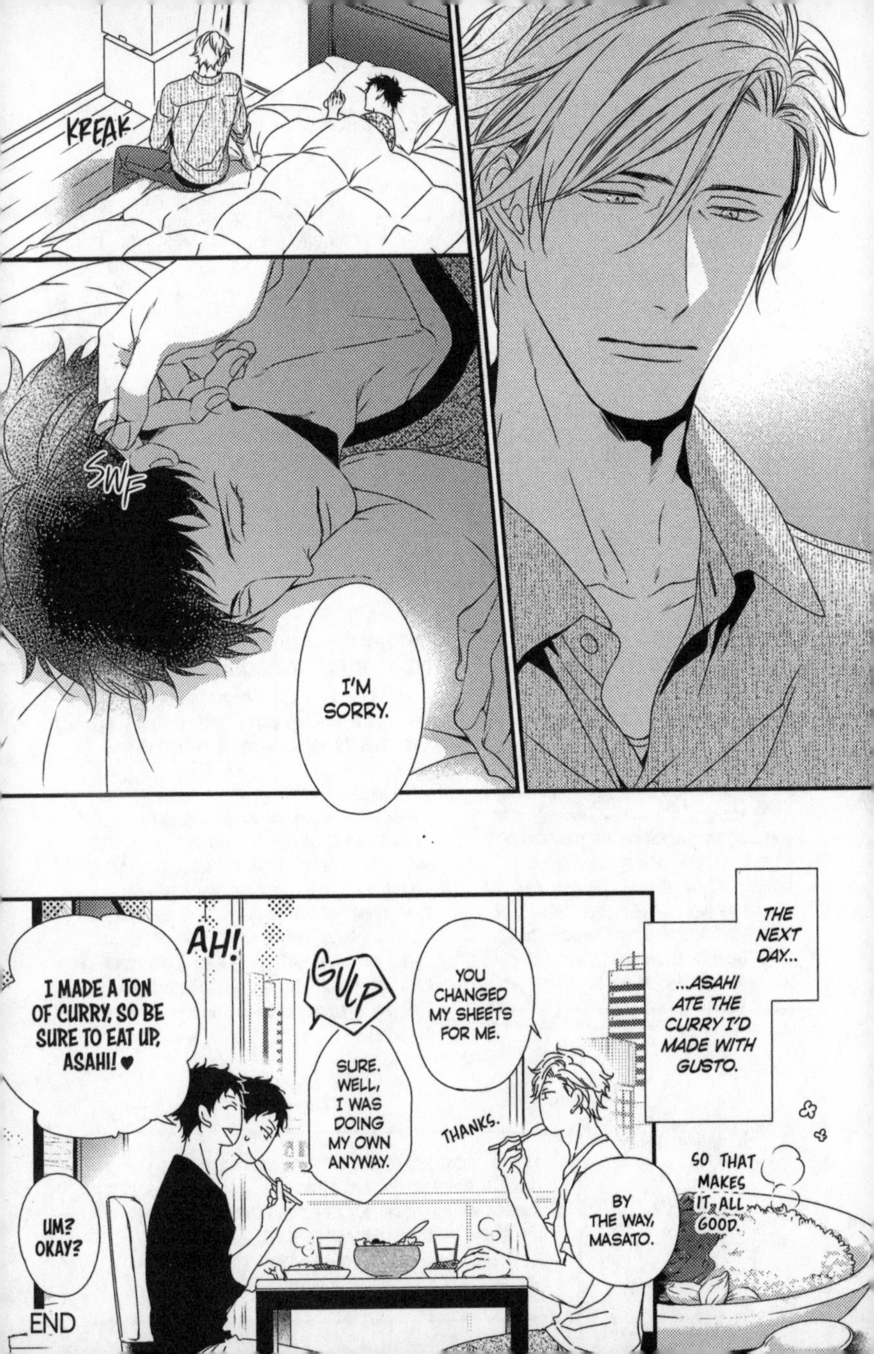
KREAK
SWF
I'M SORRY.
THE NEXT DAY...
...ASAHI ATE THE CURRY I'D MADE WITH GUSTO.
SO THAT MAKES IT ALL GOOD.
YOU CHANGED MY SHEETS FOR ME.
SURE. WELL, I WAS DOING MY OWN ANYWAY.
THANKS.
BY THE WAY, MASATO.
GULP
AH!
I MADE A TON OF CURRY, SO BE SURE TO EAT UP, ASAHI! ♥
UM? OKAY?
END

✥ THE LOVE NEST CAST BACKSTORIES ✥

ASAHI YAJIMA (AGE 38)
DOB: APRIL 21 / BLOOD TYPE: O / 185 CM

IF ASKED WHAT HE WAS LIKE IN HIGH SCHOOL, HE'D SAY HE WAS A DILIGENT STUDENT WHO FOCUSED ON HIS PART-TIME JOB AND STUDIES, BUT BECAUSE HE WAS ALWAYS HAVING TO CLEAN UP AFTER NARU'S SHENANIGANS, HE GOT USED TO FIGHTING AND WAS ACTUALLY SEEN AS A PROPER HOODLUM. TO THIS DAY, HE COMPLAINS ABOUT IT. HE LIKES ALCOHOL, BUT HE'S NOT VERY GOOD AT HOLDING HIS LIQUOR. HE'S PARTICULARLY FOND OF JAPANESE SAKE AND CAN HANDLE UP TO TWO CUPS. FOR BEER, HE CAN HANDLE THREE TO FOUR CANS. HE LIKES MOVIES ABOUT ANIMALS AND WILL, WITHOUT FAIL, GO TO THE CINEMA TO SEE ONE THAT'S PLAYING. HE HAS STAMINA WHEN IT COMES TO SEX, BUT IT TAKES TIME TO GET HIS SECOND WIND. HE'S HUNG.

MASATO HOZUMI (AGE 30)
DOB: FEBRUARY 2 / BLOOD TYPE: B / HEIGHT: 180 CM

HE WAS ON THE TENNIS TEAM IN MIDDLE AND HIGH SCHOOL AND EVEN PARTICIPATED IN NATIONALS. HIS FIRST CRUSH WAS ON A TEAM UPPERCLASSMAN IN JUNIOR HIGH. EVER SINCE HE WAS LITTLE, HIS MOM HAD BEEN VERY BUSY, LEAVING HIM IN CHARGE OF THE HOUSEWORK. TO BECOME MORE EFFICIENT, HE STARTED LOOKING INTO HIGH-PERFORMANCE GADGETS, WHICH IS HOW HE BECAME SUCH A FAN OF APPLIANCES. ON HIS DAYS OFF—AFTER HAVING PERUSED THE ELECTRONICS STORES—HE GOES IN SEARCH OF A CAFE FOR A TASTY COFFEE AND SWEETS. (HE INVITES ASAHI BUT GETS TURNED DOWN 90% OF THE TIME.) SINCE HE'S ALWAYS ON HIS COMPUTER FOR WORK, HIS HOBBIES INCLUDE READING PAPERBACKS AND DOING SUDOKU. HE'S SOMEWHAT OF A ROMANTIC, BUT HE ALSO LIKES TO GET DOWN AND DIRTY. HIS SENSITIVITY IS PROPORTIONATE TO THE AFFECTION HE HAS FOR HIS PARTNER.

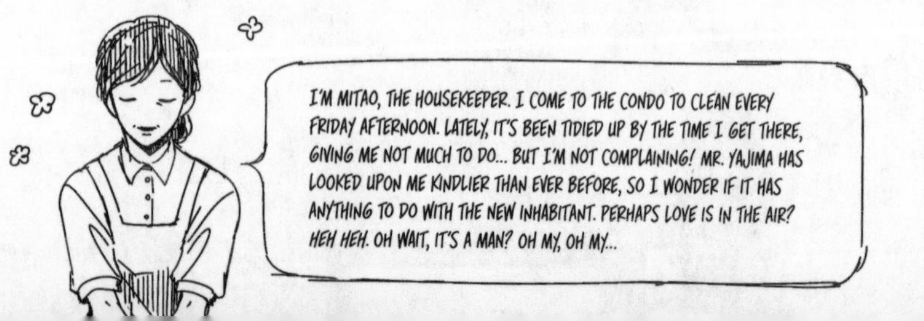

I'M MITAO, THE HOUSEKEEPER. I COME TO THE CONDO TO CLEAN EVERY FRIDAY AFTERNOON. LATELY, IT'S BEEN TIDIED UP BY THE TIME I GET THERE, GIVING ME NOT MUCH TO DO... BUT I'M NOT COMPLAINING! MR. YAJIMA HAS LOOKED UPON ME KINDLIER THAN EVER BEFORE, SO I WONDER IF IT HAS ANYTHING TO DO WITH THE NEW INHABITANT. PERHAPS LOVE IS IN THE AIR? HEH HEH. OH WAIT, IT'S A MAN? OH MY, OH MY...

IKUO ARIMURA (AGE 28)

HE WANTS TO MEET YOSUKE'S PARENTS AT LEAST ONCE, BUT YOSUKE WON'T HEAR OF IT. THE DEPARTMENT STORE HE WORKS AT HAS MOVED HIM TO A BRANCH IN THE CITY CENTER, SO HE'S MAKING PREPARATIONS FOR THAT. HIS CURRENT WORRY IS HOW TO KEEP HIS RELATIONSHIP WITH YOSUKE FUNCTIONING THROUGH IT ALL (MANY DAYS HE SHOWERS HIM WITH SO MUCH AFFECTION THAT HE PHYSICALLY HITS HIS LIMIT AND ENDS UP REGRETTING IT). HIS IS A SIZE BEYOND COMPARE.

YOSUKE ITO (AGE 26)

HE REALIZED ONCE THAT SOMEBODY WAS STALKING IKUO AND DROVE HIM AWAY (WITHOUT IKUO EVER EVEN FINDING OUT). HIS CURRENT WORRY IS HOW HE DOESN'T HAVE ENOUGH STAMINA TO KEEP UP WITH HIS NIGHTLY EXPLOITS WITH IKUO, AND WHEN HE TOLD MASATO THAT HE'S SERIOUSLY CONSIDERING JOINING A GYM, HE GOT LAUGHED AT. AFTER, MASATO WOULDN'T STOP FLOODING HIM WITH INVITATIONS TO JOIN HIS GYM, AND HE FELT LIKE KICKING HIMSELF FOR HAVING EVER OPENED HIS MOUTH.

MARIE KURODA (AGE 30)

SHE WAS TRULY WORRIED ABOUT MASATO AFTER HE WAS HURT SO BADLY BY A PRIOR RELATIONSHIP, BUT SINCE HER GIRLFRIEND HIYORI HATES HIM, SHE'S KEPT HER DISTANCE. FOLLOWING WHAT'S HAPPENED WITH YOSUKE, SHE'S TAKEN TO LOOKING AFTER MASATO AGAIN SINCE HE'S SEEMED TO CHANGE HIS WAY OF THINKING.

HIYORI MOMOSHIRO (AGE 33)

SHE'S USUALLY CALM AND QUIET, BUT AT THE HOSPITAL WHERE SHE WORKS, SHE'S SEEN AS A ANGEL IN A WHITE COAT WHO'S AS SCARY AS A DEMON. SINCE MASATO WAS THE TYPE TO BLINDLY HURT THOSE AROUND HIM, HIYORI DIDN'T WANT HIM COMING NEAR MARIE AND MADE AN EFFORT TO DRIVE HIM AWAY. BUT LATELY SHE'S STARTED TO EASE UP A BIT.

About the Author

Yuu Minaduki is the creator of over a dozen boys' love manga, some of which have French, Spanish, and German editions. She is a Leo born on August 7 in Saitama with an O blood type. You can find out more about Yuu Minaduki on her Twitter page, **@toriniku_y.**

Love Nest

Volume 1

SuBLime Manga Edition

Story and Art by **Yuu Minaduki**

Translation—**Christine Dashiell**
Touch-Up Art and Lettering—**Deborah Fisher**
Cover and Graphic Design—**Alice Lewis**
Editor—**Jennifer LeBlanc**

Printed in the U.S.A.

Published by SuBLime Manga
P.O. Box 77010
San Francisco, CA 94107

10 9 8 7 6 5 4 3 2 1
First printing, September 2022

PARENTAL ADVISORY
LOVE NEST is rated M for Mature and is recommended for mature readers. This volume contains graphic imagery and mature themes.

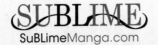

SuBLimeManga.com

For more information

on all our products, along with the most up-to-date news on releases, series announcements, and contests, please visit us at:

 SuBLimeManga.com

 twitter.com/**SuBLimeManga**

 facebook.com/**SuBLimeManga**

 instagram.com/**SuBLimeManga**

 SuBLimeManga.tumblr.com

SUBLIME
MANGA

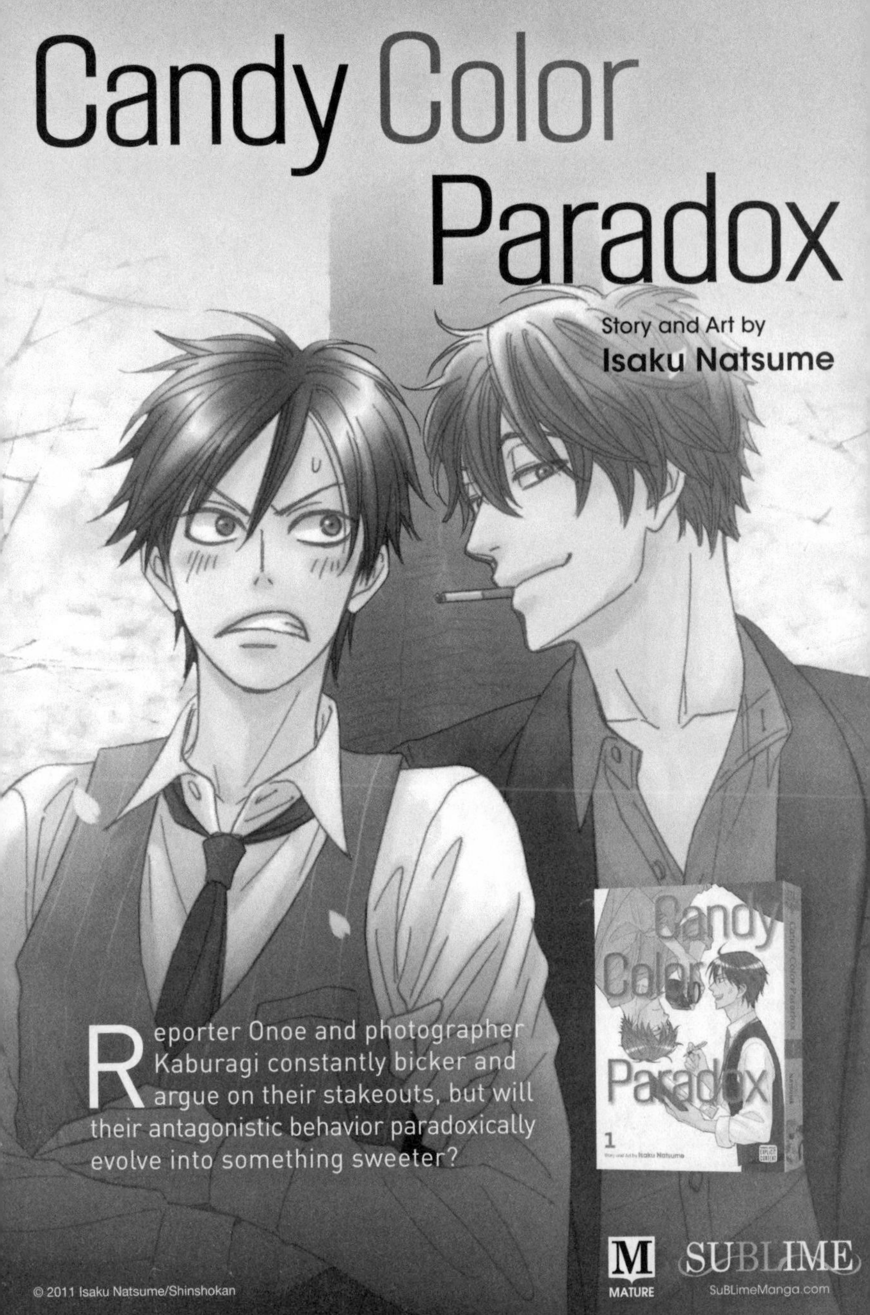
Candy Color Paradox
Story and Art by
Isaku Natsume
Reporter Onoe and photographer Kaburagi constantly bicker and argue on their stakeouts, but will their antagonistic behavior paradoxically evolve into something sweeter?
Candy Color Paradox
1
M
MATURE
SUBLIME
SuBLimeManga.com
© 2011 Isaku Natsume/Shinshokan

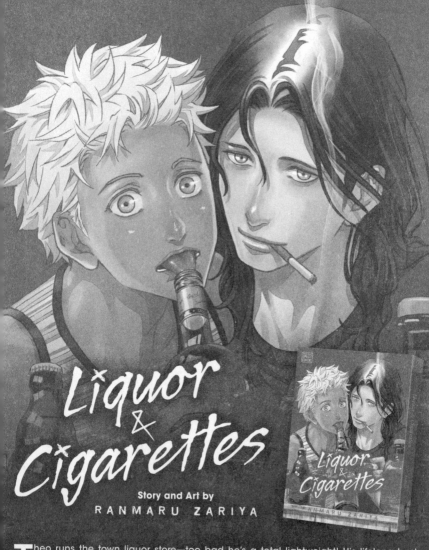

Liquor & Cigarettes

Story and Art by
RANMARU ZARIYA

Theo runs the town liquor store—too bad he's a total lightweight! His lifelong best friend, Camilo, runs the cigarette store across the street, and recently, he's been making his attraction to Theo quite clear. Unsure of how he feels about dating a man, Theo accepts Camilo's offer of a trial run at dating, and with a little liquid courage and a lot of heavy petting, Theo sees a whole new side to his childhood friend. Will these new experiences clarify his feelings or only serve to further muddy the waters of love?

MATURE

SUBLIME
SuBLimeManga.com